THE SOCIETY OF THE MUSLIM BROTHERS

THE SOCIETY OF THE MUSLIM BROTHERS

Richard P. Mitchell

With a Foreword by John O. Voll

OXFORD UNIVERSITY PRESS
New York Oxford

Oxford University Press

Oxford New York Toronto
Delhi Bombay Calcutta Madras Karachi
Kuala Lumpur Singapore Hong Kong Tokyo
Nairobi Dar es Salaam Cape Town
Melbourne Auckland Madrid

and associated companies in
Berlin Ibadan

Published by Oxford University Press, Inc.
198 Madison Avenue, New York, New York 10016-4314

Oxford is a registered trademark of Oxford University Press, Inc.

Originally published in 1969 by Oxford University Press in the Middle Eastern Monographs series (advisory editor Albert Hourani).

First issued as an Oxford University Press paperback, 1993.

Library of Congress Cataloging-in-Publication Data
Mitchell, Richard P. (Richard Paul), 1925–1983
The Society of the Muslim Brothers /
Richard P. Mitchell ; with a foreword by John O. Voll.
p. cm.
Originally presented as the author's thesis (Ph.D.)—Princeton University, 1960.
Reprint, with new introd. Originally published: 1969.
Includes bibliographical references (p.) and index.
ISBN 0-19-508437-3
1. Jam'īyat al-Ikhwān al-Muslimīn (Egypt)
2. Islam—Egypt—History—20th century.
I. Title. DT107.82.M5 1993 322.4'2—dc20 93-20368

4 6 8 10 9 7 5

Printed in the United States of America
on acid-free paper

To Alita

Joshua, Jessica, and Jeffrey

FOREWORD

The roles of religion in society and world affairs have changed dramatically in the part thirty years. The ways that scholars understand those roles is also being transformed. These two processes of change interact and reflect the new and emerging dimensions of religious life on a global scale at the end of the twentieth century. In the 1990s it is important to be aware of these processes of change, and the reprinting of Richard P. Mitchell's *The Society of Muslim Brothers* provides an appropriate occasion to look at both the changing roles of religion, as reflected in the history of the Muslim Brotherhood, and the challenges posed by those changes for scholars trying to understand contemporary religious life. Important aspects of the general issues of scholarship relating to religious movements can be highlighted and better understood by reference to the analysis presented in Mitchell's book.

The most direct challenge to scholars is explaining and analyzing the resurgence in the late twentieth century of religion, especially in a form that is often called "fundamentalist." This resurgence is not confined to a single major tradition of world religion but is, in many ways, a complex global set of phenomena.[1] Most studies of "fundamentalist" groups in Muslim societies that were done in the 1950s and 1960s, before this resurgence, now seem out of date and their basic analytical and methodological assumptions antiquated. However, a few major works from that period continue to be used and are an important part of the *current* literature in the field. This seminal study of the Muslim Brotherhood in Egypt by Richard P. Mitchell, published in 1969, is an important example of such studies with continuing validity and utility. In the 1990s, it continues to be cited as "the best history of the Muslim Brothers" in the era from the establishment of the organization in 1928 until its suppression by Gamal Abd al-Nasir in the mid-1950s.[2]

Scholarship in the 1950s and 1960s was undertaken within the framework of distinctive modern worldviews. Many aspects of these scholarly perspectives made it difficult for scholars to understand or even perceive the global resurgence of religion in a "fundamentalist" form. Some of these problems are not just simply minor methodological ones but reflect deeply held assumptions about the nature of modernity, and they continue to be a part of the scholarly scene in the 1990s.

One important dimension of this analytical perspective is a sense of tension or contradiction between modernity and religion. This takes many forms in different times and places, involving apparent conflicts between science versus religion, rationality versus faith, and the emerging modern industrial social order versus "traditional" society. While many scholars in the 1960s would have disagreed with Arnold Toynbee over many aspects of his view of world history, few would have disagreed with his statement in 1968 that "all current religions—whether tribe-bound or missionary or 'lower' or 'higher'—have been losing their hold on the hearts and consciences and minds of their former adherents." Toynbee set the beginning of this rejection of "traditional religion" in 17th-century Western Europe, and he noted that "one of the modern Western cultural influences that is making itself felt in the non-Western societies today [1968] is the modern Western attitude toward religion . . . [and] all the non-Western religions . . . are now experiencing the same crisis of faith and allegiance that the Western Christian churches had begun to experience before the close of the 17th century."[3] In intellectual terms, there was a general sense that as "modernity takes hold . . . social institutions and popular attitudes often seem to become more of a threat to, than a sustaining force for, religious belief."[4]

In the analyses of the modernization of Third World or "developing" areas during the 1950s and 1960s, it was argued that "wherever the modernization process has had an impact, it has contributed to secularization, both social and political,"[5] and secularization was seen as a reduction of the significance of religion. A widely quoted study of the "modernizing of the Middle East" by Daniel Lerner, published in 1958, gave concrete specifics of the declining role of religion as people became more "modern" and less "traditional." This was part of specific developments as well, with Lerner noting, when discussing Egypt, for example, that the "familiar process of secularization accompanies urbanization in Egypt as elsewhere."[6]

In this context, the influence of religion was a measure of the degree of modernization and development. There was a continuing assumption that religion would play an important role in "transitional" developments but that, especially in the political realm, the "general forces of secularization of culture and society" would reduce the "effectiveness" of religion.[7] These analytical positions were confirmed by examination of the most important developments in societies around the world. Specifically, in Middle Eastern and Muslim societies, secularist forces were clearly both dominant and the most successful.

The Egyptian context in which the Muslim Brotherhood developed reflected the validity of the analysis that tied growing modernization with increasing secularization of the social and political orders. In broadly political terms, the Egyptian monarchy was overthrown by a revolutionary military regime, led by Gamal Abd al-Nasir, which became a model for the radical modernizing alternative in the Middle East. More explicitly "religious" alternatives for political leadership, like the Muslim Brotherhood, lost power and visibility in the 1950s and 1960s. At the end of the 1940s the Muslim Brotherhood had been an important political force, but it lost in the power struggles with Abd al-Nasir. The organization known to Mitchell through his research was suppressed in 1954 and its leaders jailed or executed. The leading Brotherhood writer after the suppression, Sayyid Qutb, was executed in 1966 and there was little if any popular outcry.

Mitchell's own research experience brought him into close contact with these developments. In 1951–1952, he was among the first Fulbright scholars to go to Egypt and he observed the end of the Old Regime directly, viewing the dramatic burning of Cairo in January 1952, for example, from the vantage point of the Garden City House, a rooming house not far from some of the areas burned. His direct research for the book was done in Egypt in 1953–1956, the time of the highest level of conflict between the Brotherhood and the emerging revolutionary regime. He also was in the United States Foreign Service briefly, serving a short tour in pre-revolutionary Yemen (1960) and in Kuwait (1960–1962) just after its formal independence. These experiences gave him a strong sense of the persuasive power of secular nationalism and the weaknesses of the "traditional" institutions. The contrast between Egypt under Abd al-Nasir and Yemen under the old Imam was a stark one, emphasizing the secularizing nature of the processes of modernization and development.

Writing in the 1960s on the basis of this experience and the analytical assumptions of the time, Mitchell concluded that the alleged Brotherhood conspiracy of 1965, which was severely suppressed by the revolutionary regime, was nothing more than "the predictable eruption of the continuing tension caused by an ever-dwindling activist fringe of individuals dedicated to an increasingly less relevant Muslim 'position' about society; and of professional malcontents," and he concluded that "the essentially secular reform nationalism now [1968] in vogue in the Arab world will continue to operate to end the earlier appeal of this organization." In this, he noted that he was in agreement with other prominent scholars at the time, like Manfred Holpern, who concluded in 1963: "When traditional Islam reacts by transforming itself into a religio-political totalitarian party [like the Muslim Brotherhood], it can safely be challenged as a novel ideology rather than as a hallowed way of life. There will still be battles, but this particular war is over in the great majority of Middle Eastern states."[8]

It is important to emphasize that in the 1960s, these conclusions were in accord with observable political and social realities. In the following two decades, however, the situation changed dramatically, with the revival of the significance and power of activist Islamic "fundamentalist" individuals and groups and the transformation of the role of Islam in society. By the early 1990s, a major scholar could write: "What had previously seemed to be an increasingly marginalized force in Muslim public life reemerged in the seventies—often dramatically—as a vibrant sociopolitical reality. Islam's resurgence in Muslim politics reflected a growing religious revivalism in both personal and public life that would sweep across much of the Muslim world."[9] It was accurate by the 1990s to state that analysts agreed that "Islamic activism will be a major feature of regional politics into the twenty-first century."[10]

The Muslim Brotherhood in Egypt represents an interesting and important dimension in the history of this broader resurgence. In the period covered by Mitchell's study, the Brotherhood represented the only significant movement or major visible tendency of Islamic "fundamentalism" in Egypt. But the decades following the period covered by Michell saw a number of significant changes. Abd al-Nasir's policies of suppression destroyed the public apparatus of the organization and fundamentalists lost their institutional core. The most active were in prisons and gradually coalesced into a number of small militant groups. These militants were often more actively inspired by the writings of Sayyid Qutb, the leading Brotherhood writer of the 1950s and 1960s who was executed in 1966, than by the writings of Hasan al-Banna, the founder of the Brotherhood, or of Hasan Hudaybi, al-Banna's successor as Supreme Guide. These new groups became the core of the extremist "fundamentalist" fringe that emerged during the 1970s.[11]

At the same time, the Muslim Brotherhood itself also managed to reconstitute itself. During the years of the most active suppression there were a few of the old leadership who were able to maintain a support network. Zaynab al-Ghazali, the organizer of the Muslim Sisterhood, for example, was able to provide support for some of the imprisoned Brothers and was an important link in distributing the writings of Sayyid Qutb from prison before his execution.[12] After Abd al-Nasir's death in 1970 the situation became less oppressive as Abd al-Nasir's successor, Anwar al-Sadat, relaxed the controls over the Brotherhood. They were allowed to publish their own magazine, *al-Da'wah,* which expressed the views of the old leadership of the Brotherhood. From the early 1970s on, this leadership continued in the traditions of the organization to act within the limitations of the political system to Islamize the state and society through evolutionary means. During the 1970s, there were thus two different styles of active Islamic advocacy, the extremist fringes and the more mainstream Brotherhood.

By the 1980s, the mainstream tendencies gained in influence. In 1981, members of one of the extremist groups had murdered Sadat but the expected "fundamentalist" revolution did not take place. Instead, a more broadly-based affirmation of Islam on the part of Egyptians of all classes gave a new mainstream-based popular support for the Brotherhood and a variety of other Islamically-identified people and groups. A number of more fundamentalist preachers emerged as popular media stars while Islamic medical clinics and social welfare organizations flourished. The government actively suppressed the more violent and extremist fringe groups but in the early 1990s, as economic and social problems mounted, the extremist groups continued to be a visible force alongside the more mainstream groups, which came to dominate the professional associations and other non-governmental groups. Islam had become the basis for political discourse for virtually all parts of the political spectrum, and manifestations of Islamic resurgence were setting the tone for normal, not just "marginal" societal life.[13]

There had clearly been a "resurgence of Islam" since the mid-1950s. One important element in this resurgence in Egypt was the Muslim Brotherhood, and Mitchell's book provides a foundation for understanding the nature of the role of the Muslim Brotherhood in this resurgence. Ironically, he himself did not forsee this continuing vital role for the Brotherhood because the situation in the 1960s was so dramatically different from what it was to become in the 1990s.

This situation represents not only a transformation of the conditions of the 1960s, but also a significant problem for the theories which had been developed to understand the social and political dynamics of change in the modern world. Many of the important studies written in the 1950s and 1960s are now little-cited and this is related to their identification with specific theories which have been superseded. They tended to be guided by a model of modernization and development which conceived of the process as essentially unilinear and leading ultimately to a homogeneous "modern" end product; modernity was identified with secular structuring of society. While Mitchell was influenced by this perspective, it was not the core of his approach to the study of the Muslim Brotherhood. There were certain crucial value judgments and unconscious assumptions in the old development model which Mitchell did not share, and at least some of these assumptions continue to have an impact on the analysis of movements of contemporary religious resurgence in many different regions.

In general terms, the social sciences have had more difficulty in covering the religious dimensions of contemporary history than in providing insight into economic processes or concrete socio-political developments. Most social scientists themselves accept the assumptions of the secularist worldview and, as a consequence, find it necessary to "explain" religious belief as a secondary phenomenon related to "real" motivations involving material gain, class interest, or other non-religious aspects of human experience. This creates a contradiction. "Few eras have been shaped more profoundly by religious activism than the last fifteen years. But the *presumption of unbelief* is so basic to much of modern academe that it is hard for scholars to take religion altogether seriously . . . That an understanding of economic action is essential for sociologists and political scientists is all but unquestioned; that religion should be accorded similar centrality is all but unconsidered."[14]

Increasingly in recent years, however, some scholars have become aware of the importance of belief and the possible errors in analysis created by the "presumption of unbelief." People's images and beliefs create much of the social, cultural, and political realities in which we live. Nations, for example, are increasingly being understood as "imagined communities" rather than permanent "objective" entities.[15] In the context of the effective resurgence of religion at the end of the twentieth century, it is becoming increasingly necessary to recognize that many people actually believe in their religion and are not simply manipulating religious slogans for some other purposes. Mitchell was already sensitive to the reality of the faith of the members of the Brotherhood. In his section on "ideology" he noted that "in so far as what men believe to be real, is real, our concern here will be not the validity of these beliefs, but only the fact of their existence," and he noted that the major appeal of the Brotherhood was "for those whose commitment to the tradition and religion is still great, but who at the same time are already effectively touched by the forces of Westernization."[16] There is little "presumption of unbelief" in Mitchell's analysis. Speaking in the early 1980s, in the midst of the Islamic resurgence, Mitchell emphasized both the importance of recognizing belief and the difficulty for scholars in that recognition when he stated: "For many Western intellectuals (and some Easterners) to understand that man may act in the mundane world as though God were alive and well requires almost a transcendental act of will and thought process transfer. . . . [The Islamic movement] would not be a serious movement worthy of our attention were it not, above all, an idea and a personal commitment honestly felt."[17] Mitchell's willingness to assume the reality of belief may be an important part of the continuing validity of his analysis in the contemporary era of religious resurgence.

Another area of difficulty within the social sciences for understanding the religious resurgence is the identification of the audience to which the resurgent religions are appealing. An interesting analysis of the difficulties of sociologists in understanding the upsurge of evangelical or fundamentalist Christianity in the United States identifies some "theoretical barriers" in sociological analyses of the 1970s. Early studies which located evangelicalism among the lower classes and "disinherited" groups provide the basis for a transformation of empirical generalizations into theoretical constructs in which "evangelicalism is perceived as *by definition* the religion of the disinherited."[18] The result of this is that "the bias toward perceiving evangelicalism as a lower-class phenomenon combined with the middle class identification of sociologists (and other professionals) at the very least does not make it likely that they will be attuned to its emergence in their midst."[19] Similarly, in the Middle East, there is a tendency for scholars and secular intellectuals, both foreign and local, to assume that the core of the fundamentalist movements is in the uneducated lower classes who could be roused to "fanatic" religious fervor[20] and that modern educated middle-class professionals would not find fundamentalism appealing, except for opportunistic reasons. For example, the author of a widely-read discussion of Middle Eastern politics in the late 1980s states that those who advocate an increasing role for Islam in politics and society "tend to be traditionally or perhaps hardly educated, and they include the Sunni Muslim Brothers in Egypt and Syria, Tunisia and Algeria."[21]

From this perspective, it is difficult for the analysts to explain the strong appeal of the activist Islamic movements among the modern educated professionals. In Egypt in the 1990s, the Muslim Brotherhood has become the dominant force in the major professional associations, controlling the syndicates of doctors, engineers, pharmacists, dentists, and lawyers. The Muslim Brotherhood victory in the ruling council elections of the Egyptian Bar Association in September 1992 was viewed by many as "one of the most significant political events in a decade."[22] While various Islamic activist groups have considerable appeal in urban lower-class areas, like the Imbaba district in Cairo, the dominant character of the Islamically-active elements in Egyptian society is not that they are illiterate and poor, even though that is what secular middle-class analysts might expect.

Mitchell's study makes it clear that the appeal of the Brotherhood to modern educated Egyptians is not a recent phenomenon. In an analysis of the people who were involved in arrests and trials in the late 1940s and early 1950s, Mitchell concludes that rural membership and members from the urban lower classes were seldom more than "a backdrop for the urban activists who shaped the Society's political destiny," and that the sampling of membership suggests "urban, middle class, *effendi* [modern-educated professional usually in the civil service] predominance among the activist membership."[23] This basic understanding of the composition of the Brotherhood's membership and its appeal has not been superseded by current events and developments. Mitchell continues to provide a basis for understanding the actual dynamics of the Islamic resurgence because his study is not tied to some of the common "theoretical barriers" found in some analyses of movements of religious resurgence in the contemporary era.

Analysis in the social sciences of movements of religious resurgence faces additional problems with respect to terminology and related issues of conceptualization. There is a tendency in broader or comparative studies to use terms which have meanings identified with specific cases. This provides an effective and usable terminology but it has some dangers. Sometimes the result is that the specific characteristics involved in the term are assumed, by definition, to be part of the general phenomenon. Two of the most frequently used terms of this type are "conservative" and "fundamentalist."

R. Stephen Warner found that sociologists of religion tended to assume that Evangelical Christians in the United States were "conservative" by definition. This was the result of transforming the observation that in the past century specific movements of this type "have not been particularly oriented to protest or social change" into the generalization that all such movements in the present and future would, by their nature, be conservative. This makes it difficult for such scholars to recognize social activism among Evangelicals.[24]

Scholars studying movements of Islamic resurgence sometimes have this same difficulty. They will use the term "conservative" as a convenient label for such movements and then assume that the normal general definition of "conservative" as a "preference for the old and established in the social and political order rather than the new and untried"[25] is an accurate description of resurgence movements. When it becomes clear that these movements are in strong opposition to the *existing* social and political order, such scholars shift the emphasis to a "preference for the *old*" and see such movements as calling for a restoration of earlier conditions. The "conservative" movements are seen as Luddite responses to change or deeply reactionary, in conformity with the secularist assumptions about the processes of modernization. Such an approach makes it virtually impossible to understand the appeal and revolutionary potential of many of the major Islamic resurgence movements. "Despite stereotypes of activists as fanatics who wish to retreat to the past, the vast majority share a common call for the transformation of society not through a blind return to seventh-century Medina but a response to the present."[26] The Ayatollah Khomeini in Iran was in virtually no way a "conservative." He was actively opposed to the existing monarchical political order in Iran and proposed a system of governance which had never existed before within the Shi'i Islamic world. He was not striving for a return to medieval Muslim systems or social orders, and interpretations which viewed him as "conservative" in this way created a conceptual obstacle to understanding both Khomeini's significance and his appeal.

Although the Muslim Brotherhood has been called "conservative" by some analysts over the years, Mitchell understood their position in a way which went beyond this approach. He recognized that the goal of the Brotherhood was not conservative in the sense of attempting either to preserve existing institutions or restore past conditions. Instead, the Brotherhood aimed at "a total reform of the political, economic, and social life of the country," and this "did not mean the return to a seventh-century Islam or a particular Muslim polity."[27] In his analysis of the Muslim Brotherhood, Mitchell went beyond the "analysis by definition" of Islamic resurgence as conservative. Some individuals and groups are actually conservative; al-Azhar, the great Islamic university in Cairo, for example, tends to represent a truly conservative position of supporting existing governments regardless of their ideologies and of opposing advocates of radical and rapid change. However, Mitchell makes it clear that activist non-liberal *religious* groups like the Muslim Brotherhood are not necessarily "conservative" and that the spectrum is more complex than the simple liberal-conservative dichotomy frequently implied by the terminology of many analysts.

The term "fundamentalist" is even more complex and controversial than "conservative" when it is used to identify individuals and groups involved in the Islamic resurgence. The term "fundamentalist" initially referred to a specific Christian experience in the United States but has increasingly been applied to parallel experiences in other religious traditions. However, in any context, it is a term which carries a variety of negative connotations from the perspective of secular modernist scholarly analysis. Scholars with this worldview tend to portray a dramatic conflict "between fundamentalist and modern in history, producing a naturalizing narrative of the progressive spread of modern ideas, at times lamentably thwarted by outbursts of reactive and reactionary fundamentalist fervor."[28] The assumption involved in the usage of the term "fundamentalist" by secularist analysts is a clear contrast between "modern" and "fundamentalist," with the fundamentalist representing a negative tendency going counter to the processes of modernization and rationalism and unconsciously viewed by the analyst as a "repugnant cultural other."[29] These problems are clearly visible when scholars apply the term to Islamic movements and this has lead some to conclude that "fundamentalism" should not be applied to Islamic cases because it is "too laden with Christian presuppositions and Western stereotypes."[30]

"Fundamentalism" has been accepted, however, as a useful term for comparative study by some people. This involves carefully defining the term as a general mode or style of religious expression divorced from the particulars of the original usage of the word.[31] However, most of the time when the term is used, it involves the negative connotations of the "cultural other." The sense of the "fundamentalist" as an anti-modern "other" on the margins of modern society limits the utility of the term. The implication is that the "fundamentalists" are a marginal and relatively unimportant minority within society, and this conceptualization means that the term is not helpful when applied to groups that are large and increasingly reflect the socio-cultural mainstream of the society.

The Muslim Brotherhood in Egypt in the 1950s and 1960s was seen by many as "fundamentalist" in the sense of a marginal, anti-modern other. One important study, for example, spoke of the "rigid Islamic fundamentalism" of the Brotherhood as excluding them "from full participation in the ever expanding opportunities of secular education," and "their exclusive religious concentration on fundamentalist Islam" meant that "they could not hope to attain to a position of intellectual leadership in their own country."[32] They were described as being so anti-Western and anti-modern that their use of printing presses and loudspeakers at meetings was seen as a profound dilemma for the movement and the implication was that their primary mode of defending their faith was "by terrorism and assassination."[33] Such a portrait makes it difficult to understand how the Brotherhood could attain the position that it had by the 1980s among the modern educated professionals in Egypt.

Mitchell did not view the Muslim Brotherhood as a marginal, blindly anti-modern group and avoided using the term "fundamentalist" in his book. However by the late 1970s, as scholars became more aware of the Islamic resurgence, the term became almost unavoidable and Mitchell accepted the term as preferable to a number of constructed labels. However, he noted that there was no real Arabic equivalent for the term and he emphasized that he used the term "to suggest . . . a *style* and, above all, a mood."[34] Within this perspective on "fundamentalism," Mitchell argued in a conference in 1983 that "it is most useful to view the Islamic movement not as a narrow and specific programmatic entity with discrete beginning and ending points, but as a broader endeavor which Muslims are pursuing—a search for authenticity, a search for 'roots,' so to speak—as a necessary aspect of contending with the Muslim situation in the contemporary world."[35] This places Islamic movements at the center of the modern experience of Muslims and not on the margins as an extremist "other." As liberal secularist and radical socialist options failed in countries like Egypt, this analytical framework provided an effective basis for understanding the reemergence of the Muslim Brotherhood and the broader trends of the Islamic resurgence of the final quarter of the twentieth century.

An additional feature of Mitchell's study of the Muslim Brotherhood is that it reflects important developments in the structure of scholarly study that were occurring in the 1950s and 1960s. Among these changes were the decline of traditional Orientalism and the rise of Area Studies as ways of studying the Islamic world, as well as the growing interest among mainstream scholars in the social sciences in the study of Third World or "underdeveloped" societies. Although Mitchell did not present formal arguments on methodology or theory, his work involved specific approaches to research and the subject matter which have proved on the long run to be especially effective in understanding the religious resurgence of the late twentieth century.

Classical Orientalism provided the basis for much of what was known by Western scholars in the 1950s about the Islamic world. The subject of this older scholarship was, in the words of a major practitioner and critic of Orientalism, Hamilton A. R. Gibb writing in the 1960s, "the study of what is now generally called the 'great culture', the universal norms expressed or predicted in literature, religion and law, recognised as authoritative and paradigmatic by all its adherents, but rarely more than loosely approximated in their local groups."[36] The primary methodology was a close analysis of texts, usually ones that were seen as culturally canonical, and there tended to be a lack of awareness of diversity or concrete issues of modern political and social life.

Scholars increasingly recognized that it was important to have direct contact with the society being studied and that textual studies in isolation were not sufficient for understanding the dynamics of contemporary societies. Many social scientists came to recognize the importance of the study of countries outside of Europe and North America and developed a broad range of models and methods to interpret especially the processes of modernization. However, these approaches sometimes became abstract and ethnocentric in tone and had little foundation in the distinctive cultural realities and traditions of the societies being studied. Gibb provided a trenchant critique of these approaches: "It needs no proof that to apply the psychology and mechanics of Western political institutions to Arab or Asian situations is pure Walt Disney. The sociologist whose research begins and ends with a questionnaire and a statistical computer is not really much more useful, while the linguist who has no interest in the substantive product of the language that he studies . . . is like a man who can produce and analyse musical tones but can never hear the music."[37]

Area Studies developed to bridge the gap between the text-oriented Orientalism and ethnocentrically-developed social sciences. Effective language skills and knowledge of the specific culture and society were to be combined with the analytical skills and methods of the social sciences disciplines. Mitchell's book provides an excellent example of the positive results when the Area Studies approach is done well. Mitchell's analysis is based on a clear study of the important major texts in the history of the Muslim Brotherhood, but this is combined with direct contact with members of the Brotherhood and interaction with them. The portrait of the Brotherhood that emerges is not, therefore, simply the product of interpreting the text of what someone chose to write about the organization. Mitchell also did not start with some abstract model which he then applied to the case of the Brotherhood. Instead, he identified his approach as "a classically historical one: to attempt to capture in their deepest possible dimensions a related series of events and ideas in a period of time, a historical phenomenon, (a) within its own terms and (b) within a structure reflecting my own humanist view of man and society."[38]

Understanding religious (and other) historical movements and individuals "within their own terms" emerged as an important aspect of analysis in Area Studies and the history of religions during the 1960s. There was a growing awareness of the dangers of imposing Eurocentrically defined conceptualizations on non-European materials and there was an increasingly globalized audience for the scholarship. Area Studies scholars not only interacted with people in the regions of their specialization during the course of research; they also interacted through having their publications become part of the intellectual discussions in those regions, as well as in their own academic communities in Western Europe and North America. Growing numbers of Muslims became part of these scholarly communities as well. In this context, an analysis that presents a picture of a religious movement or leader which is not significantly recognizable by a member of the movement loses a major dimension of credibility.[39] This does not mean that the scholars should become advocates of the positions being explained, and often they can be effective critics, but it does mean that a significant effort has to be made to present the experience authentically in its own terms, whether in agreement or disagreement.

Successful studies have the capacity to become material in the internal debates of the societies studied as well as in the external scholarly and policy discussions. In this sense as well, Mitchell's book was successful. The book was translated twice into Arabic and became an important source for information and interpretation in the Middle East.[40] In one edition, an extended introduction was written by Salah 'Issa from a leftist perspective[41] and in the other edition the introduction was by Salih Abu Ruqayq, reflecting the views of an older and somewhat conservative member of the Brotherhood. In both cases, the authors entered into a real interaction with Mitchell's ideas rather than simply seeing the book as an outsider's attempt to reshape Egyptian history in a foreign mold.

The Brotherhood organization itself responded directly and relatively favorably to the book. In the mid-1970s, when the Brotherhood was permitted to publish a monthly magazine, the book received prominent coverage in a review article which was contained in two early issues. The reviewer commented on many specific points, challenging some interpretations and providing different data, but the conclusion at the end of the discussion was "Nevertheless, the monograph of Dr. Mitchell, professor at the University of Michigan and a former American diplomat who has served in many Arab countries, contains much information and is worthy of much study and consideration."[42] In the 1990s it continues to be cited by members of the Brotherhood as a source of information about the organization's history.[43]

The global resurgence of religion continues to require rethinking of scholarly approaches and the development of perspectives that go beyond the theoretical and practical barriers for understanding religion in the contemporary world. It is important to examine and utilize those studies that have stood the test of time, continuing to provide understanding of individuals and movements of religious resurgence. As a guide to developing effective approaches for study as well as a source of information about the early history of the Society of Muslim Brothers in Egypt, this book by Richard P. Mitchell continues to be "worthy of much study and consideration."

John O. Voll

University of New Hampshire

NOTES

1. See, for example, the general discussions and specific case studies in Martin E. Marty and R. Scott Appleby, *Fundamentalisms Observed* (Chicago: University of Chicago Press, 1991).

2. Barry Rubin, *Islamic Fundamentalism in Egyptian Politics* (New York: St. Martin's Press, 1990), p. 156. See also the assessment in Yvonne Yazbeck Haddad, et al., *The Contemporary Islamic Revival, A Critical Survey and Bibliography* (New York: Greenwood Press, 1991), pp. 138–139, and the continuing references to Mitchell's book in the annual editions of *Social Sciences Citation Index*.

3. Arnold Toynbee, "Preface" in John Cogley, *Religion in a Secular Age* (New York: Frederick A. Praeger, 1968), p. xvi.

4. John Cogley, *Religion in a Secular Age,* p. 71.

5. James S. Coleman, "The Political Systems of the Developing Areas," in Gabriel A. Almond and James S. Colemen, ed., *The Politics of the Developing Areas* (Princeton: Princeton University Press, 1960), p. 537.

6. Daniel Lerner, *The Passing of Traditional Society: Modernizing the Middle East* (New York: The Free Press, 1958), p. 230.

7. Donald Eugene Smith, *Religion, Politics, and Social Change in the Third World* (New York: The Free Press, 1971), p. 4.

8. Manfred Halpern, *The Politics of Social Change in the Middle East and North Africa* (Princeton: Princeton University Press, 1963), p. 130.

9. John L. Esposito, *The Islamic Threat: Myth or Reality?* (New York: Oxford University Press, 1992), pp. 11–12. This important book is essential reading for all who are interested in the broader issues involved in the interaction between the personal perspectives of scholars and the analytical conclusions which they draw regarding Islamic resurgence.

10. Robin Wright, "Islam's New Political Face," *Current History* 90 (January 1991): 35–36.

11. Helpful discussions of the emergence of these groups can be found in Gilles Kepel, *Muslim Extremism in Egypt,* trans. Jon Rothschild (Berkeley: University of California Press, 1985) and Emmanuel Sivan, *Radical Islam: Medieval Theology and Modern Politics* (New Haven, CT: Yale University Press, 1985).

12. For her own account of this, see Zaynab al-Ghazali, *Ayyam min hayyati* (Cairo: Dar al-Sharuq, 1980).

13. For a discussion of the interaction between the developments of the mainstream and extremist Islamic groups, see John O. Voll, "Fundamentalism in the Sunni Arab World: Egypt and the Sudan," in Marty and Appleby, *Fundamentalisms Observed.*

14. Craig Calhoun, "Introduction," in *Comparative Social Research: A Research Annual,* ed. Craig Calhoun, 13 (1991): pp. ix–x. Emphasis added.

15. See, for example, the influential study: Benedict Anderson, *Imagined Communities: Reflections on the Origin and Spread of Nationalism,* rev. ed. (London: Verso, 1991).

16. Richard P. Mitchell, *The Society of the Muslim Brothers* (London: Oxford University Press, 1969), pp. 209 and 331.

17. Richard P. Mitchell, "The Islamic Movement: Its Current Condition and Future Prospects," in *The Islamic Impulse,* edited by Barbara Freyer Stowasser (London: Croom Helm, 1987), p. 79.

18. R. Stephen Warner, "Theoretical Barriers to the Understanding of Evangelical Christianity," *Sociological Analysis* 40, No. 1 (Spring 1979): 4.

19. Ibid., 5.

20. See, for example, the comments of "one Egyptian observer" (unidentified) who is reported to have said that the appeal of the popular Egyptian preacher, Shaykh Kishk, "is to the illiterate or semi-literate." Derek Hopwood, *Egypt, Politics and Society 1945–1981* (London: George Allen & Unwin, 1982), p. 163.

21. David Pryce-Jones, *The Closed Circle: An Interpretation of the Arabs* (New York: Harper & Row, 1989), p. 371.

22. *Al-Ahram Weekly,* 17 September 1992, in *Foreign Broadcast Information Service,* FBIS-NEA-92-184 (22 September 1992), p. 8.

23. Mitchell, *Society,* p. 329.

24. Warner, "Theoretical Barriers . . . ," pp. 5–7.

25. Donald Cameron Watt, "Conservatism," in *The Harper Dictionary of Modern Thought,* ed. Alan Bullock and Oliver Stallybrass (New York: Harper & Row, 1977), p. 132.

26. Esposito, *Islamic Threat . . . ?* , p. 165.

27. Mitchell, *The Society . . .* , pp. 260 and 324.

28. Susan Harding, "Representing Fundamentalism: The Problem of the Repugnant Cultural Other," *Social Research* 58, No. 2 (Summer 1991): 374.

29. Ibid., pp. 373–374.

30. Esposito, *Islamic Threat . . . ?* , p. 8.

31. See, for example, the discussion of the term in Martin E. Marty and

R. Scott Appleby, "Introduction—The Fundamentalism Project: A User's Guide," in Marty and Appleby, *Fundamentalisms Observed,* pp. vii–xiii. One concrete example of a way to define "fundamentalism" as a general style of religious experience can be found in John O. Voll, "The Sudanese Mahdi: Frontier Fundamentalist," *International Journal of Middle East Studies* 10, No. 2 (1979).

32. Christina Phelps Harris, *Nationalism and Revolution in Egypt* (Stanford, CA: The Hoover Institution, 1964), pp. 230–231.

33. Ibid., p. 233–234.

34. Mitchell, "The Islamic Movement . . . ," in *The Islamic Impulse,* pp. 79–80.

35. Ibid., pp. 84–85.

36. Sir Hamilton Gibb, *Area Studies Reconsidered* (London: University of London, 1963), p. 10.

37. Ibid., pp. 13–14.

38. Mitchell, *Society,* pp. vii–viii.

39. See, for example, the important discussion from the 1950s in Wilfred Cantwell Smith, "Comparative Religion: Whither—and Why?," in *The History of Religions,* ed. Mircea Eliade and Joseph M. Kitagawa (Chicago: University of Chicago Press, 1959), pp. 38–44.

40. *al-Ikhwan al-Muslimun,* trans. Abd al-Salam Radwan, two volumes (Cairo: Maktabah Madbuli, 1977–1978), and trans. Mahmud Abu Saud (Kuwait: n.p., 1980).

41. ʿIssa's introduction was reprinted in a collection of essays: Salah ʿIssa, *al-Karithah alati Tuhaddidna* (Cairo: Maktabah Madbuli, 1987), pp. 213–276.

42. [No author listed], "Jamaʿah al-Ikhwan al-Muslimun," *al-Daʿwah* No. 3 (Ramadan 1396/ September 1976), pp. 30–31 and No. 4 (Shawwal 1396/ October 1976), pp. 32–33.

43. It was cited, for example, to show longterm trends in Brotherhood modes of operation by Dr. Essam al-Erian, who had represented the Brotherhood in the Egyptian People's Assembly in the early 1980s. Interview in Cairo, 13 January 1993.

PREFACE

For the third time since its founding in 1928, members of the Society of the Muslim Brothers in 1966 paid the ultimate price—life itself—for the 'right' to challenge organized authority in Egypt. Having begun to emerge from incarceration and from the shadows of Egypt's political life by 1964, members of the organization became involved in some kind of conspiracy against the régime of President Gamal Abd-al-Nasir. Arrests were made beginning in the summer of 1965 and for the remainder of the year and through the first half of 1966; more arrests and trials culminated on 21 August 1966 in the sentencing by the Supreme State Security Court of seven Brothers to death by hanging and a hundred or so more to prison terms of varying lengths. On 29 August the death sentences of four were commuted to life in prison and the remaining three were hanged. In the absence of adequate source material, and guided by our own personal knowledge of the difficulties which accompany research on this movement, we will delay final judgement as to the meaning of these recent events. However, we do think it possible to observe briefly and in passing that these recent executions do not, despite suggestions to the contrary by the Egyptian government, signal a general resurrection of the Society of the Muslim Brothers. Rather, it was the predictable eruption of the continuing tension caused by an ever-dwindling activist fringe of individuals dedicated to an increasingly less relevant Muslim 'position' about society; and of professional malcontents. Our feeling, for some time now shared by others,[1] is that the essentially secular reform nation-

[1] See esp. M. Halpern, *The Politics of Social Change in the Middle East and North Africa* (1965), p. 153; and also C. P. Harris, *Nationalism and Revolution in Egypt* (1964), p. 209.

alism now in vogue in the Arab world will continue to operate to end the earlier appeal of this organization.

This study is concerned with that earlier period, from its founding in 1928 through its two major crises of 1948 and 1954. It delves into the history, organization, and thought of the movement.[2] The history of the movement is preceded by a résumé of the life of the founder, Hasan al-Banna, who early in his youth began a long involvement with organizations concerned with morality and the regeneration of Islam, and at the same time developed a strong sense of the practical and applied this to his effectively developing sense of leadership.

The movement's humble beginnings among the workers of the Suez Canal Zone city of Isma'iliyya are traced through its early days in Cairo, when the essential framework of its organization was established, and through World War II, when its institutions were perfected and it experienced its first clash with authority. We see the forces at work in World War II as important elements in the appearance, in the post-war period, of the Society in the centre of the Egyptian political arena. That period revealed a fundamental conflict between the two mass parties of Egypt—the Muslim Brothers and the Wafd—as they contested for political primacy. It also

[2]We should like to note here that this study is not one of mass movements. It is the study of one such movement in depth. We have not related it to other mass movements or informed it by the theoretical literature appearing in ever greater volume on mass movements and political behaviour in non-Western societies. My approach is a classically historical one: to attempt to capture in their deepest possible dimensions a related series of events and ideas in a period of time, a historical phenomenon, *(a)* within its own terms and *(b)* within a structure reflecting my own humanist view of man and society and assumptions and hypotheses generated by the study itself. I hope that colleagues in sister disciplines, trained to view the world in different ways, will find in this largely empirical study (of which there should be more) information on which to build meaningful theoretical schemata by which we may better understand the area.

In my own study, I am in debt to the pioneering work of Husayni, *Ikhwan* (see Note on abbreviations, p. xix). Another general (ibid.) partisan, and useful work which has received less recognition is Zaki, *Ikhwan*. And, of course, it is necessary to mention the early, important, English-language work of J. Heyworth-Dunne, *Religious and Political Trends in Modern Egypt* (1950); the author, as will be noted later, was a participant in some of the history of the movement and his work must be considered a primary source. The most recent study directly concerned with the movement is Harris, *Nationalism and Revolution*. Two other important, interpretative studies of the evolving political systems of Egypt and the Near East, which examine the Society, are N. Safran, *Egypt in Search of Political Community* (1961); and Halpern, *Politics of Social Change*. Less directly concerned with the Society is L. Binder, *The Ideological Revolution in the Middle East* (1964). Primarily concerned with the religious significance of the movement are W. Cantwell Smith, *Islam in Modern History* (1957); K. Cragg, *Counsels in Contemporary Islam* (1965); and the first and yet most important of all, H. A. R. Gibb, *Modern Trends in Islam* (1947).

revealed an initial harmony of purpose (in opposition to the Wafd) between the Society and the palace, which broke down in the wake of extensive violence in Egypt between 1946 and 1948 culminating in the latter year in the murder, by a Brother, of the prime minister, Nuqrashi Pasha, the dissolution of the organization, and the officially inspired murder of its leader, Banna. We see the violence of this post-war period as a consequence rather than the cause of the actual breakdown of parliamentary life in modern Egypt, an era brought to an end by the revolution of July 1952.

For a short period after its dissolution, the Society remained underground, then emerged with a new leader and, after the 1952 revolution, with an apparently new importance, a fact which derived from a long, clandestine association of some of the officers with the Society. More apparent than real, happy relations between the two groups rapidly deteriorated over a period of two years, to end in the attempted assassination of the then prime minister, Nasir, in October 1954. Another dissolution and the hanging of six Brothers in December 1954 bring our history to its end.

The second and third parts of the study deal respectively with the structure of the Society and with its ideas and its plans for bringing about a truly Islamic order. In our conclusion, we attempt to assess the Society in the light of Egypt's recent political history[3] and of Islamic modernism.[4] We note and emphasize two points: first, much of the political violence with which the organization was justly charged was a consequence of a widely shared sense of political, economic, and social frustration which in turn was a result of a paralysis of the political process and the general evolution of Egypt's economic and social development and the international frustrations bred by Egypt's dispute with Britain and by the Palestine question. Secondly, the violence of the Brothers created an intolerable measure of sectarianism—involving Muslims as well as Jewish and Christian minorities—generated out of the critical imbalance between the recognized tradition and the actual condition of Muslim society, and the militant quality of the teachings by which the Society hoped to redress this imbalance.[5]

[3] It will become readily apparent that we have not challenged much of the accepted framework of the history of modern Egypt except where it concerns this movement. My historical study will show its debt to the work of Colombe, Marlowe, Kirk, Lacouture, Wheelock, Little, and the Egyptian historian, al-Rafi'i. Because this is not a general history of modern Egypt, I have not made it a point to display in these pages my bibliographical knowledge of that history.

[4] Similarly, I have not attempted to re-do, or even to summarize, the work so ably done on this subject by Gibb, Smith, Cragg, Adams, Hourani, Gardet, Anawati, Jomier, and Jamal Ahmed, among others.

[5] I am indebted to Professor Manfred Halpern for helping to clarify my thinking on this question of violence.

As a result of the Society's political commitment, its place in the movement of Islamic modernism lacks clarity. Although sharing in some areas the relatively catholic Muhammad ʿAbduh tradition, the Society also reflected the progressive change in the character of that movement to more rigidity and thus intolerance. Yet, we conclude, that the movement, although conservative in spirit and quantitative membership, attracted as activists largely lay and urban people, most of whom in varying degrees had already accepted the premises of modernization. That so many of these were men with no stake in an ever-increasingly secular society, over which they had no control, created the turbulence and image of radicalism which characterized the movement of the Brothers.

This study was originally prepared as a Ph.D. thesis submitted to Princeton University in 1960. The decision to undertake the study of the Society of the Muslim Brothers was made in the spring of 1952 following a few months' observation of the political life of prerevolutionary Egypt—the Egypt which had abrogated her treaty of alliance with England and was attempting, once again, by diplomacy and violence to resolve the question of her ultimate relationship with that nation. The actual research in the field began in July 1953 and ended in April 1955. The research was sporadically curtailed, often enriched, and always complicated by the growing pains of a revolutionary government, tensions between this military government and the Society of the Muslim Brothers, a cleavage within the Society itself, two official dissolutions of the Society, a struggle for power within the government in which the Society became involved, a near assassination of Nasir, at that time Prime Minister and, subsequently, six hangings and hundreds of incarcerations. The objective course and circumstances of this research were never easy and were further complicated because the study concerned a movement whose historic unfolding has been accompanied by an inordinate measure of both positive and negative hysteria which I have tried, probably unsuccessfully, to dispel.

In this revision I have not attempted, as noted, to update the work to the events of 1965–6. I have taken the liberty to delete and summarize some material and much documentation which seemed necessary at the time of the original writing. And I have not felt it necesary, in either the bibliography or text and notes, to refer to the increasingly voluminous literature on modern Egypt which has appeared since this study was written, except where my subject was central to the analysis of modern Egypt or where new information became available. In this respect, the study as originally conceived was never intended to be more than a small aspect of the history of modern Egypt.

My gratitude is great to many people and institutions. The Fulbright Foundation made possible my first visit to Egypt. The Ford Foundation generously supported the research and special thanks go to Mr Cleon O. Swayzee and his staff. Mr. John Marshall of the Rockefeller Foundation helped to support the initial writing of the study. Princeton University's Department of Oriental Languages and Literature generously supported my graduate education in general and the completion of this study in particular. I record the following names only because they were most directly involved: Professor T. Cuyler Young who encouraged me on; and R. Bayly Winder who read the study as it was written.

My thanks to friends and colleagues are many but I single out only a few. 'Chris' Carson, now of AID, will recognize many hours of debate concerning the meaning of this movement and the 'facts' about it. So, too, will William R. Brown now also of AID. Professor William D. Schorger of The University of Michigan Centre for Near Eastern and North African Studies made possible the opportunity to re-think and re-write the study. In appreciation I have given to the Centre at Michigan, to be held in a special research collection, all the material I collected while in the field. I think it to be the most complete collection extant.

Many of my graduate students were of assistance. Ahmad Joudah helped during the research in Cairo with translations and discussions about the meaning of events. He also, along with Charles D. Smith, Jr, read the completed text, checked references, and made valuable comments. James Jankowski, now teaching at the University of Colorado, did the same. Leland L. Bowie, Patricia Fincher, and Paula Ajay did the typing and proofing of this manuscript.

My thanks are also due to Miss Katharine Duff, who edited the book for press and to Mr R. E. Thompson, who made the Index.

For the end I have reserved the most important acknowledgements. To the scores of Egyptians, Muslim Brothers, and others, who welcomed and talked to me (or were hostile), from whom I learned much, my thanks are without limit. To my family, who suffered through it all, mere words would be meaningless.

June 1968 R. P. M.

CONTENTS

PART II ORGANIZATION

PART III IDEOLOGY

PART IV CONCLUSION

NOTE ON ABBREVIATIONS AND TRANSLITERATION

On the assumption that the subject of this study has had its moment in history, and that for very few of its leaders will historians reserve a place larger than a footnote, if that, we have decided to dispense with the paraphernalia of orientalist scholarship—the diacritical marks—in our text. Without meaning to denigrate the human beings in this story, we believe simply that the ephemera and trivia which constitute the bulk of our sources do not warrant the massively time-consuming and heart-breaking (for authors, typists, printers, and proof-readers) demonstration of transliteration erudition so much now the vogue. While applauding the development of a more commonly accepted 'source language', we feel that for this unorthodox study in contemporary history, some more unorthodox manner of handling documentation is justified. Thus, we have dropped most of the diacritical marks from the text, dropped the use of the definite article before names and places except where the full name is used or grammatical construction requires it, and followed the popular rather than correct spelling, in most instances, for well-known places and names. Similarly, the sources most often used in the study have been listed below in the abbreviated form in which they appear in the footnotes, again, to ease the mechanical aspect of the study. For Arabic magazines, newspapers, and pamphlets, a key letter has been used to precede an alphabetically abbreviated title: 'M' for *majalla;* 'J' for *jarīda;* 'R' for *risāla*. Likewise, references to the works most used are either alphabetically abbreviated after the author's name or in shortened title. While they have been simplified in the text, full and completely transliterated references are available either in this introductory explanation or in the Bibliography. Our style of transliteration will be obvious to those who know Arabic and irrelevant to those who do not.

1. ARABIC NEWSPAPERS

JA	*al-Ahrām*
JAK	*al-Akhbār*
JAY	*Akhbār al-Yawm*
JIM	*al-Ikhwān al-Muslimin*
JJ	*al-Jumhūriyya*
JM	*al-Miṣrī*
JSU	*Ṣawt al-Umma*
JWM	*al-Wafd al-Miṣrī*

2. ARABIC MAGAZINES AND PERIODICALS

MAI	*Ākhir Laḥẓa*
MAS	*Ākhir Sāʿa*
MDA	*al-Daʿwa*
MIDHM	*al-Idhāʿa al-Miṣriyya*
MIM	*al-Ikhwān al-Muslimūn*
MIT	*al-Ithnayn*
MJJ	*al-Jil al-Jadīd*
MMB	*al-Mabāḥith*
MMN	*al-Muslimūn*
MMR	*al-Muṣawwar*
MR	*al-Risāla*
MRY	*Rūz al-Yūsuf*
MS	*al-Shihāb*
MTH	*al-Thawra*
MTR	*al-Taḥrīr*

3. WESTERN MAGAZINES AND PERIODICALS

AA	*L'Afrique et l'Asie*
COC	*Cahiers de l'Orient contemporain*
MEA	*Middle East Affairs*
MEJ	*Middle East Journal*
MW	*The Muslim World*

4. 'OFFICIAL' *RASA'IL* AND PUBLICATIONS

RA	*al-Anāshīd.*
RBAWY	*Bayn al-ams wa'l-yawm.*
RD	*Dustūruna.*
RDFTJ	*Da'watuna fi ṭawr jadīd.*
RIJA	*al-'Ibāda—jawharuha wa-āfāquha.*
RIMTRQ	*al-Ikhwān al-Muslimūn taḥt rāyat al-Qu'rān.*
RJ	*al-Jihād.*
RM	*al-Muḥammadiyya.*
RMAUK	*Min ādāb al-usra wa'l-katība.*
RMBBM	*al-Mar'a bayn al-bayt wa'l-mujtama'.*
RMFDNI	*Mushkilātuna fi daw' al-niẓām al-Islāmī.*
RMI	*al-Mujtama' al-Islāmi.*
RMKH	*al-Mu'tamar al-khāmis.*
RNJM	*Naḥw jīl Muslim.*
RNUNA	*Niẓām al-usar nash'atuha wa-ahdāfuha.*
RNURT	*Niẓām al-usar wa-risālat al-ta'ālīm.*
RS	*Ila al-shabāb.*
RTH	*al-Rasā'il al-thalāth* (including the three following):[1]
RD	*Da'watuna.*
RIASSN	*Ila ayy shay' nad'u al-nās.*
RNN	*Naḥw al-nūr*
RTI	*al-Tashrī' al-Islāmī.*
RUIM	*al-Risāla al-ūla li'l-Akhawāt al-Muslimāt.*
Barnāmaj	*Barnāmaj thaqāfi mihani li'l-mudarrisīn.*
al-Bayān	*al-Bayān alladhi aqarrathu al-hay'a al-tasīsiyya li'l-Ikhwān al-Muslimīn.* fi Ijtima'iha ghayr al-'ādi al-mun'aqid bi'l-Markaz al-

[1] Cited as *RTH: D, RTH: IASSN,* and *RTH: NN.*

	ʿĀmm fi yawm al-jumʿa 10 dhu al-qida 1371 (1 August 1952).
LANR	*al-Lāʾiḥa al-Āmma liʾl-nashāṭ al-riyaḍī.*
LD	*al-Lāʾiḥa al-dākhiliyya al-ʿĀmma liʾl-Ikhwān al-Muslimīn*
LDQI	*al-Lāʾiḥa al-dākhiliyya li-qism al-ittiṣal.*
Manhaj al jumʿa	*al-Manhaj al-dirāsi al-Islāmī li-madrasat al-jumʿa.*
Manhaj al-usar	*al-Manhaj al-dirāsi al-Islāmī li-Ikhwān al-usar.*
QA	*Qanūn al-niẓām al-asāsi li-hayʾat al-Ikhwān al-Muslimīn al-ʿĀmma.*

5. WORKS IN ARABIC BY MUSLIM BROTHERS[2]

ʿAssāl, *BKA*	Fathi al-ʿAssāl. *Ḥasan al-Bannāʾ kamāʿaraftuhu.* 1953.
ʿAwda, *IBJAWAU*	ʿAbd al-Qādir ʿAwda. *al-Islām bayn jahl abnāʾihi wa-ajz ʿulamāʾihi.* 1952.
—*IWAQ*	—*al-Islām wa-awḍāʿuna al-qānūniyya.* 1951.
—*IWAS*	—*al-Islām wa-awḍāʿuna al-siyāsiyya.* 1951.
—*MWHFI*	—*al-Māl waʾl-ḥukm fiʾl-Islām.* 1951.
—*TJIMQW*	—*al-Tashrīʿ al-jināʾi al-Islāmī muqaranan biʾl-qānūn al-waḍʿi.* 1949. 3 vols.
Bannā, *MISI*	ʿAbd al-Bāsiṭ al-Bannāʾ. *Mata . . . ila . . . shahīd al-Islām.* [*c.* 1953].
—*TIWMI*	—*Tāj al-Islām wa-malḥamat al-imām.* [*c.* 1952].
Būhī, *IAM*	Muḥ. Labīb al-Būhī. *al-Ikhwān ayyām al-miḥna* [*c.* 1950–2].

[2] Published in Cairo unless otherwise stated.

—*IWR*	—*al-Imān wa'l-rajul*. [*c*. 1950–1].
—*MSI*	—*Ma' shuhadā' al-Ikhwān*. [*c*. 1952–3].
Ghazālī, *FMD*	Muḥ. al-Ghazālī. *Fi mawkab al-da'wa*. 1954.
—*IIS*	—*al-Islām wa'l-istibdād al-siyāsī*. [*c*. 1950–1].
IMI	—*al-Islām wa'l-manāhij al-ishtirākiyya*. 1951.
—*IMABSR*	—*al-Islām al-muftara 'alayh bayn al-shuyū'īyīn wa'l-ra'smālīyīn*. 3rd ed., 1953.
—*IWAI*	—*al-Islām wa'l-awḍā' al-iqtiṣādiyya*. 3rd ed., 1952.
—*MHN*	—*Min hunā na'lam*. 4th ed., 1954. (Tr. Isma'il R.Faruqi. *Our Beginning in Wisdom*. Washington, 1953.)
—*TFDWH*	—*Ta'ammulāt fi'l-dīn wa'l-ḥayāt*. 1951.
—*TWTBMI*	—*al-Ta'aṣṣub wa'l-tasāmuḥ bayn al-Islām wa'l-masīḥiyya*. [*c*. 1953–4].
Ḥajjājī, *IMAM*	Aḥmad Anis al-Ḥajjājī. *al-Imām*. 1950–2. 2 vols.
—*RLAT*	—*al-Rajul alladhi ash'al al-thawra*. 1952.
—*RMM*	—*Risāla min al-mirrīkh*. n.d.
—*RWR*	—*Ruḥ wa-rayḥān*. 1946.
Ḥamīd, *QSIHB*	—Fatḥi 'Abd al-Ḥamīd. *Qaḍīyat al shahīd Ḥasan al-Bannā'*. 1954.
Jundī, *QDHRTM*	Anwar al-Jundī. *Qā'id al-da'wa: ḥayāt raju wa-tarīkh madrasa*. 1946.
Khūlī, *QDIHB*	'Abd al-Khabīr al-Khūlī. *Qā'id al-da'wa al-Islāmiyya Hasan al-Bannā'*. 1952.
Mudh.	Ḥasan al-Bannā'. *Mudhakkarāt al-da'wa wa'l-dā'īya*. [*c*. 1951].
Quṭb, *AIFI*	Sayyid Quṭb, *al-'Adālat al-*

	ijtimā'iyya fi'l-Islām. 3rd ed., n.d. (Tr. John B. Hardie. *Social Justice in Islam.* Washington, 1955.)
—DI	—*Dirāsāt Islāmiyya.* 1953.
—*MIWR*	—*Ma'rakat al-Islām wa'l-ra'smāliyya.* 1952.
—*SAWI*	—*al-Salām al-'ālamī wa'l-Islām.* 1951.
Ramaḍān, *FAAI*	Sa'īd Ramaḍān. *Fi āfaq al-'ālam al-Islāmī.* [1953–4?].
—*MT*	—*Ma'ālim al-ṭarīq.* Damascus, 1955.
Sammān, *IM*	Muḥ. 'Abd Allāh al-Sammān. *al-Islām al-muṣaffa.* 1954.
Sharif, *IMFHF*	Kamil Ismā'il Sharīf. *al-Ikhwān al-Muslimūn fi ḥarb Filasṭīn.* 2nd ed. [*c.* 1952–3].

6. WORKS IN ARABIC BY OTHER WRITERS

Aḥmad, *Mīzān*	Muḥ. Ḥasan Aḥmad [*pseud.*]. *al-Ikhwān al-Muslimūn fi'l-Mīzān.* [*c.* 1947–8].
Aḥmad, *Nahḍa*	Muḥ. Ḥabīb Aḥmad. *Nahḍat al-shu'ūb al-Islāmiyya fi'l-'Aṣr al-ḥadīth.* 1952–3.
Ḥusaynī, *Ikhwān*	Musa Isḥāq al-Ḥusaynī. *al-Ikhwān al-Muslimūn: kubra al-ḥarakāt al-Islāmiyya al-hadītha.* 1st ed., Beirut, 1952. (Tr. John F. Brown *et al. The Moslem Brethren.* Beirut, 1956.)
IRHAB	[RCC]. *al-Ikhwān wa'l-irhāb.* [1955].
Rāfi'i, *Thawra*	'Abd al-Raḥmān al-Rāfi'i. *Fi 'qāb al-thawra al-Miṣriyya.* 1947–51. 3 vols.
Sādāt, *Ṣafaḥāt*	Anwar al-Sādāt. *Ṣafaḥāt majhūla.*

	1954. (Eng. ed. *Revolt on the Nile*. New York, 1957.)
Zaki, *Ikhwān*	Muḥ. Shawqi Zaki. *al-Ikhwān al-Muslimūn wa'l-mujtama' al-Miṣrī*. 1954.

7. DOCUMENTS

Qaḍiyat al-jīb	*al-Ḥukm* fi qadīyat al-niyāba al-'Umūmīyya, raqm 2294, 1950, al-Khassa b-qadīyat sayyārat al-jīb al-sādir fi 18 Māris 1951.
Qaḍiyat Majlis al-Dawla.	Majlis al-Dawla, al-qaḍiyya raqm 190, sana 'Q', Dā'irat Waqfal-Tanfīdh b-riyāsat ḥaḍrat saḥib al-'izza Muḥammad Sāmi Māzin.
Qaḍiyat al-Nuqrāshi	*al-Ḥukm* fi qaḍīyat al-jinayya al-'Askariyya, aqm 5 'Abidin, 1949, al-khāṣṣab-maqtal al-maghfūr lahu dawlat Mahmūd Fahmi al-Nuqrāshi Bāshā, al-ṣādir fi 13 Uktūqar 1949.

[The following items are not properly documents, because they are partisan publications, but despite their editorialized context they do contain parts of the above and other legal proceedings in which the Brothers were involved.]

Aqwāl wa-ta'dhīb	Dar al-Fikr al-Islāmī. *Qaḍāya al-Ikhwān*: Qaḍīyat sayyārat al-jīb; aqwāl kibār al-shuhūd waḥawādith al-ta'dhīb. [*c.* 1951].
Ḥaythiyāt wa-ḥukm	Dar-al-Fikr al-Islāmī. *Qadāya al-Ikhwān*: Qaḍīyat sayyārat al-jīb; al-ḥaythiyāt wa-naṣṣ al-ḥukm. [*c.* 1951].
Kīra, *Maḥkama*	Kamāl Kīra, ed. *Maḥkamat al-sha'b*. 1954–5. 2 vols.

THE SOCIETY
OF THE
MUSLIM BROTHERS

PART I · HISTORY

I

HASAN AL-BANNA AND THE FOUNDING OF THE SOCIETY OF THE MUSLIM BROTHERS[1]

HASAN AL-BANNA

HASAN AL-BANNA was born in October 1906, in the province of Buhayra, in the small town of Mahmudiyya, about ninety miles north-west of Cairo. His father, Shaykh Ahmad 'Abd al-Rahman al-Banna al-Sa'ati, was the local *ma'dhun*, *imam* and teacher for the mosque, and student and author of various works on the *hadith*; he had been educated at Azhar University at the time of Shaykh Muhammad 'Abduh.[2] In between his religious duties, reading, and studying, he practised the art of watch repairing, which, along

[1] The primary source for the life of Banna is his own autobiographical material collected and compiled from the pages of the Society's newspapers and magazines. The first book of memoirs, presumably gathered together by a Syrian (see *MDA* (15 Apr. 1951), 8), appeared in Beirut and was called *Mudhakkarat Hasan al-Banna*, vol. 1 (n.d.). It dealt with the life of Banna and the first few years of the history of the movement. A Cairo edition, *Mudhakkarat al-da'wa wa'l-da'iyya* (n.d.), is the original text of the Beirut edition with additions by an Egyptian which take the story to the beginning of World War II. Presumably the first text appeared in Beirut shortly after the first major dissolution of the Society in 1948 and the second in the early period of its reorganization after 1950. The Cairo edition will be used for this study and will be noted hereafter simply as *Mudh.* Because this chapter is largely based on this material, references will be noted, in parentheses, in the body of the study. Unfortunately, there are no critical sources, to our knowledge, with which to compare this autobiographical material.

For insights into the life, personality, and influence of Banna, the unofficial but authoritative journal *Majallat al-Da'wa* is useful; see especially the commemorative issues which appeared on the anniversary of Banna's death: *MDA*, 13 Feb. 1951; 12 Feb. 1952; 10 Feb. 1953; 16 Feb. 1954; 15 Feb. 1955. The best and earliest summary and analysis of the data available on Banna is Husayni, *Ikhwan*, pp. 7–8, 12–19, 40–62.

[2] Husayni, *Ikhwan*, p. 42, lists among his works two arrangements of the legists Shaf'i and Ibn Hanbal. Husayni draws his material from the only lengthy treatment of the life and background of Banna's father, in Hajjaji, *RWR*, 101–22.

with his broad classical and traditional learning and piety, he passed on to his son.

Hasan, the eldest of five sons, began his formal education at the age of eight[3] at a *kuttab* school.[4] His teacher, Shaykh Muhammad Zahran, was among the first, after his father, who profoundly affected his development.

At the age of twelve, Banna was enrolled in a primary school, where he quickly joined the first of the many religious societies to which he committed himself through the phases of his development. His teacher there—another formative influence—organized and, at first, directed the Society for Moral Behaviour, the purpose of which was to sensitize its members to moral offences. A system of increasingly burdensome fines was levied on all members who cursed their fellows and their families, or cursed in the name of religion. Within a short time, Banna became the leader of the society (pp. 6–7).

Not satisfied with this, some of the younger boys formed another group called the Society for the Prevention of the Forbidden, whose work was intended to reach deeper into the town life. One of their main activities was the composition and distribution of secret and often threatening letters, to those they regarded as living in violation of the teachings of Islam (pp. 8–9).

It was during this early part of his life that Banna witnessed his first *dhikr*, the mystic circle of the Order of the Hasafiyya Brothers. Deeply impressed, he became involved with this particular order for the next twenty years, and with Sufism in a special way for most of his life. He read avidly from the materials available on the founders of the order and on Sufism, becoming, in the meantime, an ardent member of the *dhikr* circles and a disciple of its leading shaykh (pp. 10–14).

These new associates inspired the creation of yet another organization, called the Hasafiyya Society for Charity, with the twofold aim: to fight for the preservation of Islamic morality, and to resist the work of the Christian missionaries in the town. Banna, at the age of thirteen, became its secretary, and at its head stood Ahmad al-Sukkari, a young man whom he had come to know in the *dhikr* circles, and who afterwards played an important part in developing the idea of the Society of the Muslim Brothers. It was this group which Banna himself later saw as the root and forerunner of the Society (p. 16).

Banna's last year at the primary school coincided with the out-

[3] See an account by Banna's father of his infancy and pre-school days, *MMR* (29 Aug. 1952), 16.

[4] See the recollection of these days 'in the father's Library' by his brother Abd al-Rahman, *MDA* (13 Feb. 1951), 3, 30.

break of the Revolution of 1919. As a student, he participated in demonstrations which erupted in and out of school, and in the composition and recitation of nationalistic poetry. He was afterwards to remember with special bitterness the sight of British forces in occupation of his home town at this time (pp. 22–5). He took these memories with him as he prepared, when just under fourteen, to enroll in the Primary Teachers' Training School at Damanhur, thirteen miles south-west of Mahmudiyya. His newly acquired Sufism became more intense and in 1922 he was accepted as a fully initiated member. For a time, he even adopted the tasselled turban and white outer garment of the order (pp. 14–16, 19–22).[5]

By now his whole outlook was permeated with the teachings of Sufism and with those of the towering figure of Abu Hamid al-Ghazzali (A.D. 1058–1111). The medieval master's views on learning, derived by Banna from the *Ihya' 'Ulum al-Din*, persuaded him of the futility of further formal education. At stake was the final stage in his formal training: higher education in the capital city. In his last year at the Teachers' Training School, Banna recalls struggling within himself, setting against his admitted 'love of learning' and his belief in 'the benefits of learning for individual and society', the Ghazzalian ordering of the sciences and knowledge, and the view that learning was to be confined to what was necessary 'to fulfil the religious duties and earn a livelihood' (p. 29). This attitude towards learning was a basic feature of his preaching to his first followers in the Society; and, throughout his career, it sustained and reinforced what one might call the 'practical and at the same time other-worldly' qualities of his mind. For the time being, however, his teachers persuaded him to put aside his doubts and go on to higher education. At the age of sixteen, in 1923, he left the Teachers' Training School; and later in that same year he entered Dar al-'Ulum in Cairo (pp. 28–9). Dar al-'Ulum had been founded in 1873 as the first Egyptian attempt to provide 'modern' higher learning (sciences) in addition to the traditional religious sciences which were specialities of the traditional and ancient university of al-Azhar. It became essentially a higher teacher-training school, and, with the development of the secular university system in Egypt, it became more and more traditional.

By this time Banna's intellectual and emotional apparatus was taking shape. The two continuous influences on his training so far had been classical Islamic learning and the emotional discipline of Sufism. The extra-academic influence of his father and his teachers had been more important than his formal education. He

[5] See also Husayni, *Ikhwan*, p. 47.

prided himself on going beyond the dictates of his 'academic programme'. Besides his religious studies he read widely: the literature of Sufism, biographies of the Prophet, and historic tales of heroism—defence of 'the homeland', 'zealotry in defence of religion', and 'struggle in the path of God'. It is not clear whether this last type of reading preceded or followed his awareness of Egypt's occupied status, but he clearly indicates its relationship to this awareness.[6]

All these influences in his life were given a 'practical' orientation by his teachers,[7] and 'practical' application in the numerous societies with which he became involved. A revealing instance of his religious ardour and convictions is the legendary tale, perhaps apocryphal but undoubtedly symbolic, of his single-handed and successful effort, at the age of ten, to have an 'obscene' statue of a semi-naked woman which was displayed on one of the river boats removed and destroyed by the police.[8] This propensity for action was to be shaped into new and sharper perspectives by the experience of Cairo.

Banna's arrival in Cairo coincided with the period of intense political and intellectual ferment which marked the 1920s in Egypt. Surveying the scene with 'the eyes of a religious villager',[9] Banna isolated what were to him the serious problems: the disputed control of Egypt between the Wafd and Liberal Constitutionalist parties, and the vociferous political debating, with the consequence of 'disunity', which followed in the wake of the revolution of 1919; the post-war 'orientations to apostasy and nihilism' which were engulfing the Muslim world; the attacks on tradition and orthodoxy—emboldened by the 'Kemalist revolt' in Turkey—which were organized into a movement for the 'intellectual and social emancipation' of Egypt; the 'non-Islamic' currents in the newly reorganized Egyptian University, whose inspiration seemed to be the notion that 'the University could not be a lay university unless it revolted against religion and fought the social tradition which derived from it'; the secularist and libertarian 'literary and social salons', societies, and parties; and 'the books, newspapers, and magazines' which propagated those ideas whose sole goal was 'the weakening of the influence of religion' (pp. 46–8).[10]

Banna, with friends of like mind, reacted to this picture of

[6] Beside the works listed by Banna (p. 27), *Husayni*, *Ikhwan*, pp. 7, 48–9.

[7] Ibid., p. 46.

[8] The story is told by his father among others in *MMR* (29 Aug. 1952), 16 f.

[9] Ahmad, *Nahda*, p. 105.

[10] See also Jundi, *QDHRTM*, pp. 137–9; and Husayni, *Ikhwan*, pp. 10–11.

Cairo: 'No one but God knows how many nights we spent reviewing the state of the nation . . . analysing the sickness, and thinking of the possible remedies. So disturbed were we that we reached the point of tears.'[11]

In Cairo Banna made contact with the Hasafiyya, and in his second year he joined another religious group, the Islamic Society for Nobility of Character, which organized lectures on Islamic subjects;[12] but first the one and then the other group seemed to him to be inadequate to span the gulf which he saw separating Muslims from the faith and its teaching. Out of a growing conviction that 'the Mosque alone did not suffice' to bring the faith to the people, he organized a group of students from the Azhar University and from Dar al-'Ulum who were willing to train for the task of 'preaching and guidance'. They offered their services to the mosques and also—a more important move which was afterwards to be so successful—to the 'people's institutes' (the coffee-houses and other popular meeting-places) (pp. 44–6). Some of these students, after their training in Cairo, were sent out all over the Egyptian countryside to take up their various appointments and professions, and not only to carry 'the call to the message of Islam',[13] but also, eventually, to disseminate the idea of the Society of the Muslim Brothers.

Banna's concern with the defection of 'educated youth' from the 'Islamic way of life' led him to seek the counsels of his religious and lay elders. He often went to the Salafiyya book store, at that time directed by Muhibb al-Din al-Khatib; he frequented the heir to the mantle of Muhammad 'Abduh, the Syrian Rashid Rida, editor of the magazine *al-Manar*; and he came to be a loyal admirer of Farid Wajdi and Ahmad Taymur Pasha, all partisans, as he saw it, of the 'Islamic cause' (pp. 49–50, 57–8). He carried his anxiety, finally, to the shaykhs of Azhar University, the intellectual centre of Islam, and bitterly disputed their ineffective opposition and apparent resignation in the face of 'the missionary and atheistic currents' disrupting Islamic society. The 'time for action', he felt and argued, was at hand (pp. 50–4).[14] His own early experiences had prepared him to feel keenly on the matter; for the rest of his life he carried sharp and painful memories of the

[11] *RMKH*, p. 7.

[12] See the list of religious societies in Heyworth-Dunne, *Modern Egypt*, p. 30.

[13] See RMKH, p. 6.

[14] Banna claims that out of this exchange of opinion came the two important 'Islamic developments' of 1927: the establishment of the Young Men's Muslim Association (YMMA) modelled on the YMCA and the YMHA; and the founding of the magazine designed to be a 'voice of Islam', *Majallat al-Fath*. See *MDA* (15 Feb. 1955), 18, for information, on Banna's first published articles, which appeared in *Majallat al-Fath*.

profound spiritual malaise which overwhelmed this period of his life in Cairo in his relations with religious 'officialdom'. With more clarity he began to see the kind of 'action' necessary to save Islamic society, and his own role in it.

In his last year at Dar al-'Ulum, his class was called on to write an essay on the subject 'Explain the greatest of your hopes after completion of your studies and show how you will prepare yourselves for their realization.' Banna's essay began: 'I believe that the best people are those who . . . achieve their happiness by making others happy and in counselling them.' This, he decided, could best be achieved in either of two ways. The first was 'the path of true Sufism—sincerity and work' in the service of humanity. The second was 'the way of teaching and counselling, which is similar to the first in requiring sincerity and work, but distinct from it because of its involvement with people'. 'I believe', he added, 'that my people, because of the political stages through which they have passed, the social influences which have passed through them, and under the impact of western civilization . . . materialist philosophy, and *franji* [foreign] traditions, have departed from the goals of their faith.' As a result, the heritage of youth has been a 'corrupted' faith; 'doubt and perplexity' have overwhelmed them and 'rather than faith there is apostasy'. In this situation, Banna saw his mission in life as the reversal of these trends; he would become 'a counsellor and a teacher', giving himself, by day to the children and by night to their parents, to the task of teaching 'the objectives of religion and the sources of their well-being and happiness in life'. He would bring to this mission 'perseverance and sacrifice', study and understanding, and a body willing to face hardship and a soul which he had 'sold to God'. 'That is a covenant between me and my God', he concluded (pp. 54–7).[15]

The now dedicated young man graduated from Dar al-'Ulum in the summer of 1927 at the age of twenty-one. For a short time he considered the possibility of joining one of the annual governmental missions for education abroad, but for unknown reasons he did not do so (pp. 58–9).[16] Instead, he accepted an appointment in the state school system. His assigned post was to teach Arabic in a primary school in the Suez Canal Zone city of Isma'iliyya. He remained a schoolmaster until his resignation in 1946, nineteen years later. On 19 September 1927 he left Cairo for his new home and his new job (pp. 59–61).

[15] See also Hajjaji, *RWR*, pp. 85–98, for a detailed and lyrical description of the 'anguished' writing of the essay.

[16] Members themselves have raised the important question as to what might have happened had Banna gone abroad; see *MDA* (15 Feb. 1955), 18; and Ahmad, *Nahda*, p. 104.

THE FOUNDING OF THE ORGANIZATION

From the first Banna began to take an active part in the life of the community of Isma'iliyya. Through the mosque and the school he familiarized himself with the chief personalities, religious and lay, in the town. Soon, as he had promised himself in his graduating essay, he was conducting not only his day classes, but also night instruction for the children's parents. At this time, these were mostly labourers, small merchants, and civil servants (pp. 61–2).[17] While in his early days he used the school and mosque, Banna again resorted to the coffee-houses, as he had done in Cairo, to create an audience; discussion in the mosque prompted this move. It was his practice to make his speech, notice which listeners were most affected, and take these in smaller groups to other rooms for teaching, preaching, and discussion of the cause of Islam. He also sought at this time to acquaint himself with and penetrate the sources of power in the community. These he identified as (1) the *'ulama'*; (2) the shaykhs of the Sufi orders; (3) the 'elders,' by which he meant the leading families and groupings in the broadest sense; and (4) the 'clubs' (social and religious societies). To these, in their turn, he directed his attention, seeking thereby to influence the opinion-makers (pp. 62–71).

When Banna was assigned to Isma'iliyya, he admitted that he did not know its 'exact' location, except that as for most Egyptians, the city was identified with the Suez Canal and all that it implied. His observations of the community heightened his awareness of the role assigned to the city as a focal point, both of the British military occupation and of foreign 'economic occupation'. Here were not only the British military camps, but, equally hateful to Banna, the Suez Canal Company; complete foreign domination of the public utilities; and the conspicuously luxurious homes of the foreigners overlooking the 'miserable' homes of their workers. Even the street signs in the popular Egyptian quarters, he observed, were written in 'the language of the economic occupation' (p. 73).

While his attention was necessarily focused on his new environment, he did not let himself forget Cairo, with both its sins and its hope. He maintained, therefore, his contacts with the 'Islamic groups' there, and with the friends with whom he had pledged himself to serve 'the message of Islam'. He supported the creation in 1927 of the Young Men's Muslim Association and acted as local agent for the newly founded *Majallat al-Fath*, the organ of conservative Islamic groupings at that time, edited by

[17] See also 'Assal, *BKA*, pp. 54–5.

Muhībb al-Dīn al-Khatīb, the director of the Salafiyya bookshop and one of the founding members of the YMMA (pp. 71–2).[18]

Very shortly after the founding of the YMMA in Cairo, Banna's own movement was born. In Dhu al-Qi'da, 1347—or March 1928, as recorded by Banna[19]—six members of the British camp labour force came to see him, and with their words formally launched the Society of the Muslim Brothers. What they actually said cannot be verified. What it is claimed that they said is worth noting: first, as a highly dramatized but very accurate summing-up of the inspiration and spirit of the movement; and, secondly, as a revealing insight into what came to be a major source of its strength—the relationship between the leader and the led. The account goes as follows: the men came to Banna and, after thanking him for his teaching, said:

> We have heard and we have become aware and we have been affected. We know not the practical way to reach the glory [*'izza*] of Islam and to serve the welfare of Muslims. We are weary of this life of humiliation and restriction. Lo, we see that the Arabs and the Muslims have no status [*manzila*] and no dignity [*karama*]. They are not more than mere hirelings belonging to the foreigners. We possess nothing but this blood . . . and these souls . . . and these few coins. . . . We are unable to perceive the road to action as you perceive it, or to know the path to the service of the fatherland [*watan*], the religion, and the nation [*'umma*] as you know it. All that we desire now is to present you with all that we possess, to be acquitted by God of the responsibility, and for you to be responsible before Him for us and for what we must do. If a group contracts with God sincerely that it live for His religion and die in His service, seeking only His satisfaction, then its worthiness will assure its success however small its numbers or weak its means.

Banna, duly moved, accepted the burden imposed on him, and together they took an oath to God to be 'troops [*jund*] for the message of Islam'. The name was selected by Banna: 'We are brothers in the service of Islam; hence, we are "the Muslim Brothers" ' (pp. 73–4).[20]

[18] See n. 14, above. Banna never considered the YMMA broad enough in scope to command his full and undivided attention.

[19] Dhu al-Qi'da 1347 translates correctly into April–May 1929, as observed by Heyworth-Dunne, *Modern Egypt*, p. 15, and F. Rosenthal, 'The "Muslim Brethren" of Egypt', *MW* (Oct. 1947), 278. Banna gives the above Arabic date and March 1928. Husayni, *Ikhwan*, p. 17, makes it March 1928 without, however, reference to a Hijra date. Everyone else has followed one or another without reference to the conflict. The tenth anniversary of the Society was celebrated in January 1939, making the 1929 date more appropriate, but the twentieth anniversary was celebrated in September 1948. Most members accepted 1928 as accurate, and it was incorporated in Article 1 of the Society's regulations, *QA*, p. 5, along with the Hijra date above. Cf. Harris, *Nationalism and Revolution*, p. 150.

[20] See also Husayni, *Ikhwan*, pp. 17–19; and Banna, *TIWMI*, pp. 18–25.

ISMAʿILIYYA: 1928–32

In the first three years of the life of the Society, its primary goal was the enlargement of its membership in and around Ismaʿiliyya. Banna and selected deputies pursued this goal by direct contact, touring the countryside on weekends and during vacations, preaching most usually in the mosques but also in the homes, clubs, and other meeting-places of the people. The use of the mosques gave the speakers the legitimacy and respectability they needed. Direct communication with the people in their homes, at their work, and in their places of leisure added to that legitimacy the quality of sincerity and the personal touch. Within four years, there were branches along the eastern edge of the Delta in Ismaʿiliyya, Port Saʿid, Suez, and abu-Suwayr, and on the western edge as far as Shubra Khit; there was also minor contact with Cairo (pp. 84–6, 100–8).

In Ismaʿiliyya, the centre of activity, the Society took an old house as headquarters (p. 75). Contributions (including £E500 from the Suez Canal Company) and loans from local merchants helped to finance the building of a mosque completed in 1930 (pp. 82–6, 93–6); to this were afterwards added a school for boys and a club (pp. 96–8), and a school for girls (pp. 109–10). All new branches were founded on the same pattern: the establishment of the headquarters was followed by the creation of some project or another—a mosque, a school, a club, or a small home industry—which came to serve as a focus for the interest or activities of the community.[21]

But as quickly as the Society spread, so also did there appear antipathy and resistance to it, prophetic of what was to come in later years on a scale perhaps undreamed of by Banna. At this time, in 1930, hostility was confined to complaints about the movement and its intentions towards the ministry of Ismaʿil Sidqi Pasha. The charges made—some by Christians, Banna felt—

There is some dispute about this widely accepted version of the founding of the organization. Partisans of Ahmad al-Sukkari, Banna's lifelong friend and deputy in the Society until his dismissal in 1947, argue that Banna overstates his own role in the story; that Sukkari, as early as their common involvement in the Hasafiyya Order, conceived the idea; that it grew from their common experience in the Order; and that in Cairo it took more definite shape among his friends there than Banna has suggested. After Sukkari left the organization, this view was presented but on the whole rejected by the membership. Banna has undoubtedly emphasized his centrality to the movement's inception, but it is equally true that he never concealed the part played by his long-term associates, especially Sukkari. This is perfectly clear from his own memoirs. And the question is slightly irrelevant, since no observer doubts the centrality of Banna's charisma to the Society's success.

[21] See Husayni, *Ikhwan*, p. 21; and ʿAssal, *BKA*, p. 54.

alleged among other things that Banna was (1) a communist and using communist money for his work; (2) a Wafdist working against Sidqi; (3) a republican working against King Fu'ad; and (4) a criminal violating civil-service provisions against the gathering of funds which he went on to use for illegal purposes. Banna was investigated by the ministry of education on the request of the prime minister but was 'cleared' of all charges (pp. 88–93). If nothing else, the investigation brought the organization to the attention of Sidqi Pasha, who was to have a further role in the unfolding of its history.

After the summer holidays of 1932 Banna asked for and received a transfer to Cairo. His group was already in touch with the Society for Islamic Culture in that city, which was headed by ʿAbd al-Rahman al-Banna, one of his younger and equally religious brothers, who was working in Cairo after obtaining his Higher Commercial Diploma. The two groups merged to form the first branch of the Muslim Brothers in Cairo, the merger providing the Society with an organizational entrée to the 'Islamic circles' of the capital. Most of the members of the Cairo group rapidly became leaders of the Society in its new urban setting (pp. 108–9).[22]

The need to select a deputy to replace Banna in Ismaʿiliyya was the occasion of the first dispute in the Society. Banna's own account of the dispute is as follows. After members close to him had asked him to name a deputy, his nominee was unanimously accepted at a general meeting in the mosque. Soon after, however, partisans of a rival aspirant to the post started a whispering campaign against the new appointee, complaining that the meeting had been unconstitutional, because all the members were not present. Banna discussed the matter with the dissidents and agreed to call another, a widely advertised meeting, but demanded and received their prior agreement to abide by that meeting's decision. Nevertheless, when the second meeting upheld the original appointment the dissidents resorted to new devices. First, they rumoured it about that the new appointee was such a bad manager that the loans made to the Society were in jeopardy. Banna, thereupon, with the consent of the Society's creditors, assumed personal responsibility for the whole sum involved. When his action became known, private contributions were made to him enabling him to repay it in full.

Next, the dissidents, among whom was the treasurer of the Society, preferred legal charges that Banna had misused its funds by distributing them to the newly created branches, including the

[22] See also Banna, *TIWMI*, pp. 34–6; Buhi, *IWR*, pp. 6–7; Khuli, *QDIHB*, p. 26; and *MDA* (12 Feb. 1952), 11.

one headed by his brother in Cairo. The public prosecutor cleared Banna of the charge when the plaintiff admitted that the members themselves would have supported this practice. Banna now decided that the men had obviously lost their sense of the nature of the Society and 'their faith in obedience to the leadership', and that they must be dismissed. Before he could act they resigned, only to begin another whispering campaign about the dangerousness of the Society and its 'secret works', and above all about its denial of 'freedom of opinion'. After Banna arrived in Cairo some of them attempted to discredit him with the principal of the school to which he had been transferred. Banna's friends beat them and were taken to court, but were all acquitted (pp. 119–35).

This is the only dispute in the Society in Banna's time of which so comprehensive an official account exists. Though not one single part of Banna's account is corroborated by independent evidence, it is worthy of note as typifying all the issues which periodically disturbed the Society's inner unity as it became more prominent, and which were to influence its rise to power, the course of its history, and its final demise.

II

CAIRO: THE RISE TO POWER

CAIRO: 1932–9

THE minor crisis which marred Banna's departure from Isma'iliyya did not impair the sense of elation and expectation which accompanied the move to Cairo. Banna shared his time between the demands of his school and the new organization. We have seen that the merger with the Society for Islamic Culture provided an operational starting-point for the latter. The branch in Isma'iliyya declared the transfer of the headquarters to Cairo, and continued to assist the Cairo operation financially. Banna claims to have rejected, as early as this period, offers of 'aid' in exchange for support of 'the political *status-quo*' made by Isma'il Sidqi Pasha, the perennial palace strong man and foe of the Wafd.[1]

Banna took as firm a grip of affairs as his time away from teaching would permit. He followed a regular routine: visiting the headquarters in the morning before school, after school, and in the evening. During these times he attended to all pending business, and lectured to, or merely chatted with, the increasingly large numbers of visitors.[2] The time between the sunset and evening prayer was usually set aside for formal lectures: mostly Qur'anic exegesis simplified for his first listeners, the poor of the district around the headquarters who were 'without learning and without the will for it'.[3]

From these modest beginnings, which did not especially distinguish it from the many religious societies which throve in the capital, the Society of the Muslim Brothers grew, by the outbreak of the second world war, into one of the most important political contestants on the Egyptian scene. Its membership became so diversified as to be virtually representative of every group in Egyptian society. More important, it made effective inroads into the most sought-after of these groups—the civil servants and the

[1] *Mudh.*, p. 109. The offer appears to have been made to the leader of the Cairo Society for Islamic Culture, Banna's brother. If the report is true, this is the first recorded instance of an alleged continuing alliance between Islamic groups and conservative leaders (or the palace) against the Wafd and / or communism. On the early period of the Society in Cairo, see also Hajjaji, *RWR*, pp. 228, 249–53.

[2] Hajjaji, *RWR*, pp. 253–5.

[3] Buhi, *IWR*, pp. 8, 10–11.

students—and the most neglected but potentially powerful, the urban labourers and the peasants.

A series of moves brought the Society's headquarters out of the alleys of the popular quarters to the main streets of Cairo, from little rooms to buildings and land[4] with full-time, paid secretarial and clerical staffs,[5] in keeping with its growing membership, strength, and internal and external activity. Another measure of the growth of the Society was the size and scope of 'general conferences' called periodically to discuss and plan action, or merely (and more usually) to ratify what had already been done or decided. These conferences also provide a general picture of the activity of the years 1932–9.

The first general conference, in May 1933, concerned itself primarily with the problem of Christian missionary activity and the means of combating it. A letter was sent to King Fu'ad outlining the Society's belief in the urgency of bringing the activities of the foreign missionaries under control.[6]

The second general conference, held later that year, dealt with advertising and instructional propaganda, and authorized 'a small company for the establishment of a press for the Muslim Brothers'.[7] This was followed in due course by the founding of the first official journalistic voices of the Society: first, a weekly magazine called *Majallat al-Ikhwan al-Muslimin*; and later, another called *Majallat al-Nadhir*. The press also printed what came to be the most important indoctrination texts for members—and until 1948 the chief sources for the study of the ideas of the movement—the 'messages' (*vasa'il*). Written by Banna, these either reproduced or summarized the Society's extensive communications to the governments of Egypt about the state of Egyptian society and the path of reform, or were messages written to the membership about one or another of the ideas, duties, and responsibilities of membership. The Society also began rapidly to institutionalize oral communication by instituting weekly lectures at all levels in its headquarters and branches, and by lecturing and preaching in the mosques and wherever else a group could be gathered.[8] The problem of winning adherents was for Banna the first stage through which all movements must pass, the stage of 'propaganda, communication, and information'.[9]

[4] See *Mudh.*, p. 144; and Heyworth-Dunne, *Modern Egypt*, p. 17.

[5] Banna, *TIWMI*, pp. 36–8.

[6] *Mudh.*, pp. 145, 155–63.

[7] Ibid., pp. 170–1. The date of the second conference is not certain; that given in the Memoirs, Shuwwal 1350/Feb. 1932, appears to be incorrect.

[8] Ibid., pp. 145, 148–50, 235.

[9] *RMKH*, pp. 20–1; and *RTH*: *D*, pp. 11–12 for an instance of Banna's concern with the 'scientific' use of means of propaganda.

The fourth general conference met to celebrate the coronation of King Faruq in 1937 (see below, p. 16). The third and fifth, in March 1935 and January 1939, were important organizational sessions. The third conference, in direct response to the increase in membership, tackled such questions as membership criteria and responsibilities, and the hierarchy and structure of the Society. In particular, it regularized the formations of 'rovers' (*jawwala*) which had gradually been developing out of the athletic training started in the very earliest days at Isma'iliyya.[10] After the rovers came the creation in 1937 of the 'battalions' (*kata'ib*), also with the aim of forging inner loyalties within the Society[11] and of supplying instruments for putting its ideas into effect. The fifth conference paid particular attention to these questions of the 'orientation' of the 'internal formations'.[12] Banna described 'this as the second stage of the movement, that of 'formation, selection, and preparation'.[13]

The fifth conference was also the tenth anniversary of the movement. These ten years had produced a set of ideas which, though general in form, were the foundations of the ideology of the Society and the substance of its appeal for the next ten years and beyond. These ideas were, essentially, a definition of 'the Islam of the Muslim Brothers'; the insistence on (1) Islam as a total system, complete unto itself, and the final arbiter of life in all its categories; (2) an Islam formulated from and based on its two primary sources, the revelation in the Qur'an and the wisdom of the Prophet in the Sunna; and (3) an Islam applicable to all times and to all places.[14]

Within this framework, Banna defined for the members the scope of the movement of which they were a part: 'The idea of the Muslim Brothers includes in it all categories of reform'; in specific terms he defined the movement as 'a Salafiyya message, a Sunni way, a Sufi truth, a political organization, an athletic group, a cultural-educational union, an economic company, and a social idea'.[15] Among its outstanding qualities were the avoidance of doctrinal disputes, of 'notables and names', and of 'parties and societies'; its concern with organization, programme, and action; and a steady attention to steady growth.[16] From these bases, Banna outlined the attitude of the Society to power and government, the constitution, law, nationalism, and Arabism.[17]

[10] See *Mudh.*, pp. 188–212.

[11] On the rovers, the battalions, and other matters of organization, see Part II of this study.

[12] *Mudh.*, pp. 259–64, esp. pp. 262–3.

[13] *RMKH*, pp. 21–2.

[14] Ibid., pp. 8–14.

[15] Ibid., pp. 14–16.

[16] Ibid., pp. 17–33.

[17] Ibid., pp. 33–64. On these and all other matters of 'ideology' see Part III of this study.

However, the fifth conference also looked to the future, to the dawn of 'a new life' and 'a new struggle'—to the preparation of the third stage of activity of the movement, the stage of 'execution', 'the active stage out of which the perfected fruits of the mission of the Muslim Brothers will appear'. But apparently already under pressure from his youthful partisans (as we shall see in a moment), Banna seized this opportunity of warning 'the anxious and the hasty' that the way was yet long but that there was no other; that success could only follow patience and planning; and that action, not speech, and preparations, not slogans, would guarantee the victory. He set the terms of this stage in his now famous concluding words:

At the time that there will be ready, Oh ye Muslim Brothers, three hundred battalions, each one equipped spiritually with faith and belief, intellectually with science and learning, and physically with training and athletics, at that time you can demand of me to plunge with you through the turbulent oceans and to rend the skies with you and to conquer with you every obstinate tyrant. God willing, I will do it.[18]

Internally, then, the fifth conference of 1939 suggested that the Society had assumed its fundamental shape and was sufficiently strong, in its own mind, to flex its muscles publicly albeit cautiously. Its external activity, limited only by the exigencies of an organization in growth, developed more boldly, more self-assuredly, and more inclusively as its ideas, and the instruments of those ideas, evolved more clearly and precisely.

The letter to King Fu'ad in 1933 concerning missionary activity was the forerunner of many such communications to Egyptian heads of government seeking reform in the name, and within the spirit and letter, of Islam. The most notable of these, a letter addressed in 1936 to King Faruq, his prime minister, Mustafa al-Nahhas Pasha, and the heads of all Arab governments, is a basic statement of the early propositions held by Banna; it appeared as the *risala* called *Nahwa al-Nur* (Towards the Light).[19] These letters and the publication of its weekly magazines constituted the Society's chief form of activity during its first years in Cairo.

The disturbances in Palestine between Zionist and Arab nationalism and the British provided the first occasion for active involvement, beyond propaganda, in matters 'political'. This took the

[18] *RMKH*, pp. 22–5; for the quotation, p. 24.

[19] This *risala* is reproduced partly in *Mudh.*, pp. 236–41; the letters to the prime ministers of Egypt were reproduced in *JIM* in a series appearing between 1 and 27 July 1946.

form of collecting funds to aid the Palestinian Arabs to maintain the Arab 'strike' in 1936–9, and demonstrating, pamphleteering, and speechmaking on behalf of their cause.[20] Political activity as a part of the movement's interests was officially if belatedly recognized by Banna in the first issue of the weekly, *al-Nadhir*, in May 1938, the appearance of which, he said, marked 'the beginning of their involvement in the external and internal political struggle'.[21] And the fifth conference of 1939, it will be recalled, defined the Society, *inter alia*, as a 'political organization'. This movement towards political activism seems to have been timed to coincide not only with the Society's growing sense of organizational power, but also with an auspicious trend of political circumstances in Egypt. Henceforth, Egypt itself was to receive some of the consuming political attention being directed to 'Islamic causes' throughout the Arab, South Asian, and North African worlds.

In Egypt, the political situation was dominated by the presence of the newly elevated and much loved young King Faruq, who, after a period of regency beginning in May 1936, was crowned in July 1937. His early religious attitude, inspired by one of his mentors, the rector of the Azhar, Shaykh Mustafa al-Maraghi, won for the new king the esteem of his people. The Brothers' fourth conference, as has already been noted, was called to celebrate his accession. After a long and joyous celebration—in which the rovers played their first important role as forces of 'order and security'—the Brothers gathered at the gates of 'Abidin Palace chanting a traditional oath of loyalty: 'We grant you our allegiance on the Book of God and the Tradition of His Prophet.'[22]

The other influence on Faruq, besides Maraghi, was 'Ali Mahir Pasha, an old friend of the royal family and foe of the Wafd. The new king's prestige was transferred to Mahir, who readily seized the opportunity to gain an initiative for the palace in the traditional struggle for power between the royal prerogative and the popular Wafd Party. The Maraghi–Mahir combine, with pan-Arab and even pan-Islamic overtones coupled with anti-Wafd politics, won the support of and in turn encouraged such groups as the Muslim Brothers and Young Egypt (*Misr al-Fatat*)—the 'Green Shirts' led by Ahmad Husayn Effendi. On one level, both groups, as 'popular parties', were useful as counterweights to the Wafd. Besides this, however, the activity of the Muslim Brothers on behalf of Palestine had impressed both Maraghi and Mahir, who saw in this issue, and its partisans, useful material for the enhancement of Egypt's prestige in the Arab world.

[20] See also below, p. 17.

[21] *Mudh.*, p. 150.

[22] Ibid., pp. 251–5 for an account of the celebration and the *bay'a* to Faruq.

When Mahir, one of the Egyptian representatives at the London Round Table Conference on Palestine held in 1939, returned to Cairo in March, he was welcomed by the Muslim Brothers in force.[23]

This relationship between Mahir and the Muslim Brothers took on added significance in the early war years, a matter which will be discussed later in this chapter. As the relationship became more obvious, it became the occasion for a second, and this time more serious, membership defection. Approximately in the autumn of 1939 a small dissident group left the Society to form 'the Society of Our Master Muhammad's Youth' (*jamiyat shabab sayyidna Muhammad*). Three major and separate issues were involved in the defection, but these gradually coalesced into fundamental questions about means and ends.

The first of these issues concerned the use of funds raised by Banna in support of the Arab strike in Palestine and of the Society's activities on their behalf. Most of the members accepted his argument that to spend some of this money on branches of the Society in Egypt—and thereby to make the Society itself more effective—was not to deny the Palestinians but, rather, to help them in another way. For the moment the dissidents were silenced, but their discontent was revived by the second strand in the dispute: the question whether or not the Society should eschew alliances with one or another of the established political forces in the country.

Banna had made it one of the cardinal virtues of the Society to avoid involvement with 'notables and names' and 'parties and societies'. His cordial relationship with 'Ali Mahir—widely believed to have encompassed 'aid' of some sort to the Society, an accusation repudiated but not emphatically denied by Banna[24]—provided the occasion for an airing of the issue. The dissident group demanded the dismissal of Ahmad al-Sukkari, Banna's childhood friend, and old associate in the idea of the organization, who had recently come to Cairo to assume the role of deputy to the leader. Sukkari, who was regarded as the focus of the problem of relationships with Mahir, had by this time become unofficial political 'liaison officer', a role he was to play until his dismissal in 1947. In 1939 Banna refused to dismiss him, thereby allowing the situation to become still more inflamed. Some of the dissidents were obviously moved by revulsion, not so much from politics or

[23] Heyworth-Dunne, *Modern Egypt*, pp. 23–8, 34; Royal Institute of International Affairs, *Great Britain and Egypt* (1952), pp. 56–7 (RIIA, *GBE* in later references). The Brothers' reception of Mahir was not unanimously supported, and became part of another dissension in the group as we shall see.

[24] *Mudh.*, p. 257.

political alliances as from 'Ali Mahir[25] and the thought of permitting the Society to become his instrument with which to fight the Wafd. At this time it had not yet become a contradiction in terms to be a Wafdist member of the Muslim Brothers.

The question of political alliances and political action involved the third, and most important, issue, that of the imperatives, moral and theological, by which the Society would be guided. Though temporarily settled, this last issue was never really resolved. Having joined the Society in 'defence' of Islamic values, some members took this commitment in a literal sense, encouraged by the Society's emphasis on discipline and training, physical as well as spiritual and moral. As the Society grew more powerful, and institutionalized that power in the rover and battalion systems, some of the members became inclined to demand the fulfilment of its mission. For this group, its mission was clear and uncomplicated by political considerations; it was the moral salvation of Egypt, if necessary with 'the force of the hand'. The group turned, in the context, to the Prophetic tradition which said: 'He among you who sees an abomination must correct it with his hand; if he is unable, then with his tongue; if he is unable, then with his heart. The last of these is the weakest of faith.' Banna, in this dispute, rejected the application of the Tradition in favour of the Qur'anic verse (16: 125): 'Call unto the way of thy Lord with wisdom and fair exhortation, and reason with them in the better way. Lo! thy Lord is best aware of him who strayeth from His way and He is Best Aware of those who go aright.'[26] Between 1937 and 1939 individual members had left the Society because of their dissatisfaction with Banna's attitude on this matter—one seemingly inconsistent with the teachings of the Society. One of these is reported to have made an attempt on his life. In 1939 cumulative anger over the questions of politics and the use of funds in Egypt and in Palestine, and of Banna's continuing refusal to sanction forceful reform bore fruit in the secession movement. The rigidly puritanical attitudes of the new group, the Society of Our Master Muhammad's Youth, suggests the relative importance of the moral issue in the dispute with Banna.

The defection had some immediate consequences. Banna's warning to 'the hasty and the anxious', voiced at the fifth con-

[25] Heyworth-Dunne, *Modern Egypt*, pp. 27–8, 30, only discusses this political facet of the dispute, but gives the most complete account of it.

[26] The Tradition is recorded in *Sahih Muslim* (Cairo, n.d.), i. 48, in Kitab al-Iman, Bab 83 with a variant in Bab 85. The Qur'anic verse is the translation of Marmaduke Pickthall, *The Meaning of the Glorious Koran* (London, 1930), p. 281; unless otherwise noted, Pickthall will be used throughout for translations without further reference. Khuli, *QDIHB*, pp. 73–4, presents the only available written account of the third aspect of the dispute; see also Ahmad, *Nahda*, p. 110.

ference in 1939, was made necessary as a result of this development. Feeling remained so high that the issue had another airing in 1940, which caused more defections to the new group. The most important of these was Mahmud abu Zayd, editor of *al-Nadhir*, who took with him both the magazine and the Society's licence to publish it.[27] Finally, it would appear that, because of this response (called 'immature' by later Brothers) of the dissidents to the training programme, the battalion system was deemed to have failed to achieve its purpose, and was allowed to fall into temporary disuse.

Though significant, and wearisome for Banna, the defection of 1939 and the problems it raised did not seriously retard the Society's advance in numbers and influence. The war years and their political and economic consequences for Egypt added momentum to that advance. Tendencies in the Society's thought or structure which had been implicit or potential during the first ten years of its life were clarified and took definite shape. Almost imperceptibly, amid the frustrations and chaos of these years, the Society developed into a force willing and able to play a decisive part in the post-war life of Egypt.

THE SECOND WORLD WAR

From the beginning of the second world war the history of the Muslim Brothers is inextricably associated with, and moulded by, that of Egypt. Before describing the development of the Society in detail, some account should therefore be given of general political events in Egypt and also of relations between Egypt and Great Britain. In August 1939 the prime minister, Muhammad Mahmud Pasha, resigned for reasons of ill health. 'Ali Mahir was commissioned by the king to form a new cabinet. Around him Mahir placed, among others, Muhammad Salih Harb Pasha in the strategic ministry of national defence, and 'Abd al-Rahman 'Azzam Bey in the ministry of *awqaf*, later in the ministry of social affairs and, more importantly, as head of Egypt's 'territorial army'. With General 'Aziz 'Ali al-Misri as commander-in-chief of the armed forces, and with a king duly impressed and influenced by Mahir, by Maraghi, and by the complex of ideas of pan-Arabism (and perhaps even pan-Islamism) represented by all of these names, Egypt was not in the hands of those who could be regarded by Britain as her most dependable leaders.[28]

[27] *MIM* (20 May 1954), 2.

[28] See M. Colombe, *L'Évolution de l'Égypte, 1924–1950* (1951), p. 82; G. Kirk, *The Middle East in the War* (1952), p. 40, speaks of an 'inner Cabinet' of Misri, Harb, and 'Azzam who, under Mahir, 'worked to consolidate the loyalty of the armed forces to the King, and so use them as a support of their own power'. For the historical background in this period we have relied primarily on Colombe, Kirk, and RIIA, *GBE*.

The Egyptian attitude was correct. With the British declaration of war on Germany, Egypt did what was required of her by the treaty of 1936: she

> broke off diplomatic and commercial relations with Germany, sequestered German property and interned all German subjects who could not establish an anti-Nazi record. [The government] proclaimed a 'state of siege' with the Prime Minister as Military Governor; placed the ports under British naval control; and imposed a strict censorship of posts, telegraphs, and telephones, and the press, with British participation.[29]

The government also declared its loyalty and friendship and waited to see the outcome of the war, the prospects of which, in the early stages, seemed to grow progressively dimmer for the Allies.

The news of the course of the war, added to the German propaganda effort, made difficult the British attempt in Egypt to win—short of a declaration of hostilities—a deeper commitment to the increasingly burdensome war effort, and a more active response to the dangers of the deteriorating Allied cause. The issue became serious with the entrance of Italy into the war in June 1940, and the consequent problem of security this created among the large Italian population of Egypt. Faced with a lethargic if not hostile, leadership, British authority inspired a series of changes which considerably strengthened, for the moment, the Allied hand. In February 1940 the commander-in-chief, Misri, was suddenly granted 'sick leave' for three months, which was extended for six more months in May 1940; he was then pensioned off on 7 August and replaced by a general considered by the British authorities to be more dependable. The final removal of Misri was accomplished by a new government. Following the Italian entry into the war 'Ali Mahir, at direct odds with British authority on how to deal with the new situation, 'resigned' as prime minister, being replaced, at the same time, as chief of the royal cabinet by Ahmad Hasanayn Pasha.

Hasan Sabri Pasha's new cabinet, formed on 27 June 1940, without Harb as minister of defence, lasted until his death in November. During that time, as Egypt debated a potential role as belligerent in the war, the battle of Africa was joined and Alexandria itself was bombed. Husayn Sirri Pasha assumed the reins of government in November, a fact which promised a continued amelioration of the relations between the treaty partners, despite the refusal of the Wafd and the Sa'dist parties to join the government. British successes in the Western Desert, followed by a stabilization of that front in the spring of 1941, facilitated the

[29] Kirk, *Middle East in the War*, pp. 34 f.

settling of the pattern of Anglo-Egyptian relations into a fairly efficient and co-operative operation to face up to the burdens of the war.

In May 1941, however, the relative calm was broken by the Rashid 'Ali putsch in Iraq, after which the British authority re-examined security in Egypt. 'Ali Mahir, as a potentially subversive person, was confined to his country estate by Sirri. The dismissed Misri, who had meanwhile been reached by Italian and German intelligence, planned an escape from Egypt to reach the insurgents in Iraq. He was intercepted on the night of 15–16 May with two other officers, in an Egyptian air force plane, but escaped only to be re-arrested on 6 June. On 19 May Hasan al-Banna was transferred to Upper Egypt by the ministry of education, under an Egyptian military order. On 20 May, 'Azzam Bey was replaced as head of the Egyptian 'territorial army'.[30]

Again, for a moment, the situation in Egypt seemed to be in order. Banna was allowed to return from Upper Egypt in the autumn but was re-arrested in October (see below, p. 22). In the broader picture, a poor harvest, supply shortages, and a renewal of tension resulting from the opening of a new German offensive in the Western Desert provoked restiveness in the country which focused on a palace affront at a decision of the government to break off diplomatic relations with Vichy France in January 1942. A mass demonstration of students on 1 February sparked off the resignation of Husayn Sirri's government.

The British Ambassador, Sir Miles Lampson (later Lord Killearn), visited King Faruq and complained that

> the co-operation of the well-intentioned Sirri Government with the British had been prevented by intrigue in other quarters; Axis propaganda had not been adequately checked; pro-Axis elements had been left at liberty; the students had been encouraged to demonstrate in favour of Rommel; now that the enemy were advancing in Cyrenaica, the strategic situation was full of dangerous possibilities for Egypt, Britain's vital base in the Middle East. . . . [Therefore] in accordance with constitutional practice, a Government should be formed which commanded a majority in the country and would thus be able to control the internal situation.[31]

He asked the king to call Mustafa al-Nahhas Pasha, head of the Wafd, to form a government. The king promised a conference of all party leaders with a view to forming a coalition. He was advised of the futility of such a gesture and presented with an ultimatum on

[30] On this period see especially Sadat, *Safahat*, pp. 85–92.

[31] Kirk, *Middle East in the War*, p. 209, an 'unofficial' account, but one of the fullest available.

4 February to which, after he had resisted and found his palace surrounded with British armour, he yielded. On 6 February the cabinet of Nahhas Pasha was formed.[32]

The Wafdist government remained in power almost to the end of the war, completely fulfilling the expectations of the British as to its ability and will to maintain the order and security necessary to the successful pursuance of the war. Its own internal corruption (which led to a split in its ranks) and, as the war danger receded from the Nile Valley, the emergence of old and new political tensions (especially between the palace and the Wafd) set the stage in October 1944 for a royal dismissal of the Nahhas cabinet. On 9 October a new government was formed by Ahmad Mahir, the Sa'dist Party leader. Mahir ended the war period with his declaration of war on the Axis Powers, for which he paid with his life as he read the proclamation to the chamber of deputies on 24 February 1945.

At the outbreak of war, in a letter to the then prime minister, 'Ali Mahir, the Muslim Brothers declared their support of Egyptian non-belligerency and of the confining of aid to Britain to the strict letter of the Treaty of 1936.[33] Beyond this, on the surface, the Society continued to press its cause; it also took a more active part in the nationalist agitation against Britain, the war notwithstanding. As we have already noticed, Britain reacted with firmness to this potential threat to her rear.

Transferred to Upper Egypt in May 1941 (Sukkari was transferred at the same time to Lower Egypt), Banna used his new location as a headquarters, and publicly continued his activities. His transfer caused a mild parliamentary ruffle. Wafdists seized the chance of embarrassing the government—most likely for reasons other than Banna. When the prime minister, Sirri, justified the transfer on the ground that Banna, a civil servant of the ministry of education, had been neglecting his work, the Society's headquarters prepared a brief which, supplemented by ministry of education inspection files, was presented during the parliamentary debate and appears to have refuted Sirri's observations. Banna and Sukkari were retransferred back to Cairo in September.[34] In October, however, after a mass meeting denouncing the British, both were arrested and imprisoned, together with the secretary-

[32] For an Egyptian account of the February incident, see Mustafa Mu'min, *Sawt Misr* (1951), pp. 88–110. Mu'min was a student leader at the time and was to become prominent among Muslim Brothers.

[33] *Mudh.*, pp. 280–6.

[34] Hajjaji, *RWR*, pp. 230–1; 'Assal, *BKA*, p. 55; Hamid, *QSIHB*, pp. 24–7; and Heyworth-Dunne, *Modern Egypt*, p. 38.

general, 'Abd al-Hakim 'Abidin, and a few of the members. At the same time, the government suppressed the journals of the Society—at that time *al-Ta'aruf* and *al-Shu'a'*, and the well known *al-Manar*, which Banna had recently taken over from the heirs of Rashid Rida. Meetings and any reference in newspapers to the Brothers were forbidden.[35] Again, however, within the month, the detainees were released, following an unfavourable public and parliamentary reaction as well as alleged pressure from the palace.[36] In the words of the Muslim Brothers, this was the first *mihna* ('persecution') to befall the organization. From that time, no government in Egypt avoided clashing with the Society of the Muslim Brothers.

Banna's transfer in May 1941, coinciding as it did with the banishment of 'Ali Mahir, the dismissal of 'Azzam from the command of the territorial army, and the final retirement of 'Aziz al-Misri from the command of the Egyptian army, suggested relationships between these men which had inspired the common action against them. Banna later denied that in the Mahir ministry of 1939–40 he had known the prime minister or any of the cabinet, except Salih Harb Pasha and 'Azzam Pasha. The latter two were known widely, and especially to the Brothers, for their devotion to Arabic-Islamic causes.[37] Mahir, likewise, had come to share this prestige and, contrary to Banna's assertion, had met and come to know him from 1935.[38] Beyond this there is little information, save that already noted: that there appeared to be a continuing dependency by Mahir and his associates on the Muslim Brothers for support of nationalist, pan-Arab, and anti-British policies. This complex of relationships presumably encompassed, on the one hand, the palace, Mahir, Harb, 'Azzam, Misri, and Maraghi, and, on the other, the Azhar students, the Muslim Brothers and other Islamic groups, and such organizations as Young Egypt.[39] Banna's contact with Mahir—one of the causes, as we have already seen, of defections from the Society just before the war—clearly continued during the first two years of it; but there is virtually no information as to its precise nature.[40]

35 *RNUNA*, pp. 6–7; and *JIM* (3 July 1946), 2.

36 *JIM* (3 July 1946), 2; Husayni, *Ikhwan*, pp. 26–7; and G. Kirk, *A Short History of the Middle East* (Washington, 1949), p. 200.

37 See *JIM* (13 July 1946), 4.

38 See *MDA* (10 Feb. 1953), 3.

39 See Heyworth-Dunne, *Modern Egypt*, pp. 23–8, 33–4, 36–8, followed by Kirk, *Middle East in the War*, p. 207; Jacob Boehm, 'Les Frères musulmans', *Hamizrah Hehadash* (Summer 1952), translated in *Monde non-chrétien* (June 1953), 212; Zvi Kaplinsky, 'The Muslim Brotherhood', *MEA* (Dec. 1954), 380. See also on Maraghi, *COC*, iii (1946), 511.

40 See the hints about Banna's 'historic' role during the war in *MDA* (12 Feb. 1952), 15.

Rather more is known about the relationship between Banna and ʿAziz al-Misri. Misri, like ʿAzzam and Harb, had distinguished himself by services to various nationalist and Arab causes; he had won for himself military honours and repute in the Ottoman campaigns in Tripolitania and had shared in the ferment which swept the Arabs into revolt against the Sultan of Turkey. He himself records his first meeting with the Brothers, in the person of Banna, after a visit to London in 1937. He was met at the airport, he reports, by three people in 'Islamic dress' who greeted him with words which pleased him so little that he shouted angrily: 'I want to see the Ikhwan representing the idea of renewal and renaissance, even in their clothes. . . . In their hands [I want to see] rather than prayer beads, books with which to dispute with me.' The first meeting was followed by others, in which Banna apparently persuaded Misri that the Brothers were what he sought.[41]

From 1938 to 1940 Misri presumably acted in concert with Mahir in wooing not only the Muslim Brothers, but also Young Egypt. Misri, according to Heyworth-Dunne, sought to unify the two groups,[42] which because of the growing competition between them were experiencing a strain on their relations.[43] The friendship between the two men was sufficiently strong for Banna, in 1940, to offer himself as an intermediary—the first on record—between Misri and a group of discontented young army officers which, at a later date and under different stresses, calling themselves the 'Free Officers' led the successful revolution of 23 July 1952.[44]

Anwar al-Sadat, a member of the revolutionary group, was the officer with whom Banna had his first meeting. Whom Sadat represented at that time is not clear, but he was in the army and refers to groups planning revolution. It seems highly unlikely that he had in mind the 'Free Officers' who became the rulers of Egypt. He and Banna are alleged to have met first by chance in the mess hall of a barracks outside Cairo. It was the night of the Prophet's

[41] *MDA* (12 Feb. 1952), 6.

[42] Heyworth-Dunne, *Modern Egypt*, p. 36. The name of Young Egypt was changed in 1940 to the Islamic National Party.

[43] *RMKH*, pp. 56–9. Banna was especially angry at the fact that many thought the Muslim Brothers to be a branch of Young Egypt.

[44] The major source on the relationship of the Muslim Brothers to the present military government of Egypt is Sadat, *Safahat* (Eng. trans. *Revolt on the Nile* (1957)). This first appeared as a series of articles, beginning in December 1953, in the then government daily, *Jaridat al-Jumhuriyya*, under the title 'Safahat majhula min kitab al-thawra'. *Safahat*, like other officially inspired accounts of this relationship, appeared after the public had become aware of the conflict between the two groups at the end of 1953, and was intended to convey, perhaps more than was warranted, the idea of long-standing dissociation from the Brothers. What is said by Sadat is worth recording as a first statement on the situation.

birthday and Banna was making an informal speech as part of the celebrations. The two established a ready rapport and began a series of meetings which lasted for over two years. Sadat goes on to suggest (with seeming retrospective wisdom) that as early as 1938 the idea of revolution had taken root in the army, and that the revolutionary group sought support from within the existing power structure. To this end they hoped to make contact with ʿAli Mahir and ʿAziz al-Misri, the two primary objects of British hostility after the outbreak of war.[45]

Mahir's dismissal in June 1940 put him out of reach of the group. Misri was contacted through Hasan al-Banna. In the autumn of 1940 Sadat met him in the clinic of Dr Ibrahim Hasan, a second deputy in the Society. The two discussed the plight of Egypt under the British occupation, and, despairing of all else, agreed that 'the salvation of the country could be assured only by a coup at the hands of the military', a 'distant goal' which filled Sadat with awe. After this first meeting Banna and Sadat began to reveal the 'secrets' that each suspected the other of having, and for the first time there was open talk of intentions and of uniting ranks for the common goal.[46] After this series of meetings, Misri seems to have become the central figure around whom groups from the army, the Muslim Brothers, and the police dramatized their discontents, finding in each other mutual reinforcement for their common urge to action against the British.[47]

In May 1941 Misri, with the aid of German intelligence officers and Anwar al-Sadat, made his abortive attempt to join the insurgents in Iraq. One of the two other officers arrested with him was ʿAbd al-Munʿim ʿAbd al-Ra'uf, a friend both of Sadat and of Misri and one of the army malcontents since 1939. Upon his release in the spring of 1942, and following the arrest of Sadat in August 1942 (for continued contact with German agents), Ra'uf became the chief liaison officer between the army and the Muslim Brothers.[48] Unlike Sadat, Ra'uf shortly afterwards became a full and dedicated member of the Society. His role in its history is of major importance. At the time, he acted primarily as chief missionary for the discontent in the army, bringing officers to the

[45] Since the overthrow of Faruq every group in Egypt has put conspicuously on record its recollections of long-standing hostility towards him. It is a matter of some interest, nevertheless, that Sadat's army group sought to contact Misri and Mahir, both palace men. Nationalist discontent, not revolution, was their obvious motive.

[46] Sadat, *Safahat*, pp. 33–48.

[47] Sadat in *JJ* (9 Sept. 1954), 1, 9. Sadat goes too far in speaking of Misri as the first leader of the first 'front' of the army, police, and Muslim Brothers. For similar certitude, see Harris, *Nationalism and Revolution*, p. 180, drawing her material from the same source.

[48] Sadat, *Safahat*, pp. 85–92, 105, 110.

headquarters to hear Banna and then arranging private meetings for them with him.[49] Subsequently he assumed a leading position in the ranks of the main and successful stream of army discontent which culminated in the revolution of 1952.

One other point is of importance here. Sadat, in the course of his meetings with Banna, had been overjoyed to see that the latter had already started collecting arms. Without the knowledge of even his closest colleagues, Banna had started a trickle of arms flowing to him through his agent-followers in army ranks.[50] Just before his arrest in August 1942, however, Sadat had a final meeting with Banna, during which he told all that he could about the army group and its operation. Despite the excitement shown by Banna at the revelations, Sadat felt he was not yet fully committed to the idea of the Society playing the role of civil or 'popular' support for a military movement of liberation from the British. Sadat remained convinced—even when he wrote in 1953—that although Banna was dedicated to the goal 'heart, being, mind and soul', the significant disposition of 'armament and formations' which, by his secretive behaviour, he had led Sadat to believe existed, could not be counted on, and his proffered part in that liberation on the army's terms was in question.[51] As it turned out, for the moment, the issue was academic. Further, it did not prevent more fruitful relations between the army and the Brothers as the idea of revolution gained momentum. It did, however, set a tone of suspicion which continued to prevail, with more or less intensity, in the relations between the groups as they became more involved, and which finally brought ruin to that relationship.

However important this liaison with the army came to be later for the Society, at that time it was confined to Banna alone, and its primary import lay in its relation to the larger picture of nationalist agitation and harassment of the British occupation, an activity given new point and more hopeful meaning by the pressures of the war on England and her resources. The British response was vigorous and conclusive; in retrospect the most serious of the actions taken by them was the installation of the ministry of Nahhas Pasha in February 1942. From this time on, many elements of the national movement began to develop a new and inordinately bitter focus for their agitation.

The first act of the Nahhas ministry, on 7 February, was to dissolve parliament and call new elections. At the sixth general conference of the Muslim Brothers, held around January 1941, it had been decided that, at the proper time, the Society would run

[49] *MMR* (10 Dec. 1954), 26.
[50] Sadat, *Safahat*, pp. 50–2.
[51] Ibid., pp. 80–2.

candidates in national elections. The elections called by the Wafd were considered appropriate for the first test of the Society's electoral strength. Banna declared himself a candidate for the district of Isma'iliyya, the birthplace of his movement, but no sooner had he done so than Nahhas summoned him and called upon him to withdraw. Without much debate, he consented, but 'at a price' which included (1) freedom for the movement to resume full-scale operations; and (2) a promise of government action against the sale of alcoholic drink and against prostitution. Nahhas agreed, and very shortly ordered restrictions on the sale of liquor at certain times of every day, during Ramadan, and on religious holidays. Similarly, he took steps to make prostitution illegal and immediately closed down some of the brothels. He also permitted the resumption of some of the activities of the Society, including the issue of some of its publications and the holding of meetings.[52]

The issue of the elections thus muted, in March Banna pledged his support to the Wafdist Government.[53] There was no serious nationalist agitation for the remainder of its period of office. However, relations between the Muslim Brothers and the Wafd remained unstable. At the end of 1942 Nahhas again closed down all branches, excepting only the headquarters. In early 1943 the situation was reversed, with the visit to the headquarters of a group of Wafdist dignitaries—mostly ministers—who, after a speech by Banna, declared their 'loyalty' to 'the idea' represented by the Brothers. During the remainder of the life of the ministry relations alternated between the friendly and the hostile: surveillance and censorship, followed by periods of relative freedom.[54]

The inconsistency of the Wafd reflected in part the recognition of the growing power of the Muslim Brothers, and what, from that time on, would be an ambivalent or many-sided approach to it. For the 'liberal' wing of the Wafd, the Muslim Brothers were always anathema. For the 'right' wing, headed from that time by Fu'ad Siraj al-Din, the Society was as a useful instrument against the dangerous social pressures being generated in Egypt—communism especially had flourished during the war. As minister of agriculture in this cabinet, Siraj al-Din is reported to have facilitated the spread of the movement in the countryside. And for the Wafd as a whole, no potential power could be overlooked, for

[52] Heyworth-Dunne, *Modern Egypt*, p. 40, who also points out that Banna played to the fullest the role of 'martyr' which the sacrifice of his candidacy on behalf of 'Islamic reform' had conferred on him; see also *MIM* (20 May 1954), 2.

[53] RIIA, *GBE*, p. 72.

[54] *MMB* (23 Jan. 1951), 4; *JIM* (3 July 1946), 4; and Hajjaji, *IMAM*, ii. 39–51.

the services it might render to the overriding and unabated Wafdist conflict with the palace or for the threat it would pose were the palace to make use of it.[55]

Wafdist relations with the Society were also, however, influenced by Nahhas's anxiety—given the stringent war-time definition of security—lest the Brothers should say or write anything that threatened the all-out support of the Allied cause that he had promised the British—a promise to which he remained true. Though he was unquestionably acting out of both conviction and self-interest, his identification with the British Embassy necessarily laid him open to charges of collusion with the 'imperialists'. In their treatment at the hands of the Wafd the Muslim Brothers saw a continuation of their 'persecution', begun in May 1941, by the 'British oppressor'.

After Banna's release from prison in October 1941 contact was made between the British Embassy and the Muslim Brothers. Who made contact with whom is a matter of dispute, but the fact of the contact seems established, as was its essentially unproductive consequence.[56] The point here is that the Brothers regard the failure of the British 'to purchase' them as the key to the harassment of the Society by Nahhas: first, by his rejection of Banna's candidacy for the election;[57] and secondly, in the on-again off-

[55] See Boehm, 'Les Frères musulmans', 212–13; Kaplinsky, 'The Muslim Brotherhood', 380.

[56] The Brothers have often publicly mentioned the meeting, alleging that the initiative came from the British, who were afraid of a rapprochement between the Brothers and the palace. After the ideas and programme of the Society had been discussed, the British agent, duly 'impressed', offered 'to aid the organization in the realization of its goals'. Banna, it was said, refused the offer. For versions of this story, see *RNUNA*, pp. 8–9; *JIM* (31 July 1946), 2; *MDA* (29 May 1954), 9; *MIM* (22 July 1954), 9; (29 July 1954), 9.

Heyworth-Dunne, universally reported by the Brothers to have been one of the principals on behalf of the British Embassy, comments that Banna gave out through Egyptians who were in touch with British agents that he would be prepared to co-operate 'and would be amenable to some kind of payment, . . . which made people believe that he had learnt his lesson through internment. But nothing was further from the truth. He had no intention of receiving the money of infidels; he gave much prominence to this question of being offered money during the War in his paper, the *Ikhwan al-Muslimin* (especially in 1946). Ahmad al-Sukkari had a great deal to do with this stratagem. On one occasion he asked for forty thousand dollars and a car, in return for the support of the Ikhwan. For twelve years, the Ikhwan had been fed on anti-British propaganda; it would have been virtually impossible to have asked them to work for the British' (*Modern Egypt*, pp. 38–9).

The relative quiet of the Brothers after the coming of the Wafd has led many to believe that the offer of 'aid' was accepted. Particularly convinced of this are former members of the Young Egypt group which led the great pro-Rommel demonstrations in the summer of 1942, and which the Brothers, as an organization, did not join; see Boehm, 'Les Frères musulmans', 213, and Heyworth-Dunne, *Modern Egypt*, p. 41.

[57] The British, it was argued, were (1) unsympathetic to the idea of a Muslim Brother in parliament, which would then offer an official platform for diatribes

again hostility towards them while Nahhas remained in office. So certain were the Brothers of this implacable hostility of the British towards them that in mid-1943 Banna, convinced that British intelligence was striving to bring about his exile,[58] wrote a farewell message to his followers.

This document,[59] which ranks high on the list of prescribed reading for members, contains the fruit of his first two years' experience of conflict with authority and an oft-quoted warning to members of the travail through which they might expect to pass in the face of growing external hostility. Part of it is worth quoting, both as a reflection of a basic mental attitude of the movement, and as a prediction of things to come.

The Obstacles in our Path

I would like to avow to you frankly that your message is yet unknown to many people, and that when they know it and recognize its purposes, they will meet it with the severest opposition and the cruellest enmity. You will then be obliged to face numerous hardships and obstructions. Only then will you have begun to march on the road of the bearers of missions. . . . The common people's ignorance of the reality of Islam will stand in your way. You will discover that the people of religion and the official '*ulama*' will consider your understanding of Islam a strange thing and deny your struggle on its behalf. Your chiefs and leaders, as well as people of rank and title, will envy you. One government after another will obstruct you, and each of them will attempt to hinder your activity and block your progress.

All the oppressors will exert every effort to restrain you and to extinguish the light of your message. They will win the help of weak governments and weak morals and of the hands stretched out—towards them for begging and towards you for evil and oppression. All these will excite suspicion and inspire unjust accusations regarding your message, and they will attempt to give the people an ugly and imperfect picture of it. . . .

This will lead you to the stage of trial, wherein you will be imprisoned, detained, and banished; your property will be confiscated, your special activities stopped, and your homes searched. Indeed, your period of trial may last long. . . . But God has promised that he will assist those who struggle and do good. . . . Are you resolved, my brothers, to be the defenders of God?

Ye Muslim Brothers, listen: I have tried with these words to place your message before you. Perhaps we may have a critical period of time

against them; and (2) fearful of the consequences of an election campaign in the highly sensitive Canal Zone; see *RNUNA*, pp. 7–8; and *MMB* (12 Dec. 1950), 4–5; cf. Heyworth-Dunne, *Modern Egypt*, p. 40.

---

[58] *RNUNA*, p. 10.

[59] *Risalat bayn al-ams wa'l-Yawm* (*RBAWY*), originally titled *Risalat al-Nabi al-amin*, and also *Min tatawwurat al-fikra al-Islamiyya wa-ahdafuha.*

during which we will be separated from one another. In this case, I will not be able to talk or write to you. Therefore, I advise you to study them when you can, and gather around them, for each word carries several meanings.

My Brothers: you are not a benevolent society, nor a political party, nor a local organization having limited purposes. Rather, you are a new soul in the heart of this nation to give it life by means of the Qur'an; you are a new light which shines to destroy the darkness of materialism through knowing God; and you are the strong voice which rises to recall the message of the Prophet. . . . You should feel yourselves the bearers of the burden which all others have refused. When asked what it is for which you call, reply that it is Islam, the message of Muhammad, the religion that contains within it government, and has one as of its obligations freedom. If you are told that you are political, answer that Islam admits no such distinction. If you are accused of being revolutionaries, say 'We are voices for right and for peace in which we dearly believe, and of which we are proud. If you rise against us or stand in the path of our message, then we are permitted by God to defend ourselves against your injustice.' . . . If they insist on pursuing their oppression, say to them, 'Peace be upon you, we will ignore the ignorant.'[60]

The threat, real or imagined, to Banna himself never materialized, but his words coincided with the newest internal organizational developments. Friction with the government made the Society more actively hostile to the occupying power; but also, for the first time, it nurtured hostility to the existing order of things in Egypt. It was in these circumstances that Banna moved into the final stage of his organizational planning. Late in 1942 or early in 1943 that unit came into existence which was known inside the Society as 'the special section' [*al-nizam al-khass*], and outside it as 'the secret apparatus' [*al-jihaz al-sirri*].[61] This dating, the most likely of all those possible, refers to the establishment of the unit, not the inception of the idea. Orally, the members themselves have dated the beginning of the secret apparatus anywhere from 1930 to 1947—one of the many reflections of the widespread ignorance within the Society concerning it.

As early as 1930, in Banna's first dispute with dissident members, he was being charged, by rumour and by direct accusation, with 'secret works';[62] but at this early stage the accusation undoubtedly

[60] *RBAWY*, pp. 28–31.

[61] The difference in these two phrases was unimportant except for some of those who joined the group. To them, the 'special section' was merely the less open wing of the formal organization into which only the most 'sincere' and 'ardent' servants of the cause were admitted. Because of their trust in the leadership's perception of 'right and wrong', there was no sense of the criminality which came to be attached to the words 'secret apparatus'. On this point, see the confession of the assassin of Nuqrashi Pasha in 1948 (*Qadiyat al-Nuqrashi*, p. 47).

[62] *Mudh.*, p. 128.

referred to the lack of frankness and directness so often noticed by those close to him. The classification of membership adopted at the third general conference in March 1935, besides the three degrees of (1) 'assistant' (*musa'id*), (2) 'related' (*muntasib*), and (3) 'active' (*'amil*), listed a fourth, that of 'struggler' (*mujahid*).[63] The precise meaning of this fourth category was not explained at the time. Other information would, however, suggest that Banna did not mean an 'apparatus' but merely a group of the most dedicated and active members, on whom could be placed the primary burden of serving 'God and the message'. By 1936 the rover groups had taken shape, and at the same time Banna began personally to assume the instruction of small groups of ten members in the aims of the Society. Similarly the creation in 1937 of the battalions, with its emphasis on communal training and rigorous night vigils of prayer and meditation, expressed the principle of the dedicated *mujahid* enunciated publicly in the meeting of 1935. These organizational developments corresponded in time with the beginning of the Brothers' concern for, and activity in, Palestine—the issue which, with the British occupation, was most notably identified by the members themselves with the inspiration for political activism in the Society.

But if the secret apparatus as such had not yet been set up, emphasis was laid on secrecy as to the purpose of existing formations. In a remarkable statement, made in 1938 but published only after the revolution in 1952, Banna, informing a questioning youth of the 'revolutionary' nature of the organization in matters of both 'reform' and 'liberation', reminded him that in the face of 'the law', it was a mistake to be candid, and that secrecy was necessary in the beginning of any movement to maintain its solvency and assure its survival.[64] Only after his first clashes with authority in the early years of the war was a secret organization established. When discussing the basic principles of the Society in his farewell message of 1943 he mentioned 'additional means', both negative and positive—'of which some would agree with the established practice of people, and others would rebel against those practices . . . and some would be gentle and others would be forceful'.[65] The early war-time contacts with army officers, at first independent of external matters, were later reinforced by those events which exacerbated the national feeling; together, they were direct causes of the formalization of the secret apparatus and the first stages of the resort to extra-legal action.[66]

[63] Ibid., pp. 203–5.
[64] Hajjaji, *RLAT*, pp. 16–19, 22–3, 33–5.
[65] *RBAWY*, p. 27.
[66] As late as 1954 there was uncertainty in the Society itself as to whether it was Banna or the acknowledged head of the secret apparatus from 1947 to

Inspired in the first instance as an idea by the concept of *jihad*, formalized into an organization under the pressures of nationalist agitation, the secret apparatus was almost immediately rationalized as an instrument for the defence of Islam and the Society. In 1943 it began to play the part of defender of the movement against the police and the governments of Egypt. A major motive here was already a sense of betrayal of the national leadership, brought sharply into focus by the circumstances of the war, a feeling widely shared[67] by the Egyptian nationalists, and one which under continued pressure was to direct the attention of the national movement inwards to Egypt and to Egyptians, as well as outwards against the British. In 1944 the secret apparatus also began to infiltrate the communist movement, which during the war had taken on new life and which the Muslim Brothers still considered to be one of their principal enemies.

The creation of the secret apparatus was accompanied by a new and far-reaching development in the open organization. The battalion system, having been regarded as a failure, was supplemented by a more minute, flexible, controllable, and natural form of organization, one which, by its harmony with the ethos of the organization, provided the chief instrument for mobilizing the loyalty of members. This was the system of 'families' (*usar*), the keystone of the organizational power of the Muslim Brothers, the secret apparatus notwithstanding. Late in 1943 a mass-meeting of the Society adopted a report establishing 'the system of co-operative families' (*nizam al-usar al-ta'awuni*), which, from that time on, established the dominant pattern of inner relationships. Essentially, this created an infinite number of cells numerically limited to five members. The cells were primarily indoctrination rather than administrative units, in which the Brother received at first hand, and in a co-operative endeavour, those ideas to which his membership had committed him. Added to a now formalized secret apparatus and an increasingly effective rover system, the

1953, 'Abd al-Rahman al-Sanadi, who founded it; (see *JJ* (24 Nov. 1954), 7). Kira, *Mahkama*, i. 33–4, suggests that Banna used German officers to help launch it. The above account is admittedly 'patch-work' and is inspired by the certainty which accompanies ignorance; of considerable weight in this reconstruction is a letter that came into the writer's hands in the 1954 crisis of the Society, meant by its writer, Muhammad 'Alawi 'Abd al-Hadi, for his colleagues in the leadership echelons. In attempting to analyse the problems faced by the Society in its crisis with the government in 1954, the letter throws some useful historical light on other matters of interest, including the secret apparatus and its founding.

[67] See esp. Sadat, *Safahat*, pp. 142–4.

family system completed the strengthening of the internal fabric of the Society.[68]

With the dismissal of the Wafd in October 1944, the palace selected Ahmad Mahir Pasha, the leader of the Saʿdist party, to form a new government. This was the first of a succession of what the Brothers and the Wafd called 'minority governments'.[69] From this time until the elections of January 1950 Egypt was ruled by independents and Saʿdists, reflecting the active return of the palace to the field of domestic politics and its success at excluding the Wafd from power. The situation also promised that post-war Egypt, facing critical internal and external problems and ruled by men without a semblance of popular support, was destined to pass through a lively period in its history.

Mahir immediately made preparations for a new general election which the Brothers again prepared to contest. Banna again opted for Ismaʿiliyya, and five of his chief colleagues chose other areas in Egypt intending to campaign on the basis of an 'Islamic programme'. In January 1945 the elections—believed to have been among the more obviously dishonest held in Egypt—took place, and Banna and all the other Brothers were defeated in constituencies where they had been certain of victory.[70] Besides the obvious interest of the government in winning seats for its partisans, Mahir had already shown his attitude to the Brothers by seeking, but not getting, a *fatwa* from the rector of the Azhar, Shaykh Maraghi, declaring that there were too many Islamic societies in Egypt—a move felt to be aimed at the Muslim Brothers.[71]

When Mahir made known his intent to declare war on the Axis, the Muslim Brothers, together with the great majority of nationalists, including the Wafd, protested; but, determined to secure a place for Egypt in the peace-making, Mahir persisted. On 24 February, as he read the declaration of war in the chamber of deputies, he was assassinated. Banna, Sukkari, and ʿAbidin were arrested but almost immediately released, following the investigation and the assassin's confession that he was a member of the

[68] *RNUNA*, p. 10; see also below, pp. 195–200.

[69] See e.g. Ghazali, *IMABSR*. 7.

[70] See Kirk, *Middle East*, p. 263, for a comment on the nature of the election. For the most detailed, though not disinterested, account see Zaki, *Ikhwan*, pp. 21–2. Zaki's book, originally a thesis at Cairo University for the Higher Diploma in Social Work, is offered as an 'impartial' study of the movement. His adviser on the thesis was a prominent leader of the Society (Kamal Khalifa: Harvard, Columbia, and the University of Michigan), and much of the work can be said to be an 'inside' view. Zaki's account of the elections reflects the organizational attitude of frustration at the denial, once more, of the use of the legitimate or 'official' path for propagandizing the movement. On this point, see also below, pp. 307–13.

[71] See *MDA* (10 Feb. 1953), 12–31.

National Party.[72] Banna visited the new prime minister, Mahmud Fahmi al-Nuqrashi Pasha, a close friend of Mahir and his successor as head of the Sa'dist party, to convey his condolences and to explain the mission of the Society. Nuqrashi responded with orders for the strict surveillance of the activities of the members and the organization,[73] a policy which was applied with varying degrees of severity while he remained in office.

Nuqrashi's government, from 25 February 1945 to 14 February 1946, bridged the transition from the wartime to the post-war phase of the history of the movement. The Brothers regard this government as the beginning of the 'great *mihna*',[74] which carried them over the next three years to their period of greatest power. It was a government headed by Nuqrashi which finally challenged that power.

[72] Cf. Kirk, *Middle East*, p. 266; and RIIA, *GBE*, p. 81, according to both of which the assassin was said to be from the ranks of Young Egypt. The government in 1954 made the first sustained effort to charge the Society with the crime; see e.g. *MAS* (1 Dec. 1954), 4; and *Irhab*, pp. 21–7.

[73] *JIM* (4 July 1946), 4.

[74] Zaki, *Ikhwan*, p. 23. The use of the term *mihna* was probably intended to invoke the earlier persecutions of the conservative orthodox, especially Ahmad ibn Hanbal, at the hands of rationalist (Mu'tazila)-influenced caliphs of the Ummayad and early 'Abbasid periods; see P. K. Hitti, *History of the Arabs* (1949), pp. 429–30.

III

1945–1949: APOGEE AND DISSOLUTION

THE SETTING

THE end of the war brought with it a release of tensions and lifted the lid from hostilities which had long raged beneath the controls of martial law. The death of the prime minister, Ahmad Mahir, was the initial expression of this fact. The impact of the war itself on Egypt's economic, political, and social life had manifold consequences for both the momentum and the direction of the national movement. Issawi, in a few paragraphs, has summed up the most important features of post-war life in Egypt.[2]

Perhaps the most important single factor was the imposition of a twentieth-century inflation on a social structure in many ways reminiscent of the eighteenth century. The gap between rich and poor, already great, was further enlarged; the unskilled rural and urban labourers suffered severe privations; and the salaried middle and lower middle classes, whose money incomes rose very little, were relentlessly pressed down.

Another trend which was accelerated by war-time conditions was urbanization, with its manifold social consequences. The rapid growth of industry attracted peasants to towns, raised the wages of skilled workmen, and stimulated the formation of trade unions. At the height of the war effort, Allied army workshops and services employed over 200,000 Egyptians, of whom some 10,000 were male clerks, and some 80,000 were skilled or semi-skilled workmen. In addition, several thousands found employment in services catering directly to Allied troops. All these newcomers were naturally drawn into the political life and agitation of the country, which is still mainly confined to the towns. The withdrawal of the bulk of the Allied troops after the war led to an estimated unemployment of over 250,000 and to much distress and agitation.

Into this fertile ground some potent ideas had meanwhile been sown. Egypt had done its best to stay out of the war, but it had been engulfed by the flood of propaganda pouring in from every quarter. Britain and the United States harped incessantly on the themes of democracy, social justice, and, perhaps the one which found the most appreciative audience, the upholding of national independence against Nazi (and subsequently Soviet) aggression. The Germans struck still more responsive chords, whole-heartedly supporting the Egyptian and Arab cause

[1] C. Issawi, *Egypt at Mid-Century* (1954), pp. 262–3.

against the Western Powers, promising the Egyptian upper classes the property of foreigners and assuring the peasants that their entry into Egypt would be followed by a redistribution of large estates. As for Russian propaganda, it was provided with a unique opportunity, often carried out unintentionally by over-eager British or American officials. The prowess of the Soviet Union was exalted and Russian economic and social achievements were given their due, and more. In these circumstances it was natural that there should be a rapid spreading of Socialist and Communist ideas, and an even greater spreading of deep and inarticulate dissatisfaction with the existing order, unable to express itself clearly and ready to follow anyone who promised a change.

The issues, still unresolved, of Palestine and of relations with Britain helped to embitter the internecine struggle within the country among the mass parties, and between these and the government and palace, a struggle the outcome of which was to hasten the pace of internal disorder and violence—testimony to the unrecognized but real collapse of parliamentary life and the rule of law. While the whole atmosphere transcended the Society of the Muslim Brothers, the Society's contribution to the crisis was nevertheless of essential importance, both for Egypt's future and for its own.

Inside the organization the post-war period began, auspiciously enough, on a constitutional note. On 8 September 1945 the Society met in mass plenary session and reaffirmed the principles expressed in the important fifth conference of 1939. At the same time, Banna presented a comprehensive set of statutes, *Qanun al-Nizam al-Asasi li Hay'at al-Ikhwan al-Muslimin al-'Amma*, which, although modified in 1948 and supplemented in 1951, remained the basic constitution of the Society. This gave formal recognition to an informal operative system of administration and control based on a theoretical delegation of power to, and distribution of function and authority among, the leader, the General Guide (*al-murshid al-'amm*), an advisory General Guidance Council (*maktab al-irshad al-'amm*), and a Consultative Assembly (*al-hay'at al-ta'sisiyya*). Similarly, the statutes provided the framework for administrative and technical operations and established a concrete field apparatus and hierarchy.

At the same time, as required by Law 49/1945 concerning organized charity and social work, the Society submitted its records to the ministry of social affairs for inspection. The ministry decided that the organization was 'political, social, and religious', and that the law granting welfare societies government aid would apply to only part of its activities. On the basis of this decision the Society, in effect, divided itself into two parts.

A 'section of welfare and social services' was established, with its own head, regulations, hierarchy, and organization, empowered to deal directly with the ministry of social affairs on matters of mutual interest. In so doing, Banna was creating a legal basis for the protection of the services of the Society from the caprice of the precarious political order.

The creation of the new section reflected a great upsurge in the activity of the organization in this as well as all other fields to which the movement dedicated itself in its effort to exemplify its belief in the totality and applicability of Islamic teachings. Night and day schools and institutes, which offered both technical and academic programmes, were established for boys, girls, and adults. Some small industries were founded, both to relieve post-war unemployment and to dramatize the viability of 'Islamic economics'. Welfare activity was supplemented by social work, largely in rural areas, and medical work in the form of hospitals, clinics, and dispensaries. These and other related matters will be discussed later, for whatever may have been their value as an ideological stimulus to members, they counted for much less in the post-war life of the Society than its total involvement in the political problems and conflicts which were at that time the primary issues in Egypt.

POLITICS AND THE NATIONAL MOVEMENT

The Wafd, after the war, though by no means deprived of all of its traditional strength, had, however, lost its unique role as the principal voice of articulate nationalist discontent. Its acceptance of power at the hands of the British in 1942 had significantly altered its image in the eyes of youthful nationalists. Added to this was the corruption of Wafdist rule which had revealed itself in the defection of its secretary-general Makram 'Ubayd Pasha, and in his publication of the famous dossier called *The Black Book.*[2] Besides costing the Wafd some of the aura of purity which had surrounded it throughout its history, these revelations, more significantly, documented the truth, only yet dimly perceived, that the Wafd, traditionally a 'middle-class' stronghold, was being dominated in its leadership by men whose interests lay rather with the ruling élite. Whatever motions towards progressive legislation might be made by the Wafd, its leadership began to speak more obviously in the accents of vested interests, and more fully to share in the general lethargy of the ruling groups when

[2] See Kirk, *Middle East*, pp. 269–72, for a brief summary of the charges.

action was called for to relieve the increasingly explosive economic and social pressures which beset the Egyptian people.[3]

With the end of the war, the Wafd's haste to establish leadership in the national movement was in part an attempt to alter its image of collaboration with the British.[4] It was also partly due to traditional Wafdist enthusiasm when out of power; but especially to the challenge flung at the Wafd by the Muslim Brothers. That group had seriously eaten into traditional Wafdist strongholds: the university, the civil service, and the countryside; and their new prestige and power boded ill for the Wafdist conflict with the palace. The resurgence of the Wafd was strengthened by the fact that, in recognition of the social forces at play in Egypt in the post-war world and as long as the party was out of office, the 'left wing' was gradually allowed to be its dominant voice.[5]

The palace, too, had suffered a crucial blow from the event of February 1942. The king never again recovered the position from which he had commanded and received the affection of his people; this was especially true among his young army officers, who most sharply felt the sting of his capitulation to the British show of force.[6] He became, in fact, the object of an ever-growing antipathy, because in his personal life he offended against all the traditional virtues, and in his political life he ever more closely identified himself and his throne with the British and with the conservative ruling élite.

Even before the war ended, the political situation assumed recognizable and traditional forms as the palace asserted itself at the very first occasion and dismissed the Wafd. Thenceforth, as long as it was possible, the palace continued to express its aversion to the Wafd by calling upon none but members of the Sa'dist Party or independents to form the governments which attempted to resolve the successive crises of the times. The 'minority' governments, as the opposition called them, commanded no popular support, and in the circumstances of extreme political partisanship and pressing post-war problems, they could rule only by forceful use of the police arm or by skilful manipulation of the opposing forces. The conservative heads of government, whether former Wafdists or traditionally hostile to the

[3] See Issawi, *Egypt*, p. 261. [4] RIIA, *The Middle East* (1954), p. 189.

[5] See Heyworth-Dunne, *Modern Egypt*, p. 43; Kaplinsky, 'The Muslim Brotherhood', 380. M. Alexander, 'Left and Right in Egypt', *Twentieth Century*, cli (Feb.1952), 121, describes the Wafdist press as 'the main Communist conquest' in Egypt at the time. Zaki Badaoui, *Les Problèmes du travail et les organisations ouvrières en Égypte* (1948), p. 149, in an analysis of the forces operating in post-war Egyptian life, describes the Wafd as 'the most important of the parties of the left'. See, finally, RIIA, *GBE*, p. 90.

[6] See Sadat, *Safahat*, pp. 52–4, 95–6, and 143.

Wafd, shared the palace antipathy to Wafdist rule and therefore joined fully in the battle, more especially since the spread of radical thinking in Egypt had been rendered a more acute problem by what appeared to be increasing communist prestige in the Wafd itself. In the setting, it was almost natural that liaison should be made with the Muslim Brothers. It was equally natural, given the inherent but not readily perceived contradictions in such a liaison, that it could not last.

The Muslim Brothers, as already noted, from the beginning of their emergence into prominence had been courted by conservative groups. ʿAli Mahir's pan-Arabism and pan-Islamism, while undoubtedly aimed at the British, also embodied the traditional view of Islam as a bulwark against social and economic radicalism in word and deed. This view partially explains Wafdist—or 'right-wing' Wafdist—overtures of friendship in 1943 and 1944, and appeared to underlie the attitudes of the palace and the heads of minority governments. The same forces which had pushed the flexible Wafd into its 'progressive' post-war policies, inspired powerful reactions among the conservatives, most notably a concerted and widespread programme of repression of communists, communist and front groups, and allegedly communist newspapers and periodicals which began under the ministry of Ismaʿil Sidqi in 1946.[7] In this campaign the Muslim Brothers, bitterly antagonistic to the communists, could join wholeheartedly. Their press reported the course of the governmental campaign in a daily column entitled 'The Fight against Communism'. The 'intelligence' of the Society passed on information useful to the government in its continual round-ups of real and suspected communists, especially in labour and university circles.[8]

But Banna, while vehemently repelled by communist doctrine, had in fact made an appeal with his movement to the same groups which might have been attracted to it, and for the same general reasons of discontent; he did so, however, in 'Islamic' terms. This religious orientation partially obscured the activist reform attitudes, real and potential, in the movement; and these attitudes created a posture which in many respects was ultimately incompatible with the perpetuation of the political, economic, and social *status quo* to which the ruling groups were dedicated. This truth, only dimly perceived, ensured that the liaison between the Muslim Brothers and the conservative rulers would be both unstable and tenuous. For the moment, however, the Society could be used

[7] RIIA, *GBE*, pp. 85, 90–1; Badaoui, *Les Problèmes du travail*, pp. 158–9; and Colombe, *Égypte*, pp. 249–51, for Sidqi's anti-communist campaign.

[8] See *MAS* (1 Dec. 1954), 4–5; and, for further detail, p. 281 below.

without thought of the fulfilment of its revolutionary implications, because for the moment, the palace, the conservative heads of government, and the Muslim Brothers shared common foes: communism and the Wafd. For Banna, there was another dimension. With a now powerful organization to support him, he could not only assert more firmly the ends to which his work was dedicated—the reform of Egypt through its Islamization and the evacuation of the British—he could also think more precisely about the means to those ends, thoughts which inevitably included the share of the Muslim Brothers in the distribution of power in the country.

How this common interest was translated into formal relationships is not clear. Most members of the Society would reject any suggestion that Banna had anything to do with the palace or its governments, but close associates of his assert that he was by no means implacably hostile to Faruq, and that one of his greatest dreams was to be welcomed into the royal presence. Evidence given for this was that in his description of the future of Islam, talk of the institution of the caliphate was so nebulous and far in the future as to be without real meaning. In talking about Islamic reconstruction, it is said, he deliberately generalized his views within the terms 'the Islamic system' (*al-nizam al-islami*) without much specification as to what this meant in terms of government theory and practice. His attempt to be inoffensive on this score may have been a devious ruse to conceal ulterior motives, or merely an effort to avoid unnecessarily arousing the royal wrath; it seems to be more true that he himself continued to be loyal to the throne, and that he hoped, in fact, to achieve his reforms through it.

The reconstruction of this attitude is based mainly on a sifting of private views, impossible as yet to document. One source, the recollections of Anwar al-Sadat about the background of the revolution of 1952, adds some important, though as yet unprovable, information relative to actual contact. Sadat, it will be recalled, was arrested in August 1942, but escaped in November 1944, one month after the dismissal of the Nahhas cabinet. Almost immediately he resumed the contacts with Banna which had begun in 1940. Sadat records his surprise, when, after a number of meetings with him, Banna made an unusual explanation and request. He told Sadat that he was disturbed that 'the king and the foreigners' had come to fear his movement: the former for the Society's stand on traditional Islamic views of fealty [*bay'a*] rather than heredity as the source of kingly authority; the latter because of fear of the loss of their work, properties, and rights if the movement was successful. Banna felt that if the king were reassured then foreigners would be too. He concluded by asking Sadat to arrange for him to meet the king. This was to be done through the close personal friend of Sadat and personal physician of Faruq, Yusuf Rashad. Sadat, uneasy about his own peculiar status of escaped prisoner, finally consented and went to Rashad, who agreed to make the attempt. Rashad, to Faruq's displeasure, made two different and unsuccessful attempts to secure permission to meet Banna, but some months later the king reversed his decision and ordered Rashad to meet Banna and report the conversation back to him. Rashad did so, and persuaded of Banna's 'sincerity' towards Faruq, conveyed his view to the king, who merely roared with laughter: 'Hasan al-Banna has made a fool of you'.

All this presumably took place in 1945. Sadat completes the story with the following words:

> This is what Yusuf Rashad told me.
>
> He also told me years later that the king said to Ibrahim 'Abd al-Hadi at the end of his term in 1945: 'We erred in smashing the Brothers. We should return to the old policy.'
>
> I asked Yusuf Rashad what the old policy was.
>
> He said: 'Believe me . . . I don't know . . . but it seems that another contact was made between Hasan al-Banna and the king by some path other than me . . . and that the king for a short period in 1946 took a certain position *vis-à-vis* the Brothers . . . then changed it after the Palestine war. . . .'
>
> He said this . . . then he said: 'Allahu A'lam'.[9]

What the 'other' path was—or who—remains a mystery, as does any information about the nature or intensity of the relationship. A constantly recurring story is that Banna was consulted prior to the appointment of Isma'il Sidqi Pasha as prime minister in February 1946.[10] A continuing relation seems to have been indicated by the essentially friendly attitude of the Society to the early period of the ministry of Nuqrashi Pasha which succeeded that of Sidqi in December 1946. And shortly after the appointment of Ibrahim 'Abd al-Hadi as chief of the royal cabinet in February 1947, Banna was invited for the first time to attend a royal banquet.[11] The conversation reported by Sadat between 'Abd al-Hadi and

[9] Sadat, *Safahat*, pp. 99–102. Most of this story has been verified by Yusuf Rashad in *MDA* (15 June 1954), 6. According to Sadat, at one of their meetings, Banna had with him his 'military adviser' Mahmud Labib, who was, however, kept out of the secret of the palace liaison.

[10] See *MAS* (1 Dec. 1954), 4–5, an account intended to prove Banna's 'treason to the people's movement'.

[11] Whether Banna attended the banquet is in dispute, but oral evidence suggests that he did; see *MDA* (5 Jan. 1954), 13, which takes a negative stand on the issue.

the king supports the wide spread view that the former was important in whatever links existed between the latter and Banna. Sadat also, correctly, records that the Palestine war was a turning-point in this relationship.

What all this meant in practical terms throughout 1946 and 1947 is difficult to determine. The Society of the Brothers was obviously conceived of as an instrument against the Wafd and the communists. Banna appears to have received from Sidqi official courtesies which would have encouraged it in this role. Among them were the following: a licence to publish the official paper of the Society, *Jaridat al-Ikhwan al-Muslimin*, beginning in May 1946; privileges in the purchase of newsprint at official rates, which meant a saving of from 20 to 30 per cent of the black-market rates; privileges for the rovers (use of the national uniform purchased at a discount, and of government camps and facilities; and grants of land for buildings in the countryside). The appointment of Muhammad Hasan al-ʿAshmawi, who had long been a partisan of religious education in the secular schools and a friend of the Society, to the post of minister of education in the Sidqi cabinet seems to have been in the same order of things. Financial 'aid' may have been direct but more likely was channelled through the ministries of education and social affairs as legitimate government contributions to the education, social, and welfare services of the Society.

Whatever these arrangements may have been, in the light of events they meant virtually nothing. The Society's press maintained an almost unrelieved hostility to the governments and their works, matching at times the shrillness of the Wafdist organ. Government–Society clashes were almost continuous, especially in labour strikes and nationalist riots. The liaison with high authority was clearly a matter of 'high policy' with Banna and a few chosen colleagues. For the agitated membership there could be no question of serious or sustained links with palace governments. The nature of the clashes—labour and nationalist agitation and challenges to security—was a constant reminder of the essential incompatibility of the forces in alignment; the truth of this fact was dramatically emphasized in the violence and fury which marked its breakdown, beginning in 1948.

Thus the relations between authority and the Muslim Brothers were not much more than a temporary convenience. Between the Muslim Brothers and the Wafd, on the other hand, there was a genuine conflict, the more important because of its implications. The progressive weakening of the Wafd's prestige was accompanied by a weakening of the symbols of parliamentary life and a correspondingly large increase in the strength of extra-parliamentary groupings and in extra-legal activity. The ensuing violence was to encompass all the internal forces in the country; but as the Wafd and the Muslim Brothers were the only mass parties, it was their conflict that dominated the scene. Battle was joined on many fronts: in their most important newspapers, *al-Ikhwan al-Muslimin* and *al-Misri*, later *Sawt al-Umma*; in the countryside, in the form of intensive recruitment or fence-building; in labour agitation; and in the universities for control of the student body. The national movement, of course, was the focus of the struggle.

With all this in mind it is possible to go on to trace, with only enough of the detail of Egyptian history to make it meaningful, the course of the Muslim Brothers as they stepped forth into the centre of Egyptian political life.

The end of the war in May 1945 was the signal to align forces for another phase of the nationalist struggle with Great Britain. The Wafd leaped in as early as July 1945 by submitting to the British Ambassador a memorandum on the aspirations of the Egyptian people. The Muslim Brothers showed their intention by convening a 'people's congress' in Cairo and in seven major centres of the countryside[12] in early October to debate the national cause and to frame demands; thus serving notice on the Wafd, the government, and the British of the ambitious and universal role it expected to play. It was not until December 1945 that the Nuqrashi government formally requested the opening of negotiations on evacuation and the unity of the Nile Valley.

The Brothers' meetings just preceded the opening of the academic year at the universities, which were, as usual, the major focus of national agitation, and which would also be the scene of the most important part of the struggle between the Wafd and the Muslim Brothers. The university students, although united in their loyalty to the national cause, and on all important occasions acting in concert, were in fact bitterly divided over control of the national movement.

In Fu'ad (now Cairo) University, the main cleavage was between supporters of the Wafd and of the Muslim Brothers. The communists were in tactical alliance with the Wafd; the Brothers were most usually supported by the National party, the Young Egypt party of Ahmad Husayn, and a number of smaller groups of various political shadings. The first move was made by the Wafd when a group calling itself the 'Nationalist Committee' summoned

[12] Husayni, *Ikhwan*, p. 88.

a 'General Conference of Students on the National Demands' to be held on 7 October. On the day before the Muslim Brothers, in the first of many such manœuvres, called and held a student meeting which resolved to submit a memorandum to the government outlining the minimum demands of the national movement. At the meeting called for the 7th, the representative of the Brothers presented the resolutions of the earlier meeting and asked for the concurrence of this one, in the name of 'student unity'; immediately upon the heated rejection of the request, the Brothers withdrew from the meeting and dissociated themselves from the work of the group. They returned to its meetings in December, however, when elections for the leadership of the Nationalist Committee were held; but they unsuccessfully contested the Wafdist plank. From then on, given a 'mandate' by the students, the Committee changed its name to the 'Executive Committee'.[13]

Dissension was momentarily halted when on 26 January 1946 the British answer, cool and non-committal, to Nuqrashi's note arrived.[14] The students, infuriated by what was regarded as an affront to Egyptian sovereignty, pushed aside their differences and closed their ranks for a general student conference to draw up resolutions of protest. On 9 February a memorandum was dispatched to King Faruq demanding the immediate opening of negotiations. That same day, to give point to their views, the students began 'a peaceful march' on 'Abidin Palace. On the way they were dispersed by force by the police; the event, much disputed but now historic in the annals of the student movement is called the 'massacre of 'Abbas Bridge'. Every group in Egypt, including the Muslim Brothers whose leader in the university, Mustafa Mu'min, led the march, invoke on every appropriate occasion the memory of those 'martyred' at the bridge 'in the cause of Egypt and at the hands of the British-controlled Egyptian police'.[15]

On 10 February the king, scheduled to come to the university for the royal opening of the new dormitory, University City, arrived to find a sullen student body which refused to greet him. That afternoon, through his chief of royal cabinet, Ahmad Hasanayn, he invited all the student leaders to the palace for a conference at which he not only disclaimed any association with

[13] See RIIA, *GBE*, pp. 90–1, for part of the story; see also the vitriolic anti-Brothers tract, Ahmad, *Mizan*, pp. 80–3.

[14] Colombe, *Égypte*, pp. 228–9, and 243–6 for texts of the notes exchanged.

[15] The quotation is a summary of the student view. For two accounts of the incidents, see Colombe, *Égypte*, p. 229; and Rafi'i, *Thawra*, iii. 180–1. Those who fought the Muslim Brothers during this period with charges of 'treason' to the national movement find it difficult to explain the Brothers' share in this incident and other bloody events of this time; see e.g. Ahmad, *Mizan*, p. 83.

the police operation of the day before, but also hinted at the demise of the Nuqrashi government. On 11 February, a huge demonstration, also headed by Mustafa Mu'min, marched from the university to the palace, this time under police 'protection'. On 14 February the Nuqrashi ministry fell. The incident at the bridge was the last of a series of internal cabinet crises which made his continuance in power, for the moment, impossible.[16]

Isma'il Sidqi Pasha was called to form the new government and he immediately lifted the restrictions imposed on demonstrations by the preceding one: the palace felt that the people should be allowed to express themselves.[17] The arrival of the Sidqi government, and what appeared to his opposition to be an alliance between him and the Muslim Brothers, intensified the activity and the dissension in the national movement.

Immediately after Sidqi's appointment, the Wafd made a serious effort to enlarge the front it commanded by combining the students and industrial workers in a group called 'the National Committee of Students and Workers', an offspring of a communist-directed 'Workers' Committee of National Liberation'. The latter group was formed in October 1945, to direct the industrial strikes at the textile centre in Cairo, Shubra al-Khayma, about which more will be said shortly. The National Committee of Students and Workers without delay called a nation-wide strike for 21 February, 'the day of evacuation and unity of the Nile Valley', a strike which turned into one of the worst and bloodiest riots of the period, as students clashed with the police and the British forces who were still stationed in Cairo. In the preparations for the strike, the Brothers refused to join for many alleged reasons, the important one being the domination of the Committee by 'foreign elements', i.e. communists. A delegation from the Committee visited Banna to enlist his support and received the obviously unreal answer that 'the Muslim Brothers are not ready'.[18] It was clear that he would neither co-operate with communists nor be led by the Wafd. He was immediately charged with destroying the national movement at the behest of Sidqi Pasha. On the day of the strike the Muslim Brothers were, of course, out in full force, with the major focus of their independent activity in Alexandria. Whatever Banna might have promised Sidqi, it clearly could not have included the diversion of the national fervour of his followers.[19]

[16] On the fall of the cabinet, see Colombe, *Égypte*, pp. 229–30; and *JIM* (5 July 1946), 4.

[17] RIIA, *GBE*, p. 86.

[18] Ahmad, *Mizan*, pp. 84–5; RIIA, *GBE*, pp. 90–1.

[19] The following unconfirmed story is told by one of the characters in it. Banna, it is said, asked for and received from his colleagues on the Guidance Council a resolution of support for Sidqi's new government. Presumably on

On 27 February, in another attempt to outmanœuvre the Wafd, Banna, in the daily *al-Ahram*, published an appeal for a 'unified' committee to organize yet another nation-wide strike on 4 March, 'the day of national mourning' for the victims of the 21 February riots. The appeal went unanswered except for derisive accusations, again, that Banna was leading a counter-nationalist movement inspired by Sidqi 'to quiet the situation'. Banna went ahead and formed his own 'Higher Executive Committee' from a number of minor groupings. The strike went off peacefully, except in Alexandria, and included all groups in the country although under their own separate commands.[20]

During the next month university dissensions continued to be focused on Wafdist control of the students' voice, the Executive Committee. When the Brothers failed to unseat its leadership in another vote test, they created yet another competing group of the minority parties,—the 'National Committee'. But they continued the attempt to win control of the Executive Committee until on 17 April, during a celebration of the French evacuation of Syria, a verbal duel occurred, in which the Brothers openly charged the Wafdist front with 'communist affiliations'; the pitched battle which followed destroyed any possibility of a united front and set the stage for the further disintegration of relations between the two mass parties.[21] However, the university itself, in traditional manner, was no longer a problem for the government, because spring had come, and the examinations were now in sight.

Tension between the groups now focused, as did the attention of the government, on the paralysing strike at the huge textile centre of Shubra al-Khayma. It had begun in September 1945, under the leadership of communist-inspired trade unionists who had just returned from a conference in Paris of the World Federation of Trade Unions. On 8 October three members of the Egyptian delegation to that conference formed the 'Workers' Committee of National Liberation' which took the lead in the strike. Although they were arrested in January 1946, and their successors were continually harassed in the Sidqi campaign against

the occasion of the 21 February strike, Banna privately ordered one of the leading 'demonstration lieutenants' to call the Brothers out on the streets, in violation of Council policy. When confronted by the Guidance Council by what appeared to be insubordination on the part of the leader of the strike, Banna, without admitting his part, agreed to an investigation of the event, but successfully delayed and manœuvred the issue into oblivion.

---

[20] On these events, see RIIA, *GBE*, p. 86; Rafi'i, *Thawra*, iii. 184–7; and *JIM* (5 July 1946), 4.

[21] See Ahmad, *Mizan*, pp. 88–91; Rafi'i, *Thawra*, iii. 187; *JIM* (5 July 1946), 4, (3 June 1946), 2.

the left, contact was made with the Wafdist-communist coalition at the university, which resulted in the National Committee of Students and Workers already mentioned.

Workers in the Shubra area who were Brothers joined the strike soon after it began; and early in the New Year it won the support of the Brothers-dominated Tramways Union Syndicate. However, after the 4 March demonstration the Brothers withdrew all formal and informal contact with strike leaders.[22] As in the university they incurred the wrath of the communists and Wafd for breaking the common front against the government-supported management. There they had been charged with sharing Sidqi's anti-nationalist sentiments and thus with being 'tools of the imperialists'; here they were accused not only of 'strike-breaking' but also with 'spying' on the workers and thus with being 'enemies of the working class' in the service of the 'capitalists and exploiters'.[23] The Muslim Brothers, of course, denied these charges, and explained how well they understood the role of labour.[24] The charges and denials hurled back and forth did not seem to alter the fact that the Muslim Brothers did not, after March, co-operate with the communist-dominated committee in charge of the strike; The Society did, however, continue the strike of its own workers at Shubra and in Alexandria, exacerbating for months to come its relations with the government.[25]

These relations had grown more tense, in any case, when in April 1946 Sidqi declared his intention of beginning negotiations with the British. The Brothers' newspaper was from the first among the most vocal in articulating national demands. Periodically, like the other groups in the country, the Brothers were ordered out into the streets to remind Sidqi of his 'obligations' to the nation. The atmosphere of the negotiations was made difficult by charges of 'political deception' to every declaration of British friendship and mutuality of interests. Mass meetings were called regularly to take note of the situation at each interval in the talks.[26] Incidents in Alexandria on 31 May and 1 and 8 June were followed by arrests and then sporadic harassment of the meeting-places of

[22] RIIA, *GBE*, pp. 85–6; W. J. Handley, 'The Labor Movement in Egypt', *MEJ* (July 1949), 283.

[23] See Boehm, 'Les Frères musulmans', 218, 220; and Ahmad, *Mizan*, pp. 38–50. A recent addition to the leftist literature on Egypt is Anouar Abdel-Malek, *Égypte, société militaire* (1962). While primarily concerned with an analysis of the present régime, it does briefly consider the matters under discussion for this period on pp. 32–4.

[24] See e.g. *JIM*, 3, 14, 17 June 1946. For further treatment of the Brothers and labour, see below, pp. 277–82.

[25] See *JIM*, 24, 25, 27 July and 6 Oct. 1946.

[26] See e.g. *JIM*, 8 May, 3 June, and 1 Sept. 1946.

the Brothers in July and August; mosque prayers were put under surveillance; and the rovers were denied freedom of movement in September. During that same month, after continuous denunciation of Sidqi's 'persecution' of the Society, Banna warned him: 'What God has joined together none can put asunder.'[27] The sense of righteous power was gaining momentum.

Despite these developments, the Wafd press continued to elaborate the theme of the Banna–Sidqi alliance. In early July the bitterness generated between the two mass parties exploded in a series of pitched battles between the youth of the two groups, as they attempted to break up each other's meetings in Isma'iliyya and Port Sa'id. In one of these an exploding bomb nearly killed Banna.[28] Each group, of course, accused the other of provocation. The Wafd, seizing on the event and on a series of threatening letters allegedly directed to leading Wafdists, addressed a memorandum to Sidqi warning him that it would 'take the law into its own hands if the authorities did not put an end to acts of Fascist terror committed by the Brothers'. Specifically, it demanded the dissolution of 'the phalanxes of the Muslim Brothers', i.e. the rovers.[29]

The vitriolic press campaign which the Wafd directed at Banna—especially the charge of intimacy with the government—was having its effect, meanwhile, in the Society itself. In its newspaper, Banna repeatedly had to deny the accusations. In June he called a special meeting of the members to explain his position *vis-à-vis* Sidqi. He gave the members the traditional explanation that the Muslim Brothers neither opposed nor supported any government as such, because the Society was not a political party in the accepted and corrupted sense of that word. Any money coming to the Society from Sidqi was a legitimate government contribution to its welfare agencies. He similarly repudiated as ridiculous the notion that he had 'interfered' in the labour movement and as a result had benefited the 'capitalist exploiters of the people'.[30]

During the following months these reiterated themes rang more convincingly to members as relations between Society and

[27] *JIM* (1 Sept. 1946), 1, 3. See also ibid., 14 June, 9, 11 July, 28 Sept. 1946.

[28] See *JIM*, 7, 8 July 1946. See also *JWM*, 7 July 1946; *JSU*, 25 Aug. 1946; and *COC*, vii–viii (1946), 321–2.

[29] See Boehm, 'Les Frères musulmans', 212–13; *JWM*, 9 July 1946; *JSU*, 17 Sept. and 19 Oct. 1946. The Wafd argued its position from laws passed in 1933 and 1938 forbidding any political party to have at its disposal formations of a military character. Wafdist youth, while not at this time organized in formations similar to the earlier Blue Shirts of the party at which the above laws were aimed, were nevertheless performing the same functions with reasonable skill.

[30] *JIM* (3 June 1946), 1; and p. 47, n. 24, above.

government became more obviously strained. This, together with pressures from within the organization, led in August or September to secret meetings between Siraj al-Din, the leader of the right wing of the Wafd, and Ahmad al-Sukkari, first deputy of the Muslim Brothers and its political liaison officer. The purpose of the meeting was to achieve 'understanding' and 'the resolution of conflicts'. Both groups denied that any 'treaty' had been signed between them,[31] and indeed, while tensions were curbed at the time, not until much later, in 1949–50, did any cordiality develop in their relations. Inside the organization, however, the meetings stimulated the schism which broke the oldest and strongest friendship in the Society, that of Banna and Sukkari, as will be described presently.

The meeting of the Wafd and Muslim Brothers was, significantly, timed to coincide with the rapidly approaching climax of the Anglo-Egyptian negotiations. After weathering a cabinet crisis (1–12 September) and three months of fruitless negotiation in Cairo, Sidqi went to London on 17 October 1946. Between the opening of the national question and his departure, the national movement had passed from the stage of insisting on the terms of negotiations to that of demanding that no negotiations at all should take place until after evacuation. Banna sent a letter to the king and to Sidqi pleading for 'an invitation to the nation to *jihad*',[32] and an economic, cultural, and social boycott of England. In a message to 'the people of the Nile Valley', he prophetically announced: 'The government of Sidqi Pasha, in its insistence on negotiations, does not represent the will of the nation; any treaty or alliance concluded by it with Britain, before evacuation of her forces, is void and does not bind the nation.'[33] The day before Sidqi left for England, the Brothers gave point to the warning by calling for major demonstrations all over the countryside and in cities.[34]

Sidqi returned to Cairo on 25 October with the outlines of the Sidqi–Bevin draft treaty, only to have what was regarded as a victory break down completely owing to misunderstandings by both parties about its terms.[35] The nationalists greeted the draft with unqualified hostility. Its terms became known—unfortunately for its chances of acceptance—at the beginning of the autumn session at the universities. On 16 November the students joined in a 'National Front of Students of the Nile Valley'; the harmless initial activity of speechmaking and sending letters of protest to

[31] Ibid. (15 Oct. 1946), 2; and *JSU* (11 Sept. 1946), 2; see also Boehm, 'Les Frères musulmans', 212.
[32] *JIM*, (8 Oct. 1946), 1.
[33] Ibid. (10 Oct. 1946), 4.
[34] Ibid. 16, 17 Oct. 1946.
[35] For two views, see RIIA, *GBE*, pp. 92–7; and Rafi'i, *Thawra*, iii. 195–213.

members of parliament and the government became, within a week, daily riots which by 25 November exploded into orgies of fire—English books, stores, trams, and trees—and attacks on security and British forces in all the major centres. In part this day had been foreseen for over a month in the campaign of the Brothers for a 'cultural boycott' of the English which had been declared formally on 21 October, and which included a mass collection of English-language books to be consumed on 'the day of the fire' which finally took place on 25 November.[36] The event was sufficient, in the explosive first month of the academic year, to inspire the student community as a whole to participate and extend the horizons of the day.

The government struck back sharply. The university and the newspapers were closed, Cairo was placed under virtual siege, and numerous arrests were made from among Wafdists, communists, socialists, and the Muslim Brothers. On 27 November Ahmad al-Sukkari, Banna's deputy, who had been arrested and released on the 25th, was re-arrested for inflammatory speeches praising the rioters. Hasan al-Banna at the time was on the pilgrimage. Continuing arrests followed continuous rioting in the next week, which included, more prominently, attacks on British establishments and personnel and on the Egyptian police.[37] By 8 December, the rioting had served its purpose: having failed in his mission to sell the treaty to Egypt, Sidqi Pasha resigned. King Faruq called once more upon Mahmud Fahmi al-Nuqrashi Pasha to form a cabinet on 9 December.

Formal resistance to the idea of the treaty was continued through the so-called 'Liaison Committee' composed of the groups in opposition to it; the Muslim Brothers refused to join, arguing that the committee lacked 'sincerity'. The Wafd, of course, revived the charge that Banna was obstructing the national movement by allying himself with the government, a charge given surface substance by what was to follow. Meanwhile, on 25 January 1947, Nuqrashi broke off negotiations and declared his intention of bringing Egypt's case before the Security Council of the United Nations.

Many months earlier the Muslim Brothers had recommended this course.[38] They therefore, decided to send a mission of their own with Nuqrashi, because, as they put it, 'two voices are louder than one'.[39] Their representative, Mustafa Mu'min, left Cairo on

[36] *JIM*, 21 Oct. and 24 Nov. 1946.

[37] Ibid. 28 Nov., 1, 2, 4 Dec. 1946; Colombe, *Égypte*, pp. 233–6; and *COC*, vii–viii (1946), 323–4, 340.

[38] *JIM.*, 8 May 1946.

[39] Mu'min, *Sawt Misr*, p. 1. This is a book of recollections about modern Egypt and impressions of the United States gathered on this trip in 1947. When

26 July. In the United States he travelled and spoke on behalf of the Egyptian cause and made himself heard at the United Nations itself. On 22 August, while a resolution recommending a resumption of negotiations was being discussed, he delivered an impassioned speech from the spectators' gallery and produced a document, signed with students' blood, which repudiated negotiations and demanded the complete evacuation and immediate reunification of the Nile Valley. Expelled from the debating chamber on this and on a later occasion, Mu'min returned before the end of the Security Council sessions on Egypt, and, with the aid of a New York maritime union which included some former Egyptians, produced a 'demonstration' outside the United Nations building.[40]

From Egypt Banna sent telegrams not only of support to Nuqrashi but of demands to the Security Council and to the heads of delegations. He rapidly and vehemently repudiated the rejection of Nuqrashi as the legitimate voice of Egypt, which was telegraphed by Mustafa al-Nahhas, head of the Wafd, to the Security Council. This, for the Wafd, was evidence of the 'treason' of the Muslim Brothers to the national cause.[41] It shows the strength of the feeling aroused that Banna himself led some of the popular demonstrations during August.[42]

The Security Council adjourned on 10 September with the Egyptian question still unsolved.[43] On his return Nuqrashi was met by the Muslim Brothers in force and greeted with that combination of super-patriotism and hypersensitive warmth reserved for defeated heroes. The inaction of the Security Council heightened the nationalists' sense of frustration. The 'internationalization' of the Egyptian question had done little more than accentuate the international isolation of Egypt and reinforce the already deep mistrust of the Western countries. This mistrust and frustration became even more important when on 29 November 1947 the Security Council decreed the partition of Palestine. A new phase in the life of Egypt and the Muslim Brothers was under

the problem of the official delegation arose, a Cairo daily carried a cartoon depicting all the country's leaders marching to the United Nations; among them was Hasan al-Banna, who was crossed out, however, because, the cartoon explained: 'The members of the Security Council are Christians and do not like the Muslim Brothers'. (See *MAS* (29 Jan. 1947), 13.) This was less a slur on the Muslim Brothers than a reflection of the state of mind of even the most Westernized of Egyptians as they viewed Egyptian relations with the West.

---

[40] Mu'min, *Sawt Misr*, pp. 1–4, 295–325 and accompanying pictures. See also *NYT* (23 Aug. 1947), 1, 4; (27 Aug. 1947), 11.

[41] As also for the later revolutionary government; see *Irhab*, pp. 91–2.

[42] *COC*, xi–xii (1947), 212–13; *MDA* (13 Feb. 1951), 22.

[43] For two versions, see RIIA, *GBE*, pp. 99–107; Rafi'i, *Thawra*, iii. 222–34.

way. Before resuming that story, however, something must be said about developments inside the Society.

INTERNAL SCHISMS

Inside the organization, 1947 marked a year of crisis and schism. A morals charge against the secretary-general and a serious policy dispute between Banna and his deputy resulted in a number of resignations and dismissals which partially paralysed the administrative apparatus, and which, coinciding with the increasingly strong pressure of external events, enhanced the role of the secret apparatus.

Late in 1945 Banna was advised that his secretary-general, 'Abd al-Hakim 'Abidin (also his brother-in-law), was taking advantage of his position 'to violate the homes and honour of some of the Brothers'. For some weeks the allegations did not go beyond Banna, the complainants, and a few of the top leaders. One of Banna's two deputies, Ibrahim Hasan, was commissioned to conduct a secret and informal investigation. Before the issue could be settled, however, the news leaked to the membership and by mid-1946 was causing serious repercussions. A first proposal from Hasan—to dismiss both 'Abidin and the four members of the Guidance Council who had accused him—proved to be unacceptable. Banna was thereupon compelled to appoint a committee of investigation composed of leading members. After months of 'hearings', during which further complaints were voiced, the committee, although 'it could not reach agreement' on the validity of the charges, urged that 'Abidin should be dismissed from the Society 'as a measure of purification'. One of the angry members of the committee in his report described the defendant as 'the Rasputin of the Society of the Muslim Brothers'.

The Guidance Council decreed the dismissal of 'Abidin by an 8–1 vote of those present. The matter then went to the Consultative Assembly, which, apparently under persuasion from Banna, established a new committee responsible to it for a new investigation. The vote on the new report brought an acquittal for 'Abidin. Banna seems to have succeeded in convincing a majority of the assembly that 'for the sake of the Society', the vote should be 'not guilty'; he promised, in return, to send the accused away and, after a period, to demand his resignation. Involved in the decision of the second committee, it has been argued, was the important fact of Banna's family relationship with 'Abidin and the dishonour to himself which would have followed a conviction. The resignation was forthcoming, but in calmer times Banna persuaded the

Guidance Council to reject it. The failure of the leader to dismiss the secretary-general, however, cost him one of his oldest members; in April 1947 Ibrahim Hasan resigned in protest.[44]

Hasan's departure from the Society was followed in a few months by the dismissal of the other deputy, Ahmad al-Sukkari. The occasion was a policy disagreement over relations with the Wafd. As political liaison officer, Sukkari's chief contacts were with the Wafd. In the post-war situation of conflict his role took on greater significance, especially among those who felt that conflict with the Wafd was inevitable, but who questioned its desirability when it served the palace—as it seemed to do in 1946. Banna, as we have already seen, felt compelled repeatedly to deny Wafdist allegations concerning his relations with the governments of Sidqi and Nuqrashi through 1946 and 1947. The serious violence of early July 1946 between the two parties inspired second thoughts in the minds of some, and was partly responsible for the negotiations between the spokesmen for the groups, Siraj al-Din and Sukkari, in the three months following the clashes. The meetings certainly reflected a common desire to wreck the Sidqi–Bevin draft treaty, then almost completely negotiated; for Sukkari, however, there was also the deeper problem of the ultimate relationship between the two mass parties.

This was not a new issue in the thinking of the leaders of the Society; Banna, it was said, had accepted in principle the idea of a coalition if the Wafd would adopt the programme and principles of the Society. Sukkari, the 'political thinker', had enunciated a clearer and more concrete view: that the Society of the Brothers could be a power in Egypt only in organic union with the Wafd; that to exercise influence on an electorate or have authority, it must work through and rely on a (secular?) political party. The Wafd, the only party with a popular following, was that party. Sukkari envisaged the role of the Muslim Brothers as the 'spiritual' fulfilment of the Wafd. He also saw himself as 'political' leader of the Muslim Brothers, and Hasan al-Banna as their 'spiritual' guide, working together as part of an irresistible union of the 'people's parties'. Sukkari, quite apart from the sincerity or intensity of his

[44] On this story, see the only available public although partial accounts in Kira, *Mahkama*, ii. 31–5; and *JJ* (23 Sept. 1954), 1, 8, and 4. The latter account omits any mention of Banna's hand in the overruling of the first by the second committee. Both of these accounts, from government sources, are regarded by the Brothers as unfair, but they do not, in fact, differ materially from accounts given by Brothers themselves, except in the omission of the interesting defence made by 'Abidin and his partisans: that in entering the homes of the Brothers he did so honourably fulfilling his informal role of wife-seeker and marriage-arranger for the community of the Brothers; and that personal rivalries and jealousies were the real cause of the dispute.

views on union with the Wafd, had, in effect, decided to challenge Banna's role as leader of the Society. His underlying motive, as was the case with Ibrahim Hasan and an unrecorded number of other leading members, was rebellion against Banna's continued exercise of arbitrary power. The regulations formulated in 1945 were admittedly designed to herald a gradual abdication by Banna of his position, and the distribution of his power and functions to appropriately established governing units; the process did not occur fast enough. The issue assumed greater urgency—and perhaps this was the reason why Sukkari focused his dispute on the question of union with the Wafd—when Banna, out of all accord with the forces at work in the movement, seemed to have made the Society an instrument of the palace.

The airing of the differences between the two old friends remained a private issue, during 1946, at the top levels of the Society. The public explosion of the ʿAbidin affair, together with Banna's questionable attitude and responses to it, and the mounting uneasiness about the external relations of the Society coincided in time to produce a serious crisis. Both issues converged on Banna. Shortly after Hasan left in April 1947, Banna brought Sukkari before the Consultative Assembly and presented the questions posed by him. The assembly acquiesced in the leader's desire—made known from behind the scenes—that Sukkari be dismissed.[45]

The departure of Hasan and Sukkari at almost the same time created a real, if not apparent, problem of administration and morale. One member says that the dispute gave 'the enemies of the Society' ammunition with which to attack it, dissipated all the energies of 'the public organization' (*al-hay'at al-ʿamma*), and prevented it from 'facing up to [outside] events'. In the circumstances, this observer notes, Banna was compelled to take 'this burden' on his shoulders 'with the aid of the special section which was bound to him personally'.[46]

The activation of the secret apparatus was, in fact, hastened by this paralysing crisis in the leadership. It is significant that the man chosen by Banna to replace Hasan and Sukkari as his deputy was the first head of the secret apparatus, Salih ʿAshmawi. What happened after this is difficult to determine with precision. The secret apparatus by this time appears to have become fully structured, with appropriate rules delineating functions, com-

[45] Alexander, 'Left and Right in Egypt', 125, mentions as one of the issues of the dispute Banna's acceptance of money from the British in 1946. The dispute as we have described it has not been publicly treated to our knowledge; the above account is from oral sources from both sides.

[46] See Appendix A attached to the original version of this study.

mands, authority, and responsibilities, and appropriate symbols, oaths, and equipment. Its numbers, never very large, were qualitatively increased by recruits from among army officers, probably including some of those who later participated in the revolution of 1952. Banna's relationship to the group was technically that of supreme leader, but he kept in touch with it through selected representatives. The leadership of the apparatus itself passed from 'Ashmawi to 'Abd al-Rahman al-Sanadi, whose assumption of extraordinary and ambitious powers raised questions of communication peripherally attested to by periodic changes of unsuccessful liaison officers between him and Banna, by the final assumption of that role by Banna himself, and in comments attributed to Banna about some of the activity for which the secret apparatus was later responsible.[47]

PALESTINE

Of events outside the Society, the Palestine question became the most pressing, following the adoption of the United Nations resolution on partition in November 1947. The Society had first become directly involved in Palestinian affairs when Banna's brother 'Abd al-Rahman visited Palestine in 1935 and met Haj Amin al-Husayni, mufti of Jerusalem and chairman of the Supreme Muslim Council of that time.[48] The visit reflected the predictable concern of the Muslim Brothers—as Egyptians, as Arabs, and as Muslims—for the cause of Palestine. 'Abd al-Rahman al-Banna had been the chief and most articulate spokesman of that concern from the earliest days of the movement in Cairo.[49] The first formal act of support came during the Arab general strikes of 1936–7. At the third general conference, in March 1935, Banna had appealed for money to assist the cause of the Arabs and had established a committee to propagandize the issue through telegrams and letters to the authorities concerned, and through the press, pamphlets, and speeches. These devices were supported by public demonstrations on behalf of the strikers in Palestine and with the dispatch of supplies and equipment.[50]

The war years provided little opportunity for communications

[47] For hints that this was the case, reinforced from oral sources, see Kira, *Mahkama*, i. 33–4; Muh. al-Tabi'i, *et al.*, *Ha'ula' hum al-Ikhwan* [Cairo, 1954], pp. 52–3; and also D. Peters, 'The Muslim Brotherhood', 9. See also below, pp. 55, 73.

[48] *Mudh.*, p. 213.

[49] See 'Abd al-Rahman al-Banna, *Thawrat al-damm* (1951), for a number of articles on Palestine from the earliest of the Society's official journals.

[50] See above, p. 15–16, and *Mudh.*, pp. 222–7, 241–2, 262; *RNUNA*, p. 6; Banna, *TIWMI*, pp. 37–8. Sharif, *IMFHF*, p. 42, claims that 'volunteers' were sent to aid the Arab strike. In *MMB* (26 Dec. 1950), 9, the mufti testified to the accuracy of this claim.

though there seem to have been contacts with Amin al-Husayni. Immediately after the war relations were resumed through missions sent from Egypt not only to spread the message of the movement but to inspire resistance to Zionism. Among the missions were 'technical' personnel to assist in the establishment and training of Palestinian rovers. Most prominent of these was Mahmud Labib, a retired army officer who had contributed his services to the Society and became 'deputy for military affairs'; he was sent to Palestine to assist in the military training of civil groups. Along with other Brothers, he was asked in 1947 by the British authorities to leave.[51]

Even now, however, the major activity was in the field of propaganda in the Arab world at large and in Egypt. The question of Palestine was kept alive and kept foaming by continual reference to it in the press, in pamphlets, in public speeches, in popular meetings, and in demonstrations. When the mufti, Haj Amin, arrived in Cairo in 1946, the Muslim Brothers' newspaper led the successful appeals to the government to grant him asylum.[52] From the end of the war Banna had been in close contact with the Arab League and especially with its head, his old friend 'Azzam Pasha, on the issue; after the partition decision in November 1947, he joined with other 'Islamic personalities' like Salih Harb Pasha of the Young Men's Muslim Association and Muhammad 'Aluba Pasha to form a 'Committee of the Nile Valley' to collect money and arms for the 'volunteers' now being openly recruited 'to save Palestine'. Mustafa Mu'min was the Muslim Brothers' representative on this committee.[53]

In October 1947 Banna ordered the branches of the Society to start preparing for *jihad*; on the 20th, the first 'battalion' (*katiba*) went on display. The rapid 'mobilization' was possible, of course, because the first members of this and the other 'battalions' sent from the Society were already trained members of the rovers and the secret apparatus.[54]

It was Banna's feeling, shared by 'Azzam Pasha and the mufti, that governments as such should not be involved in the Palestine question beyond the diplomatic and political support they could give the Arabs of Palestine; that if fighting became a necessity, it should be left to the Palestinians themselves and to 'volunteers'.

[51] *JIM*, 14 June, 11 Aug., 17, 23 Oct., 15, 24 Dec. 1946; Sharif, *IMFHF*, pp. 43–6; 'Assal, *BKA*, p. 43, n. 1; *Aqwal wa-ta'dhib*, pp. 30–1.

[52] *JIM* (21 June 1946), 1; on propaganda work in the Arab countries, see *JIM* (21 May 1946), 3; and *MDA* (17 Feb. 1951), 22.

[53] *Aqwal wa-ta'dhib*, p. 32. The Society was in 1954 charged with misuse of the funds collected for Palestine; see e.g. *JJ* (22 Nov. 1954), 3.

[54] See *MDA* (13 Feb. 1951), 22; and *JJ* (12 Nov. 1954), 4.

In this way, it was felt that the issue could be kept an 'internal issue' and thus preclude the involvement of international bodies.[55] The plan was never officially accepted by Nuqrashi's government; but pressed by the League, which was prepared to finance it, he did permit the official training of volunteers, provided it was done by an army officer. The League, for its part, organized a volunteer movement all over the Arab world, including North Africa, and supplied all those who came with arms and training.[56] The Brothers, on their own initiative, personal and collective, added to the growing store of arms;[57] and they themselves were trained and armed, privately, it would seem, by army-officer members of the secret apparatus.

On 25 April 1948, weeks before the official war began, the first battalion of volunteers set out for al-'Arish, on the frontier, and was joined by its commander, an officer on leave from the army, Ahmad 'Abd al-'Aziz. They were later joined by other officers, including Kamal al-Din Husayn and Salah Salim, later of the original revolutionary junta; like 'Aziz, they had left their units to join the battle with the volunteers. These officers and others of like mind still in the army continued to be a source of training and equipment for the Brothers throughout the Palestine War.[58]

How many of the Brothers were involved in the Palestine War is not known nor are their activities clear. However, a few general points can be made.[59] Even before the arrival of the 'official volunteers' of the Arab League, Brothers were engaging Zionists in the Negev, and learned, in their attempts to take some of the settlements, some early and bitter lessons about warfare.[60] After the arrival of Ahmad 'Abd al-'Aziz, and after the formal opening of hostilities in May, a number of minor engagements occurred, which seem to have been no more than harassing missions directed

[55] *MDA* (13 Feb. 1951), 22; (15 June 1954), 6.

[56] Sharif, *IMFHF*, pp. 62 f., 101, 103; *Aqwal wa-ta'dhib*, pp. 44–5. See also Boehm, 'Les Frères musulmans', 222–3.

[57] *Aqwal wa-ta'dhib*, pp. 3–16, 31, 44; *MMB* (16 June 1950), 8–9, 16.

[58] See *JJ* (9 June 1954), 4; *MMR* (14 Nov. 1952), 12–13; *MJJ* (20 July 1953), 4–5. Sadat, *Safahat*, pp. 176–7, says: 'The Free Officers felt it a duty to train the youth who volunteered for the battle, to volunteer with them and to lead them during battle.' Sadat records (pp. 177–82) the meetings in the home of Banna with the Free Officers, including Gamal 'Abd al-Nasir, for purposes of uniting effort.

[59] Sharif, *IMFHF*, is the only work by a Brother about the Palestine war. Other information is scanty and/or confusing.

[60] See esp. Sharif, *IMFHF*, pp. 80–101. Following these first engagements it was decided to use guerrilla tactics rather than direct assault on Zionist positions. The bodies of the first twelve 'martyrs' were brought back to Cairo and given large public funerals; see *MDA* (13 Feb. 1951), 22, 31; and Buhi, *MSI*, pp. 24–36, for some short sketches of the lives of these and others of the volunteers for Palestine.

at Zionist positions and of little note, except for the contributions to the Arab defence of Jerusalem and Bethlehem, both before and after the first truce of June–July. ʿAziz was killed accidentally by an Egyptian sentry's bullet in August 1948, and was replaced by a new commander, who brought with him a new battalion of volunteers to join the remnants of the first. All seem to have been sent to the Jordan sector of the frontier, where, because of differences with the Jordan authorities, they remained virtually immobilized.[61]

The Brothers' most notable achievement was the assistance they rendered to the besieged Egyptians caught in the 'Faluja pocket', created by the Israeli advance after the second truce had broken down in October 1948. In the field the Brothers helped to run supplies through to the encircled forces; in Cairo the Society joined with others to press the Egyptian government for more volunteers to relieve the trapped garrison. Nuqrashi refused,[62] and it was only in the following February, after the armistice agreements, that the pocket was relieved.

The Faluja excitement reached its highest pitch in November 1948. Early in the next month the Society of the Muslim Brothers no longer legally existed. On the night of 8 December the forces of the Muslim Brothers in Palestine were ordered into camps. Next morning they found themselves surrounded by Egyptian troops; they were then informed of the decree, which had just been made public, dissolving the Society. According to the historian of the Brothers in the Palestine War, the commander-in-chief of the Egyptian forces, Fu'ad Sadiq, gave them the choice of laying down their arms and returning to Cairo, or staying at the front, under controls, and continuing to assist the army. Most of them elected to stay, inspired, he suggests, by their devotion to the task in hand and by a message from Banna pleading for calm and order.[63] Following the Rhodes agreement and the realignment and redeployment of forces on both sides, these, their arms confiscated, joined their Brothers in Cairo in 'the persecution'.[64]

VIOLENCE AND DISSOLUTION

Underlying the order dissolving the Muslim Brothers in 1948 was the belief that the Society was planning imminent revolution. More immediately, however, the order related to the stream of

[61] Sharif, *IMFHF*, pp. 109–72.

[62] Ibid., pp. 145–6, 160–6, 173–9; *Aqwal wa-taʿdhib*, pp. 38–40; *MDA* (7 Oct. 1952), 15. The question of the Faluja pocket was finally settled with the transfer of the area to Israel and the evacuation of the garrison to Egypt by the Rhodes Armistice Agreement of 24 February 1949; see Rafiʿi, *Thawra*, iii. 256. Among the defenders of Faluja was Gamal ʿAbd al-Nasir.

[63] Sharif, *IMFHF*, pp. 146–7, 179–85.

[64] *Aqwal wa-taʿdhib*, pp. 5–16.

violence which shook Egypt from 1945 onwards, in which the role of the Muslim Brothers, although not unique, was the most dramatic and, from the point of view of the government, the most potentially dangerous.

The violent struggle for primacy between the Wafd and the Muslim Brothers was itself part of a larger picture of violence involving all the organized and unorganized groups in the country in their challenges to each other and to the governing authority. Mutual antipathies were exacerbated by the passions and sense of frustration aroused by the conflicts with Zionism and the British. The so-called 'minority governments' had little or no ability—or will—to attract any significant popular following. Their resort at times to the Muslim Brothers as an instrument against the Wafd can be seen as an attempt to compensate for this, but such manœuvres could be no more than temporary, since, whatever the intentions of their leaders, the Muslim Brothers were in the vanguard of the forces which precipitated the crisis. In retrospect these years can be seen as the beginning of the final phase of the breakdown of parliamentary life and the rule of law in Egypt, which culminated in the revolution of 1952. Disorder, destruction, violence, and bloodshed, inspired by any and all groups wielding a minimum of power, official or unofficial, were the costly accompaniment of that breakdown.

The assassination of Ahmad Mahir, in February 1945, followed his declaration of war on the Axis and reflected the widespread resistance to what were regarded as the pro-British sentiments of Mahir and the Sa'dist party. His assassin, as already noted, only admitted to being a member of the National party.

That event was followed in December 1945 by an abortive attempt on the life of Nahhas Pasha by a young nationalist named Husayn Tawfiq; in January 1946 he succeeded in killing the war-time minister of finance, Amin 'Uthman Pasha, widely accused of being a 'British agent'.[65] The assassin confessed readily to the murder and to the attempt on Nahhas; later he made known his associates, including among them Anwar al-Sadat, who was imprisoned for thirty-one months but later released after acquittal by a court. Since the revolution of 1952, he has continued to boast of his share in the responsibility for this death and for his organization of 'a murder society to liquidate others holding like treasonable views'.[66] The case was celebrated in Egypt as the

65 See Rafi'i, *Thawra*, iii. 265–6; Issawi, *Egypt*, p. 268. RIIA, *GBE*, p. 81, describes 'Uthman as 'the principal intermediary between Nahhas and the British Embassy during the Wafdist Government' of 1942–4.

66 H. Lehrman, 'Three Weeks in Cairo', *Commentary* (Feb. 1956), 103; see also Sadat, *Safahat*, pp. 159–60.

'political assassinations case' and again received front-page treatment when 'Uthman's assassin made his escape in June 1948, taking with him the good wishes of the great numbers who supported his 'patriotic' act.[67]

In their confessions the group involved in the 'political assassinations case' admitted plans for other murders and violence to be directed at the British—a field of operation always attractive to the nationalists. From 1946 onwards, in the large cities until after evacuation,[68] and then in the Canal Zone whither the troops were withdrawn, bomb assaults on the British in their passing cars, establishments, or enclaves were common. In this, it would seem that all groups vied with each other. The Muslim Brothers, apparently, used this kind of operation as 'training tests' for the personnel of the secret apparatus. It is some indication of their state of mind that they were just as ready to use Egyptian police posts for target practice.[69] 'Imperialism' and 'government' were becoming more consciously one and the same 'enemy'.

In May 1946 and in May 1947 two theatres in Cairo, the Cinema Metro and the Cinema Miami, were partially destroyed by bombs; in both bombings the loss of life was confined to Egyptians. In the first instance, no accusations were made; arrests following the second explosion and the subsequent trial—called the 'Cairo bomb trial'—cast guilt on the group arrested for the first bombing and for other attempts on British and Egyptians during the period. The group called itself *Rabitat al-Shabab* and primarily included Wafdists.[70]

In the autumn of 1947, after the Security Council had dismissed the Egyptian case and during its debate on Palestine, paramilitary formations for the National Party, for the Wafd, and for the Young Men's Muslim Association appeared publicly in Cairo—all boasting arms, munitions, and explosives to be used in Palestine and against the British, but also, apparently, for use against fellow Egyptians. Colombe, describing the situation at the end of 1947, says: 'Tentatives incendiaires à l'aide de bouteilles enflammées lancées dans les vitrines des magasins, explosions, assassinats et attentats à la bombe, deviennent les faits courants de la vie politique intérieure.'[71] The year ended in December with almost

[67] See Heyworth-Dunne, *Modern Egypt*, p. 39 and n. 39; see also Rafi'i, *Thawra*, iii. 218–19, 267.

[68] The Citadel was evacuated on 4 July 1946, but the last troops left the Qasr al-Nil barracks on 29 March 1947; see Rafi'i, *Thawra*, iii. 218–19.

[69] Ibid., p. 266; *JIM* (6 May 1946), 3, and the two subsequent issues; and *Qadiyat al-Nuqrashi*, p. 110.

[70] Heyworth-Dunne, *Modern Egypt*, p. 99. Cf. *JM* (4 Jan. 1949), 6, for a denial of Wafdist ties; and *Irhab*, pp. 28–40, for an accusation of the Brothers.

[71] M. Colombe, 'Où va l'Égypte', *AA* (no. 4, 1948), 35; see also *COC* (1947), 212; and (1948), 224.

daily demonstrations in the two capitals, Cairo and Alexandria, in protest against the Security Council's decision of 29 November to partition Palestine, which, like almost all demonstrations related to Palestine, took a decidedly destructive, anti-foreign turn.[72]

1948 was the year for the Muslim Brothers. In January the government announced that in a secluded spot in the Muqattam hills on the outskirts of Cairo it had discovered 165 bombs and cases of arms, which were confiscated after a battle between the police and some young Muslim Brothers who were training in the hills. The young men claimed to have hoarded the arms for Palestine—'bought from the Arabs [i.e. Bedouin] for the Arabs'. Their leader, Sayyid Fayiz, unbeknown to the government a leader of the secret apparatus, was arrested and, together with the others, immediately released.[73] Arms-gathering 'for the Arabs' and 'training', thus apparently vindicated, went on apace.

On 17 February 1948 attention shifted, for the moment, to the capital city of the Yemen, San'a and the *coup d'état* by the so--called 'Free Yemeni Movement' which cost the life of the aged Imam Yahya and three of his sons. Persistent rumours were soon circulating that the Muslim Brothers were involved. They were undoubtedly in touch with the 'Free Yemenis'. As early as 17 February 1947 Banna had cabled to the then crown prince, Sayf al-Islam Ahmad, urging action 'to raise the Yemeni social level'; five days later a mission was appointed and sent to the Yemen with 'this purpose' in mind.[74] The other interest of the Brothers in the Yemen was indicated by a telegram sent on 15 March 1948, in the midst of the post-coup crisis, by Banna to Sayf al-Islam Ahmad, now the victorious new Imam, urging his acceptance of 'the arbitration of the Arab League' on the basis of a new constitution drawing its support from 'the national will' (lit.: *qawa'id al-mithaq al-qawmi*), and in which the ruler would be 'a constitutional Imam'; he also supported the view that the rebel leader should be accepted into the government as 'leader of the consultative assembly' (*ra'is li-majlis al-shura*), thus establishing in the Yemen a 'constitutional government'.[75]

To what extent this interest in the 'reform' of the Yemen expressed itself in actual planning and participation in the event with the leaders of the movement, al-Sayyid 'Abdullah ibn-Ahmad

[72] See 'Developments of the Quarter', *MEJ* (Apr. 1948), 205.

[73] *JM* (22 Jan. 1948), 6; *Haythiyat wa-hukm*, pp. 26–7.

[74] *MDA* (13 Feb. 1951), 31.

[75] *Irhab*, pp. 49–50. Heyworth-Dunne, *Modern Egypt*, pp. 17–18, described the coup as an attempt to establish 'a constitutional government based on Islamic laws'. Ghazali, *MHN*, p. 106, praised the 'revolt against the priesthood' in the Yemen.

al-Wazir and the sixth son of the aged Imam, Sayf al-Haqq Ibrahim, is not, however, clear. Missions before and after the coup have been interpreted as part of a plot directed from Cairo; money was allegedly sent—or preparations were being made to send it—to Banna by the dissidents either for the purchase of equipment or in return for the aid of the Society.[76] Until, however, more information becomes available, not much more can be said than that the Society did support the goals of the Free Yemeni Movement, and actively worked on behalf of the dissidents after the failure of the coup brought the issue before Arab public and official opinion.[77] The Brothers have not made much effort to refute allegations of complicity with the 'Free Yemenis', and freely admit their interest in 'reforming the Yemen'. While essentially unrelated to the crisis in Egypt, the events in the Yemen and the involvement of the Brothers necessarily had their effect there.

In Egypt, on 22 March, events took a tragic turn with the news of the assassination of a respected judge on his way to work: Ahmad al-Khazindar Bey was killed because he had sentenced a Muslim Brother to prison for the youth's attacks on British soldiers in a club in Alexandria. The two assassins, members of the secret apparatus of the Society, were soon captured, and on 22 November, 1948 they were sentenced to life imprisonment with hard labour. Banna had been interrogated but released for lack of evidence.[78] His intimates have since reported his revulsion at the act and his fear that the members of the secret apparatus had ceased to be under his control. There is some slight evidence that the latter concern was real, as has already been noted;[79] but the general view in the Society is that Banna cannot be completely exonerated, if only because he himself failed to practise restraint with regard to the sentence passed by Khazindar. Whether or not he was directly involved, and irrespective of the fact that members of the Society, without exception, join in repudiating the act, they had always before their minds the confusing 'fact' that the judge had imprisoned a 'patriot' whose 'crime' was an attack on the 'hated occupier'. The Egyptian historian Rafi'i deplored the fact that in this case and in that of the murder of Amin 'Uthman, which was being tried at the same time, the courtrooms, filled with lawyers

[76] See Heyworth-Dunne, *Modern Egypt*, pp. 17–18 and n. 17, for information derived mostly from *The Times*; *Irhab*, pp. 42–51, for a categorical and detailed charge of complicity in the affair. For the other side, see *MMB* (12 Dec. 1950), 5; and *MDA* (13 Feb. 1951), 31.

[77] See 'Developments of the Quarter', *MEJ* (Apr. 1949), 183.

[78] See *MAS* (24 Nov. 1948), 6–7; *MMR* (12 Nov. 1954), 13; *COC*, xiv–xv (1948), 132.

[79] *JJ* (13 Nov. 1954), 10, and above, p. 55.

of all political shades, were allowed to become 'platforms for the glorification of murder and crime'.[80]

The major events of the next nine months were interspersed by two more attempts on the life of Nahhas Pasha: in April, following explosions in the Sa'dist club and in the buildings of the Sa'dist newspapers, *Dar Akhbar al-Yawm*;[81] and in November, during which attack two of Nahhas's body-guards were killed.[82] The Wafdist leader accused in the first instance the secretary of Ibrahim 'Abd al-Hadi, the Sa'dist head of the royal cabinet, and in the second the secretary of the Sa'dist prime minister, Nuqrashi.[83] Even these events, however, were overshadowed by the now intense interest in the course of the war in Palestine and the incidents generated by it.

On 13 May, two days before the official entry of the Egyptian army into Palestine, the government declared martial law throughout the country. A number of measures were enacted pursuant to it as national security precautions. On 27 May the government announced that special permission was now required for Egyptians and foreigners before leaving the country. Another decree controlled the amount of wealth which could be taken out of the country; it also forbade the transfer of property to the Sudan. On the 31st the government ordered the 'seizure of property belonging to persons arrested or interned in connection with the Palestine war, and to organizations connected with such persons'. This had followed upon large-scale arrests and imprisonment of suspected communists and Zionists. These ordinances, which mainly affected the Jewish community, were the government's contribution towards heightening the insecurity and tension already being exacerbated by the war between Arabs and Jews. The first violent manifestation of popular reactions occurred five weeks after the fighting began.[84]

On 20 June some houses in a part of the Jewish quarter were blown up, an event officially explained as an accidental detonation of fireworks! On 16 July a single Israeli plane appeared in the Cairo skies and dropped bombs which exploded in a poor quarter

[80] Rafi'i, *Thawra*, iii. 266–7.

[81] Ibid. 267–8; *COC*, xiii (1948), 30; *COC*, xiv–xv (1948), 132. See also Tabi'i, *Ha'ula'*, pp. 49–50, where the Muslim Brothers are also charged with sending threatening letters to the same publishing house; this is probably true.

[82] 'Developments of the Quarter', *MEJ* (July 1948), 321; ibid. (Jan. 1949), 66.

[83] *MMB* (23 Jan. 1951), 2.

[84] 'Developments of the Quarter', *MEJ* (July 1948), 321–2. For fuller and more pointed discussions of the matter, see S. Landshut, *Jewish Communities in the Middle East* (1950), pp. 33–4; and L. Resner, *Eternal Stranger* (1951), pp. 114–16. Landshut gives more consideration than does Resner to the relationship between the tensions aroused by the Palestine question and this outbreak of anti-Jewish violence in Egypt.

of the town. On the 17th an air alert set off anti-foreign rioting. On the night of the 19th an explosion in the lower part of the main thoroughfare, Shari' Fu'ad, destroyed parts of two large Jewish-owned department stores, Cicurel and Oreco. The press, taking its lead from the government, put the blame on 'Israeli bombs' dropped as Cairo underwent another air alert. That morning the Egyptians had been told of the first truce on the Palestine front. During the last part of July and early August other Jewish-owned businesses (Benzione, Gattigneo, and the Delta Trading Company), and the Marconi Telegraph Station (regarded as a centre of Zionist communications) were either destroyed or damaged by explosions. On 22 September another explosion destroyed another part of the Jewish quarter, and on 12 November the building of the Société Orientale de Publicité, widely believed to have aided Zionist activity, was destroyed by a bomb. In all these events the cost in property damage was high and scores of people were killed or injured.[85] At the time no arrests or accusations were made.

Meanwhile, in October, the government discovered a cache of arms and munitions in Isma'iliyya on the estate (*'izba*) of Shaykh Muhammad Farghali, the leader of the Brothers' battalions in Palestine. And on 15 November all attention focused on the Muslim Brothers. On the afternoon of that day a jeep rolled to a halt in front of a house in Cairo just when policemen happened to be passing. Noticing that it happened to be unplated and loaded with crates, the policemen challenged the two dismounting passengers, who immediately took flight but were stopped a short distance away by crowds which formed after the police started shouting 'Zionists!! Zionists!!' Within a few minutes a third man carrying a briefcase, on his way to what must have been the rendezvous, aroused suspicion and was similarly stopped by the crowd and arrested by the police. The third man's flat, which was the meeting-place, revealed three more of the group, and within a few hours the number arrested had reached thirty-two. Papers and documents from the jeep, from the briefcase, from memorandum pads, diaries, wallets, and other personal records in the homes of the arrested men provided the first public disclosures of the existence of the secret apparatus of the Muslim Brothers. With all this to add to the evidence from the January arrests in the Muqattam hills, the assassination of Judge Khazindar in March, and the confiscation of arms on Farghali's *'izba* in the previous October, the government began to put together the first serious

[85] See, for figures and pictures, *Irhab*, pp. 61–82, 93; see also Rafi'i, *Thawra*, iii. 267–8; *JM*, 20, 21, 29 July, 1, 4 Aug. 1948; Resner, *Eternal Stranger*, pp. 116–24; and Landshut, *Jewish Communities*, pp. 35–41.

case against the Society and to prepare the ground for its dissolution.

On 28 November, Banna, who had been away during most of October and early November on the annual pilgrimage, was arrested, on the basis of evidence found in the jeep, on a charge of being implicated in the destruction earlier in the month of the building of the Société Orientale de Publicité. He was, however, released almost at once, and set about in earnest, through direct contact and through the good offices of people friendly and otherwise to both sides, to reduce tension between the government and the Society. But events moved too fast.[86]

On 4 December widespread riots at the university against the proposed armistice talks on the Palestine war brought out the full force of the police headed by its hated Cairo commander, Salim Zaki. During a pitched battle with students who had stationed themselves on the roof of the Faculty of Medicine and were pelting the police with whatever could be thrown, including explosives, Zaki was killed by a bomb thrown in his direction. Although in the circumstances of a mass riot it would have been impossible to determine who was actually guilty ('everyone wanted to kill him'), the Muslim Brothers were at once officially accused. Strangely enough, no arrests were made in the case until 26 January 1949.[87]

Following the accusation the newspaper of the Society was ordered to close. On 6 December it was already clear what the government had in mind, and Banna worked feverishly to forestall the event, even attempting to contact the king and the chief of the royal cabinet, Ibrahim 'Abd al-Hadi. At 10 p.m. on the night of the 8th the deputy minister of the interior, 'Abd al-Rahman al-'Ammar, assured Banna that something would surely save the situation. At 11 p.m., while Banna and many of the members waited in the headquarters for the outcome, the radios broadcast the order of the ministry of the interior dissolving the Society of the Muslim Brothers throughout the length and breadth of Egypt. Police immediately surrounded the headquarters and arrested everyone in it except Hasan al-Banna.[88] The wealth of the Society was placed in the hands of a special agent of the ministry of the interior to be disbursed for welfare and social services on the

[86] *Haythiyat wa-Hukm*, pp. 23–7; cf. *Irhab*, pp. 96–7.

[87] *JM* (26 Jan. 1949), 1. Those arrested received twenty years of hard labour in prison. See *Qadiyat al-Nuqrashi*, p. 111, for more information on the Zaki case. Safran, *Egypt*, p. 205, takes the incident out of context thereby enlarging its significance as the prelude to uprising. The exclusion of this incident from the roster of charges made retroactively by the RCC in 1954 was related to the belief of many that Anwar al-Sadat was involved.

[88] For pictures and details of the event see *MMB* (12 Dec. 1950), 1, 16.

order of the ministry of social affairs. Commenting on the event, the organ of the Sa'dist government, *Akhir Sa'a*, said: '[The government] had done with a Society that could be regarded as its strongest opponent. This was not just a party but rather resembled a state with its armies, hospitals, schools, factories, and companies.' Commenting on the strong protest against the government decree made by the Copt Makram 'Ubayd, the only political leader in the country to do so, *Akhir Sa'a* noted that Banna must have thought that 'Makram Pasha had become the last Muslim Brother'.[89]

The memorandum presented to the prime minister by the ministry of the interior—the decree of dissolution—contained the government case against the Society. There were thirteen counts. The first, based on a 1942 investigation, held that the Society intended 'the overthrow of the political order' through the 'terrorism' of its militarily trained 'rover units'. Two charges held the Society responsible for the death of two people and the injury of others in 'battles with opponents of theirs' on 6 July 1946 and 27 February 1948. Three of the charges had to do with arms and training: the arrest on 10 December 1946 of members engaged in 'the manufacture of bombs and explosives' in Isma'iliyya; the discovery and confiscation of arms and the arrest of members training in the Muqattam hills on 19 January 1948; and the discovery of arms and documents on the estate of Shaykh Farghali in Isma'iliyya on 22 October 1948. These charges, said the indictment, testified to the intent of the Society 'to embark on widespread terroristic activity of pressing danger to the security and existence of the state'.

Two further counts levelled at the group were direct charges of violence: on 24 December 1946, when bombs were thrown at 'numerous establishments in the city of Cairo' followed by the arrest of two members of the Society and the conviction of one of them; and the undated 1948 bombing of the King George Hotel in Isma'iliyya in which 'numerous people', including the criminal, were hurt. One item listed a general charge of 'numerous clashes of the members of this Society with the police, not only in resisting them but in aggression against them as they fulfilled their task of preserving order and security'. Another accused the Society of using 'threatening letters to companies and commercial establishments for purposes of extorting funds from them on the pretext that [the money] was an advance on the subscriptions to its paper'. The final three counts, interestingly, held the Society responsible

[89] *MAS* (15 Dec. 1948), 5. See Rafi'i, *Thawra*, iii. 269–70, for an argument against the wisdom or legality of the decree of dissolution, an argument in part made successfully by the Society later in the courts; see below, pp. 72–9.

for violence among labourers and farmers in the countryside: on 18 January 1948 for 'setting fire' to 'the woods of a property owner near Kafr Badawe'; on 3 February 1948 for 'instigating the local people near Kafr al-Baramun to agitate for higher wages' and for 'moderate rents', and for 'demonstrating' with inflammatory slogans and resisting the police with 'firearms and stones'; and on 16 June 1948 for 'inspiring the workers' of a village belonging to the ministry of agriculture 'to strike in support of the demand for possession of this land'.[90] The decree contained no reference to the important events of 1948, events which afterwards constituted the legal case of the government against the Brothers.

The fearlessness with which Nuqrashi pursued his course following the decree was equalled only by the tenseness which seized Egypt. Banna, still at large though under strict surveillance, kept on trying to save the situation, primarily by direct bargaining with the prime minister, who, in turn, refused to see him.[91] Banna knew better than anyone whither the situation could lead, for among those arrested on 15 November after the discovery of the jeep were the leaders, and some but not all of the members, of the secret apparatus. Whatever else the dissolution had done, other important arrests and his own isolation had completely shattered the chain of communications in the organization and thus all means of control. On 28 December the anticipated came to pass. As Nuqrashi entered the ministry of the interior, he was saluted by a young man dressed in the uniform of an officer, who then fired one shot into his back as he passed and another into his chest as he turned to face his attacker. Nuqrashi died a few minutes later. The assassin, 'Abd al-Majid Ahmad Hasan, was twenty-three years of age, a member of the Society since 1944, and a third-year veterinary student who had attended classes up to the day before the event.[92] The mourning at the funeral of Nuqrashi was accompanied by bitter—and prophetic—shouts by his followers demanding 'Death to Hasan al-Banna'.[93]

[90] See *Irhab*, pp. 99–102, for a reproduction of the decree of dissolution; *MDA* (16 Apr. 1952), 13, for some legal details. One account of the behind-the-scenes aspect of the decree from a knowledgeable source has it that Eastern European *émigrés*, in the employ of first British and then Egyptian (palace?) intelligence, were instrumental in spreading the notion that the Brothers were in fact tools of international communism and must be suppressed. Yusuf Rashad was among those in the palace entourage who resisted and fought the idea, but the king by October was already persuaded, and from that time pushed Nuqrashi on to the action. Certainly the last three counts of the indictment—in the light of the other known deeds of the Brothers—need some rationale.

[91] Hasan al-Banna, *Qawl fasl* (1950), pp. 37–8.

[92] See Rafi'i, *Thawra*, iii. 271–2; *Irhab*, pp. 102–8; *MRY* (5 Jan. 1949), 8–9; *MAS* (29 Dec. 1948), 3–4.

[93] *MMB* (23 Jan. 1951), 2.

A new government was immediately formed by Nuqrashi's close friend, Ibrahim 'Abd al-Hadi, chief of the royal cabinet and now head of the Sa'dist party. Always identified with the palace, 'Abd al-Hadi, in the next six months, became a name identified by all Egyptians with official terror, and won for himself the unqualified hatred of virtually every segment of articulate opinion, in particular of a group of young officers in the army who were planning revolution. As will be seen, 'Abd al-Hadi was the first of the old political leaders to be brought before the Revolutionary Tribunal established by the army junta, mostly for his deeds in this period.

Banna tried once more to make peace with 'Abd al-Hadi, offering as his terms co-operation with the government in the restoration of order and security in return for the waiving of the ban on the Society, the release of its confiscated assets, and the freeing of the arrested members.[94] A 'mediation committee' was established which included Salih Harb Pasha, Zaki 'Ali Pasha, Mustafa Mar'i Bey, Muhammad al-Naghi, and Mustafa Amin, friends of both sides. Banna also wrote a pamphlet, with the consent of the government, entitled *Bayan li'l-nas*, in which he repudiated the assassination of Nuqrashi.[95] Banna seems to have been aiming at the release of the leaders of the lower echelons and of the secret apparatus who alone could restore some kind of order to the chain of authority and controls.[96] He is said to have admitted to the mediators that after the death of Nuqrashi 'a dangerous situation' existed, that he could not deny the 'errors' of the Brothers, and that he was so shaken by what had come to pass that he himself felt the need for the dissolution of the Society.[97]

The prime minister was not convinced of Banna's reasoning and released no one. Negotiations collapsed after an attempt on 13 January 1949 to bomb and destroy the courthouse in which the records of the jeep investigation were kept. A long-time member of the secret apparatus, Shafiq Ibrahim Anas, was arrested shortly after the bomb, given to a servant for delivery within, was discovered and exploded outside the court.[98] Banna again hastened to repudiate the act in a public letter to the ministry of the interior and to the members at large. The letter contained a statement about the perpetrators of violence which was painfully and angrily received by his followers: 'They are neither Brothers, nor are they Muslims.' This letter, together with a *fatwa* from the Committee

[94] Hajjaji, *IMAM*, i. 116–17.
[95] Ibid. i. 37; 'Assal, *BKA*, p. 82.
[96] See Banna, *Qawl fasl*, pp. 39–40, for his statement about the situation. The above is my own interpretation of his attitude.
[97] See *JJ* (16 June 1954), 10; and Husayni, *Ikhwan*, p. 36.
[98] *Irhab*, pp. 109–11; *JM* (15 Jan. 1949), 1; *JJ* (28 May 1954), 8.

of High *'Ulama'* of the Azhar denouncing the Nuqrashi murder as 'anti-Islamic', was given wide prominence by the government. Banna further made a public appeal to 'those young ones' to cease from writing threatening letters and committing acts of violence; he added that he would regard any further misdeeds by anyone who had any relation with the Society as 'directed at my person', and that he would insist on bearing the full legal consequences himself.[99] Banna was presumably prompted by a letter, among others, which had appeared in the press from unidentified Brothers threatening to kidnap Nuqrashi's two children and hold them as hostages for the life of his assassin.[100]

Towards the end of January the contacts between Banna and the government ceased. The prime minister issued a decree prescribing the death penalty for anyone seized carrying bombs and explosives; widespread new arrests were made. For 'Abd al-Hadi the problem was to break the secret apparatus before it could commit any other violence, and to this end he brought to bear the full governmental apparatus, legal and illegal, including physical and mental torture in the prisons. As humiliating to the Brothers as all the alleged abuses of family and personal honour was the decision to hang in their cells the following Qur'anic verse:

> The only reward of those who make war upon Allah and his messenger and strive after corruption in the land will be that they will be killed or crucified, or have their hands and feet on alternate sides cut off, or will be expelled out of the land. Such will be their degradation in the world, and in the Hereafter theirs will be an awful doom.[101]

Banna, meanwhile, giving up hope for a settlement with the government, wrote a small pamphlet, *Qawl fasl*, clandestinely distributed, denouncing the decree of dissolution; it also gave the Brothers' version of what happened to them in this period. In

99 *MRY* (13 Feb. 1949), 11; *JM* (4 Jan. 1949), 5. A widely reported story has it that the members of the Society were so angry with Banna that a letter from the prisons was delivered to him saying: 'We think that the manifesto is a government manœuvre; however if it is true, we will demand an accounting from you when we are free.' Rumour of this message was the foundation of the view later held by some that Banna was assassinated by his own men. See below, p. 71, n. 103.

100 *JM* (22 Jan. 1949), 1; *MAL* (19 Jan. 1949), 3.

101 *Qur'an* 5: 33. On the point of torture, see Ghazali, *MHN*, p. 38; and Zaki, *Ikhwan*, p. 27; *Aqwal wa-ta'dhib*, pp. 53–79; *Haythiyat wa-hukm*, pp. 38–42, 79–85; Buhi, *IAM*, *passim*; and *MDA* (6 Feb. 1952), 16. It seems to be true that torture is an accepted device of the Egyptian police no matter what the regime; there seems no reason for not accepting the general proposition of torture at this time, although some questions might be raised about the lurid details. See Hamid, *QSIHB*, pp. 90–2, for a summary of the later (1953) findings of the Revolutionary Tribunal against 'Abd al-Hadi on this count.

effect, he denied or qualified all the charges made against the Society in the original decree of dissolution, explaining them away as fabrications or distortions. He added some comments on the various events before and after the decree. The arms in the possession of the Society, he insisted, were officially recognized by the government itself as part of the arrangement between the Society and the Arab League, and involved no secret activity or intent other than their use in Palestine. The explosions in the Jewish establishments, even if proved to be at the hands of the Brothers, had not been—and could not be—proved to have been by order of the leadership. He added that these events must be seen as a consequence of the Palestine war and the clearly doubtful loyalties of some of 'our Jewish compatriots' and 'leading Egyptians'. Though he expressed sorrow at the death of Ahmad al-Khazindar, he maintained that the Society could not be held responsible for the acts of its members. He reminded the public that the judge had laid himself open to criticism from young people by sentencing young patriots to prison for attacks on the English. The death of Nuqrashi was also to be regretted, but he recalled that 'there was no Society to be questioned, no leaders to plan, for they were either in prison or under surveillance; it was the reaction we feared'. Similarly, as regards the bombing of the courthouse, he reminded the public of his 'strong repudiation' of the deed and insisted again, in effect, that with the leadership unable to assert its authority, 'the only ones responsible for these acts are those who commit them'.

He went on to describe the 'persecution' to which the members of the Society had been subjected in the mass arrests without accusation: torture in the prisons, loss of work, jobs, and property, and unwarranted search and censorship. The real reasons for the dissolution of the Society he listed as foreign pressure, preparation for negotiations with the British and the Zionists, a wish to divert attention from the failures in Palestine, preparation for coming elections, and the hidden fingers of 'international Zionism, communism, and the partisans of atheism and depravity'. He denied the charge that the Society of the Muslim Brothers had 'become political' and that it was planning 'the overthrow of the political system'. A final section summarized 'the contributions of the Muslim Brothers to the Nile Valley, the Arab countries and the Islamic nation'.[102]

[102] This pamphlet, *Qawl fasl*, has already been referred to (n. 96 above); it appeared in quantity only in 1950, but it made its first press appearance in *JM* late in 1949, a fact which suggested a pre-election Wafdist manœuvre to discredit the Sa'dists and win the support of the Brothers. It was reproduced again in *MMB* (12, 19 Dec. 1950); and, in part, in Hajjaji, *IMAM*, i. 9, 62 ff.

The little pamphlet was Banna's last written work. On 12 February 1949, in the late afternoon and after being mysteriously summoned to the headquarters of the Young Men's Muslim Association, he was shot in the street outside the building as he was entering a taxi and died a few minutes later in the near-by hospital. Banna had prophetically told his associates that the failure of the government to arrest him was his official death warrant. Evidence presented in the numerous investigations and trials held later indicated with little doubt that the assassination was an act planned, or at least condoned, by the prime minister (with the probable support of the palace), and executed by members of the political police. Those involved were all brought to trial, but only when the army officers reopened the case after the revolution of 1952. In 1954 sentences were passed on the four principal accused: the chief hand in the crime (Ahmad Husayn Jad) received life imprisonment with hard labour; two other officers (Mahmud 'Abd al-Hamid and Muhammad Mahfuz) received fifteen years in prison; and one (Muhammad al-Jazzar) received one year.[103]

Banna went to his grave escorted by tanks and armoured cars. Again, only the Copt, Makram 'Ubayd Pasha, defied the government and broke the police lines surrounding the home of the deceased to join the immediate family, the only mourners permitted by the government to attend the funeral.[104]

The certainty with which 'Abd al-Hadi was shrouded with guilt and the terrible sense of loss felt by the members assured no immediate end to the crisis. The king, it was reported, temporarily

[103] The material covering the event and the subsequent investigations and trials is copious, but it did not seem worth while to elaborate on the event and the subsequent legal activity related to the crime. Virtually all the books by Brothers since 1950 make mention of the death of Banna in more or less detail; of these, see Banna, *MISI*, pp. 13–29; Hajjaji, *IMAM*, i. 30–78; 'Assal, *BKA*, pp. 75–93. The criminal investigations by the various governments were brought together by the lawyers for the Banna family in a work called *Mahadir al-tahqiq wa-mudhakkarat al-niyaba fi qadiyat ightiyal al-imam al-shahid Hasan al-Banna'* (3 vols., 1954); the printing of these volumes was completed only shortly before the 1954 dissolution and the fate of most of the copies is in doubt. As indicated above, after the revolution of 1952 the first serious investigation and trial were begun. The court hearings were planned for June 1953, delayed until September, and interrupted again in December, when the lawyers for the plaintiff, Banna's father, challenged the competence of the court. The hearings were resumed and finally ended with the sentencing by the court on 2 August 1954. For full newspaper coverage of the course of the trial, see *JJ* from its first issue of 7 December 1953 through 2 August 1954; for a summary of the proceedings and statistics of the trial, see *MIM* (5 Aug. 1954), 9. The other explanation already alluded to (n. 99 above), that Banna was killed by one of his own men, was given circulation by the Sa'dist *Dar Akhbar al-Yawm*; see Boehm, 'Les Frères musulmans', 215; cf. *JJ* (30 May 1954), 3.

[104] See *MMB* (23 Jan. 1951), 5; and 'Ubayd's own words in *MDA* (12 Feb. 1952), 6.

gave up public praying.[105] The prime minister redoubled security precautions for himself and throughout the country; his first move after the death of Banna was to inaugurate a new wave of arrests. On 9 March Egyptians learned that the government had evidence that the Muslim Brothers had a hand in the assassination of the Imam Yahya of the Yemen in February 1948.[106] During April a number of 'cells' were uncovered and another wave of arrests took place. On 5 May the long-awaited attempt on ʻAbd al-Hadi occurred: after carefully observing the prime minister's movements to and from his home in the Maʻadi suburb of Cairo, a group of Brothers stationed themselves in a strategic spot and dispatched a stream of bombs at a car which turned out to be a similar model used by the leader of the Lower House of Parliament. Hamid Juda escaped injury and ten members of the Society were immediately apprehended.[107]

This was the last major development of the time, bringing to an end almost six months of what has been described as a period of 'unbearable tension, terror, and tyranny'. The near-killing of Juda inspired more arrests; by the time Ibrahim ʻAbd al-Hadi left the government on 25 July 1949, there were an estimated 4,000 Brothers in the camp-prisons of Tur, Huckstep (a former American barracks near Cairo International Airport), and ʻUyun Musa.[108] Out of the year-long crisis, which shook the very existence of the organization in its head-on collision with the government, four well-defined court cases were set in motion: (1) the jeep case; (2) the Nuqrashi murder case; (3) the 'cells case'; and (4) the Hamid Juda case. The last two, in the light of an essentially favourable decision on the jeep case—and with the Saʻdists out of power—were never pressed to a conclusion. In October 1951 twenty-five prisoners—most of those involved in the two trials—were released. The remainder, together with all other Brothers involved in all the cases, were released after the revolution in 1952. The most instructive of the trials was that of the 'jeep case' but the Nuqrashi case came for trial earlier and was almost as important.

For over three weeks after his arrest, Nuqrashi's young assassin, ʻAbd al-Majid Ahmad Hasan, refused to lead the authorities to his associates or even to admit more than a long-past contact with the Society. The explosion in the courthouse on 15 January was a turning-point: the repudiation of that deed by Banna as well as his public chastisement of the membership, coupled with the *fatwa* of

[105] *COC* xvii (1949), 42.
[106] *MAS* (*MAL*) (9 Mar. 1949), 1.
[107] *Irhab*, pp. 113–20; *MAS* (*MAL*) (6 Apr. 1949), 1.
[108] *COC* xvii (1949), 42–3; *COC* xviii–xix (1949), 138–9; Kira, *Mahkama*, i. 38. Some of the Brothers escaped to Cyrenaica and received asylum there.

the '*ulama*' denouncing the events as anti-Islamic, so demoralized the young man that he started the chain of confessions which led to the rapid arrest of his accomplices and the ending of the investigations preparatory to trial.[109]

Because the country was under martial law at this time, a military court was established, consisting of a carefully selected group of lawyers for both prosecution and defence. With the change of government in July 1949, lawyers from both the Wafd and the Muslim Brothers joined or replaced the primarily Sa'dist lawyers for the defence. The government's brief against the assassin included a vast amount of material aimed at showing the guilt of the entire organization for its plans to overthrow the government. In sum, it argued that the violence of the six months preceding the death of Nuqrashi was the planned prelude to the act of murder and the signal for rebellion. The training programme of the Society—military and spiritual—was presented as evidence of the intention of the leaders to indoctrinate and train for violence; on this score, the 'documents' submitted by the government included some of the *rasa'il* written by Banna for the instruction of the members, and letters found in the headquarters from members asserting their loyalty to the cause of the Society. Finally, the secret apparatus was charged with having as its primary function the effecting of 'the goals of the Muslim Brothers by force'.

However much drama this added to the trial, the primary issue was still the murder charge. It seemed clear from the proceedings that the decision to kill Nuqrashi was taken after the dissolution of the Society on 8 December and that the plan was perfected by the 18th; the assassin merely waited for some practice runs and then the appropriate moment. The defence pleaded, in the first instance, 'madness' and then the 'undue influence' of the teachings of the secret apparatus. The court rejected both pleas and the young man was condemned to death. Sentence was executed on 25 April 1950.

Fundamental to the proceeding was the attribution of responsibility for the death of the prime minister. The government, although it never arrested Banna, made a determined effort to show that, indirectly as technical head of the secret apparatus and directly through his position of command, he must bear final responsibility. The opposing view is that events 'got out of hand', and that Banna lost control of the 'extremists'.[110] — he (Banna) argued this too / by saying he didn't have responsibility for them

[109] *Qadiyat al-Nuqrashi* is the official court document in the case and was housed at the time of our research in the Council of State building in Cairo. Our summary is based on this document, especially pp. 2, 19–22, 49, 65–9, 89, 114–24.

[110] See 'Developments of the Quarter', *MEJ* (Apr. 1949), 183; Werner

In the hearings two names appeared to figure prominently. The first, al-Sayyid Sabiq, a young Azhar shaykh, seems to have been the 'spiritual' inspiration for the act. Nuqrashi's dissolution of the Muslim Brothers was seen by him as an 'aggression against Islam' and tantamount 'to closing down hundreds of mosques'; he also appears to have been the source for the story that the headquarters of the Society was to be transformed into a police precinct for the distribution of licences for prostitution! Along with these 'Islamic' motivations were other more mundane factors involving 'betrayal' by 'the leaders and the rich' in Palestine and in dealings with the British.[111] Although he was described at the time—even by some of the members—as 'the blood mufti' [*mufti al-dima*'], he was acquitted for lack of evidence of being concerned in the crime itself.

The other name was that of Ahmad Fu'ad, a young police officer and a secondary leader of the unit of the secret apparatus which was involved in the crime. After the deed he fled from Cairo, pursued by the police, and was shot to death in a gun battle in the town of Banha. All evidence points to him as the prime mover in the decision to kill the prime minister, and the chief architect of the plan. This view is partly confirmed by the judge's closing words at the trial: 'It is my greatest sorrow that the engineer of the crime is not present, that he preferred the bullets of the police to the verdict of death which this court would most certainly have decreed.'[112]

Because of its scope, the 'jeep case' was regarded by the Muslim Brothers as the centre of their legal battle with authority; because of its outcome, it is held to be a total vindication of the Society and its works. The trial, indeed all-inclusive, grouped together the major issues: the capture of the jeep in November 1948 and the subsequent seizure of the briefcase full of documents; the discovery of the cache of arms on the *'izba* of Shaykh Farghali; the murders of Judge Khazindar and Nuqrashi; and two other charges of arms concealment. The case first came before a military court but the defence demanded a delay until the termination of martial law. It then passed to a civil court in June 1950, which merely examined the records of the investigations and released eight of the accused. The real trial of thirty-two of the members of the Society

Caskel, 'Western Impact and Islamic Civilization', in von Grunebaum, ed., *Unity and Variety in Muslim Civilization* (Chicago, 1955), p. 348, where it is argued that the murder was done 'certainly by a member of the Ikhwan but hardly with the knowledge of Banna who was too intelligent not to foresee the consequences'. Cf. Tabi'i, *Ha'ula'i*, pp. 52–3.

[111] *Qadiyat al-Nuqrashi*, pp. 19–22, 57, 122.
[112] See *MMR* (12 Nov. 1951), 13.

began on 2 December 1950. The presiding judge, Ahmad Kamil Bey, was assisted by Mahmud 'Abd al-Latif Bey and Zaki Sharaf Bey. The trial lasted three and a half months.[113]

There were four major counts in the indictment. The first point was the crux of the case: that the accused joined in a 'criminal conspiracy' among themselves and with others, whose goal was 'to take power by force'; that thirteen among the thirty-two had banded together in a 'terrorist unit' with a formalized command and a highly disciplined membership, well-trained in the use of arms and techniques of terror. Eleven sub-charges detailed the elaborate 'plans' for revolution, which included the use of murder, theft, and arson, and of sabotage against government installations, communications, utilities, banks and private property, and civil and military personnel. The last three of the major counts detailed charges of stockpiling explosives and unlicensed firearms, and the unauthorized use of radio equipment.[114]

The prosecution argued that the organization, after it grew strong, assumed 'political goals'; the secret apparatus was created and the rover group was trained to assist it in the ultimate political goal of taking power. From 1946 the Society sought to call attention to itself by violence directed against the British or manifested during the Palestine agitation. They were thus responsible for the attacks on Jewish property in Cairo between June and November 1948. Palestine was merely a façade to cover their real intentions of arming and training for revolution in Egypt. To support this argument the prosecution produced the documents discovered in the jeep and all others made available to the government in the course of its many clashes with the Society; also some of its *rasa'il* and other public statements. The jeep papers were the main source of information about the organization of the secret apparatus which was presented as evidence in itself of preparedness for insurrection. Among those papers also were maps, memoranda, and directives which clearly pointed to the responsibility of the secret apparatus for the terror inflicted on the Jewish community through the summer and autumn of 1948; training manuals on arms, munitions, military organization, and guerrilla warfare in Arabic and English added, for the prosecution, certainty to the view that the secret apparatus was designed for revolution. Prosecution evidence purporting to show the real

[113] Circumstances prevented the writer from seeing the official court document, *Qadiyat al-jib*, for more than a few hours; its important points and facts were summarized in *Haythiyat wa-hukm*. See *Haythiyat wa-hukm*, pp. 13–17, for line-up of defendants and lawyers; for further general statistical data, see *MMB* (26 Dec. 1950), 8–9; and *MDA* (30 Mar. 1951), 4, 5.

[114] *Haythiyat wa-hukm*, pp. 18–19.

intentions of the Society included the important *risalat al-ta'alim* which was used by the battalions and rovers, and letters and other written statements that had passed between members. Among these was a 'plan' found in the headquarters, presented by the prosecution as a fundamental proof of the preparation for a coup.[115]

The defence argued its case along the two lines set out by the prosecution: specific acts of violence; and insurrection. To the first group of charges two main arguments were put forward: (1) that the young men who committed the violence deviated from the rules established by the leaders; (2) that the organization could not be held responsible for the acts of its 'extremist' members. What was wrong was not the secret apparatus, but its insubordinate members, 'some individuals . . . misunderstood their training . . . and created of themselves a terrorist organization'.[116]

The second and more general charge of insurrection was denied categorically. Arms, training, and the literature on weapons and warfare only showed the militant interest of the Society in the defence of Egypt, Arabism, and Islam against Britain and Zionism; further evidence for this was the list of Brothers 'martyred' in resistance to Britain in Egypt and Zionism in Palestine. The defence refuted the contentions of the prosecution that the members were being indoctrinated to violence. '*Jihad*', as taught by the Society, meant defence against 'imperialism and unbelief (*kufr*)'. Similarly the defence paid heed to the clarification of the Qur'anic verse used by the prosecution as evidence of criminal intent: 'Make ready for them all that thou canst of [*armed*] force and of horses tethered, that thereby ye may dismay the enemy of Allah and your enemy. . . .' (8: 60). This, the defence argued, did not mean 'force' in the sense of violence but rather 'strength' in the sense of might, to be rallied under the banner of Islam in its defence. The prosecution's much emphasized document alleged to form a 'plan' for revolution, was shown by the defence to be an essay prepared for a competition in a students' magazine, which portrayed the student's image of 'Islamic Society'.[117] Much of the case for the defence consisted in showing the 'peaceful' intentions of the Society as evidenced by the social, educational, medical, welfare, and spiritual services it rendered to the community in the name of Islam.[118]

Two themes occupied the special attention of the defence: the

[115] *Haythiyat wa-hukm*, pp. 34–6, 46–60.

[116] *Qadiyat al-jib*, i. 97–8.

[117] Ibid., pp. 99–100; *Haythiyat wa-hukm*, pp. 32–3, 55–6.

[118] Much of this part of the defence is elaborated in press accounts of the trial; see *MMB* (23 Jan. 1951), 1–9, 16; *MDA* (6 Feb. 1951), 12–13; (20 Feb. 1951), 12–13; (27 Feb. 1951), 12–13.

tyranny of the Sa'dist government; and the hand of the British in the dissolution of the Society. On the first point the argument was mainly supported by reports of the torture to which the Brothers were subjected in the prisons, intending thereby to undermine the force of the confessions in the hands of the prosecutor. To support the second point, a young lawyer member of the Society startled the court one day by producing documents, later published in English, which purported to show an exchange of communications and a demand by the British Embassy in the name of the American and French Embassies for the dissolution of the Society.[119]

The court pronounced its verdict on 17 March 1951. Its findings represented a remarkable success for the battery of defence lawyers. The court first methodically outlined all the evidence and documents presented to it. It rejected, as part of the evidence, some of the confessions of the accused because of the 'improper' devices used to obtain them; it chastised the government, in fact, for violation of 'the rights of citizens'.[120] After reviewing the case made by the prosecution and the history of the Society, the judges argued that the prosecution had confused two matters: (1) 'training in the use of arms and in guerrilla warfare'; and (2) 'the terrorist orientations of some of its members'. The resultant error was to describe 'the special section [i.e. the secret apparatus] in its entirety as a terrorist society'. The court saw 'the special section' as a training apparatus in line with the avowed goals of 'liberating the Nile Valley and all Islamic countries'; it did not imply or call for 'crime' and was not concerned if 'some of its members created of themselves a criminal conspiracy for deeds of murder and destruction'. The literature on military organization, weapons, and guerrilla warfare presented as evidence of revolution by the prosecution was not being used for training

[119] The story as presented is briefly as follows: On 10 November 1948 the senior representatives of Britain, France, and the United States met at Fayid, on the Great Bitter Lakes in the Suez Canal, and agreed jointly to request the dissolution of the Muslim Brothers through the British Embassy. The meeting was inspired, it was said, by a memorandum presented by a group of foreigners residing in Egypt, mostly Greek, to the British Ambassador, asserting that they no longer felt 'security for their lives in Egypt'; the meeting resulted in an extended series of negotiations between the British and Egyptian governments which led ultimately to the order of dissolution. For information on the documents presented to the court, see *MMB* (12 Dec. 1950), 5; for reproductions in English of the documents, see *MDA* (31 Jan. 1951), 1; for a defence of their validity, see *MDA* (12 June 1951), 8–9. Banna, *Qawl fasl*, p. 26, claims to have been told by the deputy minister of the interior of the tripartite intervention; see also Hajjaji, *IMAM*, i. 111–19. Resner, *Eternal Stranger*, p. 120, reports that protests were lodged by the three governments in November 1948, with threats of British occupation backing them, unless order was restored.

[120] *Haythiyat wa-hukm*, pp. 34–42, 79–85.

terrorists, but—like the plans for destroying bridges, communications, and transport—for planning resistance operations against the British. The court took particular notice of the praise expressed by the two commanders-in-chief of the Egyptian army in Palestine (Ahmad al-Mawawi Bey and Ahmad Fu'ad Sadiq) for the contribution of the Brothers to the Palestine conflict and thus for the usefulness of the training they had undergone.

Examining the documents presented by the prosecution, the judges argued that these were often presented out of context, or unsigned, or untraceable, or irrelevant to the organization; such evidence was not admissible as proof of plans or intentions. As for the 'plan' for revolution the judges upheld the defence contention that it was a harmless student-competition essay which happened to be at the headquarters of the Society merely because one of the judges in the contest was receiving entries there; the prosecution was reminded that it had omitted to note all the pertinent information about the essay and had misconstrued what it had noted.[121]

The court, thereupon, found 'a criminal conspiracy to overthrow the form of government, on the basis of the evidence and investigations, to be without foundation'; it agreed, however, that 'in the case of some of them', the papers found in the jeep established a connection with the violence of the summer and autumn of 1948 and thus 'a criminal conspiracy for murder and destruction'. Before sentencing, the court explained its leniency: asserting their belief in the respectability of the goals of the movement, the judges recognized that under the influence of the emotions generated in the post-war world by the continuing British occupation and the Palestine question, some of the members 'lost their balance'. 'Desiring to shorten the way' they repudiated the path established by the leaders for realization of the Society's goals. For all of this, the court felt that together with punishment should go mercy. Five of the defendants received three years in prison, twelve two years, and one one year. The remaining sixteen were acquitted.[122]

[121] *Haythiyat wa-hukm*, pp. 46–74, 81. The essay was entitled '*al-Nizam al-Islami fi'l-'asr al-hadir*' and was presented by the prosecution as a plan for 'dictatorial socialism'. The court described the contents of the essay as a picture of an 'Islamic republic' which would be a 'parliamentary democracy' of elected representatives and a president whose term would be for life. A 'judicial power' would be established independent of the executive and would be charged with guaranteeing the rights of the citizens. The state's chief concern would be to protect its citizens from poverty, sickness, and ignorance. Annexes to the essay discussed the problems of rural reform and highway construction.

[122] Ibid., pp. 74–8, 85–95. For short biographies of all of those sentenced, see *MDA* (30 Mar. 1951), 4–5, 12–13. For a view similar to that of the courts, see Rafi'i, *Thawra*, iii. 264. Cf. Heyworth-Dunne, *Modern Egypt*, pp. 74–7, for the view that the Society was planning a coup, but that Banna 'came out into

On a later occasion the chief judge in the trial, Ahmad Kamil Bey, admitted that after the jeep case he was persuaded to become a member of the Society.[123]

the open too soon'; for views similar to this, see Issawi, *Egypt*, p. 268; RIIA, *GBE*, p. 117; Colombe, *Égypte*, pp. 267–9; and Boehm, 'Les Frères musulmans', 214–15. Safran, *Egypt*, pp. 204–5, sees the organization taking 'advantage of the relaxation of the usual public security controls' to begin mobilizing and 'to plot the complete overthrow of the regime'. We think this view an over-simplification of events, as our text indicates. As we shall see, by 1954 the RC, whose members at the time of the violence of 1948 were probably applauding the events, took a different view; see Kira, *Mahkama*, i. 34.

[123] *JJ* (17 June 1954), 3.

IV

RE-FORMATION: THE SECOND PHASE

THE RETURN TO LEGALITY

THE government of Ibrahim ʿAbd al-Hadi was replaced on 26 July 1949 by that of Husayn Sirri Pasha, in which the Wafd participated until November, when a new cabinet was formed, parliament was dissolved, and preparations were begun by Sirri to hold new elections. On 3 January 1950 the Wafd emerged victorious at the polls and formed the new government on the 12th.[1] The palace had bowed to the inevitable.

The return of the Wafd marked a swing of the pendulum in favour of the outlawed Society, although the release of prisoners had begun after Husayn Sirri's accession to power in July 1949. Detainees in the Palestine area were returned in small groups, subjected to investigations or minor detentions, and then released.[2] The organization, while it remained technically illegal, began regrouping under the leadership of the former deputy, Salih ʿAshmawi. Its rapid recovery was largely due to its having continued to operate as an organization in the prisons; grouped together in mass concentrations, it was a simple matter to re-establish the former patterns and relationships.[3] Those who escaped abroad continued to spread the message, especially in Syria, Jordan, and Pakistan;[4] their reports of sympathy among other Muslims for the 'ordeal' of the Society and of new conquests for the idea added to the sense of new life and eternal mission. The task of those outside the prisons—those never arrested and those released—was, as one of them put it, to 'compel the state to recognize the inhabitants of the caves who were outside the laws and the constitution'.[5] This they did by wisely seeking the support of the Wafd.

From the time of the departure of ʿAbd al-Hadi, in mid-1949, the Wafdist daily, *al-Misri*, took up the cause of the Muslim Brothers by persistent inflammatory references to the assassina-

[1] See Colombe, *Égypte*, pp. 269–72; Rafiʿi, *Thawra*, iii. 283–94.
[2] Sharif, *IMFHF*, p. 237.
[3] See Buhi, *IAM*, *passim*, esp. pp. 22–5, 66–7.
[4] See *MMB* (7 Nov. 1950), 13.
[5] *MDA* (29 Dec. 1953), 6.

tion of Banna and the subsequent half-hearted investigation, following up the known clues whenever possible, obviously with an eye both to discrediting the Sa'dists and to winning the support of the Brothers for the coming elections. In challenging the Sa'dists, the Wafd was, of course, also challenging the palace; in making the focus of the attack the officially inspired murder of the leader of the Muslim Brothers, it was not only endearing itself to the Brothers, but also assuring itself that the post-war palace policy of liaison with the Society against it would not be repeated. The fact that the chief negotiator for the Wafd was the leader of its 'right wing', Fu'ad Siraj al-Din, indicated that the traditional view of the Society as a bulwark against the left still persisted; it would appear, too, that Siraj al-Din was strengthening his hand against the 'left wing' of the Wafd itself.[6]

On the side of the Brothers, the drive for the return to legality overrode all considerations. The ideological obstacle of 'support for a political party' was in part reduced by the fact that the Wafd, as against the Sa'dists, represented a 'majority party'.[7] Asked by an Associated Press correspondent about support of the Wafd, the spokesman of the Society, 'Ashmawi, said: 'The Wafd is the popular party of Egypt and its followers come from the same classes as the partisans of the Muslim Brothers—the popular classes. There is then, no competition between the Brothers and the Wafd.'[8] Mutual benefits and needs, for the moment, required the submergence of the intrinsic hostility with which the two mass parties faced each other. The cordiality, predictably, was short-lived.

In the negotiations between the groups the Muslim Brothers' representative was Mustafa Mu'min. Siraj al-Din, acting for the Wafd, as minister of the interior held the better cards. His conditions for the return of the Society to life included (1) formal activity might not be resumed till martial law was ended; (2) informal activity might be resumed without delay but under a new name; (3) the old name might only be used after the lifting of martial law and the full return of the Society to legality. Mu'min, anxious to resume the functioning of the Society under any conditions, was disposed to accept the Wafdist offer; he went so far as to recommend a new name: 'The Islamic Renaissance [*al-nahda al-islamiyya*].' However, other leaders of the Society, 'Ashmawi especially, rejected the suggestions both that the name should be changed and that there should be any delay in the

[6] See Kaplinsky, 'Muslim Brotherhood', 381; Boehm, 'Les Frères musulmans', 215–17. [7] See Hajjaji, *IMAM*, i. 56–61.
[8] *MMB* (19 Dec. 1950), 1.

legalization of the Society. The election returns were hardly in before the Society was accusing the Wafd of betrayal.

As an aside to the dispute with the Wafd, another one, inside the organization, led to the dismissal of Mustafa Mu'min. After 'Ashmawi had rejected the Wafd's terms, Mu'min persisted in championing the arrangement proposed as the only one immediately feasible. In so doing, he left himself open to the accusation of having sold out to the Wafd. 'Ashmawi seized on this, as well as on a number of articles written by Mu'min for the Wafdist press on Islamic 'reform', to begin a campaign against him, focused on his pretentions to the leadership, his agreement with the Wafd, and his 'unorthodoxy'. 'Ashmawi ordered that no branches should invite Mu'min to speak, and towards the end of 1950 called a secret session of the Guidance Council and succeeded in winning an order for his dismissal on grounds that he had 'deviated from the Brothers'.[9] The feud which had begun simmering between Mu'min and 'Ashmawi while the Brothers were still in prison—one ground for which was Mu'min's proposals for 'democratization' of the Society—was only the first of the events arising out of the problem of the succession to Banna.

The controversy with Mu'min provided 'Ashmawi with a convenient focus around which to dramatize the dispute with the Wafd; in his organ, *Majallat al-Mabahith*, throughout 1950 he seized every chance to remind the 'people's government' of its broken promise to liberate the Society from its legal limbo and to attack the officially inspired harassment of its rapidly stirring activity. The government had further angered the Brothers by continuing to make official reference to the organization as 'the dissolved society' and by pushing through parliament Law 50/1950, which set the date for the ending of martial law and all its decrees except those pertaining to the Muslim Brothers.[10]

Towards the end of the year the minister of the interior let it be known that the government was contemplating replacing the decree of dissolution with a new 'Societies Law' under which full information on each member, complete with photograph, would have to be registered with the authorities. As the Muslim Brothers were the only group in question, the law was seen as directed at

[9] For published hints about the above account, see *COC*, xxii (1950), 198; Alexander, 'Left and Right in Egypt', 125; and *MMB* (31 Oct. 1950), 9.

[10] See esp. *MMB* (7 Nov. 1950), 5; *MDA* (31 Jan. 1951), 3, 8; (27 Feb. 1951), 1; (10 Apr. 1951), 1. The National party and the Wafdist Kutla, meanwhile, had seized the opportunity of embarrassing the Wafd and helped to exacerbate the matter by extending public support to the Brothers for the abrogation of the decree of dissolution; on this see *MMB* (31 Oct. 1950), 1, 9; and *MDA* (27 Feb. 1951), 1.

them. To the Brothers it was both unnecessary and unduly restrictive; moreover, it was a repressive law replacing a repressive military decree, in its effect giving parliamentary sanction to the 'illegal' military order for dissolution.[11]

The government, however, was determined to push through the law and on 16 April 1951 it came before parliament. On the 18th, while it was being debated, 'Ashmawi ordered a mass demonstration in front of the parliament building. After public speeches condemning the law, a formal memorandum of protest was presented to the government and the demonstrators were dispersed by their own leaders.[12] Within a few days the law was duly passed and the Society made it known that it would not register.

On 1 May 1951 martial law legally ended. The Guidance Council met immediately and declared the Society of the Muslim Brothers in existence. All over the country the banners of the Society were raised; government security forces went into immediate action, tore them down (with any other symbols of the Society), and occupied the headquarters.[13] The Brothers persisted; on 17 May the Consultative Assembly met for the first time since dissolution in temporary headquarters; and on the 20th the Brothers notified the government and then held their first mass meeting since dissolution.[14]

The showdown between the government and the Society was occasioned by the public notice given by the minister of the interior of his intention to buy the headquarters building[15] of the Society for a police station. To prevent this, as well as to clarify the legal situation posed by the original decree of dissolution in 1948 and the qualifications which were applied in the law ending martial law in 1950, the Society brought a suit in the Council of State against the prime minister, and the ministers of the interior and of finance.

Pending in the Council of State since November 1948 was a suit brought by Banna himself and the secretary-general, 'Abd al-Hakim 'Abidin, against the government for an injunction against the closing of the two branches in Port Sa'id and Isma'illiyya in that month. The case, which had been dropped with the assassination of Banna, was now reopened with a new plea in 1951,

[11] *MDA*, 22 May, 10 Apr. 1951.

[12] See *MDA* (24 Apr. 1951), 1–2, 4, 10–13.

[13] *MDA* (1 May 1951), 14; (8 May 1951), 8–9; (15 May 1951), 1.

[14] Ibid. (26 June 1951), 8–9.

[15] A 1951 estimate by the department of buildings placed a value of £E3,000 on the land and £E11,500 on the buildings; the Society argued that its intangible value as 'the abode of memories' was inestimable. On this matter, see a summary of the problem in an Egyptian legal journal—'Mahkamat al-qada' al-idari: Majlis al-Dawla', *Majallat al-Muhamat*, xxix/4 (Dec. 1951), 511–12.

presented on behalf of the Society in the name of ʿAbidin. The case was heard in the injunctions section under the presidency of Judge Sami Mazin Bey on 15 August 1951.[16]

The proceedings, though primarily concerned with the Society's legal status, became involved in arguments over the legal justification for the dissolution decree and subsequent measures. The arguments put forward by the Society were finally upheld in a decision delivered on 17 September. The order for the sale of the headquarters was revoked, and it was recommended that the Society's funds and property should be returned. The effect of the decision was to give legal sanction—the highest in Egypt—to the existence of the Society. On 18 December the government released its confiscated property, including its press and all its buildings.[17]

A NEW LEADER

Inside the organization, throughout this time, the first and most pressing issue was that of the succession to Hasan al-Banna. From the time of his death, authority naturally passed to the second-in-command, Banna's deputy since 1947, Salih ʿAshmawi. It was widely assumed among the members-at-large, on the basis of his active leadership through the days of crisis under both Saʿdists and Wafdists, as well as because of his long and intimate contact with and service to the organization and Banna, that he would be officially appointed Banna's successor. That this was not to be the case proved to have dangerous consequences for the Society in a few years' time.

That ʿAshmawi wanted to be the new leader seems established though it was constantly denied.[18] There were other contenders: notably ʿAbd al-Rahman al-Banna, Hasan's brother; ʿAbd al-Hakim ʿAbidin, the secretary-general; and Shaykh Hasan al-Baquri, a member of the Guidance Council and later member of

[16] Circumstances prevented my perusing for more than a few hours the mass of unarranged and disconnected papers relating to the case in the files of the Council of State building. It is not possible, therefore, for me to give detailed references. In the early papers connected with this case, known here as *Qadiyat Majlis al-Dawla*, some of the leading Wafdist lawyers were involved in the defence of the Brothers. Besides the political advantage to be gained, the Wafd wished to combat a dangerous legal precedent—palace-supported dissolutions of opposition parties. After the Wafd came to power its lawyers withdrew from the proceedings.

[17] See a legal summary in 'Mahkamat al-qada' al-idari', *Majallat al-Muhamat*, 512–14; for more detailed data (beyond the official file above noted), see *MDA*, 26 June, 17 July, 21 Aug., 25 Sept. 1951, 17 Mar. 1952, and 18 Dec. 1951.

[18] See e.g. *MDA* (19 Jan. 1954), 3. It is unbecoming in the circle of the Muslim Brothers—in line with the Society's understanding of Muslim tradition—to aspire to position and authority.

the revolutionary government, who together with 'Ashmawi kept the Society's morale and organization going in 1949 and 1950, and whom many believed Banna had chosen to succeed him.[19] Mustafa Mu'min fell out of the race with his dismissal in 1950.

During the period of 'travail', another name linked with the work of 'Ashmawi and Baquri in keeping the organization intact was that of Munir al-Dilla, a relative newcomer to the Society. His joining, in 1947, has been described as the introduction into the movement of 'Cadillacs and aristocracy'; he became a devoted follower of Banna, and from his wealth as a landowner in Upper Egypt he contributed generously to the cause. For this, and because of his dedicated service to the organization in its time of crisis, his voice was strong in the debates surrounding the selection of Banna's heir. It was in his home and at his inspiration that the name of Hasan Isma'il al-Hudaybi, a judge of more than twenty-five years' standing, was first mentioned as a candidate for the post of general guide.[20]

Little information is available on the reactions of the other aspirants to this suggestion or to the intensive campaigning on all levels of the organization by the partisans of the idea, but it seems to have been generally agreed that the movement could ill afford an almost certain split in the ranks should any one of the contenders be appointed, and that, temporarily, a leader should come from outside the organization. Equally compelling were some of the positive advantages listed by Hudaybi's supporters: that the appointment of a judge would placate the judiciary and the legal world—where the death of Judge Khazindar had not been forgotten—and help the cases of the Brothers still pending before the courts; that the palace would be assuaged (Hudaybi's brother-in-law was chief of the royal household), and would thus help to hasten the return to legality; and that the Society needed' 'a new face, new blood, and a new personality to appear before the community'.[21] The gist of all these considerations was that the Society needed respectability, and Hudaybi was a respectable man. As 'Ashmawi afterwards put it: 'It was necessary that the names of the terrorists, which had been made by the press the subject of stories of fear and terror, should disappear for a while.'[22] For most of the

[19] See *JJ* (16 Jan. 1954), 1, 3; Kira, *Mahkama*, i. 39.

[20] See *MRY* (31 Oct. 1953), 12; *MDA* (19 Jan. 1954), 3; and *JJ* (23 Nov. 1954), 10, for Dilla's own words. See also Khuli, *QDIHB*, 64–5, for an old-time member's assertion that Banna himself selected Hudaybi.

[21] *MJJ* (7 Dec. 1953), 8; see also Kira, *Mahkama*, i. 39, and ii. 14–15; and *JJ* (16 Jan. 1954), 1, 3.

[22] *MDA* (29 Dec. 1953), 16; *MRY* (31 Oct. 1953), 12. The extent or even reality of palace pressure in this appointment is not clear; cf. Husayni, *Ikhwan*, pp. 113–15; Halpern, *Politics of Social Change*, p. 149.

old hands, this was a necessary but temporary compromise with circumstances.

The arguments among the members and the negotiations with Hudaybi were concluded in October 1951, when his appointment was officially announced.[23] Little information has been made available about his life. In a short press interview, he said that he was born of ordinary worker parents in 'Arab al-Sawaliha in the Shibin area and had his earliest education in the village *kuttab* where he memorized the Qur'an. At the age of ten, he decided that he would like to be a lawyer, though his father had already decided to send him to the Azhar. He got his own way in the end and enrolled in the law school after completing his secondary education. He recalls that in college he was not a good student, and (a remarkable admission for a political leader in Egypt!) that he successfully avoided every demonstration while in school, except for the funeral of Mustafa Kamil. He graduated from the law school in 1915 and entered the law office of Hafiz Ramadan, deceased head of the National Party. He married after he had received his licence to practise. Noteworthy in this episode was his rather proud admission that he himself had asked for his wife's hand, and when her father suggested that perhaps his father should make the request, he had answered: 'My father presented himself when he wished to marry my mother. . . . As for me, I present myself, since I am the groom, not my father.' He knew, he says, that this would not annoy his father for 'he did not live in his generation; indeed, many of the traditions which had imprisoned that age had ceased to be within his consideration'.

Affairs did not move smoothly in Cairo, so he decided to move to the countryside, to Suhaj, where within a year he was earning a living. He lived through and participated in the Revolution of 1919, though with apparently less enthusiasm than most Egyptians. Obvious from his recollections was a life-long distaste for violence and for public displays. This continued to be an important aspect of his life in the Society. In 1924 he received his first appointment to the bench and spent the next twenty years as itinerant judge in the provinces of Egypt.

In 1944, he recalled, he first met some of the younger Muslim Brothers, and within a short time came to be one of Banna's close friends as well as a reverent admirer. About the first speech he heard Banna give, Hudaybi says:

> How many speeches have I heard, hoping each time that they could speedily end. . . . This time, I feared that Hasan al-Banna would end

[23] *MDA* (30 Oct. 1951), 1; *JJ* (14 Nov. 1954), 10; (19 Nov. 1954), 7.

his speech. . . . One hundred minutes passed, and he collected the hearts of the Muslims in the palms of his hands . . . and shook them as he willed. . . . The speech ended, and he returned to his listeners their hearts . . . except for mine, which remained in his hand.

His contacts with Banna inspired him to place his 'mind along with his heart in the service of the Brothers'. This does not seem to have meant official membership. When his appointment was announced he resigned from the bench.[24]

To make this appointment the Society by-passed its own regulations requiring that the leader must be a member of the Consultative Assembly and win three-quarters of its votes. The nomination was in fact made by the Guidance Council and approved by the Assembly without reference to a three-quarters vote, a required four-fifths quorum, and other considerations in the by-laws. Moreover, at the request of the new leader, the Council and Assembly appointed as his deputy a lawyer and a recent member, 'Abd al-Qadir 'Awda—also in technical violation of the by-laws. Within six months Hudaybi asked for the creation of a new post, that of vice-guide (*na'ib*) to be filled by Muhammad Khamis Humayda, an old leader from al-Mansura. This was partly because of a dispute with his original choice for deputy, 'Awda, and partly because his health compelled him to delegate work to subordinates. For the membership this was a new and disturbing departure; equally disturbing to those who regarded the appointment as a temporary one was the immediate reshuffling of some top commands,[25] and an immediate challenge to the still-existent secret apparatus.

The shuffling of leadership—which invariably replaced venerable old members with relative neophytes in the Society—seemed to the older members unduly hasty and imperious, presumptuous, and offensive. Hudaybi's right to appoint subordinates receptive to his policies was disregarded because of the mood which surrounded his appointment. This was neatly summed up in some of the words Hudaybi heard almost immediately upon his appointment: 'We want nothing from you; you need not even come to the headquarters. We will bring the papers for you to sign or reject as you will. . . . We only want a leader who will be a symbol of cleanliness.'[26] Hudaybi tried to seek out the 'elders' but, regarding him with suspicion, they would not respond to his appeals. And from the very first his failure—his inability—to bring to the role the 'personal' approach and to inspire confidence created an

[24] This information comes from an interview in *MJJ* (5 Jan. 1952), 12–13, 24.
[25] *MJJ* (7 Dec. 1953), 8; *JJ* (19 Nov. 1954), 7; (23 Nov. 1954), 9, 10.
[26] Kira, *Mahkama*, ii. 16.

insoluble problem, for the strength of the Society depended on its leader's possessing those very qualities. All these difficulties were magnified many times in Hudaybi's attempt to settle the problem of the secret apparatus, whose members considered themselves the élite of the Society.

Almost immediately after his appointment, Hudaybi stayed at home for over a month and then asked that his acceptance of the post be reconsidered. This followed upon his discovery that the secret apparatus was still in existence. Immediately he made known his repugnance to the violence which marked the years 1946–9, and his unwillingness to have any part in perpetuating the instrument of that activity. About those events he said, 'the mistakes of the past can be repaired'. About the secret organization he said: 'There is no secrecy in the service of God.' 'There is no secrecy in the Message and no terrorism in religion.'[27] In so saying, he not only alienated the members of the secret apparatus, but he also discredited the nobility of purpose with which these events were viewed by the actors in them, thereby challenging some basic and traditional views in the Society on both means and ends. He further crystallized a problem which in Banna's time had only been incipient: the challenge to the overt leadership posed by the 'élite'—leaders and members of the secret apparatus. As ʿAwda afterwards put it, the secret apparatus was an error 'administratively' because it created a 'dual' and often contradictory leadership.[28]

The tensions posed by these and other matters relating to the appointment and behaviour of the new leader were exacerbated over the next few years as the Muslim Brothers played their role on the Egyptian scene, and finally came to a head when external circumstances posed even greater problems for the Society itself. For the moment, the Society addressed itself to its role in the unfolding of another phase of the Anglo-Egyptian dispute.

NATIONALISM AND REVOLT

On 8 October 1951 Nahhas Pasha committed Egypt to the historic and complicating unilateral abrogation of the Anglo-Egyptian Treaty of 1936 and the Sudan Condominium of 1899. Standing before parliament, he completed his speech with the words, 'For the sake of Egypt I signed the treaty of 1936, and for the sake of Egypt, I ask of you this day to abrogate it.'[29] On the following day *Majallat al-Daʿwa* proclaimed the Muslim Brothers'

[27] *MRY* (7 Dec. 1953), 12; Kira, *Mahkama*, i. 41–2; ibid. ii. 19; *JJ* (19 Nov. 1954), 3; (17 Nov. 1954), 9.
[28] *JJ* (1 Dec. 1955), 5.
[29] See Mu'min, *Sawt Misr*, pp. 380–95, for one account, which includes the text of the speeches.

support for the declarations and immediately joined in the clamour for 'armed struggle' and '*jihad*'. On 17 October, following the first clash of Egyptians with the British forces, the Brothers in the Isma'iliyya area officially declared a *jihad* against the British.[30] On the 18th Hudaybi, who had been at the helm of the Society for some time, permitted the release of the information of his appointment as the new leader. In the circumstances, and in the light of what was to happen, the announcement seemed deliberately timed to seize control of the situation. It became widely known shortly after this that *Majallat al-Da'wa* was not to be regarded as the official journal of the movement. This was partly because its editor, Salih 'Ashmawi, the aspirant to the post of leader, had already emerged as Hudaybi's chief antagonist, but chiefly, at the moment, because its attitude as regards the national movement ran contrary to the inclinations and policy of the new leader. That the paper did, however, represent the feelings of the rank and file became painfully apparent in the next few months, as the official pronouncements of the leadership blatantly contradicted what the members were in fact contributing to the national cause.

Immediately after the first clash with the British in October, the nationalist demonstrators, who daily filled the streets, began demanding arms, training, and the creation of 'liberation battalions' to fight the enemy. The fact that the government had abrogated the treaty and had prepared few, if any, plans regarding what was to follow was already becoming embarrassingly apparent. By 1 November the movement for battalions was well under way in the universities, mostly under the impetus of the Muslim Brothers. When on 14 November the minister of the interior announced that the government would take over the job of arming and training the battalions, it was widely believed that this was a manœuvre designed to control them rather than to make them more effective. The Muslim Brothers were being trained not only by army officers in the public camps set up in the universities and secondary schools but also privately by these and other officers, some or most of whom had connections with a group in the army who were now calling themselves the 'Free Officers'. These were also providing the Brothers with the arms which they were to carry into the Canal Zone. An estimated 300 volunteers—some of whom were from the secret apparatus—actually found their way into the Canal Zone from December onwards, and participated in the harassment of British personnel and positions.[31]

[30] Boehm, 'Les Frères musulmans', 218–19; *MDA* (13 Nov. 1951), 8–9.

[31] Mohammed Neguib, *Egypt's Destiny* (1955), p. 94; *JJ* (17 Nov. 1954), 9, 10; (12 Nov. 1954), 4.

In what appeared to be an inexplicable contradiction of facts Hudaybi, on 23 November, denied that the Society had any battalions of its own preparing to fight in the Canal Zone, or that the Brothers would participate in the 'movement of the liberation battalions'; for the Muslim Brothers there was the single task of spreading their message peacefully. This was in part a public reprimand for a public statement by one of his higher subordinates which was intended to dissociate the Society from what appeared to be Hudaybi's indifference to the Suez issue.[32] A journalist, seeking explanation of the surprising contradictions in word and deed, quizzed a close associate of Hudaybi and received the answer that the policy of the Society was as enunciated by the leader; beyond that, each member was free to serve the nation as he saw fit.[33]

One of the factors involved in the situation was Hudaybi's personal antipathy to violence and his conception of the battalion movement as an essentially futile endeavour. Another factor, hinted at in the above statement, was that the leadership was giving 'protection' to the organization by making no 'official' inflammatory or provocative statements. The memory of Palestine and the crisis which followed it was still strong in the minds of many of the Brothers, for whom the preservation of the Society to fulfil its message was the supreme consideration; Hudaybi's leadership provided a timely official focus for organizational timidity and even outright fear of action. It was among the perennial activists'—primarily those in or connected with the secret apparatus—that the Society's official policy met with resistance, and added to the growing list of grievances against the new leader. In the meantime, Hudaybi was providing even more ammunition for his opponents.

On 13 November Egypt organized herself into a mass silent demonstration against the continuing impasse with the British. On the next day, 14 November, Hudaybi, at the king's invitation and in a royal car, called at the palace. He stayed there forty-five minutes and on his way out uttered to reporters appropriate words of homage to the ruler of Egypt. *Majallat al-Daʿwa* reported the visit and noted, with implications not lost upon its readers, that it was the first official meeting between His Majesty the King and the General Guide of the Muslim Brothers'.[34]

[32] Muhammad al-Ghazali, the prolific writer of the Society, was the recipient of the public rebuke and also of a private one; he was later to lead a 'revolt' against Hudaybi. See *MDA* (12 Jan. 1954)), 3, 14; *MRY* (31 Oct. 1953), 13.

[33] *MAL* (18 Jan. 1952), 4.

[34] *MDA* (27 Nov. 1951), 7. As we have already seen (pp. 40–2, above) it is probably not true that this was the first contact of the Society with the palace. It

In terms of Hudaybi's reputation, the meeting was ominous, for it not only appeared to reverse the Society's traditional feeling of hostility to the palace, but also coincided with an increasing determination on the part of the king to move against the Wafd, and, indirectly, against the national movement. This view was reinforced when on 24 December, Hudaybi sent a message of congratulations to Hafiz 'Afifi Pasha, appointed by the palace to head the royal cabinet, a move understood by the national movement as an indication of the royal intent to bring its activity to a halt. In the Society indignation ran high at the appointment and Hudaybi's recognition of it.[35]

By these actions and by another visit to the palace on 16 January 1952 on the occasion of the birth of the crown prince, Ahmad Fu'ad, Hudaybi further heightened the doubts in the minds of those who were concerned about what the Society did. He acted as he did either because of royal commands, or from a conviction, inevitably influenced by his long legal career, of what convention required of the leader of one of Egypt's more important organizations. For the Wafd, the spectre of the palace in accord with the Muslim Brothers was again on the horizon. The Wafdist leaders made known to the Society that they were affronted by the failure of Hudaybi to make courtesy calls on them also.[36] Within the organization, perplexity mounted as the opposition grew.

Meanwhile, on the political front, delirious joy was giving way to anger and bitterness by the turn of the year. The abrogation of the treaty of 1936 had not, after all, resolved the national dispute; the British were still in the Canal Zone and seemed determined to

was true, also, that along with Hudaybi's name on the palace register for that day, there were thirteen others from the Muslim Brothers and all from the leadership. Since it was the policy to deal with the palace, the call seems to have been one in the name of the Society. Among the thirteen names were two who made the most of the 'charge', Salih 'Ashmawi and Muhammad al-Ghazali. Both later denied the evidence—pictures of the registers with signatures—presented by the government in the press. On this matter, see *JJ* (8 Sept. 1954), 4–5; (9 Sept. 1954), 1, 9. In an interview after the revolution, Hudaybi insisted that he was summoned to a meeting with the king; (see *MMR* (24 Oct. 1952), 15). *MRY* (31 Oct. 1953), 12 (a magazine both informed about and hostile to the Society) reported that Hudaybi infuriated the king by departing from the meeting with his back to the royal presence.

[35] See *MDA* (12 Jan. 1954), 3, 14; and *JJ* (9 Sept. 1954), 4. In the university the Brothers were among the most riotous of the students who, in the day the news was announced, broke into angry demonstrations during which the king was publicly cursed and denounced; so unusual (and obscene) was this outburst that the police entered the campus proper—again unusually—and did battle with the students.

[36] See Kira, *Mahkama*, i. 40–1; *MDA* (29 Dec. 1953), 6; and *MDA* (5 Jan. 1954), 13.

stay there, the liberation battalions notwithstanding. The demonstrations which in October had paraded their national defiance of the British and extolled 'the hero of the nation', Nahhas Pasha, had slowly turned into vitriolic anti-government riots which damned 'the criminal' Siraj al-Din, minister of the interior, the symbol of the serious doubt which now existed about the sincerity of the Wafdist government's action in abrogating the treaty. The failure of the government to take serious measures commensurate with the crisis, the king's appointment of 'Afifi Pasha to his royal cabinet, and the more stringent controls placed on the expression of the national passion confirmed the notion that the British were about to win another round in the Anglo-Egyptian dispute. All of this was directly articulated in a short, well planned, highly charged demonstration which followed a mass funeral on 14 January to mourn the return of one of the first 'martyrs' of the liberation battalions in the Canal Zone. 'Umar Shahin of the Muslim Brothers was mourned that day as a symbol not only of a bloody foreign occupation but also of a humiliating national betrayal.[37]

The impasse in the national question was broken on 25 January. On that day British forces in the Canal Zone, attempting to disarm some of the Egyptian auxiliary police, directed 'a major assault' at those defending—on the orders of the minister of the interior, 'to the last man'—the Isma'iliyya police headquarters; over forty were killed in the ensuing battle. The next day, 26 January 1952, the heart of modern and westernized Cairo was left a charred ruin in the wake of the most devastating riot in modern Egyptian history. In the early morning members of the auxiliary police in Cairo marched across the bridges to the university in Giza and with the students and soldiers and officers collected along the way, returned to the city and to the parliament where demands were voiced for an immediate declaration of war on Britain. At the same time other groups, well organized and well equipped, began the systematic burning of the centre of the city. The fire consumed department stores, cinemas, bars, nightclubs, social clubs, luxury food and clothing establishments, novelty shops, automobile showrooms and garages, airline offices, and the like; the fire lumped together, in one massive rejection, the British, the West, the

[37] For pictures and stories, see *MDA* (15 Jan. 1952), 12; and *MAL* (16 Jan. 1952), 3. The memory of Shahin was commemorated by the RCC after the revolution in the use of his name for one of the newly constructed villages of the Liberation Province (see *MJJ* (6 Apr. 1953), 10–11). The significance of this in assessing the historic relationships between the Brothers and the army officers should not be overstated; Shahin was and is a national student hero in his 'martyrdom'.

foreigner, the wealthy, and the ruler—king and pasha alike. As Issawi has so aptly put it: 'The writing on the wall had, for many years, been plain to see, but during the riots of 26 January 1952 its meaning may be said to have stood out in letters of fire.'[38]

The Wafd did not have the opportunity to declare war, though during the day its spokesmen promised to do so. In the late afternoon, after most of the damage was done, the king called in the army; that evening, martial law was declared and the government of Nahhas Pasha was dismissed. 'Ali Mahir was entrusted with the job of forming a new cabinet and restoring order to the gutted city and confidence in the government of Egypt.

Among those arrested immediately was Hasan al-Hudaybi, but he was also immediately released. As an organization, the Muslim Brothers were, without question, not responsible for the planning and execution of the fire; equally without question individual members were involved,[39] as were thousands of other Egyptians with and without party affiliations, either as torch bearers or appreciative audience. Hudaybi, within a day, had issued a statement repudiating the fire and those who 'erred' in thinking that such action would rid the country either of the English or of its moral problems so long as the causes of immorality were 'permitted by law'. Repudiating all similar activity in the past, he affirmed that the Society would continue its fight in 'legal ways' to change those laws. This was followed almost immediately by a note to the government making formal representations for the lifting of martial law, the restoration of civil liberties, and the release of political prisoners.

In an effort to bring the national movement under control, Mahir brought the volunteers back from the Canal Zone. In answer to continuing pressure from the university, however, he was compelled on the political side to invite the nation into a 'national front', and on the military side to continue and formalize the programme of training battalions with the avowed aim of creating a 'popular' reserve force.[40]

On 1 March, partly because of his unwillingness to suspend the

[38] Issawi, *Egypt*, p. 271.

[39] Ibid. for some other possibilities; Kaplinsky, 'The Muslim Brotherhood', 384, accepts the notion of the Brothers' responsibility for organizing 'Black Saturday' (he errs in calling it 'Black Friday'); so, also, do Caskel, 'Western Impact and Islamic Civilization', 348, and most other commentators on the fire. The best account of it is in RIIA, *Middle East*, pp. 197–8. There is no evidence to support this view beyond the circumstantial fact that the Brothers presumably were against bars, cinemas, and the British. The Cairo government, reflecting a widely held view there, arrested Ahmad Husayn, leader of the Socialist party. Harris, *Nationalism and Revolution*, pp. 142, 192, alternates between Young Egypt and the communists.

[40] This information is drawn from the daily press of Egypt, largely *MAL*.

Wafdist parliament,[41] Mahir was dismissed; a new cabinet was formed by the most recent Wafdist defector and a former minister of education, Ahmad Najib al-Hilali Pasha. He immediately set in motion a programme of 'purifying' the government from corruption—a perennial post-Wafd move and one regarded by the nationalists as a royal manœuvre to distract attention from the national cause. However, Hilali was serious, sharing with many Egyptians the feeling that Egypt would be liberated from her occupation only when she came to the conference table purged of her own corruption. The leader of the Brothers, when asked about the new government and his programme of reform, remarked somewhat noncommittally that the Society had not changed its traditional view of non-identification with any ministry but would welcome any real reform of the nation.[42] As to the problem of the British, Hudaybi, a few days later, told Hilali Pasha that Brothers expected that he would 'work for the expulsion of the English from Egypt in a reasonable time'.[43] After the dissolution of parliament on 23 March, and the selection of 18 May as an election date, Hudaybi, apparently now more convinced of the prime minister's sincerity and seriousness of purpose, noticeably warmed up in a long letter detailing, in traditional terms, the views of the Society on national problems; he again demanded the abrogation of martial law.[44] It was also announced that the Society would not participate in the coming elections. Various reasons were given by Hudaybi and by other spokesmen for him, for the Society, and for themselves: dissatisfaction with the election laws; dissatisfaction with the timing of the elections, which would cause 'disunity and hate' in the midst of the 'national struggle'; unwillingness to participate in, and thus be sullied by, elections as they were conducted in Egypt; unwillingness to risk coming to power in a society so corrupted as was Egypt; unpreparedness of the Society for an election battle.[45] Whatever the real reason from among this range of possibilities, the issue died out with the continued postponement of the date on which the elections were to be held.

On other issues, relations between the Society and the Hilali government were unusually friendly. The government sent official representatives to functions of the Society,[46] and there were exchanges of visits between Hilali and Hudaybi.[47] This cordiality was reflected in the virtual cessation of the agitation at the university. Hilali continued Mahir's policy of clearing the volunteers

[41] See Neguib, *Egypt's Destiny*, p. 103.
[42] *MAL* (14 Mar. 1952), 3.
[43] *MDA* (18 Mar. 1952), 3.
[44] *MAL* (26 Mar. 1952), 3, 7.
[45] Ibid. (27 Mar. 1953), 3; (14 Apr. 1952), 3; *MDA* (1 Apr. 1952), 1; and *MMR* (4 Apr. 1952), 10.
[46] *MAS* (14 May 1952), 6.
[47] *MDA* (15 Apr. 1952), 3.

out of the Suez area, but he permitted, with almost total freedom, the continued operation of the training camps within the university. The students, demonstrating their 'victory' over the government attempt to crush the liberation battalions, regularly rode around the campus in an amphibious-type jeep and, in front of the administration building, sprayed their machine guns around its famous dome. Similar reports of armed students testing explosives and spraying arms fire around the campus came from Alexandria University. The students involved were in the vast majority from the Muslim Brothers.

At the same time, however, in what appeared to be the other side of a bargain, the university demonstrations and opinion at large were brought under control. Hilali needed quiet while he pushed on with his programme of reform, and also attempted to re-establish negotiations with the British; at the university he was given assistance by the Brothers. In control of the student unions the Brothers were in a position to direct university activity; this they did by organizing and planning 'programmes' for the expression of opinion about the issues of the day in the university auditorium. 'Ushers' placed at strategic places through the hall assisted in keeping the audience in step with the programme, sometimes by physical means. After a few meetings the speech-making died away and the students turned to their books, after almost a full year of rioting. Among other things, the examination period was coming up. As in earlier days, the Society, and especially Hudaybi, reaped the wrath of their opponents for 'treason' to the national cause in and out of the university.[48]

Bringing the university under control was perhaps the prime minister's only solid achievement. After it became clear that his reform intentions were serious, he met not only with no co-operation but with positive obstacles, from the palace as well as from the Wafd. His inability to make headway on this score, as well as his failure to persuade the British of the need for some gesture to justify his reopening negotiations, led to his resignation on 28 June. Husayn Sirri was called to form a new government on 29 June but he too resigned on 20 July over the issue of 'exiling' General Muhammad Neguib to the frontiers. Neguib had been elected earlier in the year president of the Army Officers' Club in defiance of the royal choice, Husayn Sirri 'Amir. Hilali Pasha was recalled and on 22 July announced his cabinet, which included the king's choice as minister of war and navy, his brother-in-law, Isma'il Shirin. By this action the king, determined to assert his

[48] See Boehm, 'Les Frères musulmans', 219–20. We were fascinated observers of this scene.

royal prerogative after his defeat in the Officers' Club, provoked the sudden decision for the long-planned, long-awaited day. On the morning of 23 July the Free Officers, with Muhammad Neguib at their head, occupied the city of Cairo and all strategic points, bringing to an end the reign of the dynasty of Muhammad ʿAli.[49]

The background to the July revolution in Egypt is peripheral to the story of the Muslim Brothers except that, from its earliest days, the revolutionary currents coming from the army sought and received the sympathetic support of that Society—more correctly, of certain of its leaders. Material with which to reconstruct that story is still scanty, and unhappily now much distorted, a fact deriving from the breakdown in relations between the groups in pre- and early post-revolutionary days. However, enough information is available to make a beginning on this very important problem. For, besides its own historical importance, the army coup of 1952, in the history of the Muslim Brothers, was the first significant challenge to the idea which had given the Society its momentum. Coinciding, as it did, with an organizational crisis, the revolution, and what it implied—or what Brothers thought it implied—for Egypt, put to a major test what had hitherto been regarded as an almost invincible attraction and power. On 23 July 1952 the Muslim Brothers joined with the rest of Egypt in celebrating the dawn of a new era; twenty-nine months later, six of the Society's members died on the gallows, and the organization was destroyed almost beyond repair. Before going on to those events, an attempt will be made to reconstruct their background.

We have already recorded that the earliest contacts of Hasan al-Banna with army discontent came as early as 1940, in the person of Anwar al-Sadat, a member of the junta. Sadat, it was observed, was probably not then in touch with the group or groups which later joined together to become the 'Free Officers', the backbone of the revolution. The importance of these contacts was that they put Sadat in touch with ʿAziz al-Misri, the unemployed, nationalist commander-in-chief of the armed forces, and that they encouraged Banna to proceed with his own plans for secret revolutionary activity. Out of them, too, came the beginning of the long and dedicated commitment to the Society of ʿAbd al-Munʿim ʿAbd al-Ra'uf, the friend of Sadat who was arrested with Misri in his abortive attempt to escape from Egypt in 1941 and who replaced Sadat as liaison man between the officers of the army and the Muslim Brothers when the latter was arrested in 1942. ʿAbd al-Ra'uf, seems, too to have been one of the first and most active

[49] See esp. Sadat, *Safahat*, pp. 220–30.

members of the group which came to be called the Free Officers; in its highest councils, he remained the chief propagandist and protagonist of the Muslim Brothers.

Assisting 'Abd al-Ra'uf in the task of recruitment for the Society in the army was another officer, Mahmud Labib. Labib had retired from the army in 1936, having distinguished himself in Egyptian operations in the Sudan; he came to know and work with Banna as early as 1941. He was unofficial adviser to Banna on 'scouting' activities until 1947, when he was appointed as a deputy in the Society for 'military affairs' and sent into Palestine to help train and recruit volunteers there. In the Palestine war, he was technical head of the 'volunteer divisions' and Banna's personal representative on matters relating to the war. He died on 18 December 1951.[50] Labib's most important contact with the Free Officers was made in 1944 and with no less a personage than Gamal 'Abd al-Nasir.

The meeting between the two was arranged by a friend common to both, at Labib's request. It took place in the summer of 1944, on the Tea Island in the Cairo zoo. Labib, doing most of the talking, spoke of 'liberation' and the need for the army to begin taking an active part in the affairs of the nation, to assist in its salvation. He interspersed his discussion of the problems of the country with observations about the need for 'faith' and about 'our organization'. Nasir asked what this meant in practice and was told: 'Begin to organize in the army groups which have faith in what we believe so that when the time comes, we will be organized in one rank, making it impossible for our enemies to crush us.' It was as a result of this meeting that Nasir, profoundly affected, presumably began 'to design the plan'.[51]

[50] Above, pp. 55–8; see *MDA* (25 Dec. 1951), 9, for a report on his life and death. He left behind him ten volumes of memoirs which were scheduled for publication but have never appeared. For other material on and by Labib, see *MMB* (31 Oct. 1950), 16; (16 Jan. 1951), 8–9, 16; Sharif, *IMFHF*, pp. 45–6, 102; and Khuli, *QDIHB*, Introd., pp. 80–1.

[51] Hilmi Salam, 'Hadhihi hiya qissat thawrat al-jaysh min al-mahd ila al-majd', *MMR* (31 Oct. 1952), 12–13. This is one of a series of very important articles under this title by the author, who is believed to be reporting Nasir's own recollections; they appear in *MMR*, nos 1464–74. Their importance is greatly increased by the fact that they appeared early in the period of the revolution and are therefore uninhibited by the urgency of later events to minimize affiliations with the Brothers. This particular episode, for instance, is omitted from the later work, Sadat, *Safahat*, which purports to treat all the relations between the officers and the Brothers. The event is also reported by Brother sources orally and in *Hatta ya'lam al-nas* [1954], p. 6; this pamphlet is one of the few available which explains the position of the Brothers on the many issues raised with the government at a later date; it came from the pens of the heads of the Muslim Brothers in Jordan, Iraq, and the Sudan. A partial English reproduction appeared in a Pakistan student paper, *The Student's Voice*, iv (16 Oct. 1954), 1.

Whether or not this recollection is correct, it would appear that from this time on, the man who in fact came to lead the army revolution was in touch with the Muslim Brothers. Nasir was joined by others in his own and other cliques in the army, one of which was led by Rashad Muhanna, whose group later merged with that of Nasir to become the nucleus of the Free Officers. Muhanna, afterwards appointed the officer member of the regency council, appears (although with less certainty than is usually noted) to have shown sympathy for the Society, in idea if not in membership.[52] Other important recruits were Kamal al-Din Husayn and Husayn al-Shafi'i, both of the junta.

'Abd al-Ra'uf continued to be an important figure in the conversion of officers. He would bring his converts to Mahmud Labib for 'instruction in the message' which, when completed, was followed by appropriate oath-taking in appropriately darkened rooms, securing thereby the allegiance of the officers to the Muslim Brothers. The oath they took signified their entrance (primarily) into its secret apparatus. In February 1946, at a meeting of Nasir's group in which the post-war situation with special reference to leaders and parties was under discussion, the leader was asked: 'Can we expect good [*khayr*] from the Muslim Brothers?' Nasir answered: 'Yes, much good [*khayr kathir*].' For the revolutionaries, the Muslim Brothers emerged from the war with high prestige, and thus became the logical associates in the plan for alliance between the army and a 'people's' party, working together with no open ties, 'until the appropriate time'.[53]

During this period, however, and over the next few years, some of the officers came to feel disenchantment with their new allegiance. The 'Abidin case raised questions about Banna's purity of motive; the subsequent resignation of Ibrahim Hasan confirmed those suspicions. Similarly, the dismissal of Ahmad al-Sukkari—with all its implications of 'treaty' with the palace and the governments, especially that of Sidqi Pasha—caused some stir in the ranks and some resignations.[54] Of perhaps greater import were the organizational problems encountered by the officers. Those who had joined expected to be of assistance in the military training of members; often they found themselves enmeshed in the existing operation, enrolled in classes and being instructed by

[52] See Salam, 'Qissat thawrat al-jaysh', *MMR* (31 Oct. 1954), 16–17, on the relations between the Nasir and Muhanna groups. On Muhanna's loyalty to the Society, see Neguib, *Egypt's Destiny*, pp. 32; D. Haydon, 'Egypt's Surprise Dictatorship', *National and English Review*, cxxxix (Oct. 1952), 212. Muhanna is also claimed by the Wafdists as well as by the Brothers.

[53] Salam, 'Qissat thawrat al-jaysh', *MMR* (7 Nov. 1954), 12–13; (14 Nov. 1952), 12; see also Sadat, *Safahat*, pp. 98–9, 111.

[54] See Sadat, *Safahat*, pp. 171–4; *MTR* (23 Nov. 1954), 4.

civilians in the use of the rifle. In this and in other issues of organization and policy, they found it impossible to break through the wall of hierarchy; like all members of the Society, they were told 'to have confidence in the leadership'.[55] It is difficult to assess how far the relationship was subjected to strain over these matters. At a later date such criticisms were to provide ample ammunition with which to discredit the Society, but at the time they were probably no more than irritants, considerably soothed by the Society's dedication to, and participation in, the Palestine war.

That phase of the relations between the officers and the Brothers has already been dealt with, especially the supply of arms and the training of the volunteers. Nasir, again, was a central figure in the operation as was Kamal al-Din Husayn, who was at the front with the volunteers. Some complaints were voiced later, concerning the foolhardiness of the first Brothers in battle regardless of army orders and operational plans, complaints which echoed earlier doubts about the possibility of co-operation, but which at the time seemed rather more like the result of patriotic fervour. It seems to be true that the Brothers won the affection of the officers at the front, including the commanders of the forces;[56] by their very presence in Palestine, prepared to fight and die, the Brothers appeared to the officers as a conspicuous contradiction to the mood of isolation and betrayal which they came to experience. Their shared experiences in battle, especially at the siege of Faluja, established for some and reinforced for others shared attitudes about things related and unrelated, especially about those responsible for the humiliation suffered in Palestine. After the revolution, the junta included in the 'Palestine Cemetery' a monument listing volunteers from the Brothers who had fought in the Palestine war.[57] The admiration worked both ways: one Brother who fought in Palestine said after the revolution that he was happy that God had willed that 'the great victory' (i.e. the revolution) had occurred 'at the hands of our noble comrades (*al-zumala' al-kiram*)' who had 'fought with us in Palestine'.[58]

The services of the Free Officers to Palestine led to the near arrest of their leader, Nasir, in May 1949, in the course of the purge instituted by the government of Ibrahim 'Abd al-Hadi. Following his return from the Faluja pocket in Palestine, and while on leave in Cairo, Nasir was summoned by the commander-in chief of the armed forces, 'Uthman al-Mahdi Pasha, and taken

[55] Sadat, *Safahat*, pp. 156–8; *MMR* (10 Dec. 1954), 26.

[56] Above, pp. 57–8. See also Sharif, *IMFHF*, pp. 173–91; *Aqwal wa-ta'dhib*, pp. 16–29, for the words of the commanders; see also Husayni, *Ikhwan*, pp. 126–7.

[57] See *MAS* (11 Mar. 1953), 10.

[58] Sharif, *IMFHF*, pp. 5–6.

to call on the prime minister. He was there charged with (but denied) 'having trained groups of the Muslim Brothers in the use of arms'. To a question by the prime minister about his relations with the Society Nasir answered: 'like the relations of 20 million Egyptians to all the parties'. Pressed for clarification, he went on to say (in the face of ʿAbd al-Hadi's vow to him to avenge the death of Nuqrashi and to sacrifice his own 'neck' to prevent the Brothers from ruling Egypt) that some Egyptians liked the Saʿdists, some the Wafdists, and some the Brothers. He added, 'I am one of those latter.' In the course of the meeting, left for a moment to himself while the prime minister busied himself elsewhere, he rid himself of some papers he recalled having on his person. The meeting ended with ʿAbd al-Hadi unsatisfied, but unwilling to press charges.[59] This was only one of the many clues, made available after the revolution, about the attitude of the Free Officers towards the dissolution of the Society—and by indirection the acts of violence which inspired the move—and towards Nuqrashi, ʿAbd al-Hadi, and the palace.

In December 1950 the Free Officers were almost uncovered and arrested following public protests about 'their intervention in political matters'. The first commander of the Palestine forces, Fu'ad Sadiq, and the man originally scheduled to be the front-leader of the revolution, was the focus of the charges and was very nearly brought to trial.[60] Why he was not may possibly have been related to a Wafdist design to frighten the palace with the threat of revolution. The king himself allegedly received late in 1950 a report that 33 per cent of his army officers were bound to the Muslim Brothers.[61] The near-exposing of the officers' plot brought the two groups closer; anticipating the worst, Nasir made arrangements secretly to transfer stores of arms to be concealed on the estate of Muhammad al-ʿAshmawi, the father of his close friend in the Society and recipient of the arms, Hasan al-ʿAshmawi.[62] The younger ʿAshmawi (not to be confused with Salih ʿAshmawi, of the *Majallat al-Daʿwa*) was one of the ardent supporters of Hudaybi's appointment and, later, one of his defenders.

[59] Sadat, *Safahat*, pp. 188–9, gives a more noncommittal, less detailed account than the earlier reference in Salam, 'Qissat thawrat al-jaysh', *MMR* (5 Dec. 1952), 16–17.

[60] See Neguib, *Egypt's Destiny*, p. 30; and 'Developments of the Quarter', *MEJ* (Spring 1951), 201.

[61] *MDA* (29 Dec. 1953), 6; see also D. Peters, 'The "Muslim Brotherhood"—Terrorists or just Zealots?', *Reporter*, viii (17 Mar. 1953), 8, reporting in 1953 that 'army officers admit that nearly a third of their ranks participate in the Brotherhood's activities'. In October 1952 the king announced from abroad his view that the Muslim Brothers had a hand in the revolution; see *MMR* (24 Oct. 1952), 15.

[62] See *JJ* (17 Nov. 1954), 9; (1 Dec. 1954), 4.

Finally, not long before the revolution, the Free Officers again armed and trained volunteers for the 'liberation battalions', mostly Brothers, sent into the Canal Zone. Isma'iliyya was the headquarters of these activities; the chief contact man was the head of the local branch of the Society, Shaykh Muhammad Farghali.[63]

The fire of 26 January 1952 was a turning-point in the planning of the Free Officers. The revolution date set for 25 March was delayed and the event finally occurred on 23 July, following the attempt of the palace to impose its will on the officers' club. What was the role of the Brothers in those dramatic first days? Most of the observers who have commented on the first days of the uprising have asserted that a clear link existed between the army junta and the Muslim Brothers. One account, obviously reflecting information from within the Society, is typical:

> Without the enthusiastic support of the Moslem Brotherhood, Mohammad Naguib's movement might already have met the fate of the half dozen Egyptian governments that preceded it in the year 1952. The Brotherhood was a full participant in Naguib's coup last summer and much of his success since then can be attributed to . . . their support.[64]

On the question of the 'support' of the Muslim Brothers, there is little doubt; most Egyptians supported the revolution. 'Participation' in the coup, however, is another matter. Much material has been made available on the continuous and often intense contact of the army officers with the Society, but little on plans for the day of the revolution itself. The army government has denied that there was anything more active or positive in the contacts between the officers and the Society than with other groups in Egypt, contacts made and then repudiated.[65] As for the Muslim Brothers, the officers point to the fact that 'Abd al-Mun'im 'Abd al-Ra'uf, the perennial member of both groups and the chief protagonist of

[63] Above, pp. 88–9; *JJ* (19 Nov. 1954), 8; Husayni, *Ikhwan*, pp. 127–8; see also *JJ* (17 Nov. 1954), 10. The latter reference is to the trials of members of the Society in 1954, during which the following exchange took place between the officer-judge and the Brother recipient of arms, Shaykh Muhammad Farghali: Farghali was talking about receiving arms in 1951 (from the army?) for 'the movement'. The officer-judge, Gamal Salim, asked abruptly, 'Which movement?' Farghali replied, 'For the revolutionary movement [of the army]'. The judge's reaction brought an immediate apology from the witness. These arms were later (see below, p. 127) 'discovered' by the government and 'exposed' as part of the arms caches by which the Society was allegedly preparing revolution.

[64] Peters, 'Muslim Brotherhood', 8; see also Haydon, 'Surprise Dictatorship', 212–13; M. Colombe, 'Onze mois d'évolution de l'Égypte', *AA*, xxiii (1953), 10–11.

[65] See e.g. Sadat, *Safahat*, pp. 142, 159–60, 216–19, 234, for relations with the communists and Wafdists. This is an important point which the story of relations with the Muslim Brothers should not obscure.

union between them, was accepted into the 'Executive Committee of the Revolutionary Command Council' in 1950 but was dismissed in 1951 because of the Council's rejection of his views.[66] The officers have only indirectly faced up to the issue of the participation of the Society in the revolution by pointing out, much later, that from 23 to 26 July, until the king was deposed, no official pronouncement of support came from the Society. There was indeed none; Hudaybi remained in Alexandria, silent. The explanation of this fact appears to be not, as the government later suggested, that Hudaybi, from the first day, was fighting the revolution and dared not move until 'his sovereign' was stripped of power, but rather in the nature of the arrangement and the situation which surrounded the rebellion of the army officers, as it has been put, 'on the backs of the Muslim Brothers'. The following is a brief summary of the information available to this writer on the Brothers' share in the July revolution.

Three names emerge as those of possible messengers from within the Society of the news that a revolt of army officers was imminent, and that it sought the support of the Muslim Brothers. The first, and probably most important, was Salah Shadi, the leading member of the Egyptian police in the Society, a close friend of Nasir, and supporter of Hudaybi. The second name was that of Hasan al-'Ashmawi, similarly closely associated with both Nasir and Hudaybi, and the recipient of the arms to be hidden on his father's estate in 1950 when the army plot was in danger of discovery. 'Abd al-Rahman al-Sanadi, the head of the secret apparatus and likewise close to Nasir, was the third among those most likely to have known of the revolutionary plan. Another possibility—not necessarily exclusive of the others—was that Rashad Muhanna was delegated by the Revolutionary Council to seek the aid of Hudaybi and the Muslim Brothers. Nothing emerges clearly about what happened next, particularly the attitudes assumed by Hudaybi. The fact that two of his strongest supporters, Shadi and 'Ashmawi, were deeply committed to the idea and the operation presumably won him over; on the other hand, his relations with Sanadi were already so cool over the issue of the secret apparatus that he appears to have shown no response to the latter's pleas for extraordinary action. However, since the issue of the revolution and the Society involved so much more than the secret apparatus, his reaction to Sanadi could not have been a decisive factor; there seems little doubt that Hudaybi

[66] *JJ* (18 Oct. 1954), 10; (15 Jan. 1955), 9; (16 Jan. 1955), 3; and *MTR* (25 Nov. 1954), 4. A guess would place 'Abd al-Ra'uf's fall from grace shortly after the July revolution.

acquiesced, albeit cautiously, in the participation or non-opposition of the Society in the forthcoming events.[67]

Two elements were involved in Hudaybi's caution. The first was his own avowed antipathy to violence and disorder, the likely corollaries of a revolution. Equally important was his image of the means and ends of the Society of which he was now leader. The official policy of the Society in the nationalist agitation of the previous year was a clue not only to official timidity but also to the larger questions of power and authority. Banna and the Society had as a traditional platform that the Society should exercise power only when the nation had been truly 'Islamized', and thereby prepared to accept the principles for which the Brothers stood; Hudaybi fully accepted this policy and, perhaps more consistently, operated within its terms. The question of participation in the revolution posed the problem as directly as anything could have done. While his response appears to have been cautiously in the affirmative, he warned his followers that participation meant responsibility and that, as he told them, 'Power corrupts the soul'. His ambivalence on the immediate issue remained a constant thorn in his relationships both in and out of the Society.

Whatever might have been Hudaybi's personal part in it—and it is very possible that the entire matter could have been negotiated without his knowledge—an agreement of sorts was reached between the two groups concerning the part the Muslim Brothers would play on the day of revolution. This plan attempted to foresee all the possible contingencies in which a well-disciplined, well-trained 'civil army' could be of use. First, the members of the Society were to take upon themselves the protection of foreigners and foreign establishments (including places of business and diplomacy), of minorities (homes, churches, and synagogues), and of strategic centres of communications in the city. The intent was to frustrate any attempts by any group to exploit the anticipated confusion of the day. Along with this, the Society would establish a network of intelligence over the movements of 'suspicious' and 'potentially treasonous' Egyptians. Secondly, should immediate popular enthusiasm for the army movement be lacking, the Society would fill the streets to spark it off and ensure immediate popular acceptance of the coup. Thirdly, if the police failed to co-operate with the army, the Society would dispatch its rovers to join in whatever fighting ensued, and to assist in the maintenance of order and security. Fourthly, if the movement, despite all precautions, failed, the Muslim Brothers would assist in the protection and escape of the Free Officers. This last

[67] See *Hatta ya'lam al-nas*, pp. 6–7.

contingency was presumably the primary responsibility of Hasan al-'Ashmawi. A fifth, although less certain, part of the arrangement had to do with a possible British intervention. Shadi was allegedly provided with arms and instructed to place at strategic spots on the road from Suez members (as civilians, to arouse no suspicions) with equipment and orders to harass and obstruct any potential reoccupation by the British forces from the Canal Zone. Of the entire scheme, very few members needed to be, and were, aware.

After 23 July members of the Society recalled with pride (at a later date, with bitterness) their share in the first three days of the revolution in helping 'to maintain order and security', and in giving the revolution its successful start.[68] But the fact that it was not necessary to invoke most of the provisions of the agreement perpetuated its secrecy even among the members of the Society. Another reported reason for secrecy was the agreement among all concerned that open participation of the Society would assure automatic Western intervention in the revolution and its destruction.[69] The government's later attempt to disassociate itself from the Society for this and other reasons was regarded as the junta's servile truckling to the foreign embassies and became a foundation stone in the wall of hostility which rapidly arose between the two groups. At the moment—given the long association of the army officers with the Society (which, with a certain vagueness as to details, was now the common property of the hitherto unknowing membership-at-large) and the real and potential role of the members in the events of 23 July (which although not of major importance did dramatize its unique relationship to the revolution —the Society came to regard the events of 23 July as 'our revolution'. From this auspicious beginning flowered the events which led to the second and more permanent dissolution of the power of the Muslim Brothers.

[68] *Hatta ya'lam al-nas*, pp. 5–8 for the only partial written account of the above arrangement. At the later trials of 1954, when a witness was asked about the anticipated role of the Society in the uprising allegedly planned in collusion with Muhammad Neguib and dissident army officers, he answered: 'the one that they undertook in the army movement of 1952—general support, protection of the movement and installations'. For this obviously careless slip by the censor, see *MAS* (24 Nov. 1954), 6. See also Husayni, *Ikhwan*, p. 128 and n. 346.

[69] See Neguib, *Egypt's Destiny*, p. 110, for a statement along these lines.

V

REVOLUTION AND DISSOLUTION: THE LAST PHASE

THE SHORT HONEYMOON

ON 26 July the Consultative Assembly of the Society, in extraordinary session, drafted and then released on 1 August a report of its proceedings which featured an expression of pleasure at the success of 'the blessed movement' of the army officers in liberating Egypt. The bulk of it consisted of a statement of the views of the Society on the multiple problems of reform—moral, political economic, and social—facing the Egyptian people at the beginning of their new era.[1]

'Abd al-Rahman al-Banna, Hasan's father, set the tone of the initial personal reaction of the members. Appearing at the headquarters of the Society for the first time since the death of his son, he went into the mosque and broke the ranks of those praying on his way to the *minbar*. Turning to face them, he said:

> O ye Brothers, this day your message has come forth. . . . This is a new dawn for you . . . and a new day for the nation. Anticipate the dawn, O ye Brothers . . . embrace Neguib and help him with your hearts, your blood, and your wealth. Be his troops . . . for this is the message of "Hasan" for which God has willed success. . . .[2]

Apart from the issue of joint action in the revolution, Banna was expressing a widespread view of the Society as the 'inspiration' for the army movement, the 'consciousness' which created the very idea of rebellion against the oppressions of Egypt; the revolution was the 'echo' and the 'offspring' of the Society of the Muslim Brothers.[3] The view was given prominence in the books written after the revolution by members of the Society in which the writers saluted 'the blessed movement' and its authors as the

[1] *al-Bayan, passim*; the details of the report will be dealt with in appropriate places. For a press report on the meeting and results, see *MMR* (8 Aug. 1952), 33.

[2] *MAS* (6 Aug. 1952), 6.

[3] See e.g. *MMR* (24 Oct. 1952), 15; *MDA* (16 Feb. 1954), 7; (30 Mar. 1954), 6; and *Hatta ya'lam al-nas*, pp. 5–6.

fulfilment of their long-awaited goals and the fruit of their long and painful endeavour.[4]

The cordiality had a firm foundation. In the first flush of revolution, the Revolutionary Command Council (hereafter RCC) abolished the secret-police section of the ministry of the interior and thoroughly discredited it. Among the victims of that purge was the most hated of its agents, Muhammad al-Jazzar, notorious for his 'specialization' in the affairs of the Muslim Brothers and his involvement in the death of Banna. It was announced, too, as one of the first acts of the new regime, that the unsolved case of the murder of Banna would be seriously investigated. The arrests which followed the uprising were noted by one observer as including known 'enemies of the Brothers'.[5] The appointment of Rashad Muhanna as one of the three regents for the infant monarch and the release in October of political prisoners, most of whom were of the Society, intensified the heady atmosphere of goodwill.[6]

On the other side, the RCC won the support of the Muslim Brothers in the university for the abolition of the student unions; this move cost the new government much support there and revived the traditional antipathy towards the Brothers of the Wafdist and communist students who almost from the start adopted a hostile attitude towards the régime. On 15 November 1952 the tension broke into a bloody riot with knives and broken 'coke' bottles after a member of the Society called for 'open war' against 'red communism'; twelve were reported injured and scores were arrested.[7] Similarly, the government won the Society's agreement to abrogate the popular celebrations on the Prophet's birthday in December, and other religious birthdays. Both the university unions and the religious celebrations were regarded in this first year—or so the Society understood it—as 'expressions of disunity'.

These measures could be, and were later on, explained by the government as part of a larger picture of setting aright the tyrannous behaviour of the *Ancien Régime* as it affected all Egyptians. It seemed to most observers, however, and above all to the Society itself, that there was a special fund of goodwill consciously reserved for the Muslim Brothers. On the surface, this continued to be true for at least another year. But from the very beginning, basic conflict marked the inner, private relationship of the Society

[4] See e.g. Sharif, *IMFHF*, pp. 5–6; Khuli, *QDIHB*, pp. 87–8; Ghazali, *IMABSR*, pp. 5–6; and esp. Hajjaji, *RLAT*, *passim*, and p. 23.

[5] Haydon, 'Surprise Dictatorship', 212; see also *MMR* (8 Aug. 1952), 30–1.

[6] See Neguib, *Egypt's Destiny*, pp. 136–8, 146–50; *MMR* (8 Aug. 1952), 30–1; (17 Oct. 1952), 20–1.

[7] See the report in *NYT* (16 Nov. 1952), 63; see also *MAS* (19 Nov. 1952), 22, for pictures and speeches at the university.

to the 'blessed movement'. In the secret dialogue that ensued, the primary antagonists were Hasan al-Hudaybi and Gamal 'Abd al-Nasir.

Right from the start of the revolution, beginning with the official declaration of support made on 26 July, the Brothers made reiterated pronouncements, publicly and also privately to the government, about the need for establishing government on the basis of Islam. This was, of course, natural and to be expected. Still more annoying to the RCC were Hudaybi's views about the first major project of the new regime—land reform. For what were called 'technical and economic' reasons, he joined with prime minister 'Ali Mahir in placing the limit to landownership at 500 feddans rather than the 200 recommended by the officers. The Mahir ministry fell on 7 September ostensibly because the prime minister felt that the army should shoulder full authority, partly, however, because of his unwillingness to decree land reform as envisaged by the RCC. The new cabinet formed by Neguib did so;[8] but of more relevance to the present study was the crisis with the Muslim Brothers which followed the creation of Neguib's ministry.

Probably against Neguib's desire,[9] but under persuasion from Nasir, the RCC decided to invite members of the Muslim Brothers into the cabinet. What happened escapes precise detection, but it appears to be true that Hudaybi was notified of the RCC's decision to ask three Brothers to join Neguib's cabinet, one of whom would be Shaykh Hasan al-Baquri. Hudaybi agreed, and without consultation with the Guidance Council recommended the names of Hasan al-'Ashmawi and Munir al-Dilla, both of whom were rejected by the RCC. Hudaybi then informed the Guidance Council of the government offer but not that names had already been put forward and rejected; the Council decided unanimously not to enter the government. Baquri, who had already been appointed, since Hudaybi had raised no objections to him in the first place, conveniently absented himself from the meeting, but was dismissed from the Society the day his appointment was made public. The appointment of Baquri and his dismissal from the Society were the only aspects of the matter which were public knowledge at the time.[10] Immediately it appeared as though the

[8] *Hatta ya'lam al-nas*, p. 8; Neguib, *Egypt's Destiny*, pp. 163–7. Cf. J. Landau, *Parliaments and Parties in Egypt* (1953), p. 192, for the unrealistic suggestion that Hudaybi's stand was due to his interest in the 'maintenance of the *Ancien Régime* and the retrograde character of the Egyptian village'.

[9] See *JJ* (23 Nov. 1954), 10.

[10] See Kira, *Mahkama*, i. 43; cf. *Hatta ya'lam al-nas*, pp. 9–10. A possible

Muslim Brothers were withdrawing their support from the regime, a serious matter in those early days.

At a later date the deputy of the Society, explaining the Council's decision not to enter the government, made two points: (1) the fear that the Society would lose its 'popular' quality, i.e. sully itself with power; (2) the fear, hinted at by Neguib in his resistance to the idea of Brothers in the cabinet, of bringing down the wrath of foreigners and minorities on the regime and thus complicating its problems.[11] Other more mundane considerations seemed to be operative: (1) behind each ministry stood an army officer who had the real power;[12] (2) with only three ministries, the Brothers would invariably be outvoted, and would be compelled to lend their names to decisions that, in conscience, on certain matters they could not support. Hudaybi may have changed his mind between the original offer and the meeting of the Council; he may have shared some of the objections to accepting the offer of authority; but his apparent willingness to forgo these objections, if men loyal to him were appointed, suggests other motives, namely his deep mistrust of Nasir and his works. The cabinet *débâcle* reflected a growing personal antipathy between the two which later knew no bounds. At the time it effectively split the Society's attitudes towards the government; one group in support, another, led by Hudaybi, passively hostile. In some branches, following the event, orders were received that the attitude of the Society towards the government would henceforth be 'negative'.[13]

Hudaybi's handling of the issue appeared to the RCC not only as duplicity but as evidence of his hostility. But while Nasir was angry, it was primarily with Hudaybi himself; and the revolution was not yet strong enough to dispense with him and possibly jeopardize the much-needed support of the Society. With the

variant of this episode goes as follows: Hudaybi was presented with a list of three names for his signature—Baquri, Salih 'Ashmawi, and 'Abd al-Qadir 'Awda. Since the two last had already emerged in the Society as his antagonists, the offer would then appear to him as an effort to undermine his authority in the Society. He would then have proposed Dilla and Hasan al-'Ashmawi, both friends of Nasir's but loyal to him. Since the government at a later point was clearly determined to undermine Hudaybi's position, this interpretation seems worth bearing in mind. Whichever view is accepted, the government rejected 'Ashmawi because he was 'too young' and Dilla because he received no recommendations from his superiors in the Council of State; on this point, see *JJ* (19 Nov. 1954), 4; and *JA* (28 Sept. 1954), 7, 11.

---

[11] *JJ* (19 Nov. 1954), 4–5.

[12] See *Hatta ya'lam al-nas*, pp. 10–11.

[13] See *JJ* (19 Nov. 1954), 4. One of the branches which received the order was that in Tanta. It was dominated by the family of a member of the RCC, Husayn al-Shafi'i; it was also one of the branches most deeply divided over the issue of Hudaybi's leadership.

virtually complete alienation of all the other organized political forces in the country, it was still imperative, for the tasks that lay ahead, that the Society should be kept loyal to the army government, or at least not be forced into opposition. The further events in Egypt pushed the officers into exercising a more repressive control over the nation, the more they needed the support of the Society; at the same time, however, it became impossible for them to avoid injecting more irritants into their relationship with it.

On 14 October, a month after the cabinet crisis, Rashad Muhanna was dismissed from the regency. The action, the result of a disagreement about the power focus in the government between the RCC and the regency, appeared to resurrect an earlier, pre-revolution lack of harmony between the groups represented by Nasir and Muhanna. The RCC was also resisting Muhanna's strongly held views on the necessity of promulgating an Islamic constitution. His dismissal was followed by arrest, release, and arrest again in January 1953, after once more waging a campaign for an Islamic state following the abolition of the Constitution of 1923 on 10 December 1952. With other 'counter-revolutionaries', he was tried on 30 March 1953 and sentenced to life imprisonment.[14] Whatever his precise commitment to the Society, Muhanna was a highly placed advocate of one of its basic propositions. His removal, and the purging from the RCC by Nasir of others of the original revolutionaries connected with the Society, raised further doubts about Nasir.[15] And these doubts were only partly mitigated when representatives of the Society were appointed to serve on the Constitutional Committee of fifty members set up on 12 January 1953.[16]

The new year brought new sources of friction. On 16 January the government ordered the abolition of all existing parties and groups except the Society of the Muslim Brothers. In a related move, on 23 January—at the six-month celebration of the revolt—it announced the creation of the Liberation Rally (*hay'at al-tahrir*). A government-supported 'people's movement' to implement the slogan of 'unity' in the nation, the Rally was also to become the nucleus of a political organization to replace the abolished

[14] See Neguib, *Egypt's Destiny*, pp. 175–8; Sadat, *Safahat*, pp. 228, 239; *COC*, xxvi (1952), 168–9.

[15] See *Hatta ya'lam al-nas*, p. 4. Chief among the comrades in mind were 'Abd al-Mun'im 'Abd al-Ra'uf (see above, pp. 101–2), and Ma'aruf al-Hadari, who distinguished himself in the Faluja episode of the Palestine War and was a member of both the Society and the Free Officers.

[16] The members selected were Salih 'Ashmawi, 'Abd al-Qadir 'Awda, and Muhammad Kamal Khalifa. See *MMR* (16 Jan. 1953), 38 and *MDA* (24 Feb. 1953), 1, 3, for a description of the opening session on 21 February and summaries of the opening speeches.

parties.[17] As it turned out—perhaps not merely by accident—it also became the nucleus, along with other more obviously military organizations later created, of the regime's 'civil security forces'. This was much what the Society had feared at the time, for obviously the creation of the Liberation Rally challenged its role as 'civil protector' of the regime. It also proposed to challenge the Society's position as popular voice on the ideological level, for the government intended to make the Rally its instrument to win over the hesitant and doubtful nation to the cause of the revolution.[18]

While publicly denying hostility to the idea of the Rally, the leaders of the Society were nevertheless arguing privately with the regime against the one-party notion that it implied, and also, more to the point, questioning the 'need' for the Rally.[19] Nasir and the RCC contended that the two organizations need not conflict, that there was room for another one, and that there was no reason why the Muslim Brothers should not 'fuse' with the Liberation Rally. The latter point was put forward by Neguib as one of the reasons for exempting the Muslim Brothers from the decree dissolving all political parties.[20] That story, however, had other aspects.

In accordance with the law of 10 September 1952 ordering the registration of all parties, the Society had already submitted appropriate documents to the ministry of the interior and declared itself to be, among other things, a political party. The decision to do so brought about Hudaybi's temporary resignation, a matter presently to be discussed. The Society's exemption, despite this action, from the decree dissolving parties can only be explained by its having been party to the decision to issue it. Members believed this to be the case. Whatever might be the conflict between them, on the issue of the abolition of parties the two groups could readily agree. For the Brothers, this was the first and most fundamental step towards political reform. For Nasir, the hard realities of ruling Egypt had imposed this reshaping of political institutions; in such a move only the Muslim Brothers could be relied on for support in the now irrevocably alienated political community. Nasir seems to have been personally responsible for advising the Society and the ministry of the interior to make the technical

[17] See Neguib, *Egypt's Destiny*, p. 181, for a statement on the goals and intentions of the Liberation Rally.

[18] See *Hatta ya'lam al-nas*, pp. 21–2.

[19] *MMR* (5 Feb. 1953), 16; Kira, *Mahkama*, i. 44; *Hatta ya'lam al-nas*, pp. 13–14.

[20] Neguib, *Egypt's Destiny*, pp. 183–4; see also *JJ* (15 Jan. 1954), 5; cf. *Hatta ya'lam al-nas*, p. 15. Neguib blames the failure of the Liberation Rally on the 'subversive influence' of the Muslim Brothers. Of the explanations possible—including popular indifference and even hostility by this time—the resistance of the Brothers was probably the least important.

changes in the earlier registration that would put the organization in the clear legally.[21] The feelings of the regime towards the Society remained positive but their basis shifted from friendship to need.

Policy makers in the Society apparently saw it this way, for on the day after the decree was published a small delegation visited Nasir to congratulate the government on its move and to discuss the future situation in the country; the terms of the discussion suggested to the government a demand by the Muslim Brothers for a commanding voice in affairs of state.[22] It was immediately clear that the exemption of the Brothers from the decree had both objectively and subjectively created a new power situation in Egypt. The fact that the government was unprepared to accept the implications of its move became another crucial factor in the privately disintegrating relations between the two groups.

Publicly, for almost the whole of 1953, the façade of cordiality was successfully maintained. The escape of the Muslim Brothers from the drive against the parties appeared to have ensconced them in a position of primacy in the country. Leading members of the government—including both Neguib and Nasir—took part in the annual pilgrimage to the tomb of Hasan al-Banna—the martyr of the nation as he was called—on 13 February 1953, the fourth anniversary of his death.[23] In August a member of the Society, al-Bahi al-Khuli (who was pro-government) was appointed both liaison officer between the Society and the Liberation Rally and the Rally's new director of 'religious guidance'[24]. In September Hudaybi publicly denied any misunderstanding with the régime. In that same month the government established the Revolutionary Tribunal to try former political leaders. Its first case, that of Ibrahim 'Abd al-Hadi, was particularly concerned with his role in the death of Banna and the persecution of the Brothers in their last conflict with authority.[25] As late as October the municipality of Alexandria was reported to be considering renaming one of the

[21] See *MMR* (23 Jan. 1953), 38; *MJJ* (13 Dec. 1954), 13; and Kira, *Mahkama*, i. 43–4. The government presented its part in the event as an attempt to 'save' the Society, for which generosity the Brothers showed only ingratitude.

[22] See esp. *JJ* (5 Jan. 1954), 5; cf. *Hatta ya'lam al-nas*, pp. 12–13. The confrontation was probably neither as total as the government contended nor as harmless as the Society insisted; see the important testimony of one of the delegates in *JJ* (23 Nov. 1954), 10.

[23] See *MMR* (20 Feb. 1953), 38, for pictures of Neguib weeping.

[24] *MRY* (10 Aug. 1953), 4.

[25] This fact did not help the government in non-Brother relations. Hudaybi actually took private issue with the government's policy of creating special courts; his refusal to rejoice, along with the majority of the Brothers, over the fate of 'Abd al-Hadi, the most hated of the Society's enemies, caused much disquiet in the Society. (See further on this point below, pp. 116-18.) On the court proceedings during 'Abd al-Hadi's trial, see Amin Hasan Kamil, ed., *Mahkamat al-thawra* (Cairo, 1953), i. 1–19, 61–188, and *passim*.

main thoroughfares of the city 'Shari' Hasan al-Banna'.[26] Also in October the government created the National Guard, timed and designed to call attention to the seriousness of purpose with which it viewed the halting negotiations with the British government over the Suez issue; to the camps established by the government came large numbers of the Brothers.[27]

There were, however, public suggestions of disorder behind the façade. Beginning about April, in a move patently designed to dissociate the name of the government from the Muslim Brothers, an official campaign 'to unify the nation' was inaugurated with the conspicuous display of a new slogan: 'Religion is for God and the nation is for all.' In July, on the first anniversary of the day of the revolution, the Brothers were conspicuously absent from the centre of the celebrations, and, where present, were notably indifferent, or suggestively punctuated speeches by the leaders of the revolution with their own unmistakable slogan. Also, from about the late spring onwards, the Society had begun publication of a small newsletter which appeared irregularly over the year; it carried official organization business and the official views on matters of interest not otherwise available because of the rigid press censorship. In one which appeared in July or August, Hudaybi praised the government for its good intentions, but also expressed his hope that it would see the wisdom of seeking the support and protection of the people from 'the heart' and not base its power on 'force and laws'. As a contribution to this goal, he sought the lifting of martial law and the repeal of press censorship.[28] In the same issue, in reply to written questions from members about his attitude to the negotiations with the British, Hudaybi said:

> The British do not see that negotiations will lead to the settlement of the Egyptian question. If some people want to negotiate, they cannot be stopped. If they arrive at a solution which satisfies us, that is good; if not, then it is our duty to resist that solution.[29]

It was in fact this issue, the negotiations, that further poisoned the relations between the RCC and the Muslim Brothers. Hudaybi's statement was not only a view of things to come; he was also not, at the time, being candid with members; since the spring he had been in contact with both the government and the British Embassy on this very problem.

There seems to be no doubt that, either in February or April

[26] *MJJ* (26 Oct. 1953), 6.

[27] See *Hatta ya'lam al-nas*, p. 15. It was clear that some of the members in joining were combining patriotic motives with service to the Society. Infiltration for purposes of spying was a problem for both the government and the Society.

[28] *Ila al-Ikhwan*, no. 8 [1953], 7.

[29] Ibid. no. 8, 4.

1953, Trefor Evans, Oriental Counsellor of the British Embassy, sought and received an interview with Hudaybi for the ostensible purpose of sounding him on the forthcoming negotiations for the evacuation of the British forces. What transpired at that meeting remains unestablished but both the government and the Society have made some comments on the matter, which became public only after 1954 when the government used the meeting as a central fact in its case for the dissolution of the Society. The government in its first accounts of the matter reported the meeting as 'secret negotiations' between the Society and the British 'behind the back of the revolution'. Hudaybi was charged with having accepted certain conditions to evacuation which had tied the hands of the Egyptian negotiators and made the British more obstinate in their stand. The most important of these was his alleged agreement to a resolution of the problem of the availability of the base by the creation of a joint Anglo-Egyptian committee to facilitate reactivation after a United Nations decision as to a 'danger of war' situation. Later, after the government had signed its treaty with the British, in answer to the criticism directed by the Society at the treaty, it enlarged the argument against Hudaybi, charging him with having demanded less in 'his negotiations', and with having 'accepted what the nation would have rejected', namely: conditions to evacuation, the principle of joint defence with the West, and military experts to maintain the base.[30]

The Society made known its position much later on, in answer to continued press attacks on 'Hudaybi's secret treaty'. It totally denied all these charges and put forward its own version: that the prime minister was informed prior to the meeting with Evans; that Hudaybi reaffirmed the traditional stand of no negotiations before evacuation, and accepted, in principle, the possibility of a 'secret agreement with the British to aid us in the event of a Russian attack on us, their entry to be on our request, their departure on the end of the mission'; that the meeting was followed by a report to leading members of the junta (including Nasir) and that there were then expressions of pleasure at Hudaybi's stand; and that the proceedings of the meeting were also reported to Sulayman Hafiz, the minister of the interior, and to Mahmud Fawzi, minister of foreign affairs. It was felt, too, that one of the British intentions in seeking the meeting was to probe the attitude of the Society to the military junta and that to this manœuvre the Brothers had dealt a resounding rebuff.[31]

[30] *JJ* (15 Jan. 1954), 5, 11; (28 Aug. 1954), 1, 9; and (16 Sept. 1954), 1, 5.

[31] Hudaybi's own account can be seen in a letter appended (K) to the original version of this study. See also *Hatta ya'lam al-nas*, pp. 15–18. Hudaybi's

The third party, the British Embassy, when the government revealed 'the plot' between them and the Society, and elaborated it to include a meeting in January 1954 with M. J. Cresswell, the minister plenipotentiary, denied all the charges and implications except that Trefor Evans had met members of the Muslim Brothers, as 'a normal part of . . . his duties'.[32]

What conditions Hudaybi accepted we do not know; there is every reason to believe that Nasir was informed both before and after the meeting with Evans, and it is technically important to set the event in context. But it is also important to observe that the later charges against the Society, while helpful in the effort to discredit Hudaybi, were not merely distortions after the fact. They reflected an immediate anger that Hudaybi, in talking with the British, was transgressing his proper bounds; not only did the Society's entrance—even though at the request of the British——into the negotiations add difficulties for the Egyptian negotiators, but it also provided leverage for the British side. This latter was especially important, if the British, as seemed to be the case, sensed the potential conflict between the government and the Society. The British, in seeking out the views of the Muslim Brothers, were in effect recognizing the voice of the Society in the affairs of the nation; Hudaybi, in agreeing to the talks, was perpetuating that notion and thus weakening the hand of the government. What appeared to the government to be the beginning of a serious challenge was reinforced by the next event.

In May, following a temporary break in the talks between the two governments, Salah Salim, then minister of national guidance and Sudanese affairs, as well as unofficial spokesman for the RCC on foreign affairs, went to see Hudaybi to ask about the attitude of the Muslim Brothers towards the possibility of hostilities with the British before the Egyptian armed forces could be prepared; he had in mind 'unifying' the groups in Egypt readily available to do battle with the British. Hudaybi's unstated negative was enshrined in the following 'logical' but irrelevant verbiage:

> We Muslim Brothers do not recognize geographical boundaries in Islam. Our concern is with the welfare of Islam, and we will engage, in its defence, in battle which includes the Muslim world in its entirety. For example, it may not be to the interest of Islam that a battle should

position that the government was advised is without doubt true; the point was given substantial support, indirectly, in an official article on the evacuation agreement in *MTR* (9 Oct. 1954), 6–7.

---

[32] *NYT* (15 Jan. 1954), 5.

begin in the Canal, but rather . . . in Tunis first. . . . We have our plans, our goals, and our independent commands which address themselves to this spacious field. It is not necessary that their vision should be bound by local problems in Egypt.

This much was reported by the government.[33] Hudaybi seems to have added to this 'reservation' a more genuine concern: that the government ought really to decide whether it seriously intended to fight the British, or rather whether it was planning to use the Brothers as a threat to the British in order to resume the ruptured negotiations. For Hudaybi, it was 'a matter of conscience', as it was put, that he should have to order into the Canal Zone Brothers, some of whom would surely lose their lives, as sacrifices to a policy of negotiation which at that time, and in the light of history, seemed doomed to failure.

Related to the suspicion about the government's intentions *vis-à-vis* the British was a suspicion about its intentions *vis-à-vis* the Society. Antipathy between the two groups was by this time at a point neither could ignore, despite continuing surface cordiality and the efforts of 'neutrals' on both sides to patch up the disputes. When Salah Salim asked for Hudaybi's commitment of the Brothers to battle in the Canal zone, he was also asking—because it was a government sponsored and organized operation—for information about the forces, real and imagined, at the disposition of the Society. Under the circumstances this could be seen as a government manœuvre to invite the Muslim Brothers into a 'patriotic struggle' which would at the same time bring within the government's control the only civil power left in the country which might conceivably threaten its existence. That this was a part of the government's thinking is evidenced by the request, made apparently for the first time officially in May and continuously thereafter, for the immediate abolition of the units of the Brothers' secret apparatus which, the government contended, existed in the armed services and in the police force.

These events behind the scenes quickened the pace of conflict. The creation of a National Guard in the following October could be explained as part of the conflict with Britain, but also as the first step towards creating a counter-weight to the Muslim Brothers. At the same time, the RCC began actively to throw support to a group of dissidents in the Society who were seeking to unseat Hudaybi. The dissolution of the Society in January 1954 followed the government's failure in November 1953 to turn to its advantage the public explosion of this schism.

[33] *JJ* (15 Sept. 1954), 1, 9, along with a scathing denunciation of Hudaybi.

INTERNAL SCHISM (NOVEMBER–DECEMBER 1953)

For a handful of old and strategically placed members, Hudaybi's appointment as the successor to Banna was, as has already been noted, viewed as a temporary compromise. Out of this mood was created the framework for the disintegration of the Society. The range of problems which arose reflected, at their root, the anger of the old members in the hierarchy that 'the intruder' Hudaybi seemed to challenge their precedence in the order of things and, thus by implication, their long, often painful, and always passionate commitment to the Society. This resentment evolved into harsh, personal antagonisms in which the real problems often went out of focus and from which the organization split into cliques. From the point of view of organization, the basic problem was an all-important loss of confidence in the leadership, a factor so integral to the dynamic of the Society as to have crippling consequences. In the dialectic of the Brothers, the Society suffered its crisis following the destruction of its basic 'spirit of love and brotherhood'. The problems raised by the disintegrating relationship between the Society and the government brought the conflict to the fore.

Personally, one of Hudaybi's greatest problems was in living up to the image of Banna, an attempt which he consciously refused to make, but one which the old members never let him forget. Hudaybi, for instance, not only summered in Alexandria but, even worse, he went swimming and rested on the beach. Again, his not-too-common visits to the branches were arranged, it seemed, so that the branches of Upper Egypt received him in the winter, unlike Banna, who chose to visit that area, the hottest in Egypt, in the dead of summer. To this un-Banna-like behaviour were added what were described as deliberate affronts to the memory of the first leader: Hudaybi's continued refusal to give up friends in the hated Saʿdist party; his unwillingness to accept another title, that of *ra'is ʿamm*, rather than *murshid ʿamm* which some felt belonged to Hasan al-Banna alone; and his alleged unwillingness to permit the display of pictures of Banna in the branches of the Society. To these specific matters was added the more general charge that Hudaybi's general behaviour as regards the palace and some of the ministries indicated that under his direction the Society had become 'a party of aristocrats' and ceased to be 'the popular movement of Hasan al-Banna'.[34]

More serious were the grievances concerned with administration and organization. From the very beginning, Hudaybi's in-

[34] *JJ* (16 Jan. 1954), 1, 3; (26 Jan. 1954), 3; *MDA* (5 Jan. 1954), 13, 16.

sistence on secrecy in the talks surrounding his appointment, and his refusal to take over immediately once the appointment was made, or to resign his job, or to permit the publication of his name were irksome—and to some members insulting. His condition for taking on the job, that ʿAwda should be his deputy, was interpreted as a device to 'rid' the top level of the two chief contenders for the leadership, Salih ʿAshmawi and Ahmad Hasan al-Baquri, and as a personal affront to them. Similar feelings were aroused by his refusal to recognize the weekly, *Majallat al-Daʿwa,* edited and owned by ʿAshmawi, as the official voice of the Society.[35] The fact—like most of the above problematic only after the event—that both he and ʿAwda were appointed unconstitutionally was another point of contention, and so was his demand for the creation of a new post, that of 'vice-guide', after his early falling out with his chosen deputy, ʿAwda.

All these things reflected the bitterness of the old members that 'new faces' had taken over the organization in deliberate and tactless disregard of their own peculiar status; they also reflected to these members what came to be an important focus of the conflict, Hudaybi's 'imperious usurpation' and 'dictatorial abuse' of power in the Society. The allegation was specifically based on what was said to be his arrogant disregard of the 'right' of the Guidance Council to decide the destiny of the Society and his 'unconstitutional' and arbitrary dissolution of branches for reasons of incompatibility with the new leadership. As a result there was, for the first time (whatever the sincerity of it), open questioning about the formal distribution of power in the organization and its important corollary, the hitherto seriously unchallenged tradition of 'absolute obedience' (*samʿwa-taʿa*). The backdrop to all the grievances was the general sense of a movement in stagnation; not only had the membership decreased, but the Society itself had become, under Hudaybi, 'a movement of words, not of action'. This seemed to refer to two things: the new leader's apparent resistance to political activism; and the spate of books by members and friends, dealing with the problems of the Society, Egypt, and Islam, which began to flood the bookstands after 1950. In sum, Hudaybi had offended the sensibilities of the members, violated the Society's constitution and precedents, and also relegated its aims to obscurity and deprived the mission of its spirit and purpose.

That Hudaybi continued to command the loyalties of the vast majority of members indicated that these problems disturbed only small groups in the Society. However, the really important policy

[35] On this point, see esp. *MJJ* 19 Oct. 1953), 3.

differences did raise general, albeit for a long time undirected, questioning and doubt. These included such major issues, dating from before the revolution, as the relationship of the Society to governments and the national movement, and the equally pressing internal question of the continued existence of the secret apparatus.

It will be recalled that Hudaybi's attitude to the Suez question in 1951 and early 1952 had caused much questioning both inside and outside the Society as to the nature of its role *vis-à-vis* the national movement. Hudaybi's visits to the palace, his official recognition in the face of universal hostility to it of the appointment of Hafiz 'Afifi Pasha to be chief of the royal cabinet, and his friendly consultations with the post-Wafdist governments of Mahir and Hilali not only raised doubts about his feelings for the national movement but, more importantly, created the suspicion that he was identifying the Brothers with professions of loyalty to the *status quo*. We have already seen that the setting was more complex, and that Hudaybi's behaviour mirrored, in part, official timidity, his pronouncedly legalistic approach to his role of leader, and his hesitancy with regard to political activism, especially when this bounded on violence.[36] The revolution of 1952 posed the political problem more directly than ever before, in so far as the Muslim Brothers for the first time were, in effect, the protégés of authority.

Inside the Society the first debate over the question came with the government order of 9 September 1952 for the registration of all parties. Basically the dispute turned on whether the Society of the Muslim Brothers was a 'political party' or a 'religious society'. In the new order in Egypt in which the Muslim Brothers seemed to hold a position of high prestige, the implications of the question were larger than they had been heretofore. On 4 October the Consultative Assembly met to debate the question. Hudaybi's position that the Society was not a political party (not that it had no political role) was not accepted by the consensus, which voted to make the necessary registration as a political party. Hudaybi, who was absent from the meeting on grounds of ill health, had actually resigned in anticipation of the Assembly's decision. He was persuaded to return, once again with the argument that a succession struggle would be detrimental to the welfare of the Society. The struggle, indeed, had already begun: it was anticipated, in his absence, and on the basis of his position in the dispute,

[36] On this general discussion the most useful published sources include *MDA* (5 Jan. 1954), 1, 13, 16; (12 Jan. 1954) 3, 11, 14; *MJJ* (7 Dec. 1953), 8, 9; (13 Dec. 1954), 7; *JJ* (16 Jan. 1954), 1, 3; (30 Jan. 1954), 3; (26 Jan. 1954), 3; Kira, *Mahkama*, ii. 16–17. See also Ch. IV. for details.

that an attempt to unseat him would be made by his chief antagonists,[37] the leaders of the secret apparatus and their partisans in the upper ranks of the hierarchy; and it was around the question of the secret apparatus that the dispute about political activism continued to express itself.

It will be recalled that Hudaybi immediately upon his discovery of the continued existence of the secret apparatus demanded its abolition. Its then leader, 'Abd al-Rahman al-Sanadi, refused to obey the order requesting the names of its members and location of its materials.[38] For Sanadi and his followers, this was an issue as basic as the existence of the Society itself: to dissolve the secret apparatus was not only 'to violate the concept of *jihad* in Islam' but also to divest the organization of its major instrument of 'defence'. Hudaybi held that while bodily training and physical fitness were an integral part of the movement's training programme, the primary emphasis should be on 'intellectual' and 'spiritual' training; such a programme should properly be carried out not through a secret apparatus but through the already existing and important system of 'families', which represented 'the spirit of brotherhood in Islam'.[39] That the attack on the secret apparatus also involved awareness of the problem of dual leadership and conflicting authority was recognized, as we have already seen, by the technical objection of Hudaybi's deputy, 'Awda, that it was an 'administrative mistake'.[40]

Sanadi's unwillingness to concede to Hudaybi brought about the latter's resignation. This was withdrawn when it was decided to refer the problem to a committee of three influential members, which was also, apparently, to persuade Sanadi to accept Hudaybi's policy. However, though between November 1951 and November 1953 two new leaders were appointed to the secret apparatus by the committee, neither of them was able to undermine Sanadi's control over its members; some members were simply not known, and the others remained loyal to their old leader. Sanadi retaliated by throwing his full weight behind Hudaybi's antagonists in the other more general disputes and by undertaking a surreptitious pamphlet campaign intended to discredit him. The latter's reaction was to accept Sanadi's challenge and begin an organized counter-movement to win for himself the loyalty pledged to

[37] In *MMT* (24 Oct. 1952), 15, Hudaybi refused to give the reasons for his resignation, but did indicate that it did not much matter whether he stayed or went. *MDA* (5 Jan. 1954), 14, confirms this observation by Hudaybi, an observation which he shortly thereafter denied having made.

[38] Kira, *Mahkama*, i. 47.

[39] *JJ*, 18 Nov. 1954, 3, and 20 Nov. 1954, 3.

[40] See above, p. 88.

Sanadi.[41] It was against the background of disintegrating relations with the government that the dispute escalated.

Throughout 1953 hints of crisis in the Muslim Brothers appeared so persistently, and speculation was so widespread, that the leadership was compelled to reassure members by a special notice to them about the 'lies' about the Society appearing in the press.[42] But by August members of the Consultative Assembly began holding small unofficial and informal meetings to weigh the problems—internal and external—which had now assumed dangerous proportions. An extraordinary meeting of the Assembly, held on 3 September, turned into a general airing of all grievances, including—what now became known to many for the first time—the crisis of September 1952 over appointments to the cabinet, and Hudaybi's meetings with representatives of the British Embassy. Much of the debate was spent in a heated argument about relations with the government: ʿAwda, whose appointment had earlier been made a condition of Hudaybi's accepting the post of leader, had now become a principal spokesman for those who sought to soothe relations with the government; he was also the main target of Hudaybi's charges that there had been indiscretion in revealing 'the secrets' of the Society to the government.[43] This phase of the controversy ended with another meeting of the Assembly on 8 October, during which Hudaybi pitted his strength against his opponents on the issue of elections to the Guidance Council, and won handsomely. He followed up this victory by beating off attempts to end his control of the organization by limiting the tenure of the General Guide to a three-year period (which would have meant his vacating the post at once); he then sought and received from the whole Assembly the all-important oath of loyalty, the *bayʿa*.[44]

Despite public shows of friendship and cordiality between the warring factions, the October meeting and the elections marked a

[41] See *JJ* (18 Nov. 1954), 3; (25 Nov. 1954), 3; Kira, *Mahkama*, i. 47–8; and *MRY* (7 Dec. 1954), 12–13. Sanadi, apparently, did concede some names and once resigned in favour of a replacement; he apparently did so as part of a plan to gain time.

[42] See e.g. *Ila al-Ikhwan*, no. 8 [1953], 4. *MDA* (14 Apr. 1953), 4, also carried denials on behalf of the Society. Cf. Banna, *MISI*, 7–8, 9–10; this army member of the Banna family was among the first in 1953 publicly to question the motives of the 'small leadership' (Hudaybi) in the failure to support 'the blessed movement' of the army. Articles in *MTH* (21 Oct. 1954), 10, and in *JA* (28 Sept. 1954), 7, 11, confirmed the anger of the family of Hasan al-Banna with the situation into which Hudaybi had led the Society.

[43] *MJJ* (14 Sept. 1953), 12–13; *JJ* (16 Jan. 1954), 3; (17 Nov. 1954), 10; *MDA* (5 Oct. 1954), 7. *MDA* (8 Sept. 1953), 1, reports the meeting but only the general resolutions taken on general and public matters.

[44] *MJJ* (7 Dec. 1953), 8–9.

turning-point on many levels.[45] In the long view, real pressure for organizational reform began here. Reform had two aspects: (1) immediately, the problem—based on the view that both the Assembly and the Council were rubber stamps of the 'unrepresentative' will of the leader—of creating the instruments by which the Society's policy towards the government could be reversed; (2) the longer-range problem of the 'democratization' of the Society's administrative apparatus. While the impetus for reform seemed to derive mainly from the friction between Hudaybi and his enemies, that friction had deeper roots: the problems raised by the succession of Hudaybi to leadership in an organization which was authoritarian because its first leader was so, and which had depended for its functioning not on law but on the personal magnetism of its leader. Although, even in Banna's time, questions were raised about it, now men who for various reasons had completely accepted the concept of 'absolute obedience' began examining its implications. As the informal basis and intangible sources of strength of the organization began to disappear, attention was directed to the letter of its constitution, and what was now regarded to be its 'unquestioned intent'. In the minds of some, Banna became the original democrat. This reaction was neither faulty memory nor total perversion of fact, but rather resulted from the differing images of the two leaders: as expressed by one member, 'We gave to Banna our loyalty; Hudaybi could not command it.'

On another level, the events of the October meeting galvanized the opposition into closer, more unified action. Hudaybi and his partisans were accused of crude, irregular, and extraordinary 'intervention' and 'electioneering'; the elections, thus viewed, were regarded as improper and unrepresentative. This was the mood of the opposition when about this time it became clear that Hudaybi was on the verge of breaking the mysterious riddle surrounding the membership and organization of the secret apparatus. His October victory in the Assembly was about to be crowned with a similar success in the struggle to win over the secret apparatus. On 20 November, however, the Brothers were startled to read in the press of the death, by means of a bomb sent via a box of pastry, of Sayyid Fayiz, a prominent figure in the events of 1948 and 1949, and now second in command of the secret apparatus. On the 22nd the Guidance Council held an all-night session and the next morning announced the expulsion of four members of

[45] See *MDA* (13 Oct. 1953), 4, for a unique picture of the two antagonists, Hudaybi and 'Ashmawi, chatting pleasantly in the offices of *Majallat al-Da'wa*. The issue of 5 January 1954 of this magazine is crucial for this entire discussion.

the Society: Ahmad Zaki Hasan, Mahmud al-Sabbagh, 'Abd al-Rahman al-Sanadi, and Ahmad 'Adil Kamal. All were members of the secret apparatus. At the meeting of the Council, the 5–5 tie vote on the issue of expulsion had been decided by Hudaybi's casting vote. The secretary-general dispatched a memorandum to all branches asking that there be no requests for explanations. The press, in handling the issue of the death of Fayiz, had made no reference to his affiliations, but for those of the general public who did not remember, *al-Ahram* placed the news about Fayiz next to that about the expulsion of the four Muslim Brothers, and to the daily report of the Banna assassination trial.[46]

Correspondents seeking some light on the expulsions pressed a spokesman of the Society for an explanation; he avoided most of the questions, specifically refusing to comment on the possibility that the events had anything to do with any 'crime'. A few days later, *al-Ahram* received from 'an informed source in the Muslim Brothers' information that the expulsions were punishments for 'numerous reports' of the misbehaviour of the four towards 'the message and the Society'.[47] This was to remain the official explanation. Of the many stories which appeared from that time on, the one most widely believed, with many variants, was that Fayiz was killed by one or all four of the other members of the secret apparatus, or on their orders, on the day on which he was scheduled to turn over to Hudaybi a report detailing the long-concealed data on the apparatus.[48] On the expulsions, Hudaybi later said to a massed audience of followers, 'we are silent out of mercy towards them'.[49]

If the government investigated the murder, it did so secretly; there were no arrests and no charges. It seems reasonable to assume that it must have had an interest in the events; on the night following the expulsions, Nasir and some of his colleagues on the RCC had dinner with Hudaybi and other members of the Guidance Council.[50] *Majallat al-Da'wa*, now identified openly as the voice of the anti-Hudaybi forces, made no mention of the Fayiz murder; but its editor, 'Ashmawi, was not quiescent. The opposition, now assured that Hudaybi was determined to have his own way, decided on a plan of action to remove him from control of the Society.

On Friday, 27 November, following the noon prayer in the

46 *JA* (23 Nov. 1953), 7.
47 Ibid. (25 Nov. 1953), 6, 11; (29 Nov. 1953), 6.
48 See esp. *MAS* (10 Nov. 1954), 9; for an official hint, see Society of the Muslim Brothers, *al-Qawl al-fasl* [cited subsequently by title] (1954), p. 4.
49 *JA* (29 Nov. 1953), 11.
50 *MJJ* (7 Dec. 1953), 8–9.

Cairo mosque of the Brothers, the anti-Hudaybi faction met in secret session. At 5 p.m. a group of twenty-one dispatched themselves to the home of the General Guide and demanded but did not receive his resignation. From there they went to the headquarters of the Society, where another group had already gathered; about seventy in all, they occupied the buildings and closed and chained the gates. They let it be known that they planned to stay until Hudaybi and the Council changed the order ousting the four members to a mere suspension pending: (1) the establishment of a committee to investigate; (2) the suspension of the Council until its future could be determined by the Assembly; and (3) the creation of a committee (themselves) to run the organization until the Assembly could meet. The communiqué was telephoned to all the branches and to the press.

Some of the 'neutral' members of the Council attempted to break the barricades but without success, whereupon a meeting of the leaders was called at Hudaybi's home. At 1 a.m. the Council issued a communiqué to the press repudiating the action, denying rumours that Hudaybi had resigned, and calling a general meeting of members for the next day. Both sides appealed to Nasir during the night for his aid in healing the breach—and in keeping the matter out of the press. Nasir rejected the possibility that he could interfere with the press (!), but he did arrange a truce which satisfied both parties. At dawn the rebels unlocked the gates of the headquarters and came out. The agreement had included a promise that both sides would join in restoring quiet at the headquarters that day, and that an investigating committee would be established. Whether the investigation would apply to the four expelled members or to those who protested against their expulsion became a serious point of contention. The former interpretation was held by 'Ashmawi and the government, the latter by Hudaybi and his friends.[51]

At 3 p.m. on the next day, 28 November, the general meeting was convened at the headquarters. From near and far, all who could came and joined the throng; the dissidents with their leaders were also there. At 4 p.m. Hudaybi arrived and received a thunderous ovation from the rank and file, which was taken as a renewed *bay'a* for him and a mass popular repudiation of 'Ashmawi. Next, the top leaders delivered a series of emotional and angry speeches of support for the General Guide. The Council sat through the night with the leaders of the coup with no information

[51] *JA* (28 Nov. 1953), 6, for the events of the day; *al-Qawl al-fasl*, pp. 20–39 for the headquarters version; and for the events as seen by 'Ashmawi, *MDA*, 1, 8, and 15 Dec. 1953.

revealed except that another meeting was called for the next day, that the twenty-one men who invaded the home of the leader were suspended, and that the question of the original four expulsions was still being discussed. On 29 November the Council announced its decision to suspend four of the dissidents pending investigations by appropriate membership and discipline committees: three of the four, including ʿAshmawi, were leaders of the coup; the fourth, Sayyid Sabiq, had been declared, or had declared himself, the new leader of the Society. Over the next few days, however, the disciplinary proceedings continued, and on 9 December it was decided to expel three of the accused, ʿAshmawi, Muhammad Ghazali, and ʿAbd al-ʿAziz Jalal from the Society. Next day the Consultative Assembly was convened and the entire case again reviewed with the guilty members. The Assembly confirmed the Council's decision, but at the same time as it reaffirmed its confidence in Hudaybi, it established a committee of five to study the revision of the constitution of the Society.[52]

ʿAshmawi made public his regret over his expulsion and asserted that the expulsions took place without accusation, without investigation, and without trial, and that Hudaybi was a dictator. All the expelled members pledged themselves to continue their work 'on behalf of the message' in their private capacities.[53] Hudaybi followed up the events by expressing his thanks to the rank and file for support, and his forgiveness for those who regretted and repented; he also pleaded that the Society should now close its ranks and forget the incident. There was a shake-up in some of the important sections of the organization,[54] but also some attempt to patch up some of the disputes which had sapped its strength in the past two years. The leadership finally decided to publish some of the records of the events of the past month in a little pamphlet, partly in answer to the charges that Hudaybi's behaviour was arbitrary. The conclusion, nowhere else alluded to, was that the former head of the secret apparatus, Sanadi, was the most prominent figure behind the scenes in the attempted coup.[55]

The main problem after the crisis was what should be done with the secret apparatus, now that its leaders and their partisans were out of the Society. It will be recalled that Hudaybi's hope of dissolving it met with resistance not only from its leaders but also from its members. One of his major problems had been the

[52] *JA* and the new government-sponsored daily *JJ* contain most of this information.

[53] See e.g. Ghazali, *FED*, p. 218; and issues of *MDA* from this time.

[54] See *Ila al-Ikhwan*, no. 9 [1953], 8.

[55] *al-Qawl al-fasl*, pp. 37–9.

simple impossibility of knowing who the members were. Another was the extent to which the idea of the secret apparatus had been imbedded in its partisans' minds.[56] Gradually, during his conflict with Sanadi, a compromise idea developed among his advisers and was put into effect after Sanadi's expulsion. A few days later the secret apparatus was dissolved and reconstituted 'on a new basis'. A new leader, Yusuf Tal'at, a grain merchant and long-time member of the Society from Isma'iliyya, was appointed as its head.[57] He was given one basic directive: to give it the 'proper orientation'—which meant bringing it out into the open by gradually enlarging its membership and integrating its activity with the family system in the open Society—and to purge it of terrorism. Tal'at's job, as the deputy afterwards put it, was 'to divest the unit of its nature and give it another',[58] in effect, to preside over its dissolution. His major problem was to make the older members accept the new idea and the new leadership in the Society. As it turned out, the course of events was fatal to the attempted reform. In January, following the dissolution of the Society, whatever might have been the intentions of Tal'at and some of those above him, the idea of destroying the secret apparatus came to seem, at the least, ill timed, if not rash. The old argument of the secret apparatus as an instrument of 'defence' had never seemed more cogent than when the Society was entering a new phase of 'persecution'.

CONFLICT: THE FIRST ROUND (JANUARY–MARCH 1954)

Having overcome the internal crisis for the moment, the Society resumed its weekly meetings and other activities in mid-December 1953. Some of the opposition, as we have seen, had sought and received the leader's forgiveness for their transgression of the oath of loyalty. The leaders of the coup remained intransigent, continuing to plead their case against Hudaybi in the pages of *Majallat al-Da'wa*. Without question, however, Hudaybi had won a resounding victory over his challengers. And this was so because in supporting him the members were not only fulfilling the obligation of the *bay'a* but also expressing their views about the situation with the government. The event had brought into the open a government policy which seemed to have been formulated in the autumn

[56] See esp. *JJ* (24 Nov. 1954), 8; (26 Nov. 1954), 10.

[57] *JJ* (17 Nov. 1954), 4; (19 Nov. 1954), 3; *MAS* (24 Nov. 1954), 6; and *MTR* (7 Dec. 1954), 13–16, for an elaborated and hostile story of Tal'at's life.

[58] *JJ* (17 Nov. 1954), 3; see also ibid. (12 Nov. 1954), 5; (19 Nov. 1954), 3; and (24 Nov. 1954), 8. Tal'at reported later that Hudaybi had said to him at the time, in the Egyptian colloquial: 'do without the spirit of gangdom' (*balash ruh al-'asaba*).

and put into effect from that time: bringing the organization under control from within by discrediting Hudaybi and then removing him. Hudaybi's victory over the dissidents was, therefore, a blow to the government as well; it prompted its decision to dissolve the organization shortly afterwards. The occasion, in a literal sense, was ready-made.

On 12 January, 1954 the students of the university, led by the Muslim Brothers, met for their annual commemoration of the 'martyrs' of the university. During the speech-making, an army jeep appeared carrying a loudspeaker and passengers identified as belonging to the leadership of the government-sponsored Liberation Rally and Youth Formations. Outside the gates of the campus, members of the Liberation Rally of neighbouring secondary schools gathered and waited. The jeep loudspeaker, a short way from the crowd already assembled, began issuing nationalist speeches in tune with the spirit of the day. A request for them to depart or move further away from the assembled group of Brothers was followed by an exchange of words and slogans and then a battle, which brought the students outside the gates into the campus with banners and weapons, and which ended in scores of injuries and the burning of the jeep.[59]

That evening, at the weekly meeting of the Muslim Brothers, the air was charged in a way clearly discernible at moments of anticipated crisis or danger.[60] On 13 January the cabinet decided to dissolve the Society of the Muslim Brothers, but in order to brace the security forces and bring Upper Egypt under control, the information was only released at 12.45 a.m. on the 15th. The Society of the Muslim Brothers was declared a political party and therefore subject to the law of January 1953 abolishing these. The decree referred to the aim of the revolution to liberate the country from corruption and imperialism, and to the course of relations between the government and the Society. It recalled Hudaybi's failure to come forward on 23 July and declare himself for the revolution; his resistance to the land-reform law; the government's gesture in reopening the Banna murder case and releasing the political prisoners; the crisis over the ministerial appointments; the government's saving of the Society from the law on political parties of January 1953, and the subsequent demand by the

[59] Many eyewitness versions of the incident support the notion that it was government-provoked. *JJ* (13 Jan. 1954), 1, contains the cryptic announcement by the ministry of the interior that it was investigating a 'battle' between 'two groups' at the university.

[60] The main speaker that night at the headquarters and at the university that day was Navab Safavi, the leader of the Persian Fada'iyin Islam, who arrived in Egypt on 10 January and announced: 'I killed Razmara'; see *JJ* (11 Jan. 1954), 1.

Brothers for control over affairs of state; the resistance of the Society to the formation of the Liberation Rally; the meetings with the British; the subversion in the army due to the secret apparatus; and finally the incident at the university. In order, therefore, to destroy Hudaybi and his clique, who were planning 'to overthrow the present form of government under the cover of religion', the Society was dissolved. Simultaneously it was announced that the schools, hospitals, and clinics of the Society would continue to operate under different names; and that there had been 450 arrests and 20 immediate releases.[61]

The Communist party immediately released a pamphlet extending its hand to the Brothers for a common struggle against 'the fascist dictatorship' of Nasir and his 'Anglo-American props'. The pamphlet also appealed to members to repudiate their old leaders, who, by their earlier willingness to work with the RCC, had shown that they, too, were 'fascist imperialists'; and the Brothers were invited into a new 'national front'.[62]

On the next day, and for a few days during the month, the government initiated a press campaign against Hudaybi and 'his clique'—not against the Society as such. The campaign was centred on all the complaints brought against Hudaybi from within the organization, especially his failure to live up to the image of Banna, and his perversion and neglect of 'the essence of the message'. Only one item, the 'discovery' of a cache of arms on the estate of one of the members, bore any relation to the charge of 'revolution'. It became so widely rumoured that these were the arms which the members of the army group, before the revolution, had put there themselves,[63] that the charge earned the government some ridicule and strengthened the picture of the Society in 'persecution'. None of the other items in the bill of particulars received any serious consideration, nor were there any frontal attacks on the Society. These facts strengthened the widespread notion that Hudaybi was the prime target, and that the RCC intended to reconstitute the Society under more amenable leadership. Nasir's visit, together with other dignitaries in the army, government and members of the Society not arrested, to the grave of Hasan al-Banna on 12 February, and his eulogy of the man and his works, served to strengthen this idea.[64]

[61] *JJ* (15 Jan. 1954), 1, 5, 11, or any other daily paper; all carried the same account. A translation of the decree of dissolution was made in 'Documents', *MEA* (Mar. 1954), 94–100.

[62] See the organ of the Communist Party, *Rayat al-Sha'b* (13 Jan. 1954), *passim*; and *al-Talaba* (21 Jan. 1954), 2.

[63] *JJ* (18 Jan. 1954), 5; and above, pp. 100–1.

[64] *JJ* (13 Feb. 1954), 1; and *MDA* (16 Feb. 1954), 1, 7. 'Ashmawi's paper, *al-Da'wa*, continued to appear after the order dissolving the Society, a fact

The organization, technically disbanded, continued to operate in an unofficial way under the unofficial leadership of ʿAbd al-Qadir ʿAwda. Members who had not been arrested met in small sessions in each other's homes; they also immediately organized an aid network for the families of those in the prisons. While the government arrested some of those caught doing this, it did not seem seriously bent on hampering the operation. In February, at the ceremonies at Banna's tomb, ʿAwda had publicly enunciated his view that the revolution had realized the goals of Hasan al-Banna.[65] Privately, with others, he had begun a series of talks with the government in an effort to win back legality for the Society; in this respect he sought and received permission to visit the prisons and plead for the resignation of Hudaybi. Other plans under discussion included the founding of a new, strictly 'religious' organization under the leadership of ʿAbd al-Rahman al-Banna.[66] Everything came to a halt, however, in the wake of the political crisis which enveloped Egypt, involving the popular hero of the revolution, General Muhammad Neguib, and its real power, Colonel Gamal ʿAbd al-Nasir.

In its essential form the crisis between Neguib and Nasir involved a demand by Neguib for power commensurate with his rank. More than a mere struggle for power, the conflict was the expression of differing views, as explained by Neguib, on the way Egypt should be run. For the older man—perhaps he was too old to be a genuine revolutionary—the alienation of every segment of the community as the revolution ran its course became more and more intolerable. Neguib was not prepared to pay the price in popularity that governing towards the enunciated goals of the revolution demanded.[67] Nasir, on the other hand, of another generation and with perhaps more profoundly felt convictions about the plight—and the future—of Egypt, had been readily disabused of whatever magnanimity he brought to the early days of the revolution and whatever illusions he may have had about the ease of guiding Egypt to her millenium.[68] Having declared the revolution and effected the surface changes, Nasir found that to make it continuous and significant no quarter could be given to

which assured observers that the Society would arise again. With the issue of 19 Jan. 1954 the paper abruptly ceased its attacks on Hudaybi and made an appeal for 'unity'.

---

[65] *MDA* (16 Feb. 1954), 1.

[66] Ibid. (5 Oct. 1954), 7; Kira, *Mahkama*, i. 52; ii. 23–5.

[67] See Neguib, *Egypt's Destiny*, pp. 213–16.

[68] See Gamal Abd El-Nasser, *The Philosophy of the Revolution* (Cairo, [1955], pp. 20–6, 48–52.

those who would oppose it—actively, passively, or with indifference. As hostility to the régime became more acute and repression became more necessary, the dispute between the two leaders became more intense. In the circumstances, it came to rest on the question of who was to have final authority in the country and to what end that authority was to be used.

The crisis came into the open with the resignation of Neguib on 23 February and its acceptance by the RCC on the 24th. That night Neguib's house was surrounded, and on the 25th the newspapers carried the first announcements of the cleavage in the army junta. By 26 February at 5 p.m., after near insurrection in support of Neguib and a virtually spontaneous popular uprising, the RCC was compelled to announce the reinstatement of Neguib in the presidency. For those who had hopefully predicted and prayed for a split in the ranks of the ruling officers thanks to which their régime might be overthrown—and there were many—the time seemed ripe. Along with every other victim, and potential victim, of the RCC, the Society of the Muslim Brothers flexed its muscles.

On the morning of 27 February, Sunday, the day after Neguib's dramatic return to office, great crowds surged through the streets celebrating the victory of their hero. The students formed their own demonstrations, and, as was predictable, the celebration for Neguib became the occasion for anti-Nasir, anti-RCC demonstrations. For most of the articulate elements in the country, Neguib merely symbolized the opposition to Nasir; in few, if any, circles could he be described as the founder of a counter-revolution. His role was that of catalyst for the opposition, who readily seized upon the situation for their respective and often conflicting interests. The largest group of students was stopped at the Khedive Isma'il Bridge by security forces who hoped to drive them back to Giza across the river. Tensions mounted and in the confusion an officer gave the order to open fire. The barrage left a score of wounded (the numerous figures given are so contradictory as to make any certainty impossible), and turned a demonstrating crowd into a frightened, but raging mob. Part of the crowd dispersed across the bridge towards the university. Another group marched in the opposite direction towards Republic Palace (formerly 'Abidin Palace) where they joined another huge crowd receiving the greetings of President Neguib from the balcony. The new arrivals brought with them handkerchiefs dripping with the blood of the victims dropped by the police fire, which they waved dramatically in the air as they demanded from Neguib an immediate investigation and punishment of the 'butchers'. The star leader of the sanguinary expedition and its most vocal member was ʿAbd al-Qadir ʿAwda, who, up until now, had been considered by the RCC one of their leading supporters. Neguib invited him up on the balcony and finally quieted him with an agreement to investigate; the crowd was then ordered to disperse.[69] During the remainder of the day ʿAwda delivered speeches and distributed pamphlets hostile to the regime and in defence of Hudaybi and all he had done over the last year. Like so many others in Egypt during those days, ʿAwda completely misread the situation and miscalculated the staying power of Nasir and the RCC; for him, it proved to be a fatal error.[70] That evening 117 people were arrested, 45 of whom were Muslim Brothers, including ʿAwda, the remainder being from the Socialist, Communist, and Wafdist parties. For the incident at the bridge, six Muslim Brother students were held.

The crisis did not end with the return of Neguib, for the basic problem, the possession of authority and the manner of using it, remained unsolved. On 9 March the government announced that General Neguib would be reinvested with the offices of prime minister and head of the RCC. Hudaybi about this time wrote from prison to Neguib, asking for the release of the Muslim Brothers in order that the situation might be 'stabilized'.[71] Neguib, on the 15th, denied the existence of any such letter;[72] but privately promised the Brothers that he would 'consult with others'. ʿAshmawi's organ, *al-Daʿwa*, joined the chorus for the release of the Brothers, describing the dissolution order of January as 'an error.'[73] Meanwhile, the universities had exploded into daily demonstrations demanding the return of the country to parliamentary life, in line with Neguib's promises, and the withdrawal of the officers from government to their barracks. The university was unanimous in its voice and united in its action until 25 March. On that day, in what turned out to be a brilliant manœuvre by Nasir, the RCC announced that the revolution would come to an end and that the country would resume normal parliamentary life. On the same day the ministry of the interior ordered the

[69] See Neguib, *Egypt's Destiny*, p. 229, for his version of the events at Republic Palace. In *JJ* (1 Dec. 1955), 5 ʿAwda insisted that he was there only to disperse the crowds.

[70] *MDA* (5 Oct. 1954), 7. Kira, *Mahkama*, i. 52, shows clearly the sense of betrayal felt by the RCC, a fact evidenced by his ill treatment in prison. On this point *JM* (28 Mar. 1954), 1, reported an official request by ʿAwda's brother for an investigation of the ill treatment. As a Wafdist journal, *JM* was full of useful information in this period of no censorship, a fact for which it paid dearly when censorship was reimposed, as we shall see in a moment.

[71] *JM* (16 Mar. 1954), 1. This issue was rapidly confiscated by the government because of this report.

[72] *JJ* (17 Mar. 1954), 1. The denial was false.

[73] *MDA* (16 Mar. 1954), 1, *passim*.

release of Hudaybi and the Muslim Brothers, in accordance with a decree abrogating the January 1953 decree abolishing political parties. Censorship was totally lifted from the press.[74] Anyone who had anything to say, to their misfortune, now had a chance to say it.

The Muslim Brothers received the special attention of the government. In private negotiations for their release, it was agreed that their moneys and real estate would be unfrozen and that no restrictions would be placed on their activities. It was also agreed—and this had an important bearing on subsequent events—that all prisoners, military as well as civil, belonging to the Society would be released. Finally, the RCC was to issue a statement explaining the reasons for the dissolution order of the previous January. Hudaybi announced that, henceforth, the Society would be a 'support' for the government. On the night of the release, Nasir met Hudaybi at the latter's home; it was resolved then that 'a Committee of Liaison with the Government' should be established to negotiate outstanding differences.[75]

The pressing problem of the Society's position on the explosive internal question explained the soft handling given to the Brothers; it was answered the next day in two different places. After visiting King Saʿud—then in Egypt and regarded as instrumental both in the return of Neguib and in the release of Hudaybi—and after visiting the hospitals where the Brothers hurt in the bridge incident lay, Hudaybi spoke at a meeting at the headquarters of the Society using as his themes the need to 'close ranks' in the nation, and to have 'a clean representative life'. An official statement to the press reiterating the same themes carried the news throughout Egypt, with its implication that the Muslim Brothers would not lend their support to the movement, which would resuscitate the 'corrupt' parliamentary life of the *Ancien Régime*.[76] The official stand was given point at the university when, immediately after the release of the Brothers from prison and the announcement that the political parties would be allowed to resume their legal existence, the participation of the Brothers—hitherto vociferous and constant—in student demonstrations, became first cautious and

[74] *JM* (26 Mar. 1954), 1.

[75] Ibid.; *MDA* (30 Mar. 1954), 3.

[76] *JJ* (27 Mar. 1954), 1, 6, 9, 11. All those previously ousted from the Society were present at the first meeting at the headquarters. *MAS* (31 Mar. 1954), 6, reported details of the attempts by all other groups in Egypt, especially the Wafd, to influence the thinking of the Brothers. *MAS* by this time was regarded as a semi-official voice of the government, often expressing official hopes; this article concluded its report with a hopeful observation: 'The overwhelming current among the Brothers is the protection of the goals of the revolution and resistance to every effort to return it to the rear.'

then nonexistent. Those who continued to speak emphasized their dedication to the cause of 'clean parliamentary life'; not one raised his voice on behalf of the return of political parties. When the Brothers withdrew, the university movement against the government collapsed. Speeches continued for a few days but the spirit sagged; one last burst of enthusiasm carried a few diehards out of the university compound to meet the troops which surrounded the campus, brought them to within the sound of cocking rifles in the hands of soldiers with orders to shoot and a determination to do so, and then burned itself out. The tensions and anxieties of the past fortnight and those last few moments almost visibly poured out of the pores of the students as they wended their way back to the grassy campus and sat weakly on their pride in almost welcome defeat.

The Muslim Brothers, in remaining loyal to their principle of parliaments without parties and incidentally reaping political advantage, brought upon themselves the wrath and contempt of their fellows at the university. The communists, who in January had extended the hand of friendship in their common struggle against the 'fascist dictator', now turned in full fury on them, charging with the Wafd another betrayal in the 'national cause'. Some of the Brothers themselves were disturbed at the turn of events, feeling at the time more enthusiasm for overthrowing the régime than for standing on principle. During the question-and-answer period of the following Tuesday meeting, Hudaybi was asked the meaning of the talks between the government and the leaders of the Society. He answered: 'They are concerned with the welfare of Egypt. We are concerned with the welfare of Egypt and Islam. We met and talked in general about the things which concern the people of the nation.' Whatever else was talked about, there was virtually unanimous agreement among the angry opposition that a 'bargain' was struck which saved the regime's life, and that by withdrawing from the 'united front', the Muslim Brothers bore the full responsibility for its perpetuation. Both government and Society leaders had good reason for what they did. The Muslim Brothers could well point to the strong ideological compulsion in their position and also to their political need at the time; the government could argue ideological reasons, but there was, also, a pressing tactical consideration, made manifest in what was to follow.

On 28 March after three full days of complete and uncontrolled freedom for the opposition, Nasir moved. On that day 'popular demonstrations' erupted in the streets demanding the retention of the revolution and its goals, and the continued abolition of the political parties. Great crowds—members of the government-controlled labour and transport unions, and the young men of the paramilitary government formations, sparked off and directed by the effendis of the Liberation Rally—surged from place to place in the city, often in government-supplied trucks, and made their point, more often than not with violence, that the government was there to stay. Among the more notable impressions left was the attack on the building of the Wafdist newspaper, *al-Misri*, and the more serious march on the Council of State where, under the eyes of armed police and soldiers, the rioters invaded the building and ejected, with violence to his person, the aged and famous jurist, 'Abd al-Razzaq al-Sanhuri, who had publicly supported Neguib's wish to return to parliamentary government. Only after the Minister of state, Salah Salim, himself came and dispersed the rioters, did the police and soldiers move from their position as observers.

That evening the government issued orders that demonstrating would in future be forbidden; and next day, in response to the clearly expressed 'popular will', the RCC decided once more to 'take upon its shoulders the full responsibility of government'[77] All the political parties were again abolished, except the Society of the Muslim Brothers, 'whose leaders promised to behave themselves', as it was put by Neguib.[78] Calm, under virtual military occupation, returned to the streets of Cairo.

CONFLICT: THE CLIMAX (APRIL–OCTOBER 1954)

Hudaybi's agreement to co-operate with the government was probably taken in good faith. Whatever this régime was, it held greater possibilities and was more desirable than a return to the old order of things, a situation which would be virtually assured by the demise of the RCC. On another level was the obvious fact that release from the prisons was contingent upon a promise of co-operation. In either case the situation reflected a necessary compromise with circumstances. Hudaybi's cautious and chastened confidence in the possibility of 'a new era of co-operation' was, however, not shared by all, especially those not ready to forgive the dissolution of the Society in January 1954, or to forget its lessons. It would appear that, in March, reorganization of the secret apparatus in its old and officially repudiated form, which had begun under the stimulus of the January decree gained momentum. Under the impact of events, some of those who had supported the

77 *MDA* (30 Mar. 1954), 1, in a front-page editorial said to the Brothers: 'This is your day; come forth.'

78 *Egypt's Destiny*, p. 235.

reform notion of disbanding the secret apparatus no longer did so. Hudaybi, having delegated to his subordinates the carrying out of the new policy, appeared to be unaware of what was happening; in effect, the old secret organization was being replaced by a new one with the major difference that its leadership was loyal to him. While official peace had been declared between the government and the Society, the instruments were being secretly forged for what was now regarded by some on both sides as an inevitable war to the end.

In April the government brought to trial some of the officers suspected of having been involved in the troubles of the previous two months. Among these were officers affiliated to the Muslim Brothers who, according to the agreement of 26 March, were not only to be freed, along with the civilian prisoners, but also to be reinstated. Negotiations between the government and Hudaybi about this broken promise failed, and the first officer brought to trial was the long-time member of both the junta and the Society, ʿAbd al-Munʿim ʿAbd al-Ra'uf. Ra'uf startled the military tribunal by asking leave to call as witnesses for the defence Muhammad Neguib and Gamal ʿAbd al-Nasir; after the court denied this request he planned and made good an escape from prison.[79] It was an inauspicious beginning for 'the new era of co-operation'. Ra'uf's odyssey after his escape is unknown, but he was to become a leading figure and planner in the newly reconstituted secret apparatus.

The trial of the officers was only the first of the alleged broken promises. Similarly, the government failed to issue the promised explanation of its reasons for dissolving the Society, and disregarded requests from the Society's leaders for official clarification on the question of the legal revocation of the January decree. In response to the angry pressures around him, Hudaybi addressed a letter to the prime minister on 4 May, which found its way in mimeograph form to the streets. In the letter he expressed his disappointment at the failure of the RCC to keep its promises concerning the order of dissolution and the release of the detainees. He added some observations about the situation in the country and suggested some measures which would lead to 'stability'. First, he recommended 'the restoration of parliamentary life'; 'modern countries' must be governed in this way, he observed, and its failure in the past was no excuse for discarding the principle; 'learning comes from actual practice in parliamentary life', he concluded. Secondly, he sought the abolition of martial law and

[79] For a brief reference to the escape, a fact not then publicized, see *JJ* (17 Nov. 1954), 4.

extraordinary measures, suggesting that they 'create an atmosphere of terror'. Thirdly he called for 'the restoration of freedom', especially the freedom of the press; 'you might', he said to Nasir, 'derive much benefit from opposition in the press'.[80] The error was not so much in making these observations as in making them public. The appearance of the letter in the form of a 'secret pamphlet' (*manshura*) was an official hint that the struggle was on again.

The letter was one of Hudaybi's last acts as leader. After presiding over the release of the first issue of the long-planned, long-awaited (and, as it turned out, short-lived) new weekly newspaper, *Jaridat al-Ikhwan al-Muslimin*, on 20 May, he made preparations for a prolonged visit to the Fertile Crescent. Before he left, it was made known that he planned to include in his itinerary a courtesy call on King Sa'ud, on the latter's invitation, to pay respects for that sovereign's intervention on behalf of the Society in March. The government, unwilling to forbid the visit to Saudi Arabia, decided at the last moment to send out a representative of the RCC, Salah Salim, then minister of national guidance,'on business' while Hudaybi was there.[81] On the eve of his departure, Hudaybi was summoned to an audience with the prime minister but refused to go. Reportedly, Nasir sought his promise not to shake the reputation of the junta in the Arab world. Hudaybi, presumably, felt that there was nothing more that could be said between them. With the emissaries he did send to Nasir that night went a message which was also relayed to those around him and the substance of which explained the reason for his journey. He is reported to have said: 'I will be out of the way for two months. Do what can be done to come to terms with each other. Our dispute is not in the interest of the country.' Regarding himself as an obstacle to peace between the government and the Society, he withdrew, selecting as guardian of the peace mission a semi-partisan of Nasir's and his own long-time competitor, 'Abd al-Rahman al-Banna.[82] In a very real sense Hudaybi's role became, thereafter, peripheral; the destiny of the Society passed into other hands.

Hudaybi's trip to Saudi Arabia, Lebanon, Syria, Jordan, and the frontiers of Israel was reported only in the new weekly journal of the Society. The more important news in the Egyptian press was the resumption of negotiations with the British for the

[80] See Appendix E of the original version of this study.

[81] For a report on the trip, see *JIM* (10 June 1954), 1.

[82] See *JJ* (17 Nov. 1954), 7. It was perfectly clear by this time that a major element in the continuing conflict was the personal antagonism between Nasir and Hudaybi.

settlement of the Suez dispute. In traditional fashion, the Brothers' journal was calling for *jihad* against the British. In equally emphatic terms, the government was being denounced in secret pamphlets not only for usurping 'the rights of the people' but also for its coming 'betrayal' of the national cause. The chief of these pamphlets, *al-Ikhwan fi'l-Ma'raka*, a small, mimeographed, magazine-type publication, bore the slogan 'the voice of the Islamic message', and claimed to report news 'with no censor on it but God'. Another pamphlet charged the government with, in effect, negotiating for 'the extension of the 1936 treaty'; also with concluding 'a secret agreement with Israel' (which provided for Israeli neutrality on the Anglo-Egyptian negotiations in exchange for Egyptian neutrality on any Arab-Israeli dispute, Egyptian withdrawal of all but 'token forces' from Sinai, and joint Israeli-Egyptian efforts to keep the Gaza frontier quiet); and with permitting the extension of 'American imperialism in Egypt' (by allowing Point Four technical aid and by granting oil concessions in the Western Desert). This pamphlet and all the others were being brought to the streets by some of the high-ranking officials of the newly reconstituted secret apparatus, and apparently with the knowledge of its former deputy head, now its head, Dr Muhammad Khamis Humayda. All this was part of a singularly intensive campaign of secret-pamphlet warfare waged by many groups, pro- and anti-government, which began with the letter of 4 May to Nasir and which continued unabated until October. The evacuation agreement opened the floodgates on pamphlets, and on more serious activity.

On 27 July, the governments of Britain and Egypt announced their joint acceptance of the 'heads of agreement' as a basis for a new treaty settling the historic Anglo-Egyptian dispute. On 31 July a Beirut newspaper carried in banner headlines the opinion of the leader of the Muslim Brothers on the agreement. The main points of Hudaybi's argument were the following: (1) the treaty of 1936 would have expired in less than two years, whereupon Britain would have been required to evacuate the base and would have been left without any legal foundation on which to return to it; the new treaty would give her that right by providing for reactivation of the base in case of attack on any of the Arab states or on Turkey; (2) the clause permitting reactivation in the event of attack on Turkey bound Egypt and the Arab states to her and therefore to the 'western camp'; (3) the provision permitting Britain to maintain air bases was a threat to Egypt and, in the air age, was a device for perpetuating control; (4) the 'civilians' expected

[83] No. 11 (July 1954), 1–5.

to assist in operating the installations were, of course, military personnel in civil dress; (5) the agreement extended the treaty of 1936 for five years and permitted 'consultation' for revision at its termination, the same kind of provision which made the treaty of 1936 eternal in effect. On all of these grounds Hudaybi 'rejected' the agreement, insisting that any agreement between Egypt and a foreign government must be submitted 'to a parliament elected freely . . . representing the will of the Egyptian people', and to a press free of censorship and free to debate.[84]

The effect in Cairo of Hudaybi's outspoken criticism of the heads of agreement was startling. Matters were not made any better by a long, more-detailed statement of criticism contained in a letter to Nasir, dated 2 August and signed by the deputy, Humayda, in the name of the Guidance Council, which was also made public via the secret-pamphlet mill. Besides criticizing the heads of agreement, this reasserted the Brothers' right to make known their views on them. Two other important pamphlets added a dramatic convulsion to the scene: one, critical of the agreement, was signed by Muhammad Neguib, and in effect dissociated him from it; the other, critical of the government generally, was signed by 'a former minister'—later identified as Sulayman Hafiz, minister of the interior in Neguib's first cabinet. Similar format, similar print, and similar paper indicated a common source: the presses of the Muslim Brothers. They had been received for publication through the hands of ʿAbd al-Qadir ʿAwda.[85]

The tension provoked by the reaction to the heads of agreement was kept under control during the absence of Hudaybi, who was still in Syria, and of Nasir, who on 7–15 August was in Saudi Arabia for the pilgrimage and for attendance at the newly proposed conference of Muslim leaders in Mecca. Hudaybi returned on Sunday, 22 August; on the same day, the government began its press campaign to discredit his stand on the agreement, primarily by reviving, in elaborated form, the image of the 'secret treaty' which he had allegedly negotiated with the British that spring, and in which, it was said, he had made more concessions than the government. Hudaybi was warmly received at the headquarters that evening and drafted his first and only reply to the charge of secret negotiations and sent it in a letter to Nasir; this also included a plea that the Brothers might be given a chance to express their views, so that 'people may judge us by our deeds, not by your words'. Again, the letter was distributed as a pamphlet.

[84] *Jaridat al-Hadaf* (31 July 1954), 1, copies of which immediately found their way to Cairo. A similar statement was broadcast over Radio Damascus.

[85] For these three pamphlets and a summary of Hudaybi's criticism, see Appendix H and I of the original version of this study.

On the following Tuesday night the traditional weekly meeting —it was the last—was tense. Hudaybi stood before the large group and repeated, for the benefit of those who had not heard him on the preceding Sunday, the details of his trip and his explanation of the talks with Trefor Evans of the British Embassy. He took up the question of the demise of the weekly journal, which had folded up after its twelfth number, explaining that rigorous censorship had rendered publication impracticable.[86] The members became more incensed as the meeting progressed, but Hudaybi exerted every effort to keep order, deliberately playing down the situation and angrily commanding silence as members stood and flung out into the tense night air slogans and epithets hostile to the government. His voice rose above its normal conversational pitch only once, as he rebuked a young man for shouting: 'Death to the traitors!' He ended his talk with a calmly worded statement, of great impact on those assembled, of his 'preparation for whatever comes', and his dedication to the principle, basic to the Society, that 'death in the path of God is the noblest of our wishes'.

This was also the last time he was seen by many of the members until he was arrested and brought to trial a few months later. During the next weekend, following an armed clash between the groups, presently to be described, Hudaybi, together with his closest advisers, Hasan al-ʿAshmawi and Salah Shadi, disappeared. He was persuaded by these and others to remove himself from the possibility of assassination or arrest. He was readily persuaded to go because of his still strong belief that he could best serve the situation by absenting himself from it. The Guidance Council legalized the absence by declaring the leader 'on vacation'. Over the next two months, the government, while making much of the disappearance of Hudaybi in its personal attacks on him, took pains to assert its lack of desire to arrest him in order to dissipate the aura of martyrdom which already had begun to surround him.[87]

From this time the government employed a twofold method of attack. First, it unleashed a massive and continuing press campaign against Hudaybi and 'his gang' and their policies. Secondly, it tightened up security and introduced stricter control, sometimes provocatively, over what little activity of the Brothers was continuing. The press campaign combined a number of often disparate, sometimes conflicting, elements: first, Hudaybi's 'secret treaty' with the British was made a central theme, with increasingly

[86] Cf. *JJ* (14 Nov. 1954), 8, for a government contention that the paper collapsed for financial reasons.

[87] ʿAshmawi's *MDA* (28 Sept. 1954), 6, took pains to recall Banna's unwillingness to flee, in the same kind of situation, in January 1949.

elaborated details which included his acceptance of 'conditions to evacuation', the principle of 'joint defence' with the West, military experts' and 'alliance with the English after evacuation'—all of this with special emphasis on the 'secrecy' of the negotiations; secondly, his 'relations' with the deposed king and 'the former ruling classes' —Hilali, Mahir, and Nuqrashi—were given full coverage, with emphasis on his 'visits' to the palace and co-operation with the *Ancien Régime*, and his failure to challenge them as he was challenging the revolution of 'the sons of the nation and the people'; thirdly, his policies were defined and identified with those of the 'Imperialists' and the 'Zionists', serving their cause at the expense of Egypt; and fourthly, he was identified with the communists in an effort to link together 'the forces of disorder'. Virtually all the old disputes were reworked and elaborated, and, together with whatever else was being said, pointed the moral that Hudaybi, 'his gang', and his secret apparatus had deviated from the original principles of the Society.

There were two other aspects to the press campaign: (1) the editorials of the official papers and journals carried answers and rebuttals to the secret pamphlets filling the streets, although they did not always report accurately or completely what was written;[88] and (2) the papers carried almost daily columns of communications, allegedly received by the government from Brothers, which repudiated Hudaybi in particular or the Society in general for their hostility to the RCC—a traditional device in Egypt for shaking confidence in a political opponent or for establishing a bandwagon movement for or against something.[89]

Interspersing this information in the newspapers or magazines was news justifying the tightening up of security. On 28 August the newspapers headlined reports from the ministry of the interior of 'aggressions against the police and the people' by the Muslim Brothers following the Friday noon prayer at their mosque in Rawda. After a speech deliberately intended to inspire violence, the report went on, the Brothers left the mosque and attacked the police and bystanders. What actually happened had a slightly different emphasis. The speech was in reality another appeal by an old student-leader friend of Nasir's for a restoration of calm and promulgation of liberties interspersed with appropriate

[88] See e.g. *JJ* (15 Sept. 1954), 1, 9; and (19 Sept. 1954), 1, 9. In the latter place, the government spokesman takes up a reference to the officers in one of the pamphlets as 'men of the coup' (*inqilab*) rather than 'revolution' (*thawra*); angered at the affront, he notes, *inter alia*, that perhaps Hudaybi thought it only a 'coup' because 'it did not deal with him as all revolutions do with traitors, deceivers and hypocrites. . . . In the very near future . . . Hudaybi will feel that what happened in Egypt was a revolution and not a coup.'

[89] See *JJ* (8 Sept. 1954), 7, 10, and almost daily thereafter.

Qur'anic and Prophetic references. The meeting had ended and the congregation had partly dispersed before a provocative attempt by army-led police (who had arrived during the services and surrounded the mosque) to arrest the speaker aroused the crowd and 'justified' the use of force, including rifle fire, to quiet the situation.[90]

On 10 September a similar event at the mosque of the Brothers in Tanta was reported: 'aggression by the Muslim Brothers against the people', a battle in the mosque during which the preacher used a knife on his antagonists. The next day the government denied in the press what had never been publicly reported, but was known in Cairo, in a matter of hours, that the government-sponsored national guard had been involved in the affair, suggesting to many observers another provoked incident. It was after this incident that the government took measures to bring the sermons in the mosques under stricter control through the ministry of waqfs.[91]

A battle in the town of Mit Ghamar between Brothers and the local police, a minor demonstration at a football match, and the storming and destruction of a clinic of the Brothers in Suez by the national guard, besides the mosque incidents, were followed by limited arrests of members. In late September and early October the police force was purged:[92] a story circulated at the time told of the arrest of a platoon of police with their officer, who, when stopped on their way to duty, were found to be loaded with the literature of the Society for distribution. Other arrests included a Brother for an attack on an army officer in the street, a group of Brothers for concealing arms,[93] and those among the Brothers who were suspected of involvement in a 'national front' with the communists.

In June, having forgotten its anger and public denunciation of the Brothers following the university *démarche* in March, the clandestine communist journal, *Rayat al-Sha'b*, announced: 'The resistance to the revolution is led by two basic forces, the Com-

[90] For the official announcement *JJ* (28 Aug. 1954), 1. The writer observed the incident from start to finish. The following week the speaker at the services used the Qur'anic verses 2 : 286 and 16 : 125–8, which preach endurance, patience, and forgiveness.

[91] See *JJ* (11 Sept. 1954), 1, for the incident, and (12 Sept. 1954) for the government denial. The government was angered by the report in *Time* 27 Sept. 1954), 25, on 'censoring sermons'; *Time* asserted 'not even Hitler or Stalin had ever attempted to dictate every word a preacher said'. The minister of waqfs, Baquri, denied locally that sermons would be written for the preachers; rather, they would be controlled by defining forbidden subjects—i.e. politics of 'the factionalist type'; see *JJ* (5 Oct. 1954), 5.

[92] See 'Developments of the Quarter', *MEJ* (Winter 1955), 57; *NYT* (8 Oct. 1954), 8. The local press did not, to our knowledge, carry the story.

[93] *JJ* (11 Oct. 1954), 1; (18 Oct. 1954), 1.

munist Party and the Society of the Muslim Brothers.' The same tract recommended that there should be a joint effort 'to bring down the government of Gamal 'Abd al-Nasir'.[94] The offer was renewed in July. The hand held out was accepted by some of the Brothers, and through July and August those involved planned a joint demonstration and protest march on the centre of the city (which was to spark off a popular uprising and bring Nasir down) to issue from the mosque of the Brothers after a Friday noon prayer. The plan was replete with signals and symbols conceived to identify the members of the conspiracy as they gathered in the mosque and its surrounding area.[95] Each time, however, it failed to materialize for one reason or another, but primarily because of last-minute persuasion, from within, and from the top of the Society, of the folly, and for the Brothers the ideological impossibility, of alliance with the communists. The only other way in which this limited co-operation worked in practice was in the agreement to help distribute each other's pamphlets, in which some Brothers were caught and arrested.[96] Only one important name was publicly attached to the liaison, that of Sayyid Qutb, at that time head of the section for the propagation of the message, editor of the Society's newspaper, and chief author of the secret pamphlets. Qutb was to become the chief spokesman of the Society after its final dissolution in 1954 and its latest 'martyr' in 1966.[97]

September in Cairo came to a dramatic peak on the 23rd with a decree from the RCC stripping of their nationality six Egyptians alleged to have destroyed the reputation of their country abroad and harmed its relations with its Arab neighbours; the charge was 'treason to the nation'. The six, all outside the country at the time, included Sa'id Ramadan, 'Abd al-Hakim 'Abidin, Sa'd al-Din al-Walili, Muhammad Najib Juwayfil, and Kamil Isma'il al-Sharif (all of them Muslim Brothers), and Mahmud abu al-Fath, a prominent Wafdist, a member of the family that owned the Wafdist paper, *al-Misri*, and considered, among other things, to be in alliance with the Brothers. All the Brothers were in Syria at the time attending a conference being held in Damascus. They were held responsible for the appearance of the pamphlets which

[94] *Rayat al-Sha'b* (29 June 1954), folio; reproduced in part in *MTR* (9 Nov. 1954), 17.

[95] See *MMR* (3 Dec. 1954), 16–17, 24, for a partial account of the liaison between the two groups. Prior information about the proposed demonstration made it possible for the writer to be on hand for the 28 August incident at the mosque. Similarly, prior knowledge may have prompted the government to deploy the force it did.

[96] *JJ* (17 Sept. 1954), 1, 9.

[97] See ibid. (16 Nov. 1954), 9; (21 Nov. 1954), 4; and Introduction, p. xiii.

issued from the conference under the names of the Societies in Iraq, Jordan, and the Sudan, pleading the cause of the Brothers against the government of Egypt, and for the intensity of the anti-RCC press of Syria, as well as for the continuous flow of news emanating from Radio Israel on the dispute in Egypt.[98] Relations between Syria and Egypt became strained over the question of the continuing activity of the Brothers in Syria—the tension caused a bitter attack on Syria in the Egyptian press and inspired a hurried personal visit by the Syrian prime minister and chief of staff of the army[99]—and over that of the future of the denationalized Brothers. The government consistently denied persistent rumours that Syria would grant, or had granted, them political asylum, but the news was correctly reported by Radio Israel on 13 October and confirmed within a day in a not widely circulated Egyptian Radio newsletter.[100] After this experience the government tightened up passport control for all suspected Brothers, a move which coincided with a minor exodus to Kuwait, Bahrayn, Saudi Arabia, and Syria.

By mid-September, Nasir had ceased appearing publicly for a while because of threats to his life. Hudaybi, when this was brought to his attention, wrote the prime minister another letter, again issued publicly as a pamphlet. In it he asked for an end to the present tensions by allowing an honourable debate on the outstanding issues in an atmosphere of freedom. He pleaded for 'cessation of the provocation' by the people and the law-enforcement authority against the Brothers: 'it is your duty', he said, 'to protect the populace, right or wrong'. Finally, with regard to threats of violence, Hudaybi assured the prime minister that he could circulate freely, 'day or night, alone . . . anywhere, without fearing anything from . . . the Muslim Brothers'.[101] Nasir seemed to agree, for towards the end of the month he was again making public appearances.

The question which troubled both observers and participants through the month of September was why, after the disappearance of Hudaybi, the continuing pamphlet warfare, the vitriolic criticism of the treaty, and the threat to the life of Nasir, the government did not invoke the decree of dissolution. Out of a number of possible explanations, three stand out. First, the negotiations with the British were in the delicate stage of near completion, and for the government to engage itself in an internal dispute—one being carefully watched by the foreign embassies—whose outcome could be both bloody and doubtful, would be folly. The second and

[98] See *JJ* (14 Sept. 1954), 1, 9; (15 Sept. 1954), 1, 9.
[99] See ibid. (19 Sept. 1954), 1. [100] *MIDHM* (14 Oct. 1954), 5.
[101] See Appendix L to the original version of this study.

third reasons were related to each other and derived from the lessons learned in the shortlived January dissolution. They were given expression in an article by the leading government voice in the press battle with the Society, Anwar al-Sadat, in answer to 'the thousands of letters and telegrams' from his 'countrymen' demanding 'the destruction of the Muslim Brothers'. In essence, he said that the recent history of Egypt (with reference, presumably, to 1948 also) had shown the basic fickleness of the people in matters like this, for whenever the Society had been suppressed it won the sympathy of the nation at large. 'A wise man', in the light of this fact, 'would not fall into the same error'. 'The people alone should do what it wants so that it will remain always wanting what it does.'[102] It would thus appear that this time the government was to prepare 'the people' for the assault when it came. Education was to precede the fact rather than follow it. The press campaign would discredit Hudaybi and his policies; the incidents would dramatize the 'aggression' of the Society against 'the people' and sensitize them to the need for appropriate action. This was the second reason for holding off the inevitable dissolution; the government would have taken up a posture of preparedness if, in fact, conflict was unavoidable.

The third reason assumed that the conflict might be localized and, perhaps, even avoided. Although not always careful in this respect, the government press continued to level its verbal barrage primarily at Hudaybi and those regarded as his partisans, particularly emphasizing his deviation from the principles of Islam and of the Society. At the same time it began a positive campaign to attach to itself an Islamic quality. In August the semi-official *al-Jumhuriyya* inaugurated a series of articles written by Anwar al-Sadat outlining the 'true' and liberal Islam.[103] Along with the usual, officially prompted Azhar pronouncements about the heresies of the Muslim Brothers, the government pressed for a reform of the curriculum of the Azhar designed to make it responsive to the needs of Egyptian society.[104] And after Nasir's return from the pilgrimage in August, great emphasis was laid in the press on his share in the creation of the 'Islamic Conference' (of Muslim leaders on pilgrimage); similarly, with the appointment of Anwar al-Sadat as its first chairman, the activity of the conference received prominent and regular coverage.[105] As respected 'Muslims', the men of the RCC could better attempt, in their attacks on Hudaybi,

[102] *JJ* (8 Oct. 1954), 12.

[103] The series was called 'Nahwa Ba'th Jadid' and ran from mid-August through September.

[104] *JJ* (2 Oct. 1954), 5; (4 Oct. 1954), 5.

[105] See e.g. ibid. (8 Aug. 1954), 1; (13 Aug. 1954), 1.

to do what they failed to do in January 1954, to place Hudaybi outside the Society in an ideological as well as in an organizational sense; to ensure the latter by succeeding in the former. The events of September and October in the organization itself give firm support to the notion that Nasir chose not to move against the organization in the hope that, after ridding it of Hudaybi and his partisans, he could win its loyalty.

Despite the appearance at the headquarters in March of all those previously dismissed in the crisis of November and December 1953, the basic issues in the conflict which had so shaken the unity of the organization still existed. The renewal of the debate on the issues followed upon the distribution of a memorandum from the headquarters, some time in May, concerning the attitude members should assume towards the wrong-doers: 'they should be boycotted and avoided'.[106] The organ of Hudaybi's opposition, *al-Da'wa*, from then on was public evidence of the unresolved status of the civil war in the ranks. The debate assumed a legal note, revolving around the contention of the anti-Hudaybi forces that in the hierarchy of power it was the Consultative Assembly which held the primacy. This view was inspired by the belief that this group alone could abrogate the orders which had separated some of the members from the Society and, more pressingly now, could reverse the policies which had made the government and the Muslim Brothers implacable enemies.[107]

The Society's official resistance to the treaty and Hudaybi's disappearance added urgency to the dissidents' demands that something should be done, and, they contended, done by the only body able to act, the Consultative Assembly. It was scheduled to have its annual meeting on 9 September. Hudaybi remained in concealment but sent a long letter to be read to the gathered members in which he reviewed the history of the relations between the government and the Society, emphasizing the promises made after March and the failure of the government to fulfil them.[108] Nothing more was done at the meeting than to read the letter and then adjourn until 23 September so that the ill-starred 'committee of liaison with the government'—hopefully established in March but made impotent by the trials of the officers in April—would have the time 'to clear the air'.[109] The Society, lines taking shape after March, split in three general ways: the first group, led by 'Abd

[106] See *MDA* (14 Sept. 1954), 16.
[107] See esp. *MDA* (20 July 1954), 7; and (28 Sept. 1954), 1.
[108] See Appendix M of the original version of this study.
[109] See *MDA* (21 Sept. 1954), 1, 16.

al-Rahman al-Banna (with the probable support of all the dissidents), was prepared to support the junta—partly because Hudaybi was seen to oppose it; on the other extreme were the partisans of Hudaybi, by now unquestionably in a mood of all-out opposition; the third group, headed by the deputy, Humayda, called itself 'neutral' and hoped that it could reconcile in some workable fashion the two other factions with each other, and the Society at large with the government.[110] Within this framework the struggle for control of the organization took place.

On 23 September, the Consultative Assembly met again. Control of the meeting, technically in the hands of the deputy, Humayda, was constantly in doubt as the two major and opposing factions made their points. Suddenly, in an apparent attempt to cut the ground from under the disputants, the neutralists introduced, and succeeded in passing, the following resolution: (1) that the RCC be applauded for its action in destroying the monarchy and feudalism and paving the way towards a better country; (2) that the RCC deserved gratitude for the efforts it expended on behalf of the nation; (3) that the government should recognize the right of the Muslim Brothers to debate with it on issues, with special reference to the evacuation agreement, and that it should understand that the Society's criticisms intended no reflection on the 'sincerity' of the RCC; (4) that both the RCC and the Society of the Muslim Brothers should work together for both 'faith and nation'. The meeting was then adjourned for a rest. What happened next is in dispute, but it would appear that other resolutions were put forward, and announced to the press that night by 'Awda as the resolutions of the whole group. They included: (1) the election of the leader for life—a frank rejection of the attempt to limit his term to three years; (2) the dissolution of the old Consultative Assembly and preparations for a new election; (3) the reform of the constitution as regards the election of members to the Assembly and the authority and responsibility of the Guidance Council. The government press presented these resolutions as the work of a 'rump' meeting, held by twenty-five of Hudaybi's supporters while the other members were absent, and therefore not representative of the views of the Assembly.[111] That the resolutions were supported by Humayda and the neutralists, and that they were accompanied by the earlier resolutions which were intended to be a conciliatory gesture to the government suggested, more correctly, that the Assembly had not yet faced the issues and had produced a compromise which would

[110] *JJ* (12 Nov. 1954), 5.

[111] On this entire development, see *JJ* (25 Sept. 1954), 1, and *passim*.

be satisfactory to no one. For the moment, however, it was the government which had suffered a 'defeat', as it was regarded in Cairo; the correspondent of the *New York Times* summed up the situation, by saying that the Muslim Brothers had 'bluntly and brazenly' defied Nasir by confirming Hudaybi for life.[112]

The administrative apparatus being now in the hands of Hudaybi's adherents, steps were immediately taken to begin elections in the branches all over the countryside. This move was followed by charges of corruption in the opposition organ, *al-Daʿwa*, and by stepped-up efforts on the part of prime minister Nasir to be done with Hudaybi. During the next three weeks he maintained close contact with all Hudaybi's opponents and also, and especially, with the neutralists, in the person of their spokesman, Humayda, in an effort to persuade them of the folly of maintaining Hudaybi in his untenable position. He did this amid the pressing last-minute preparations for the completion of the Anglo-Egyptian negotiations; on 19 October Nasir and Mr Anthony Nutting signed the new treaty which settled for the time the Anglo-Egyptian dispute.

Nasir's efforts were fruitful. On 21 October the press reported 'a coup among the Muslim Brothers'. It was said that seventy-two members had met and agreed to support the following new resolutions: (1) the General Guide was to be regarded as 'on vacation'; (2) the present Guidance Council was to be 'dismissed'; (3) all 'the decrees of separation and suspension' were to be 'abrogated', and all branches formed in the past three years were to be 'dissolved'; (4) the resolutions of 23 September were 'nullified'; (5) a temporary committee was to be established to direct the Society's affairs until the Consultative Assembly could meet to reorganize it. The 'temporary committee' included Humayda and a group of 'moderates' and also ʿAbd al-Rahman al-Banna.[113]

Hudaybi's partisans received the news with incredulity, and indicated their disapproval of the manœuvre the next day by joining in a heated brawl with the leaders of the 'coup' and their supporters at the headquarters. The Cairo press told of a battle followed by the tearful restoration of order, negotiations, and a compromise resolution in the name of 'the temporary committee', which formed a new Guidance Council, including five of Hudaybi's opponents, and ordered a delay in the elections begun after the meeting of 23 September until the new Council regained control over the organization. A meeting was called for Saturday, 23 October, allegedly to discuss matters of internal reorganization. The foreign press reported the story widely believed in Cairo, and

112 *NYT* (25 Sept. 1954), 4; (8 Oct. 1954), 9.
113 *JJ* (21 Oct. 1954), 1; *MDA* (26 Oct. 1954), 3.

more to the point, that at the protest meeting Humayda had repudiated the 'coup' of the seventy-two and had called for the meeting of 23 October to debate with them the issues separating them.[114] Although he had taken a technical stand in favour of Hudaybi, Humayda was merely avoiding an open break; from this meeting onwards he began to throw his full weight to the side of the anti-Hudaybi forces.

The conflict, though it had appeared in the press almost to have reached a solution, was far from it. The press reflected what the government wanted to be believed and its determined effort to have Hudaybi removed from within. Although in the final analysis this policy may be said to have been successful, this was for reasons other than the governmental manœuvres. The plan to discredit Hudaybi's leadership and have him removed by the organization itself had, as a concomitant effect, the discrediting of the entire leadership. Charges and countercharges of 'treason' and 'betrayal' among the members testified not only to attitudes about where one's loyalties should lie, but raised questions about where in fact they did lie. Who stood with whom against whom was a question which assumed a compelling urgency. Who in fact was running the organization was a question the answer to which depended on the prior question of loyalties. The related question: 'from whence came the orders?' was therefore also obscured. To those interested in confusing the Muslim Brothers, this situation could be regarded as an immediate victory; it also, however, released the spectre of an organization bound by fundamental rules of disciplined obedience to leadership, without a leadership. The events of 20–1 October were only the last of a series, in the same direction, in which the cumulative effect was not only the destruction of the leadership, but the parallel destruction of the chains of command, authority, and discipline. This fact was made abundantly clear by the events of the next two weeks and the prominent role played in them by the secret apparatus.

It has already been noted[115] that the intention of making the secret apparatus something other than what it had been in the past had been considerably modified by the January crisis with the government. With the release of the incarcerated Brothers in March, the secret apparatus took on new importance among some

[114] *NYT* (22 Oct. 1954), 9.

[115] See above, pp. 133–4. At this juncture we should like to recall to the reader that our reconstruction of events is based on an infinite number of bits and pieces of information which emerged during the trials of Brothers later on and were published in the press, and that these references have been drastically excised in this revision.

of those who decided that a fight with the government was inevitable. Hudaybi appears to have remained unaware of the reversion to character of the unit which had caused so much dissension within the Society; having delegated the problem to his subordinates, he regarded it as solved or in process of solution. Yusuf Tal'at, the new head of the group, seemed to have tried seriously to complete the mission assigned to him, even at the risk of his life, which was threatened by the older hands for his alleged 'treason'. In January he had accepted the advice of 'Abd al-Mun'im 'Abd al-Ra'uf on the matter of the reorganization of its units, believing, in line with the terms of reference of his appointment, that this would facilitate his 'conquering' the secret group. 'Abd al-Ra'uf presumably had other intentions. Both he and Salah Shadi seem to have begun, at this time or shortly thereafter, a new recruitment programme which quickened in tempo after the release of the Brothers from prison in March. In March, too, a new hierarchical authority was set up, in the form of a 'higher committee' to 'advise' the secret group. Its membership has been variously described, but it seems to have been led by Shaykh Muhammad Farghali of the Guidance Council and Mahmud 'Abduh, head of the Cairo regional office; its three leaders of the second rank were Tal'at for the civilian operation, Salah Shadi for the police, and Abu al-Makarim 'Abd al-Hayy for the army.

The first activities of the new group followed the January dissolution and were confined to the dispatch of threatening letters to those leaders whose non-arrest implied collusion with the government; among the recipients was 'Abd al-Qadir 'Awda. This practice continued throughout the year as the struggle within the organization continued. From May we have seen that the group carried on a full-scale pamphlet war with the government, printing and distributing as the occasion arose. And by July the notion of a 'popular uprising' seems to have become an integral part of the thinking of the inner circle of the secret apparatus.

The idea was first broached by 'Abd al-Ra'uf, in concealment following his successful escape from prison in April, and now being protected by the members of the secret unit; it was given firm support by the head of the Cairo section of the group, Ibrahim al-Tayyib. Other notions had been broached, all having at their base the death of Nasir. Twice 'Abd al-Ra'uf presented to Tal'at the idea of dressing the members of the cells in army uniforms to penetrate and then destroy the headquarters of the RCC and, presumably, the ministers. Tal'at twice rejected the proposal but the second time it was supported by Tayyib, who offered to find the arms necessary for the attack. Another plan, that of killing Nasir in person, proposed the use of a dynamite belt, to be worn by a member who would, at an appropriate time, work his way to Nasir, detonate the belt and take them both into eternity. There were no volunteers.

But the most widely accepted idea was that of the popular demonstration, because it seemed to offer the greatest degree of success. With an eye to widespread discontent with the régime among the articulate groups in the country, and what appeared to be popular indifference to the fate of the government, as well as the obvious and continuing struggle between Neguib and Nasir and what it implied for the solidarity of the army, the plan came to be outlined as follows: a public demonstration would be timed with a Neguib counter-coup which would bring out into the open any discontent in the army; the Brothers would help to spark off the 'people's revolt'; if the plan succeeded the government of the RCC would be replaced with one headed by Neguib; in the event of British interference, all approaches to Cairo would be severed and a plan for guerrilla action would be launched. 'Abd al-Ra'uf envisaged not only a demonstration but an armed one followed by a series of assassinations of the RCC.[116]

On 4 October Tal'at visited Hudaybi in Alexandria and informed him that there was much confusion and perplexity in the ranks about the desirability and form of some kind of action; he asked the leader to make a public appearance in order to clear the air and restore the sagging spirit of the Society. Hudaybi told Tal'at that it was the will of the Guidance Council that he should remain concealed, and he mentioned that he had been uneasy in the past few days regarding the possibility of violence and assassination. He added: 'If you want to join in a demonstration which is supported by all parts of the nation, that is all right'; the demonstration should, however, concern itself with 'the freedom of the press, parliament and the submission of the [evacuation] agreement to the people', and it should be 'a peaceful demonstration'. He affirmed his refusal to agree to any 'criminal act' and insisted that he would regard himself as 'innocent of the blood of anyone'.[117]

Hudaybi showed some scepticism that even the demonstration plan was feasible, but, on the lines he proposed, he advised Tal'at, if he was still interested, to contact 'Abd al-Qadir 'Awda. 'Awda was the primary contact with Muhammad Neguib; presumably, Hudaybi was concerned that the Brothers should take no

[116] For the high points, see *JJ* (12 Nov. 1954), 3, 4; (16 Nov. 1954), 9; and (24 Nov. 1954), 7, 8.

[117] The above quotations—from Tal'at's testimony—are obviously impossible to verify; we think, however, that they do reflect the sense of the situation; see *JJ* (17 Nov. 1954), 7, 8; and (14 Nov. 1954), 4, 7, 8.

action on their own without a prior move from the army. Tal'at met 'Awda, who promised to take up the subject of the visit with 'the committee', did so, and reported back that it did not then look with favour on the plan for a popular demonstration.[118] It was at this stage of affairs that, elsewhere in the secret apparatus, plans were being made to assassinate Nasir.

Early in October what was later called without clarification 'the leadership' of the secret group decided to assume 'terrorist orientations'; specifically, this meant that Nasir was to be assassinated. 'The leadership' chose Mahmud 'Abd al-Latif, a tinsmith from the Cairo section of Imbaba, to do the job. He was notified by the Imbaba section-leader, Hindawi Duwayr, a lawyer, and given three days to make his decision. On 19 October, the day Nasir signed the evacuation treaty with Britain, 'Abd al-Latif decided to accept the mission of killing him—for his 'act of treason' in signing the treaty which 'gave away the rights of the nation'. He made plans to act on the same day but the circumstances at the public gathering chosen were not conducive to the successful execution of the plan; it was, therefore, postponed to a more propitious time.

Meanwhile, on 24 October, one of the most respected members of the Guidance Council, Kamal Khalifa, visited the deputy prime minister, Gamal Salim, and extended his congratulations to the government for its successful completion of the negotiations and the signing of the treaty. It was reliably rumoured that Hudaybi had decided to issue a new statement noting his more favourable impression of the treaty as against the earlier heads of agreement. The 'committee of liaison with the government' was continuing its efforts to heal the breach. On 26 October, in the afternoon, a representative of the Guidance Council was in the office of Anwar al-Sadat seeking an appointment with the prime minister in order to try once more to resolve some of the issues in dispute.[119] That same afternoon, another highly respected, high-ranking member of the organization, 'Abd al-'Aziz Kamil, head of the family section, visited the home of Hindawi Duwayr, his friend and fellow Brother from the Imbaba district of Cairo. He was not told that earlier

[118] The committee could well have been the so-called 'higher committee' above mentioned (p. 148) but the context does not favour this construction; it could also have been a grouping in touch with Muhammad Neguib, nowhere suggested, but, in the context, a logical possibility; see *JJ* (24 Nov. 1954), 7, 8.

[119] *MDA* (26 Oct. 1954), 5, and Kira, *Mahkama*, i. 58–9. The visit was described by the government as part of the 'plot', designed to conceal the real intent of the Society that day. We think that this visit and that of Khalifa and the other developments noted in the paragraph in fact confirm our point that events had bypassed the leadership.

that morning, Duwayr, as part of a terrorist plot, had facilitated the departure to Alexandria of Mahmud ʿAbd al-Latif.[120]

That evening, as Nasir stood before a huge throng recalling Egypt's and his own nationalist struggle and celebrating its consummation in the evacuation agreement, he was fired at eight times. In a moment long to be remembered for its drama, the prime minister paused momentarily in his speech as the shots rang out and then resumed, almost single-handedly keeping order, as the fullest impact of the shots penetrated the crowd. Nasir's words at the moment, within hours, were broadcast and rebroadcast over the Cairo radio and transmitted to the Arab world:

> Oh ye people . . . Oh ye free men . . . I, Gamal ʿAbd al-Nasir, am of your blood and my blood is for you. I will live for your sake and I will die serving you. I will live to struggle for the sake of your freedom and your dignity. Oh ye free men . . . Oh ye men . . . Even if they kill me, I have placed in you self-respect. Let them kill me now, for I have planted in this nation freedom, self-respect, and dignity. For the sake of Egypt and for the sake of Egypt's freedom, I will live and in the service of Egypt I will die.[121]

Unharmed by the bullets, the prime minister finished and took leave of the crowd. As well as giving him one of his only reprieves up to that time in the hostile tussle which had marked his relations with the people he had tried to rule, the event provided him with the incontestable opportunity of being done with the Society of the Muslim Brothers. On the following 9 December, six men were hanged; thousands of other Brothers were already imprisoned, and the organization had been efficiently crushed. Those events will conclude this chapter.

CONFLICT: THE AFTERMATH (OCTOBER–DECEMBER 1954)

The day after the assassination attempt, 27 October, Nasir made a triumphal progress from Alexandria to Cairo. In the celebrations which followed his arrival late in the morning, mobs, composed mainly of members of the government-controlled transport unions, surged from the railway station, where they had greeted him, to the headquarters of the Muslim Brothers, shouting as they went 'death to the traitors', 'fire for the Brothers', and 'death to the

[120] *JJ* (12 Nov. 1954), 3.

[121] Of the many possible references to the event (including all of the dailies), see the convenient statement in *MMR* (5 Nov. 1954), 12–21. It was widely believed at the time that the government had staged the event in order to rid itself of the Society, a belief encouraged by its clumsy handling of the news.

Brothers of the Devil'. Once there, they completed the destruction of the Society's headquarters, which had been begun the evening before, after the identity of the perpetrators of the attempt had been broadcast. The crowds, 'stronger than the police', as the government paper put it, ransacked all the headquarters buildings and then set them on fire. Similar retribution was exacted from district headquarters throughout the country. 'The day ended and the people had its say', reported the government organ, which also carried an order forbidding further 'celebrations'.[122] On 29 October Nasir appeared at a rally held in Republic Square and launched the campaign which was to be waged during the next two months against the Brothers. Among other things, he said: 'The revolution shall not be crippled; if it is not able to proceed white, then we will make it red.'[123] On 30 October Hasan al-Hudaybi was arrested. That evening the government propaganda was began in earnest; Salah Salim, minister of national guidance, and from then on chief spokesman for the RCC, began the first barrage: 'I wish to inform the general public, bit by bit, about the great conspiracy which was uncovered following the act of aggression directed at Gamal 'Abd al-Nasir.'[124] For the next two months the pages of the daily and weekly press and magazines contained virtually nothing else.

The daily reports of arrests and confessions were accompanied by a detailed and gory elaboration by the government of 'the conspiracy'. The substance of the thousands upon thousands of words which comprised this story—which was elaborated out of the many confessions of the Brothers about what they hoped, anticipated, and dreamed as well as actually planned—was that the Society intended to come to power by means of a well conceived plan to destroy the two capitals of Alexandria and Cairo, dynamite all the bridges and factories in the country, cripple communications, and assassinate not only all the members of the army junta, but over 100 other army officers and civilians, and all the heads of the Arab governments. Besides all this material, in one way or another related to the assassination attempt, the press continued and accelerated the attack, begun in January and resumed in August, on Hudaybi, and this time on the organization. 'Evidence', sometimes old, sometimes new, was produced to show that the Brothers were the agents and lackeys of the monarchy, the old ruling classes, the British, the French, the Zionists, Western Imperialism, communism, and capitalism. Charges of a personal character were also directed at the Society

[122] *JJ* (28 Oct. 1954), 9. [123] Ibid. (30 Oct. 1954), 1, 3, 4.
[124] Kira, *Mahkama*, i. 71–4 for the speech.

in general and some of its members in particular; the old allegations of immorality against the secretary-general, ʿAbidin, were aired, and new, colourful ones ranging from homosexuality to adultery were added to his account and to that of Saʿid Ramadan, both of whom were still in Syria; other members were alleged to have kept mistresses, molested women in the street, and absconded with the money of the organization.[125] Underlying all this was the charge that the leaders of the Society were 'merchants of religion' either using their trusting followers for their own personal advantage or guiding them towards a primitive, barbaric 'religious state' which would be in alliance with the imperialists and capitalists. In this respect the religious authorities, Baquri, the former Brother and now minister of waqfs, and the highest body of Azhar shaykhs all dutifully condemned the Society for what the shaykhs called '*fitna*'.[126] The sense of tension and fear was perpetuated by continuing reports of new plots to destroy the government and the prime minister. By the end of November the government had announced the arrest of 1,000 members of the Society.[127]

On 2 November the RCC established the 'People's Tribunal' to try the members of the Society; its three officer members were Gamal Salim as president, Anwar al-Sadat and Husayn al-Shafʿi as his assistants. Most of the important personalities in the Society had been arrested in the first few weeks after the attempted killing: on 27 October Hindawi Duwayr gave himself up; Hudaybi was brought in on the 30th (it is not clear whether he yielded to the authorities); on 11 November Humayda was arrested for complicity with the secret apparatus;[128] Ibrahim al-Tayyib was arrested on the 12th, and Yusuf Talʿat, the head of the secret apparatus, on the 14th. When the latter was brought in the Egyptian stock market, which was reported to have collapsed after the

[125] Much of the bitterness of the RCC towards Ramadan and ʿAbidin derived from the feeling that these two men were behind the hostile press of Syria where they had lived since they were deprived of Egyptian nationality (see above, p. 141). For a note on the crisis between the two governments, see *MAS* (7 Nov. 1954), 8–9. *JAY* (13 Nov. 1954), 1, reported the recall of the Egyptian ambassador to Syria ʿAli Najib; the recall recorded the fact of crisis between the two governments and also—since the ambassador was the brother of Muhammad Neguib—foreshadowed more trouble for the president.

[126] *MTR* (23 Nov. 1954), 7. The term signifies 'sedition' or 'insurrection' which is caused by factionalism.

[127] 'Chronology', *MEA* (Dec. 1954), 406.

[128] Humayda was not expecting arrest because of his role as 'neutral', and was angered when told that Hudaybi had informed the authorities, quite correctly, that he had been delegated to deal with the secret apparatus. He told reporters: 'So long as the question has reached this stage, I am prepared to speak, and when I do, I will be speaking for history'; see *JA* (12 Nov. 1954), 1, 11. Humayda's testimony at the trials was not the history he predicted but he did say much of importance for the reconstruction of events.

assassination attempt, rallied.[129] All the other members of the Guidance Council and the leading partisans of Hudaybi had been arrested by that time; only three of those regarded as having taken a leading part in the affair are to this day at large—Hasan al-ʿAshmawi, ʿAbd al-Munʿim ʿAbd al-Ra'uf, and Abu al-Makarim ʿAbd al-Hayy.

The trials began on 9 November and the first case was that of the would-be assassin, Mahmud ʿAbd al-Latif. Three of the most prominent lawyers in Egypt—Mahmud Sulayman Ghannam, Fathi Salama, and Makram ʿUbayd—were asked to defend him, but refused, because they regarded such a 'criminal' as unworthy of being defended. The court appointed a lawyer, Hamada al-Nahil, whose only other experience with the Brothers had been to defend Banna's assassins. The accused pleaded guilty to the charges that he had committed 'acts against the present form of government' by joining in 'a criminal conspiracy' to cause insurrection and revolution, and by attempting to kill the prime minister. Before his trial ended on 20 November, nineteen witnesses, all Brothers, were called. Hudaybi was called to trial on 22 November, and then in rapid succession, Hindawi Duwayr, Ibrahim al-Tayyib, Yusuf Talʿat, and the members of the Guidance Council, bringing the date to 3 December.[130]

Very early in the proceedings the mention of Muhammad Neguib's name led to his dismissal as president of the republic and confinement to his home. His fall was foreshadowed in the recall, on that same day, of his brother, ʿAli, Ambassador to Syria, ostensibly for consultations on the state of the disintegrating relations between Egypt and that country.[131] Neguib's name, along with those of Muhammad Hasan al-ʿAshmawi, former minister of education (who was arrested) and ʿAbd al-Rahman ʿAzzam, former head of the Arab League (who was not) had been mentioned, it will be recalled, in the context of the plan for a popular demonstration discussed among some of the Brothers, who also felt that a national figure was needed to restore order to the country. When the trial ended there was no substantial evidence that any of them had been consciously involved in any part of the assassination attempt, or even for that matter aware of the role for which some

[129] See *JJ* (16 Nov. 1954), 1, 12; and *MAS* (24 Dec. 1954), 40–1.

[130] The dailies carried full accounts of the trials, but for a convenient—if edited—summary see, for the trial of ʿAbd al-Latif, Kira, *Mahkama*, i. 75–220; and for those of the remainder of the accused, ibid. ii. 39–180. The verbatim texts of the trial without editorial comment also appeared in another series entitled *Mahkamat al-Shaʿb* (Cairo, 1955), but remained incomplete in five volumes.

[131] See *JJ* (15 Nov. 1954), 1; (13 Nov. 1954), 1.

of the Brothers had cast them.[132] There is sufficient evidence that some contact existed between Neguib and the Brothers, but it is not clear what form this took or how deeply he was involved. The testimony of the Brothers was neither positive nor lucid in this respect—suggesting the absence of real planning—and Neguib was not brought to trial.[133] In his case, at least, it would appear that Nasir chose the moment of his great personal prestige to settle his unresolved conflict with the popular president once and for all. Although there were no popular repercussions to Neguib's removal, one observer quite properly noted that after he became implicated in the trials of the Brothers, an almost completely black and white situation dissolved into multiple shades of grey.

The trial itself was a memorable exhibition of the rights revolutionary governments have and take as regards the due process of law. From the very beginning it was clear that the last thing the government intended was to clarify the case and assess individual guilt. In those cases where the defence was appointed by the court, the lawyers asked questions and made comments which would have been better left to the prosecution. The chief 'judge'—Gamal Salim—conducted himself rather as chief prosecutor: he freely interrupted the answers of the witnesses if the answer displeased him; he put words into their mouths and forced—sometimes by threats—the desired answers. His questions were phrased to preclude any answer but that sought by the court; any attempt to attach niceties was halted. Sometimes he engaged in an exchange of petty insults with the witnesses; in most cases the insults came from the court alone. The court freely set one witness against the other, fabricating the testimony of one to incite another. The audience was allowed, even encouraged, to participate in laughter and ridicule and to jeer at and insult the witnesses. Most of the questioning, in this regard, was irrelevant to the crime, and included, *inter alia*, grammatical and exegetical-Qur'anic examinations intended to embarrass the witnesses.

The witnesses themselves were confused, obviously frightened, and, in most cases, not candid. The evidence was full of contradictions. This was due partly to the court's handling of witnesses, partly to the witnesses' own unwillingness to speak out. It also,

[132] See *MTR* (3 Nov. 1954), 7, for 'Azzam's denial.

[133] The failure to try Neguib was reported to be related to a visit from an indignant—and some say threatening—delegation from the Sudan; for reports on the visit and the innocuous pronouncements, see *JJ* (22 Nov. 1954), 1. The public evidence against Neguib was confined to the pamphlet which appeared under his name criticizing the treaty in August (see above, p. 137), and which had passed through the office of 'Awda; the latter's presence on the balcony of Republic Palace in February (see above, pp. 129–30) added fuel to the government case.

however, reflected the position of each witness in the Society, and thus the different levels and perspectives from which the issues at stake were viewed. The remarkable ease with which loyalties were broken and members pointed accusing fingers at each other showed how far mutual trust had been shaken. The same thing had happened in the preliminary investigations, out of which came most of the 'confessions'. The speedy collapse of the organizational fabric was partly due to torture in the prisons.[134] More important, however, was the breakdown of morale. The new secret apparatus was not old enough to have developed confidence in itself or its members, or, above all, in its leaders. In the latter case, although there was an officially recognized hierarchy, there was not, in practice, a clear and indisputable line of authority. The general organization was so deeply split by its own internecine battles that it was relatively easy to cleave it further by giving full publicity to the 'confessions' and 'betrayals'—sometimes real, sometimes fabricated—of the various members.[135] It was significant that after the papers carried accounts of the alleged 'betrayal' of Hudaybi's hiding-place, the remnant of the secret apparatus still operating sent out a pamphlet denying the allegation and affirming the continued co-operation and loyalty of members.[136] The press dramatized the point by observing that, at the trial, Yusuf Talʿat was the only man who could look Hasan al-Hudaybi in the face.[137]

The press gave complete coverage to the trial proceedings—except for some of the grosser comments of the court—accompanying the text of the testimony with vivid interpretations which did not always, or often, correspond to the information available. Separating the facts from the editorials in the news columns re-

[134] So telling were the rumours of torture in the prisons that the government published an official denial in a friendly journal, *MAS* (15 Dec. 1954), 3–6. The press was encouraged to help in disabusing the populace of the notion of torture by printing pictures about, and reporting on, the good conditions of the prisons and their inmates. See *MMR* (26 Nov. 1954), 20–1; (3 Dec. 1954), 11–15, which showed pictures of prisoners drinking tea and strolling about in the gardens; one picture showed the would-be assassin sunning himself and dangling his hand in a lily pond! Discounting the more gory of the tales told there seems to be little doubt that violence was used to extract information. The public attitude was best illustrated by a story circulating at the time: Nasir missed his fountain pen and reported the loss to the minister of the interior. In a short while the pen was found only to have been mislaid and Nasir called to report again to the minister of the interior. Incredulously, the minister replied, 'How could that be. I have already arrested a number of Brothers who have confessed to stealing your pen.'

[135] The government and the press (especially in cartoons) made much of this point; see e.g. *MRY* (15 Nov. 1954), 3; and *MJJ* (29 Nov. 1954), 4–7.

[136] See *MMR* (26 Nov. 1954), 22.

[137] *MJJ* (29 Nov. 1954), 4–7. Talʿat's testimony alone, probably, made it impossible for the government to maintain its case against Hudaybi.

porting the trials was, however, not impossible because most of the testimony was available. We have used it heavily to recreate our version of events. Given this testimony and assuming that the government, at the trials, at the previous investigations, and in the press, released all the data it possessed on the activity of the Brothers, it is possible to make some summary observations about the government's case and what actually happened.

The theme of the prosecution was simple: the assassination of the prime minister was to be the signal for a 'bloody insurrection' designed to overthrow the régime, and Hudaybi and his 'gang' were responsible for deliberately and consciously planning this. We have already seen that this was not precisely the case. The assassination attempt occurred, it would seem, as the result of inaction rather than action by the leadership of the Society. Any direct or actual relationship between it and an insurrection, or even the vague plans for a 'popular demonstration', remained unproved; it remained just as unproved that the demonstration had ever got beyond the talking stage, and it was not even clear who had been involved in the talking. The lack of planning was typified by the testimony of the head of the secret apparatus, which showed a curious ignorance of—and even indifference to—such matters as disposition of arms and questions of organizational strength and distribution. Tal'at's report to Hudaybi in the first week of October about confusion and despair in the ranks was further evidence of this.

On the whole, again assuming that everything that could be construed as damaging was made public, the Muslim Brothers would seem to have been far from fit to do battle with the government. They would probably only have risen, quite spontaneously, to support a hoped for and anticipated move from the army. It is worth recalling that Nasir and his regime had little or no support at this time. If he had fallen under the spray of bullets directed at him and the regime had subsequently fallen apart as was anticipated, the would-be assassin, who was hanged because he failed, might well have become a national hero.

The second count in the indictment, the responsibility of Hudaybi and his 'gang', was even more untenable on the evidence available. The attempt was a matter of individual or group initiative inside the secret apparatus, without the knowledge of other members, or, it would appear of its own leader, and certainly of few, if any, persons outside it. None of the witnesses except 'Abd al-Latif, the gunman, Duwayr, his superior, and Tayyib, the head of the Cairo group, had any direct light at all to shed on the attempt. The others who might have given useful information, Hasan al-'Ashmawi and 'Abd al-Ra'uf, were at large. Who actually gave the order was never clarified by the court or the witnesses; the accused confessed to having been told that 'the leadership' had made the decision to kill Nasir, but could not trace the decision back beyond their immediate superiors. Tayyib, in conveying the order to Duwayr, hinted at the concurrence of Hudaybi which he could not have had—the evidence at the trial was convincing that Hudaybi, as we have seen, was innocent of the order to kill and that he resisted such a solution of the problem. Tayyib and 'Abd al-Ra'uf had worked together to the exclusion of the official head of the secret organization, Tal'at, who also seemed to be ignorant of the actual plan of assassination. The most probable solution is that 'Abd al-Ra'uf was the chief planner of the affair, acting on his own initiative with possible—though unproved—concurrence from Shaykh Muhammad Farghali, 'adviser' to the secret apparatus on 'the higher committee' and member of the Guidance Council, and with help from Tayyib who, as head of the Cairo section, ranked high enough to relay an order from 'the leadership' to Duwayr and 'Abd al-Latif without having it seriously challenged.

The evidence not only accumulated against the possibility of an official order to kill, but also pointed to a situation in which the leadership of both the open and secret organizations was no longer in control. Tal'at recorded this fact for the secret group in reporting the contention about courses of action with Tayyib and 'Abd al-Ra'uf, their disregard of his opinions and their apparent exclusion of him from their plans. Tal'at added virtually no information of relevance to the data about the assassination, in a testimony otherwise remarkably frank and direct, because, apparently, he could not. It was Tayyib, at another point, who offered to procure arms for 'Abd al-Ra'uf, not Tal'at, who knew little if anything about any disposition of arms.

In the open section of the Society, the confusion was even more rampant. Hudaybi, in hiding, was only briefly in touch with the actual state of affairs, having delegated his authority in both groups to trusted followers. In turn, they and the other levels of leadership, friend and foe of Hudaybi alike, experienced, as the months passed, accumulated frustrations in the relations between themselves and with the membership. Through July, August, and September, as the crisis in the Consultative Assembly deepened and its cleavages became more apparent, and as the urgency of the struggle compelled the declaration of loyalties, its members met in groups to discuss the issue of the virtual transfer of authority and focus of power to the unknown and uncontrollable secret apparatus.[138] In the Guidance Council, those in disagreement with the policy of Hudaybi's partisans expressed more and more concern over the loss of that body's power and the frustration of its will. In July, with the appearance of the pamphlet, *al-Ikhwan fi'l-Ma'raka*, one of the oldest members of the Society on the Council, 'Abd al-Mu'izz 'Abd al-Sattar, resigned from the Society and agreed to return only after an order was dispatched to all branches to the effect that, henceforth, directives to the membership were to be considered valid only if issued from the offices of the Council.[139] Similarly, 'Abd al-Rahman al-Banna, another member of the Council, afterwards reported that in its last few months it had abdicated its responsibility for the course of policy and the Society's affairs.[140]

We have already seen that, on the occasion of the signing of the treaty with Britain on 19 October, another member of the Council, Kamal Khalifa, visited the deputy prime minister to convey his congratulations; that on 24 October the Council sent an emissary to the government with yet another peace overture; and that on 26 October, the day of the attempted assassination, Duwayr was visited by one of the leaders of the Society but did not inform him of the plan, already set in motion. Both partisan and enemy of Hudaybi, on the top levels, were unaware of what was to take place. They were significantly and effectively out of touch with, and control of, the membership.

The firmest testimony to the paralysis and breakdown of the formal structure of the organization came from its own members. The perplexity and ambiguity which followed Hudaybi's disappearance, and which were generated by imprecise and deliberately misleading governmental reporting of the course of the struggle between the two factions in the organization, were aggravated by the fact that, from August to October, communication in the Society on all levels was confined almost exclusively to secret pamphlets and word of mouth. The pamphlets, with few exceptions, were primarily concerned with the dispute with the government and with the general bolstering of morale. Verbal communication was complicated by scepticism and exaggeration, a function of both the highly charged situation and the aura of mistrust which had begun to sap the basic strength of the Society—mutual confidence. The trial testimony as a whole was a vivid demonstration of the variety of rumours and beliefs in both the secret and open organization concerning what this or that person among the leaders said, believed, did, or wanted.

[138] See Kira, *Mahkama*, ii. 23–6; and Appendix A of the original version of this study. [139] *JJ* (23 Nov. 1954), 4. [140] Ibid. (19 Nov. 1954), 8.

It was this widespread perplexity that took Tal'at to Hudaybi's hideaway in Alexandria in October to plead with the leader to appear publicly, in order to dispel the aura of confusion which had settled in the minds of the members. The failure to do this, in combination with all the other elements of uncertainty in the chain of authority, gave those with the will to act, the opportunity to do so. The dislocation of the Society at membership level was most dramatically pictured by one of the participants in the assassination attempt. After describing the divisions in the organization and the attempted reform of the Consultative Assembly so that it would come more truly to 'represent the Brothers', Hindawi Duwayr told of how it had 'lost the respect of the members', how it and the high command had 'lost power to direct'. In the circumstances the secret apparatus became the real focus of activity: 'Except for the secret apparatus, we found that the administrative apparatus of the Society was crippled.' Viewing the problem from the other side, the deputy, Humayda, conceded contritely that 'the leadership had failed to control the [secret] apparatus'.[141] It was an appropriately simple summing-up of the problem which had again brought the Society of the Muslim Brothers to its ruin.

On 4 December, the first judgments of the People's Tribunal were pronounced against those involved in the attempted killing and the hierarchies of both the secret and the open organization. Seven members of the Guidance Council, all advisers of Hudaybi, received life imprisonment with hard labour: they were Kamal Khalifa, Muhammad Khamis Humayda, Ahmad 'Abd al-'Aziz 'Atiyya, Husayn Kamal al-Din, Munir al-Dilla, Hamid abu al-Nasr, and Salih abu Ruqayq. Two members of the Council were sentenced to fifteen years in prison: they were 'Umar al-Talmasani and Ahmad Shurayt. Three members of the Council, all friends of the government, were acquitted: 'Abd al-Rahman al-Banna, 'Abd al-Mu'izz 'Abd al-Sattar, and al-Bahi al-Khuli. Seven members of the Society were sentenced to death by hanging: Hasan al-Hudaybi, Mahmud 'Abd al-Latif, Hindawi Duwayr, Ibrahim al-Tayyib, Yusuf Tal'at, Shaykh Muhammad Farghali, and 'Abd al-Qadir 'Awda. The death sentence for Hudaybi was commuted to life imprisonment with hard labour by the RCC on the grounds that 'perhaps he had fallen under the influence of those around him, a view supported by his bad health and age'.[142]

141 *JJ* (12 Nov. 1954), 5, (17 Nov. 1954), 3.
142 Ibid. (5 Dec. 1954), 1, 3; and *MAS* (8 Dec. 1954), 3–6, for pictures of the accused hearing their sentences.

A plea by ʿAwda that his case might be reviewed went unanswered by the government.

On 9 December despite protests from the Arab world (and in the face of considerable incredulity in Egypt), the sentences were carried out. A number of observers at the hangings recorded the last words of the accused: ʿAbd al-Latif and Duwayr repeated Qur'anic verses and showed, it was said, considerable fear; Tayyib angrily observed, 'The trial was a comedy; our enemies were our judges'; Talʿat calmly pleaded for the forgiveness of Shaykh Farghali, for whose betrayal he felt responsible, and added 'May God forgive me, as well as those who have done harm to me'. Farghali, apparently at peace with himself, merely noted, 'I am ready to die; I welcome the meeting with God'; ʿAwda ended his life with a flourish, saying 'Praise be to God that He has made me a martyr and may He make my blood a curse upon the men of the revolution'.[143]

The news of the hangings was greeted, in Egypt, in stunned and horrified silence; the government had taken the precaution of reinforcing the military patrols and garrisons around the city. Abroad, there were demonstrations of protest in Jordan, Syria, and Pakistan.[144] In Damascus, Mustafa al-Sibaʿi, leader of the Brothers there, after prayers for the dead asked for and received from his audience a pledge 'to revenge the martyrs'. Again, relations between Egypt and Syria reached a breaking-point.[145]

Events after the hangings were anti-climactic. The work of the Revolutionary Tribunal was delegated to three branches with lesser officers in charge. When the court closed its doors early in February, about 1,000 Brothers had been tried. In all, fifteen were sentenced to death, but all except the first six sentences were commuted. Over half of those tried were acquitted or received suspended sentences. Most of the Consultative Assembly were formally brought before the court but were either acquitted or given suspended sentences. For months, unnumbered Brothers, not brought before the courts or already tried and acquitted, remained in the prisons. It is worthy of note that, of all the

[143] For pictures and similar versions of the last words, see *Paris Match* (18–25 Dec. 1954), 62–5. This issue was collected from the streets by the government.

[144] See *NYT* (6 Dec. 1954), 14; (9 Dec. 1954), 5; and 'Notes of the Quarter', *MW* (Apr. 1955), 206.

[145] See esp. *MAS* (15 Dec. 1954), 5–6. The feeling was strong that because Faris al-Khuri was at the head of the Syrian government, it was not possible to move against the Brothers. The publication *Irhab*, already noted numerous times, was intended to impress Egypt's Arab neighbours with the justice of the action that had been taken. Syrian behaviour was resented as an unwarranted 'interference in the internal affairs of Egypt'.

Brothers tried, only twenty-nine were from the armed forces, and these mostly from the line. The relatively light sentences most of them received, and the fact that they were tried in the secondary courts, suggested, in the semantics of the situation, that their major crime was merely that of combining membership in the Society with service to the state; the outcome for them was all the more remarkable, since the existence of 'cells' plotting subversion in the armed forces had been one of the government's major subjects of dispute with Hudaybi, who had consistently denied their existence. Of a different order were the sentences meted out to the two officers who still remain hidden from the law: both Abu al-Makarim ʿAbd al-Hayy and ʿAbd al-Munʿim ʿAbd al-Ra'uf were sentenced *in absentia* to death by firing squad.[146]

[146] The military personnel were tried, beginning on 13 December, and their cases were before the courts intermittently until 3 January 1955: for the sentencing, see *JJ* (19 Jan. 1955), 7–8; (20 Jan. 1955), 7; and (9 Feb. 1955), 3.

PART II · ORGANIZATION

VI

STRUCTURE AND ADMINISTRATION

THE first regulations to govern the operation of the Society came into existence, according to Banna, around 1930–1.[1] On 8 September 1945 a revised code, proposed by Banna, was adopted under the title 'The Fundamental Law of the Organization of the Muslim Brothers' (*Qanun al-nizam al-asasi li-hay'at al-Ikhwan al-Muslimin al-'Amma*).[2] Within three years Banna, 'in the light of the experience of the past years', recommended a series of amendments which were drafted in the form of proposals by a special committee and adopted unanimously, after a first and a second 'reading', by the Consultative Assembly on 21 May 1948. Finally, following the appointment as leader of Hasan al-Hudaybi, the Guidance Council—acting under the authority of Article 32 of the basic statute, which empowered it to create the necessary apparatus for 'realizing the goals of the Society', and Article 62 which allowed existing Ordinances to be reviewed and modified—adopted a new series of 'General Internal Regulations' (*al-La'iha al-dakhiliyya al-'Amma*), which elaborated the earlier code.[3] These two sets of ordinances constitute the primary sources for the Society's organizational structure and its 'administrative and technical operations. The charts on pp. 164 and 177 summarize its structure on first the administrative and then the technical side.

[1] *Mudh.*, p. 148.

[2] We were unable to locate a copy of the earlier code. Rosenthal, 'Muslim Brethren', 278, refers to a code the fourth edition of which was published in 1942.

[3] Cf. Harris, *Nationalism and Revolution*, pp. 188–9, for a description of the organization after 1951, based on 'a confidential source', whose emphasis is the opposite of ours. *QA*, pp. 3–4; and *LD*, p. 2. We will henceforth insert a parenthetical reference in the text where strict summaries or quotations from either of the laws are used. *QA* will refer to the *Qanun al-Asasi* and *LD* to the *La'ihat al-dakhiliyya*; the number immediately following the letter will refer to the number of the article of the law, and the number following the colon to the page of the text. Thus *QA* 9: 11–12 refers to Art. 9, pp. 11–12 of the *Qanun al-Asasi.*

General Table of Organization

(Based on diagram in Zaki, *Ikhwan*, p. 99)

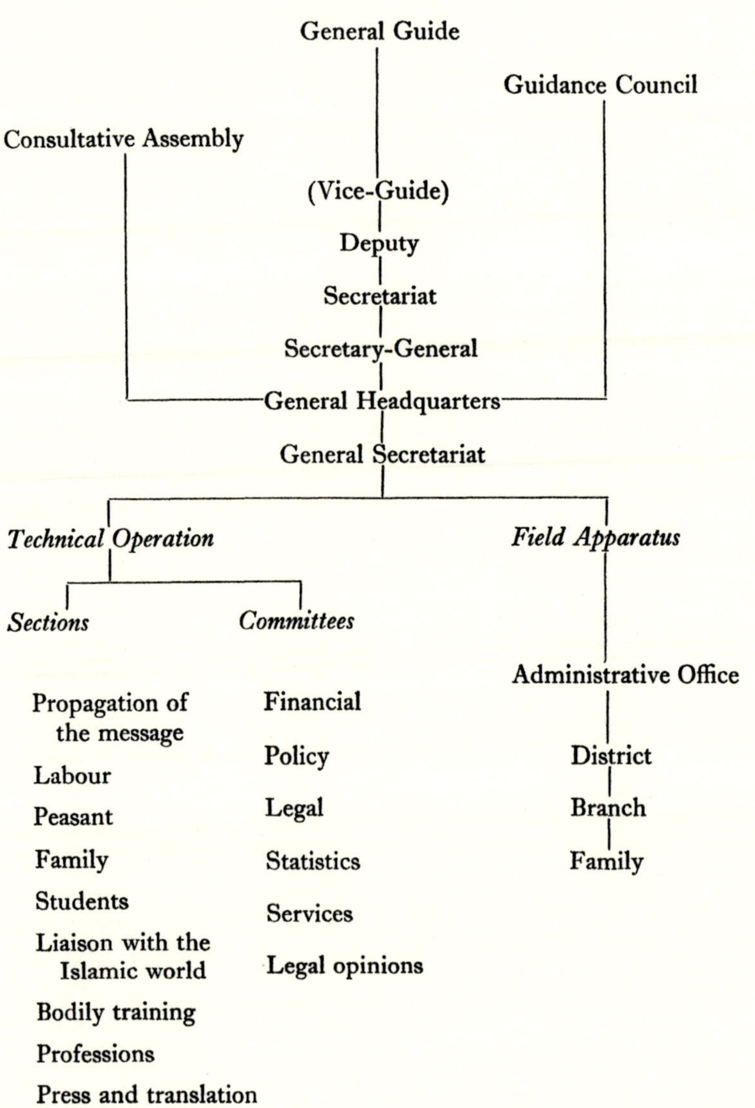

HIERARCHY

The foremost position in the Society was that of the General Guide (*al-murshid al-'amm*), who was both head of the Society and chairman of its two major governing bodies, the General Guidance Council (*maktab al-irshad al-'amm*) and the Consultative Assembly (*al-hay'at al-ta'sisiyya*; literally, the Founding Assembly). The Guidance Council was stated to be 'the highest administrative unit' of the Society 'governing policy and administration'. The Consultative Assembly was described as 'the general consultative council' (*majlis al-shura al-'amm*) of the Society and 'the general assembly' (*al-jam'iyat al-'umumiyya*) of the Guidance Council (*QA* 9: 11–12).

General Guide

The qualifications of a candidate for this post were described as follows: a member of the Consultative Assembly for five years; at least thirty lunar years of age; 'possessing the attributes of learning, morality, and practicality'. He was to be elected from among the Assembly at a meeting attended by no less than four-fifths of its members with three-quarters of those in attendance approving. If there was no quorum present, the meeting was postponed to a date not less than two weeks, not more than four, from that of the the original meeting. If again there was no quorum, then another meeting would be called within the same time limits, accompanied this time by declaration of the intention of the meeting to proceed to the election, by a vote of three-quarters of those present.

The new Guide, after the election, would take the oath to be 'a faithful guardian over the principles of the Muslim Brothers, their Fundamental Law', and to pursue the Society's interests 'according to the Book and the *Sunna*' and with the advice and opinions of those around him (*QA* 10–12: 12–14). The Consultative Assembly would take the oath of loyalty (*bay'a*) to the new Guide, and all the members of the Society would do so, both through their superior officers and at their first meeting with the new leader. The oath of loyalty read as follows:

> I contract with God . . . to adhere firmly to the message of the Muslim Brothers, to strive on its behalf, to live up to the conditions of its membership, to have complete confidence in its leadership and to obey absolutely, under all circumstances (*fi 'l-manshat wa 'l-makra*). I swear by God on that and make my oath of loyalty by Him. Of what I say, God is Witness (*QA* 4: 9).

The General Guide was required to devote all his time to the organization, especially avoiding participation, 'either personally or in his capacity as Guide', in any economic or financial venture, even one connected with the Society. With the agreement of the Guidance Council, he might pursue 'literary and educational activity'. He would be supported by the General Headquarters if he had no other income. A committee to be established from the Consultative Assembly immediately after the elections would attend to this matter.

The Guide was required to resign if he abused the duties of his office or 'lost the qualifications'. The Consultative Assembly might remove him at any meeting attended by four-fifths of its members, three-quarters of whom must agree to the action. The provisions outlined for a quorum at the time of an election would apply to the procedure for removal. The term of office was for life; in case of death or incapacity the deputy would assume authority until the Consultative Assembly could be convened, which must be done within a month (*QA* 10–18: 12–16).

General Guidance Council

The Guidance Council was legally composed of 12 members, 9 from Cairo and 3 from the provinces (*QA* 19: 16). In fact the Council, until the time of *l'affaire* 'Abidin in 1946–7, had 20 members; at that time Banna, to facilitate his official handling of the matter, reduced the number to 12, in accordance with the constitution.[4] Sometime after 1951 the number was increased to 15 members, the extra 3 to be appointed by the Council itself from the Consultative Assembly.

Candidates for the Council had to be at least thirty lunar years of age, members of the Consultative Assembly for at least three years, and endowed with 'moral, learned, and practical' qualities. Election was by secret ballot from among the entire membership of the Consultative Assembly. Votes were counted by a committee formed from among the membership of the Assembly, with preference for those who might have withdrawn their names from nomination for the Council. After the newly elected councillors had sworn to uphold 'the principles of the Muslim Brothers and the Fundamental Laws' and to fulfil the functions of the office to which they had been elected, the Assembly, in a secret ballot supervised by the vote-counting committee, would select from among the nine Cairo members of the Guidance Council a deputy, the secretary-general, and the treasurer.

Councillors held office for two years and were re-eligible. If a post was vacated, for whatever reason, it was filled by the recipient

[4] *JJ* (23 Sept. 1954), 8.

of the next largest vote in the preceding election. In the operation of the Council, a majority decision was binding on each member; a member was deprived of the right 'to criticize or oppose' once the decision took a 'legal form'. An issue to which he had taken exception might be raised again after three months, or earlier if the circumstances so changed as to justify a new debate. The member, in his actions, was responsible to his fellow councillors. For a misdemeanour he might be advised, warned, fined, suspended for one month, or expelled from the Council. An expulsion had to issue from a majority of three-quarters of those present at a meeting at which the accused had a right to be heard.

The Council presided over the operation of the Society, supervised its administration, shaped and executed its policy. It met periodically and at the discretion of the members. Extraordinary meetings might be called at the request of the General Guide, his representatives, or one-third of the members. A legal meeting was one attended by an absolute majority. Those officially excused from the meeting were counted for a quorum but not for a vote. A meeting postponed for lack of a quorum was constitutional when re-convened whatever the number present. An absolute majority at such a meeting could carry a decision. The General Guide would cast the deciding vote in the event of a tie. Meetings of the Council would be chaired by the General Guide, by the deputy in his absence, or by the 'oldest member' in the absence of the other two. The Council was authorized to create whatever committees, sections, and divisions were necessary to fulfil the goals of the organization (*QA* 19–26: 16–19; 30–2: 20–1; *LD* 31–2: 12–13; 37–50: 17–20).

Secretary-general

The secretary-general, elected by the Consultative Assembly from among the Guidance Council members, was the chief representative of the Guidance Council and the general headquarters (*al-markaz al-ʿamm*) in all 'official, legal, and administrative operations', with the exception of those functions delegated to others by special act of the Council. His tasks were to execute the decrees of the Guidance Council, supervise and direct the entire administrative apparatus of the organization, call meetings and prepare the agenda for them, and control and file the Council records. He was the major link between the Council and all other units of the Society. He chose his own staff, but they were appointed by the Council. He was 'personally responsible' for their work (*QA* 27–8: 19–20; *LD* 33–6: 13–15). This 'general secretariat' was distinct from, and apparently responsible to, the 'secretariat of the General Guide', which was responsible to the leader alone.

Treasurer

The treasurer was responsible for the financial operation of the Society as a whole and for the specific expenditure of the Guidance Council. He was required to submit a monthly report, supported by documents and records, of income and expenditure (*QA* 29: 20; *LD* 37: 16–17).

Consultative Assembly

Membership varied between 100 and 150; in the last years of the Assembly it reached 147.[5] Qualifications for membership included: active membership in the Society; at least twenty-five lunar years of age; at least five years of association with the Society; endowment with 'morality, culture, and practicality'. Each year no more than ten new members were to be admitted as replacement for ten seats annually vacated by expiration of term. Membership was to be related to 'regional representativeness'.[6] The duties of the Assembly included the 'general supervision' of the progress of the Society, and the election of the Guidance Council and of an auditor (*muraji'*). The Assembly was considered to be 'the general consultative council' of the Society, and the 'general assembly' of the Guidance Council.

The annual meeting of the Assembly was to be held during the first month of each Hijra year; its agenda would include: the Guidance Council's report on activity for the coming year; the auditor's report for the past year; the budget for the coming year; and the election of members for seats vacated by the expiration of terms. Extraordinary meetings might be called by the General Guide or the Guidance Council, or at the request of twenty members of the Assembly. The General Guide would chair the meetings; in his absence, or in matters affecting him personally, his deputy would do so (or, in the latter's absence, the 'oldest' member). An absolute majority constituted a quorum, except in cases where special numbers were prescribed. Absence of a quorum required the postponement of the meeting until a well-advertised date two weeks later; that meeting would be constitutional whatever the number present, and its decisions would be binding on a vote of an absolute majority of those present.

A committee of seven, preferably non-Cairenes, with training in legal and canonical doctrine, was to be elected by the Assembly

[5] See *JJ* (17 Nov. 1954), 4. [6] Ibid.

to supervise members' 'behaviour' and to mete out appropriate penalties. Its decisions had to be approved by the General Guide. The committee elected its own chairman and secretary and kept its own records; its meetings were constitutional with five members present including the chairman; its decisions were binding with an absolute majority. Members of the committee might hold office more than once. A decision by the committee to dismiss a member might be appealed from in a written request to the Guidance Council, which would then submit the matter to the Assembly as a whole at its next meeting. The decision of the Assembly was final. The members of the Guidance Council were exempt from the workings of the committee because of their own disciplinary procedures. The General Guide might, on his own authority, suspend any member, on condition that his order was submitted to the committee of the Assembly for review (*QA* 33–9: 22–6).

GENERAL HEADQUARTERS

These three components of the central leadership—the General Guide, the Guidance Council, and the Consultative Assembly—met and performed their various functions in the general headquarters located in Cairo, in the quarter known as Hilmiyya al-Jadida, which was also the base for 'technical' operations and the field apparatus. The leading figure at the headquarters was the secretary-general, and both his secretariat and that of the General Guide were defined as 'the officials of the general headquarters'. Other officials, in order of importance, included the supervisor (*muraqib*) and his staff, also storekeepers, library and bookshop staff, sweepers, and messengers.[7]

The headquarters building, formerly a large private house, was divided up into offices and committee rooms. While a permanent staff maintained a full day schedule, most of the work was done in the late afternoon and early evening after the completion of the outside working day for most of the members and leaders. Besides the reception rooms, the headquarters also housed a small and unpretentious mosque in one of its wings, and a library. The mosque seemed to be almost a token gesture, although it was well used, since the Brothers prayed at the prescribed time (and often at other times) wherever in the building and in its grounds they happened to be. The library was a gift of the Arabic books of Prince Muhammad 'Ali of the former ruling family, supplemented by other gifts from private collections. In 1948 it was confiscated

[7] See the charts in Zaki, *Ikhwan*, pp. 99, 101.

by the government, which after burning all the literature by the Brothers, made known plans to distribute it to other Egyptian libraries. It was finally decided, however, to present the collection to an Islamic group in Cairo called the Society for Islamic Education (*jamaʿat al-tarbiyya al-islamiyya*). The group paid the government for the bookcases. With the return to legality in 1951 the Brothers asked for and obtained the return of the collection and reimbursed the Society for Islamic Education for what it had spent on the bookcases.[8] The Library, which claimed to have 2,500 volumes covering all aspects of Islamic studies, literature, grammar, and national history,[9] was presumably destroyed in October 1954, when the mob burnt the headquarters.

TECHNICAL OPERATIONS

The Society's technical operations had two aspects. First, concerned with the administrative machinery of the movement, there were six committees (*lijan*), directly responsible to the Guidance Council: financial; policy; legal; statistics; services; and legal opinions. Secondly, there were ten sections (*aqsam*) concerned with ideology or indoctrination: propagation of the message (*nashr al-daʿwa*); labour; peasants; family (*usraʿ*); students; liaison with the Islamic world; bodily training (*al-tarbiyya al-badaniyya*); professions; press and translation; and the Muslim Sisters. Following the reorganization of 1951 the labour and peasant sections were combined, and press and translation was made a committee instead of a section.[10] The regulations provided that these committees and sections might be 'permanent' or 'temporary', that they were subordinate to the Guidance Council, and that they should be located in the general headquarters. Their activity and decisions, after authorization by the General Guide or Guidance Council, were relayed to the branches through the secretary-general. The role of both committees and sections was primarily 'advisory and investigative'. The head of each group was named by the Guidance Council; his assistants were appointed by the General Guide, on the recommendation of the new appointee (*LD* 53–6: 21).[11]

Committees

The six committees in the headquarters may be dealt with briefly. The financial committee was, in effect, an arm of the

[8] *MDA* (3 June 1952), 8–9, 14.

[9] Zaki, *Ikhwan*, p. 145.

[10] Missing from the organizational framework (*LD* 57: 21–2) was the rovers section, a matter of some import (see below, pp. 200–5).

[11] Zaki, *Ikhwan*, p. 108.

treasurer. The legal committee was charged with defending the Brothers in any court proceedings and in filing the records of these. It could not act without permission of the Guidance Council. The policy committee studied the 'general and particular political currents, internally and externally' with a view to 'defining the attitude of the Brothers towards them'. The services committee was concerned with the 'needs' of the Brothers and their satisfaction. Its vaguely worded terms of reference suggested material or financial aid. The legal-opinions (*fatwa*) committee made known the Islamic position on matters of interest to the Brothers. The statistics committee kept the records of the Brothers' activity and submitted quarterly reports to the high command. The press and translation committee concerned itself with (1) the publication of the Brothers' newspapers and magazines; (2) the collection and filing of all material in all languages which related to the Brothers; and (3) the translation of all materials necessary for 'the interests of the message' from and into Arabic (*LD* 77: 31, 82–5: 32–5).[12]

Sections

More important than the committees in the actual operation of the Society were the sections, because these were so intimately and directly involved in the orientation and training of members. The chairmanships of most of the sections were prizes which carried with them the possibility of real power within the structure, both because of the direct concern of the section with membership blocs and because of the resulting opportunity to share in policy making and in the informal distribution of power.[13] The sections functioned as follows:

Propagation of the Message. The function of this section was stated to be the organization of the propaganda of the idea of the Brothers by all means compatible with 'the spirit of Islam'. This meant: (1) 'missionaries' (*du'at*) for speeches and lectures, who were particularly well trained for 'public meetings' (i.e. outside the Society); (2) publications of a 'scientific, cultural, and athletic' nature, none of which might be issued by any individual Brother without the authorization of the section; (3) guidance—

[12] After 1950 the Society became more sensitive to the need for trained linguists and duly began a programme to tap the talents of the membership; see *Ila al-Ikhwan*, no. 9 (n.d.), 4–5.

[13] The case of the secret apparatus was only the most striking of the examples of this point. Much of the anxiety of the older members in the last years of the Society's existence was due to the control of the student groups by pro-Hudaybi people. In another sense, because of its all-important control over the instruments of communications, the section for the propagation of the message was much sought after; again, its control by partisans of Hudaybi after 1951 became a continuing source of friction.

spiritual, mental, and physical—of each Brother towards an 'Islamic preparation' by means of lectures, publications, and organized athletic activity. The section was responsible for supplying the branches with speakers and lecturers. It was also to provide every provincial division with a unified schedule of study for the missionary school which each of them was to maintain, the successful graduates of which would be elevated to the level of organizational missionaries (*LD* 58–62: 22–3).

Labour and Peasants. In its respective areas, farm and countryside, factory and city, the section was charged with sparking off among labour and peasantry the urge to create an 'Islamic atmosphere'; inspiring workers to trade-union activity on behalf of 'the protection of their rights'; organizing co-operation among workers and peasants, to support each other's needs and demands; studying the problems of labour and the peasant, and their solutions, and exerting effort towards 'bringing together worker and management' and 'peasant and landowner'; studying farm exploitation and labour organizations with an eye towards correcting abuses and returning to 'an Islamic foundation'; teaching the peasant or worker to raise his 'educational, moral, social, and health standards'; undertaking 'technical studies' for the information of the leader; and maintaining contact with the peasant and labour 'representatives' in the branches and co-operating with them (*LD* 63–5: 25–6; 66–8: 26–7).

Students. The student section was responsible for creating the 'Islamic atmosphere' in the school system of Egypt and had the same general terms of reference as the section for labour and peasants; besides this it was charged with helping students to make a more profitable use of their academic studies and also of their leisure, especially their summer vacations (*LD* 70–2: 28–9).

Professions. This section, like the two preceding ones, was intended to carry the effort to create 'an Islamic atmosphere' in word and deed into the way of life of its members. It was subdivided into committees for doctors, engineers, lawyers, teachers, merchants, agriculturalists, social workers, journalists, and civil servants. Perhaps the most important of these were the teachers' and civil servants' committees, because these were the largest professions, and because of their potential role as moulders of opinion and instruments of the creation of 'a new generation of Muslims'.

Section for Liaison with the Islamic World. This section was charged with: (1) spreading the message about Islam and the Brothers throughout the Muslim world, wherever possible through the existing 'national and Islamic organizations' in the various

Muslim countries; (2) studying the problems of the Islamic world 'in the light of the various international political currents' in co-operation with the policy committee of the general headquarters; (3) organizing an annual meeting to be attended by leaders and representatives of 'the Islamic movement' throughout the Muslim world—whether of the Society of the Brothers, or from any 'Islamic or reform organization'—to discuss matters relevant to the Muslim world and the potential unification of the rules and regulations by which the various groups governed themselves. The section would perform its work by (1) compiling files on each country which would include relevant political, economic, social, and cultural data, as well as information on the course of 'the Islamic movement' therein; (2) studying the various problems of each country through organized research, lectures, publications, and study groups; and (3) dispatching missionaries abroad to other countries and welcoming exchange missions from them.

The section was run by a chief, two deputies, a secretary, and his aide, all of whom, as the permanent staff, were authorized to establish whatever committee structure was necessary to complete the work. Six of the nine permanent committees dealt with the geographical regions of Islam: (1) North Africa; (2) East and South-west Africa (Ethiopia, Somaliland, Nigeria, and Senegal); (3) the Fertile Crescent (Syria, Palestine, Lebanon, Jordan, and Iraq); (4) Saudi Arabia, Yemen, and the independent kingdoms of the south and the Persian Gulf; (5) Turkey, Iran, Pakistan, and Afghanistan; (6) India, Ceylon, Indonesia, Malaya, the Philippines, China, and other areas of the Pacific Ocean and Far East. A seventh committee concerned itself with Islamic minorities in the Americas, the USSR, and Europe. The eighth was an advisory committee of 'older' specialists, and the ninth dealt with 'Islamic Divisions'.[14]

Scarcely a week passed without witnessing the appearance at the headquarters of one or more dignitaries and many lesser personages from all parts of the Muslim world, as official speakers or merely as listeners at the meetings. The section saw that they were duly cared for in matters of entertainment and sustenance. It also provided a kind of haven for those of the many hundreds of 'foreign' Muslim students at the Azhar and other Egyptian schools who found themselves in sympathy with the ideals of the movement. As potential missionaries for the cause after they returned to their

[14] Qism al-Ittisal, *La'ihat al-dakhiliyya li qism al-ittisal* (Cairo, [*c.* 1953]), pp. 4–10; cf. the limited description in *LD* 83–5: 29–30. The special regulations for the section also contained two annex headings but no details about the names of the officers and the budget.

respective countries, these students found themselves welcomed and whenever possible urged to join in the activities of the Society. The section also became a clearing-house for the literatures of the various 'Islamic movements' throughout the Muslim world;[15] it did, in fact, combine this material with the research undertaken by the committees of its own regional groups to produce files as complete as time, availability of material, and research techniques permitted on each of the Muslim countries as they emerged from occupation or obscurity. Finally, the section was often the official voice of the Society on public matters of importance to it: through it protests were made to the government of Pakistan for its 'persecutions' of Sayyid Abul-Ala Maudoodi and his followers there, and to the government of India when it recognized Israel.[16]

Bodily Training and Rovers. Organizationally speaking, these were two separate units, although their purpose was similar—organized and individual physical training and athletics to supplement members' spiritual and intellectual training. The original constitution of the Society issued in 1945 and revised in 1948 gives no details about these sections; the revised and expanded regulations issued in 1951 mention the section for bodily training (*LD* 76: 30), but not the rovers section, though its existence after 1951 is attested to by other sources.[17] This fact was related to the emergence of the new leadership after 1950 and was part of the dispute about the role of the secret apparatus in the Society which involved the 'athletic' or 'physical' aspects of membership. Basically, this was a question of membership indoctrination, and discussion of the issue will be reserved for that point.

Family section. The family section and its role *vis-à-vis* the secret apparatus was also part of the dispute which cleft the Society in its last years. Because of this, and since the family was, in inspiration at least, an indoctrinational rather than administrative unit, discussion of it will also be deferred.

[15] Among the literature to be gathered in the offices of the section were the following types: Jama'at al-Tabshir al-Islami wa'l-Islah bi'l-Sudan, *Taqrir* (Cairo, 1954), was an appeal for moral and financial help to the Society for the Islamization of the Southern Sudan; pamphlets on Palestine such as Sa'id Ramadan, *al-Quds fi'l-khatr bayn al-tahwid wa'l-tadwil* (Jerusalem, n.d.), and Rabitat al-Tullab al-Filastiniyin bi Misr, Lajnat 15 Mayu, *al-Shu'ub tuqadim adwa' 'ala Filastin* (Cairo, n.d.); and pamphlets from Brother-like societies in other parts of the Arab world, such as Jam'iyat al-Irshad al-Islamiyya of Kuwayit, the 'Ubbad al-Rahman of the Lebanon, and, of course, the Muslim Brothers of Syria. There were also publications of the International Society for the Propagation of Islamic Culture, written in English; the first of these was I. C. Evans, *Essentials of Islam: a Moslem Englishman Summarizes his Religion* (Cairo, n.d.).

[16] See e.g. *Ila al-Ikhwan*, no. 6 (n.d.), 5; and no. 9 (n.d.), 8.

[17] See Zaki, *Ikhwan*, pp. 129–30; *Ila al-Ikhwan*, no. 6 (n.d.), 8.

The Section of the Muslim Sisters. As far back as the beginnings of the movement in Isma'iliyya, Hasan al-Banna made known his concern about the essential role of women in his Islamic reformation, for if reform was to succeed it must begin with the individual in his family context; the mother was thus a prime instrument of the reformation. Among his first projects was the creation of an 'Institute for the Mothers of the Believers' in Isma'iliyya. This 'school', in April 1933, became the first official 'branch of the Muslim Sisters',[18] but despite the development of formal structural arrangements, there never developed among the ladies' auxiliary anything resembling the growth of the male organization. In the early years, whatever Banna thought, there was simple resistance from the male members of the Society. Ten years passed after the first branch was formed before a leadership came into existence and a headquarters was founded in 1944. At the peak of the parent Society's strength in 1948, the Muslim Sisters claimed 5,000 members. They were subjected to the same decree of dissolution the next year, and re-emerged in 1951 with the Brothers, much more highly esteemed under the new leadership, and by the members for the services they performed during the 'time of trial' of 1948–50 for the families of those imprisoned.

Unlike their more successful Brothers, the number of Sisters in the university—they were readily distinguished by their simple white hair-covering—was negligible; Brothers in varying degrees admitted, in the words of one answer to queries on the matter, that 'the Islamic feminist movement' had not been able 'to attract the educated type', that too many women had seen the movement as a 'return to the *harim*' rather than, as it was propagated, the only path to 'true female emancipation'. The Muslim Sisters in no sense gripped the imagination of the young women of Egypt as the Society for so long gripped that of so many of the young men. Its prime importance was organizational: the section provided a laboratory, however small, for working out the ideas of the Society about women; and, as members, the Sisters made useful contributions to its educational and medical services.[19]

FIELD APPARATUS

The 'field' units were the administrative channels through which the voice of the high command passed to the operating membership groups and through which the membership was welded into

[18] *Mudh.*, pp. 110, 171–2; Hajjaji, *RWR*, p. 200.

[19] For a short account of the Muslim Sisters, see Zaki, *Ikhwan*, pp. 154–64; and the first pamphlet of the Section of the Sisters (al-akhawat al-muslimat), *al-Risalat al-Ula* (Cairo, 1951).

the highly disciplined instrument it was. One of the historians of the movement has described the field or 'line' formations as 'the units for command and action.'[20]

The largest unit in the field was called the 'administrative office' (*al-maktab al-idari*) and, in extent, generally (though not necessarily) coincided with the provincial divisions used by the Egyptian government. The administrative office was then divided into 'districts' (*manatiq*), these again generally coinciding with the official provincial breakdowns. To follow governmental divisions on these two levels had the obvious value of benefiting from the communication lanes between and among the various divisions and sub-divisions already in official use. The 'branch' (*shu'ba*) was the further subdivision of the district and the most important of all the units in the Society administratively (*LD* 1–4: 3–4; *QA* 50: 31). The administrative office, the district, and the branch were identified by the names of their respective geographical locations. The chart on p. 177 shows the general appearance of the field unit.[21]

Administrative Office

The affairs of the administrative office were directed by a council composed of a chairman, a deputy, a secretary, and a treasurer. These held office either because they held the same position in the leading branch of the area encompassed by the council or because they were leading or active members of either a district or some other important group in the Society. They were appointed by the Guidance Council. In each of the administrative councils, besides the four members already mentioned who ran its affairs, was a fifth, a representative of the Guidance Council whose opinions were 'advisory' and who had no vote (*LD* 28–9: 10–12).

District Office

The district office was administered by a council composed as follows: a chairman, who was the chairman of its leading branch or a member appointed by the Guidance Council; the heads of all of the branches in the district; visitors from the branches and the administrative offices, who had no vote; and representatives of the district's most important activities. A secretary or treasurer or both for the district might be selected by the heads of its constituent branches (*LD* 24–7: 9–10).[22]

The Branches

The administrative councils and the district offices were essential liaison units and chains of command; they originated at a re-

[20] Zaki, *Ikhwan*, p. 108. [21] Cf. ibid., pp. 99–101.
[22] See *MDA* (25 Nov. 1953), 8–9, for a description of the district of Cairo.

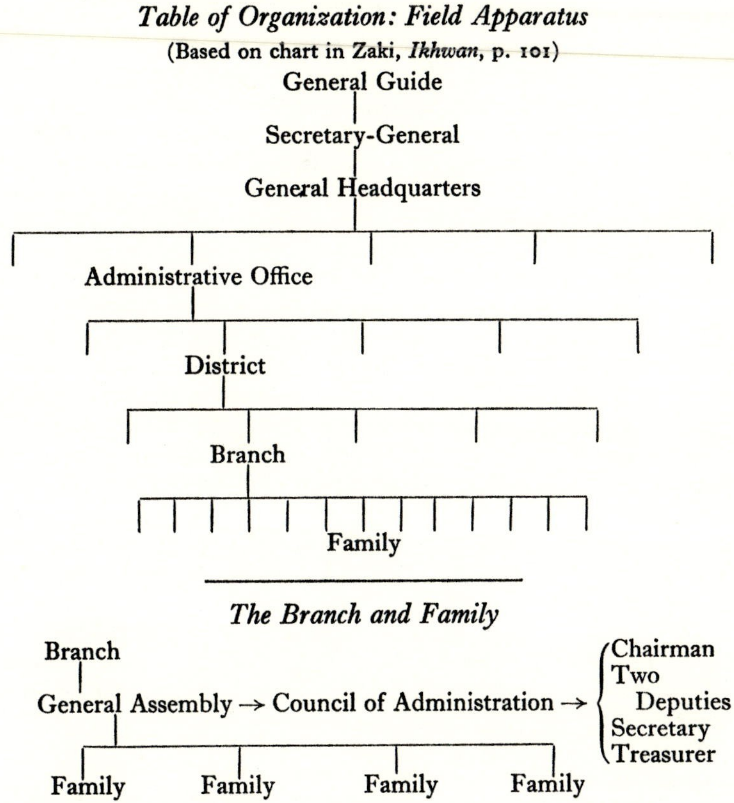

Four families constituted a 'clan' (*'ashira*), five clans a 'group' (*raht*), and five groups a 'battalion' (*katiba*).

latively late date and, where existing, their operation was a matter, primarily, of keeping records. The branch, on the other hand, was the historic grouping of members and the basic unit of administration. The officers and administrators of the Society thought in terms of administrative offices and districts; but for them, and more especially for the members, allegiance was to a branch. The supervision of the branch was in the hands of a 'council of administration', which was elected by a 'general assembly' of branch members.

The general assembly was composed of the registered and paid-up members of the branch. It held its annual meeting during the month of Muharram, but a meeting might be called at any other time by the head of the branch, by the General Guide, or at the request of one-fifth of the members. One-half of the membership constituted a quorum of any meeting and an absolute majority made a decision binding. Should the conditions of a meeting not be fulfilled, the proposed meeting would be held one week later with any number present constituting a quorum. Notifications of meetings and a statement of agenda had to be made three days in advance. The head of the branch, its deputy chief, or the oldest member would preside.

The assembly elected the council of administration (see below), and considered the budget, the accounts, and the reports on activities in the past and the coming year. The Guidance Council had to be informed ten days prior to any meeting of the general assembly and to be provided with an agenda. It was free to send a representative to the meeting. Any decisions taken by the general assembly had to be approved by the General Guide.

The council of administration of the branch was composed of a chairman, chosen by the headquarters, and two deputy chiefs, a secretary and a treasurer elected by the general assembly of the branch from among its members by secret vote every two years. Nominees for the council had to be at least twenty-one lunar years old, and members of the branch for at least one year. They might be re-elected. A chief might be relieved of his duties at the discretion of the headquarters. Each member of the council took an oath 'to be faithful to the principles of the Muslim Brothers' and to obey and execute the orders of the leadership.

The head of the branch (usually although not necessarily the chairman of the council of administration) was responsible for the activity of the branch, chairing meetings, and representing it in legal and official operations. The secretary watched over the seals, registers, and files. The treasurer was responsible, in his work, to both the council of administration and to the general assembly. Meetings of the council were held periodically, at a time set by it; the presence of half the members constituted a quorum; decisions were binding with the vote of an absolute majority; the chairman had a casting vote.

The council might create whatever divisions and committees in the branch it deemed desirable. Vacancies on the council were filled, as on the Guidance Council, by the runner-up at the previous election. The council might also dissolve the branch if it considered it 'incapable' of realizing its goals, but such a decision must be approved (1) by the General Assembly with three-quarters of the members present and two-thirds of them agreeing; (2) by the Guidance Council. On the other hand, the Guidance Council might by decree dissolve the branch, in accordance with Article

55 of the statute, if it 'deviated from the path of the message' (*QA* 40–50: 26–31; *LD* 11–23: 6–8).

The Guidance Council had also the sole right to approve the founding of new branches, directly through its representatives or through the medium of the district office. It had the right to be represented at the meetings of the council of administration of any branch, without vote, but with the authority to block any decision inconsistent with the principles of the Society, pending consultation with the headquarters, whose opinion was final. It might reject an entire elected council or any one of its members; in the latter case the rejected member was replaced by the member with the next highest number of votes (*QA* 52–5: 32–3; *LD* 22: 8).

The relationships between the three administrative units were similarly outlined by the constitution of the Society. In pyramidal order, the branch followed the district, and the district the administrative council. Communication from the lowest to the highest level passed through the hierarchy except that if a branch's complaint concerned either of its higher authorities, it might go directly to the Guidance Council if neither the district office or the administrative council relayed the complaint. Contact between branches was effected through the district office or through many district offices if the branches concerned belonged to different districts. Similarly, inter-district communication was directed through the appropriate administrative councils which, for their part, communicated with each other through the Guidance Council (*LD* 89–91: 36–7).

The regular branch, in its work and operation, might be described as a miniature headquarters. We have already touched upon its administrative instruments. The council of administration, while considerably bound by policy decisions which concerned the movement, was free to work out the branch programme. Activities followed the pattern of the headquarters sections: there was a section for propagation of the message, a section for rovers, and, depending on the locale of the branch, one for students, or workers, or professions, or peasants, singly or in combination. Each branch was requested to have a 'library' or at least a reading-room to encourage and assist the local educational programmes. Similarly, in the larger branches, some medical or clinical facilities either permanently existed or were provided periodically. (On the educational and medical work of the Society, see further pp. 283–91 below.) Operations on the branch level were conceived as 'a system of decentralization' in which the all-important activities of the 'family' could unfold.[23]

[23] See *MDA* (17 Nov. 1953), 8–9, for the working of a branch.

The academic branches were organized somewhat differently from the ordinary geographic branch, in accordance with university needs and organization. The head of the university branch was the recognized leader of the university Brothers; his was a powerful voice in the leadership echelon of the Society in general, among the student Brothers, and among other students. Control of the position was one of the most certain assurances of mobility to the highest ranks in the Society. Mustafa Mu'min, the student leader from 1946 to 1948, was in 1950–1 deemed so powerful by those in command of the Society as to be the object of their concerted hostility culminating (see above, p. 82) in a successful move for his expulsion. His successor, Hasan Duh, was at first friendly to the revolutionary junta, a fact which assured, if not complete university support for the new regime, at least (what was equally important) quiet while the régime secured its position in its first year of existence. By the same token, that power caused him to become the bitterest enemy of the regime as relations between the government and the Society disintegrated. He was the first Brother official of note to be overtly challenged by the government before the final dissolution in October 1954.[24] In the struggle for power inside the Society, the loyalty of Hasan Duh to Hudaybi assured him of the continuing support of the university and thus of the Society's most powerful segment of articulate and active opinion.

The university branch was simply and efficiently organized. Directly responsible to the university leader were the leaders of each of the various faculties; the faculties were in turn divided into groups representing each of the four years of schooling. The heads of each year-group were responsible to the faculty heads for the performance of the members of their group. This breakdown permitted an efficient organization of the university Brothers into units small enough to be rapidly assembled and large enough to be effective in their respective faculties. Liaison between faculties was in the hands of the leader of the university. Perhaps no other facet of the activity of the Brothers in the university so astounded (and infuriated) their opponents there as the ability of the leaders to communicate directions and decisions throughout the ranks of the Brothers with such speed and to have them so perfectly obeyed.

FINANCE

The revenues of the Society derived primarily from membership fees, contributions, legacies, and the profits from its economic

[24] See above, pp. 139–40; and p. 171 n. 13.

enterprises, publications, and sales of emblems, pins, seals, and the like. In the official delineation of financial responsibilities, it was proposed that the branch should contribute to the operation of the district, the district office to the administrative office and this, in turn, to the operation of the general headquarters. Each month the administrative office remitted an amount established by the Guidance Council to the general headquarters as its members' contribution to general funds. In so far as membership fees, despite all other activity, provided the main source of income, the general headquarters was, in effect, at the mercy of a strangely decentralized fiscal structure, which depended on effective provincial administration for the income necessary for its work. Throughout its history, the inefficient functioning of the system continued to bring complaints from the headquarters that the work of the Guidance Council was cramped by the excessive use of funds on the lower levels, which automatically cut the amounts forwarded to the upper level.[25]

The general outlines of the system had been developed by Banna during the 1940s when the Society had taken final structural form and become more active, making obsolete and inefficient the earlier, more informal collection of dues and gifts from the members as they could make them.[26] What appeared to be general indifference to the financial problem prompted the new leadership in 1951 to introduce new regulations providing for fixed membership dues which were collected by the family in the branch; a fixed share of these dues, on a fixed day, went to the district and thence to the administrative office and the general headquarters. All this was done with appropriate provision for inspection and control at all levels, and with ultimate review in the Guidance Council and Consultative Assembly.[27]

The problem of operating the system of quotas from the bottom to the top was the administrative aspect of the larger problem of inadequate revenue. No figures were available to me about income and expenditure,[28] or about profits—if any—from the economic enterprises. Sometimes the Society resorted to loans to finance its projects but this seems to have been confined to local affairs and the early stages of the development of the organization.[29] Another of the devices used in the 1930s was to sell members 'bonds for the

[25] See esp. *RNUNA*, p. 16.

[26] See *Mudh.*, pp. 207–8.

[27] Cf. the elaborated regulations in *LD*, 96–104: 37–43, with *QA*, 56–9: 33–4; see also Zaki, *Ikhwan*, p. 108.

[28] At the 1954 trials the treasurer of the Society testified that the monthly budget of the general headquarters for clerical and other maintenance staffs amounted to £E500; see *JJ* (19 Nov. 1954), 7; and *MAS* (24 Nov. 1954), 4.

[29] See *Mudh.*, pp. 124–6.

message', in effect, to launch intensive contributions campaigns among them.[30] One other practice, not often used, was to levy special quotas on selected provincial groups to help in the financing of some special project undertaken by the headquarters.

The only other source of funds was contributions from non-members. It seems clear that the Society did receive contributions from wealthy or well-to-do Muslims who saw some value in its work. This particular type of support seems, too, to have been largely, though not completely, rural in nature and to have taken the form not only of money gifts but also of grants of lands or buildings and material sponsorship of some of the local activities. Whatever pious, political, economic, or merely self-protective reasons inspired such aid, it was this kind of income which became the foundation of the charges by the Society's political opponents that it was the 'tool' of the 'capitalist landlords and industrialists'. The same opponents founded their charge that it was the 'tool of imperialism' on the belief that it also received 'contributions' from the British and later on from the American Embassy. On the other hand, other opponents of the Society, mostly in official positions, accused it from the beginning of its life of receiving money from Moscow.

Less is known about the contributions received by the Society than about any other aspect of its finances. It undoubtedly benefited from the attentions of various ruling-class groups who were thinking in terms of a presumed gain for their political and economic interests. Certain aspects of those interests did in fact coincide with avowed aims of the Society itself, hostility to communism, for instance; and the Society seemed to offer a powerful force in support of the symbols and ideas which had made vested interests possible. The fierceness with which the Society was repressed in 1948 and 1949 derived not only from anger over the assassination of a prime minister but also from the realization that the view of the Society held by the ruling class was suspect. It will be recalled that three of the thirteen counts made against the Society in 1948 conjured up the image of economic and social revolt.

As to the alleged foreign contributions, even less can be said. Contributions were, it would appear, offered by the British Embassy in the early part of World War II, but whether or not they were accepted must remain, along with all other allegations of foreign support, a moot point. On the face of it, the issue of whether the Society of the Muslim Brothers was, in consequence of foreign contributions, a 'tool of Western imperialism' or a Moscow agent seems hardly worth examining.

[30] See *Mudh.*, pp. 257–8; and *MDA* (22 Apr. 1952), 10.

MEMBERSHIP

The first set of criteria for membership in the Society emerged at the Third General Conference in 1935. At that time, Banna defined three degrees of membership: (1) 'assistant' (*musa'id*); (2) 'related' (*muntasib*); (3) 'active' (*'amil*). Any Muslim who declared his intention to join, signed a membership card, agreed to pay dues, and was accepted by the group was an 'assistant' member. He became a 'related' member when he proved his mastery of the principles of the movement, attended regular meetings, and committed himself to 'obedience'. He attained the degree of 'active' member with his total involvement with the movement—physical training, achievement in Qur'anic learning, and fulfilment of Islamic obligations such as pilgrimages, fasting, and contributions to the *zakat* treasury. A fourth degree of membership, that of 'struggler' (*mujahid*) was the ultimate stage, open to only a select handful of the most dedicated.[31]

The regulations of 1945, however, defined only two categories of members: 'tentative' (*taht al-ikhtiyar*) and 'active' (*'amil*). A new member spent no less than six months in the first stage, affirming in that time his fulfilment of the obligations of membership. Then he was permitted to make the oath of allegiance at the request of the branch to which he belonged. The two types of members were listed in each branch in separate registers. General conditions of membership stipulated that the candidate be (1) eighteen years of age; (2) honourable and upright; (3) able to understand the ideas of the Society; and (4) willing to pay dues. The Brother promised to pay monthly dues, and, if possible to make extra contributions, and to contribute to *zakat*. Those who could not pay were excused by the leader of the branch, after he had ascertained that they were genuinely unable to do so.

After 'contracting' to live by the laws of the Society, the member then made his oath of allegiance (the *bay'a*).

After 'contracting' to live by the laws of the Society, the member then made his oath of allegiance (the *bay'a*). The oath (reproduced on p. 165) was a contract with God to uphold the message of the Society, and to fulfil the conditions of membership, which included, above all, confidence in the leadership, and willingness 'to obey absolutely'. It will be recalled from the history of the Society, especially the period 1952–4 (Chapter 5), how important the relationship was between confidence and obedience.

A Brother who did not fulfil his duties, or who violated the Society's principles, was subject to discipline by the branch head.

[31] This later stage was probably related to the roots of the secret apparatus (see above, pp. 30–3, also *Mudh.*, pp. 203–5).

If verbal appeals did not correct the shortcoming, the branch council of administration decided whether to warn, fine, suspend, or expel him. Permission to expel an 'active' member must come from the general headquarters (*QA* 4–8: 1–11; *LD* 5–8: 4–5). The Guidance Council or branch leaders were permitted to grant 'honorary membership' to people who had 'performed services for the message' (*QA* 60: 35).

VII

COMMUNICATION AND INDOCTRINATION

COMMUNICATION

Except during its times of crisis with the government, and then only with a little more difficulty, the Society always managed to make its voice heard, whether on matters of public policy or on organizational business. This was thanks to the close attention it paid to its apparatus of communications, both with the outside world and for the indoctrination of its own members.

Newspapers and Magazines

Admittedly having learned from the West the usefulness of the technique of propaganda, Banna[1] soon thought of establishing a press, both to spread his message and to rebut the challenges of his adversaries. In time the press also came to be seen as a symbol of the possibilities of an Islamic economics; it became, in fact, the second largest of the projects undertaken by the Society.[2] It began humbly enough with a newsletter, *The Letter of the General Guide*, only two issues of which appeared, in December 1932 and January 1933.[3] Within a few months, however, Banna had succeeded in publishing the Society's first significant journal, *Majallat al-Ikhwan al-Muslimin* (the Newspaper of the Muslim Brothers). A weekly in magazine format, this was the first of the line of news publications of the Society which bore on the masthead the line: 'The Voice of the Message of Truth, Strength, and Freedom'. Its first director was Muhibb al-Din al-Khatib, proprietor of the Salafiyya bookstore and heir to the leadership of the group of that name. Banna, with £E2 in his pocket according to his own account, had persuaded Khatib to join in the venture which produced the first number in May 1933, and ran for four years.

The paper was followed, in 1938, by a 'political weekly', *al-Nadhir* (the Warner); this was regarded by Banna as the initial

[1] *RTH: D*, pp. 11–12.
[2] *MDA* (12 Feb. 1952), 22; Hajjaji, *RWR*, p. 324; Husayni, *Ikhwan*, pp. 91–2.
[3] These are in part reproduced in *Mudh.*, p. 148.

entrance into 'political struggle', internally and externally. However, after the dispute which led to the creation of the splinter group, Muhammad's Youth, in 1939 the editor followed the dissidents and took the magazine with him. It would apparently have collapsed in any case, owing to an admitted 'lack of interest' and 'a limited number of subscribers'.[4]

The Society, however, was not long without a voice, for almost immediately it came into the legacy of the old, respected voice of the Salafiyya, *Majallat al-Manar* (the Lighthouse). After the death of Rashid Rida in 1935 only three issues appeared until July 1939, when Banna pushed the publication of one more issue; six more issues over the next two years brought to completion vol. xxxv under the auspices of the Society. In 1941, in its move against the Society, the government revoked the Brothers' licence to publish *al-Manar*. At the same time it confiscated a provincial weekly magazine called *al-Ta'aruf* (the Acquainter), which was rapidly becoming another official voice of the Society.[5]

As part of their general arrangements with the Wafdist government which came to power in 1942 the Brothers were permitted to resume some journalistic activity. A weekly news magazine called simply *al-Ikhwan al-Muslimin* (the Muslim Brothers) began publication in August 1942 as a bi-weekly; it remained for the next four years, with sporadic repression, the leading organ of the Society. It was replaced from May 1946, by a daily newspaper *Jaridat al-Ikhwan al-Muslimin* (the Muslim Brothers) which continued publication until the dissolution of the Society in December 1948. The daily was the realization of Banna's early dreams and was one of the more obvious signs that the Society had come of age. November 1947 saw the publication of *Majallat al-Shihab* (the Meteor), a monthly journal of Islamic opinion and research on the model of *al-Manar*. Regarded by some as Banna's personal organ, it, too, ceased publication when the Society was dissolved in 1948.

During the period of quiescence, as the Society fought to win back its legal existence, its views found a sympathetic outlet in a long-established Islamic weekly newspaper in Cairo called *Minbar al-Sharq* (the Minbar of the East), until the appearance of a weekly news magazine, *al-Mabahith* (the Researches) (May 1950–January 1951),[6] edited and owned by Salih 'Ashmawi, at that time acting head of the Society, and afterwards editor of the magazine's successor *Majallat al-Da'wa* (the Message), also a weekly, which

[4] *Mudh.* pp. 149–50; *MDA* (10 Nov. 1953), 3.
[5] *Mudh.*, p. 273; cf. Heyworth-Dunne, *Modern Egypt*, p. 57.
[6] *MDA* (3 Apr. 1951), 6; see also Banna, *MISI*, p. 13.

appeared from January 1951 until 1956. Despite the prominent position of its editor, its claim to be an official organ of the Society, though unofficially accepted, was officially denied because of the leadership disputes in which ʿAshmawi was involved.

For some time after 1948 the Society had no official organ. A monthly learned journal, *Majallat al-Muslimin* (the Muslims), owned and edited by Saʿid Ramadan, while reflecting its ideas, never spoke in its name. After a long and apparently difficult period of planning and organization the Society, with the new leadership fully in command after the crisis of late December 1953 and January 1954, finally published the long-anticipated weekly newspaper, *Majallat al-Ikhwan al-Muslimin* (the Muslim Brothers). It first appeared in May 1954, ran a total of twelve issues until August, and then ceased publication as the atmosphere of crisis grew with the government. The Society claimed that publication was no longer feasible under the rigorous censorship; the government contended that the project was a financial fiasco.[7]

The journalistic media of the Society served many functions: simple news reporting, external propaganda, policy statements for members, indoctrination, and inter-organizational communication. Those functions were performed through less formal journalistic devices at times when its own press was not operating, either because of internal administrative or financial reasons or because of external crisis. In 1953 and 1954 before the Society was able to publish its weekly news magazine, members were kept informed of organizational directives and policy through a little newsletter entitled *Ila al-Ikhwan* (To the Brothers); and throughout its history, in response to either rigid censorship or government confiscation, resort was had to the time-honoured device of the secret pamphlet. This was especially true, as we have seen, in 1948 and early 1949, and in 1954.

Publications

The press was operated by the press and translation committee (originally a section), jointly with the section for liaison with the Islamic world and, more especially, the section for the propagation of the message. The last-named section came into its own after 1951 and was in fact the ultimate arbiter of the materials which were the stuff of the movement's ideology; its responsibility was

[7] See generally for parts of the above information, *JIM* (20 May 1954), 2; Zaki, *Ikhwan*, p. 144; and Husayni, *Ikhwan*, p. 82. The Society was woefully lacking in records of its press history; see *Ila al-Ikhwan*, no. 9 (n.d.), 6, for an appeal to members to search for copies of the past journalistic efforts of the Society so that the headquarters could compile a complete file.

to set the intellectual and spiritual tone of members' reading. Its most important job was that of collecting, systematizing, and republishing the major part of Banna's written works, especially the 'messages' (*al-rasa'il*); it then began slowly to add new material in the name of the new leader, and next, as a new departure, to commission or sanction other works. In its own name it began a new series written by its head, Sayyid Qutb, called *This is Your Message*, which was halted in its plans for development by the crisis of 1954.[8] Although the committee's production was further limited because of the policy, also dating from 1951, of encouraging each of the sections to increase its own it still had the final say on everything written or published which was used officially for the membership. The same kind of control was attempted over books appearing under the names of individual Brothers. From 1951 an increasingly large number of these appeared, dealing with the movement, its history, and its ideas, a fact which was regarded with concern by some of the leaders because so many were considered to be unrepresentative. In 1953, speaking on behalf of the section for propagation, the secretary-general (to give the warning more authority) suggested that 'Brother writers' should submit their books to the headquarters for clearance before they were published, and that failure to do so would leave their works open to 'boycott'.[9]

Lectures

The section for the propagation of the message was also responsible for programming lectures and training lecturers. In the early rural days of the movement the most useful and most effective platform available to the speakers was in the mosque, a setting which invested the speaker with an unchallenged respectability.[10] Throughout the history of the movement the mosque continued to be a principal recruiting office.

The spread of the organization into the larger towns and the influx of urban members caused speech-making to become

[8] See *Ila al-Ikhwan*, no. 9 (n.d.), 8. Only three titles in the series had appeared.

[9] Ibid., no. 8 (n.d.), 5. The point that some of the writers in the Society were taking advantage of their membership to sell books has been made by Brothers themselves. One device was to sell books in the branches at a discount. This should be considered as further evidence of the attempt of the new leadership to take control not only of the organization but of its ideas. There was good reason to believe the move was aimed, among others, at the most prolific writer in the Society (at that time an opponent of the leader) Muhammad al-Ghazali. In this context one should note that he also, by Western writers, is considered to be the most 'typical'; see e.g. Safran, *Egypt*, pp. 233 ff.

[10] Husayni, *Ikhwan*, p. 20.

secularized. It was decided to hold regular and informal meetings at specified times outside the mosques. By 1939, and throughout the life of the Society, meetings were held on Tuesday evening. The meeting-place was the general headquarters.[11]

During the early days in Cairo the subject-matter of lectures was primarily 'theological'; the speaker, usually Banna himself, sought to explain the 'true' meanings of the Prophetic revelation through copious exegesis of the Qur'an and Traditions. As the Society grew, the subject-matter broadened to include history (of Islam and of Egypt); social, economic, and political matters as they related broadly to the anticipated 'Islamic renaissance'; and, of course, the history of the movement itself. Banna, as long as he lived, was the central figure in this as in all other aspects of the movement.

From 1951 there was a noticeable change in tone and emphasis. Still fundamental, of course, to all subjects discussed was the question of Islam, its nature, meaning, and destiny, but the method of exposition was much more specific. Members were no longer satisfied with the generalized formulas which hitherto had constituted the core of the doctrine preached by Banna. This meant a more consciously 'scientific' approach to the problem of Islam. The section for the propagation of the message now began to make use of the talent available to it among its professional members in the fields of law, economics, society, education, chemistry, engineering, and zoology.[12] Besides the internal ferment, another important factor in this development was the death of Banna: the same powerful personality which had assured the successful establishment of the Society at the same time had limited its potential for growth; his absence compelled the Society to look to its hitherto untapped 'intelligentsia' to find answers to the ever-increasingly complex challenges to its premises coming from outside its ranks. Substance, not slogans, became a priority.

The Tuesday-night lectures were mass meetings; they were supplemented by lectures for special audiences, e.g. workers, students, professional men, which were held on other nights of the week in the quarters of each group in the headquarters or in the provinces. Attention to the secondary group affiliations of the membership was a practice begun by Banna in his visits to the country; its effect was to strengthen the ties of primary loyalty to the Society as the protector or fulfilment of the secondary interests.

11 Banna, *TIWMI*, p. 36; *Mudh.*, pp. 145, 217, 278–80; Khuli, *QDIHB*, p. 31.

12 See Zaki, *Ikhwan*, pp. 146–8, for a later listing of talks of more secular concern.

Missionaries (duʿat)

While the organization made more and more use of its professional talent to fill the need for specialized lectures, it still paid close attention to the core of its propagandizing endeavour, the missionary. And throughout its history the Society, in the traditional Islamic fashion, never minimized the effect of a good speaker. Banna's own power as a speaker is already legendary and needs only passing comment as one of the factors in the rapid growth of the Society; members also noticed that when choosing people for positions of authority he always had in mind their speech-making ability.

By 1938 Banna had organized formal summer classes for 'preaching and guidance' directed by himself. And by 1940 he gave his blessing to the major text used by the Brothers for instruction in preaching. Written by a member of long standing, the book dealt with the qualities of the missionary as against those of the mere preacher (*khatib*), the techniques of the work and the subject-matter of the speech, and the various media of communication open to the missionary. As sources for the study, the author cited the Qur'an, the Tradition, history, biography, and contemporary events.[13]

After 1951 the training of missionaries was reorganized. The nomination of students was no longer the responsibility of a single person (i.e. Banna), a fact again reflecting the post-Banna ethos in the leadership. Teachers were still required to be good speakers, though they were also expected to bring into what had been almost a purely theological operation more 'secular' currents of learning. The Society did, however, prefer to select members for training, who, if university-trained, were yet rurally rooted and therefore sympathetic to the needs, feelings, idiosyncrasies, dialectical peculiarities, and local circumstances of the great masses of workers and farmers who were the quantitative base of the Society. In this, too, Banna had established a precedent for the formula to success.[14]

Meetings, Chants, and Paraphernalia of Organization

As in so many other mass organizations, the atmosphere in which communication took place was as important as what was communicated. While most of the specialized lectures were given in limited quarters with small audiences, the public lectures took the

[13] al-Bahi al-Khuli, *Tadhkirat al-duʿat* (1953), *passim*, but esp. the Introduction by Banna, p. 5. See also *Mudh.*, pp. 265–6.

[14] See e.g. Hajjaji, *RWR*, p. 281; see also *RMKH*, pp. 26–7, for Banna's description of a good missionary at work.

form of mass meetings. These, as well as the ordinary organizational meetings of the massed members and the meetings occasioned by political events or holidays, became in themselves important both for strengthening members' loyalties and for proclaiming aloud the facts of unity, universality, and power, an atmosphere in which were generated both increasing hostility to the outside world and, more important, increasing internal strength. Banna exploited to the full the concept of the rolling 'bandwagon'.

Article 61 of the fundamental law stipulated that each two years a 'general congress of the heads of the branches' should be called by the General Guide, 'in Cairo or any other locale', whose purpose was to be 'familiarization and general understanding of the various matters which concern the message, and the presentation of its progress in that period' (*QA* 61 : 35). Adopted in 1945, the article merely recognized a practice which, we have already seen, was well established in general outline in the first ten years of the movement's history in Cairo. The last of these great organizational meetings in which the audience was invited to participate in 'decision-making' was that held in August 1946, when representatives of all the branches met to approve or reject resolutions presented by the governing bodies.[15] Henceforward, the business of the Society was inseparable from the politics of the nation and was reflected in the more generalized mass meeting.

Supplementing these organizational meetings and partially replacing them after their disappearance, was the smaller mass meeting which catered to the facts of geography and transport, and to members' special interests. Thus meetings were often held for students, workers, civil servants, and professional people. Similarly, to meet the needs of the provinces, there were provincial gatherings, usually convened at the district level to include a group of neighbouring branches. The pattern of all these meetings was similar: opening prayer, speeches about the movement, 'business meeting', discussion, and a terminal prayer.[16]

With the crystallization of the organization and the emergence of the Society as a voice in the affairs of Egypt by the end of the war, these meetings took on a more general, a more overt public-relations quality, and were held whenever a favourable opportunity presented itself. For example, Banna's visits to his branches were always made the occasion for a mass celebration; in the larger provincial meetings, the prestige of the affair was enhanced by the inclusion among the guests of the local dignitaries and

[15] See *JIM* (1 Sept. 1946), 1 and *passim*.
[16] Ibid.; and *Mudh.*, pp. 172–8.

officials, members and non-members alike, whose presence gave a tone of respectability to the proceedings.[17] Again, great public meetings were held to commemorate the Islamic holidays and feasts, and, wherever possible the ceremonies included participation by non-member Islamic personalities and groups.[18] 'Receptions' were arranged for visiting Arab and Islamic dignitaries and delegations, and for selected groups of educators, teachers, workers, and other potential converts to membership or at least to the ideas of the Society.[19]

The greatest effort—and for the Society it was no effort at all—was reserved for the massed 'political' meetings on behalf of the national cause. Immediately after the war, we have noted, the Society called a mass political meeting in Cairo and throughout the provincial capitals; from that time, the major public activity of the Society was in that vein. In the very choice of the name of that first meeting—a People's Congress—the Society publicly articulated the belief that its new power authorized it to speak on behalf of the nation; and while it continued to pronounce decisions under the name of the Society of the Muslim Brothers, it did so confident that this claim derived from the mandate granted by its enormous increase in membership.

Its policy was simply that of identifying the voice of the Society with that of Egypt. We have already seen that this claim did not go unchallenged in the period 1945–8 by a Wafdist-communist coalition, but few observers in Egypt would deny that it was the tenacity and singleness of purpose of the Society's nationalist programme which brought it to the pinnacle of power and underpinned its belief that, in the 1940s, it was expressing the mind and heart of most of the youth of Egypt. Here, as nowhere else, was it true that the Society's bandwagon, which began its movement with the 'disgrace' of the palace and the Wafd in 1942, picked up such speed by 1946 as to make it the dominant popular force by the time of its destruction in 1948. The principal instrument of this success was the mass public meeting (often ending in a massed public demonstration), which acted as a constant and dynamic reminder of the intensity with which the Society held its views and the vigour with which it pushed them; to both members and non-members alike, the Society came, thereby, to represent both immovable strength and irresistible force.

After the return of the Society in 1950, the types of meetings described above continued to play a part in its organizational and

17 See Heyworth-Dunne, *Modern Egypt*, p. 44.
18 See Zaki, *Ikhwan*, p. 144.
19 See Husayni, *Ikhwan*, pp. 86–7.

public life, but in a rather more restricted way. Among the reasons for this change were the decline in membership; the caution which marked the post-1949 policies of the Society; and a more general shift in its approach to its problem of communication. The new leader's distaste for public display has already been mentioned; not a good speaker, in traditional Arab terms, Hudaybi was temperamentally unsuited to all the necessary accompaniments of the mass meetings—the fiery speeches, the slogan shouting, the arousing of passions, and even the demonstrations—and therefore did not encourage the kind of situations in which Banna seemed to thrive. We have already seen the various manifestations of this outlook in the politics of the Society in 1951 and 1952, and 1954, and in the subtle changes of indoctrination techniques which the new leader tried to introduce. To some extent the failure of the Society to attract the number of members which had assured its strength in the 1940s can be attributed to this fundamental change in its former emotional approach to the 'masses'.

A gathering at which Brothers were present was never difficult to discern, primarily because of the chants that were shouted. Some of these, in their general form, were not exclusive to the Brothers. For example, the most famous of them was: 'God is Great and to Him be Praise.' Other groups had counterparts of the same formula: 'God is Great and Glory to Islam' (*allah akbar wa'l-'izza l'il-islam*) belonged most often to the Misr al-Fatat group, and sometimes to the Wafd, and even to the communists in the proper circumstances. 'God is Great and Glory to Egypt' was the slogan of all these and of the supporters of the Nasir regime, reflecting a clear clash between the 'secularists' and the Brothers over the true nature of nationalism. And these differences were more than mere preferences for words or ideas; they often were the only available recognition and action signals between and among groups and members of groups in a 'mixed meeting'. More than once the chant has served to identify a physical rallying point and then to become a battle-cry for conflicting groups.

For the Brothers, 'God is Great and to Him be Praise' was a chant of profound ideological import: it was the simplest possible reaffirmation of the unity of God and the derivative doctrines of Islam. To it was added another basic formulation of the credo, one which perhaps surpassed the short chant in its emotional import to the Brother; it was equally useful as a unique mark of the Brother. This was a combination of six short phrases, as follows:

God is our goal. The Prophet is our leader. The Qur-'an is our constitution. Struggle is our way. Death in the service of God is the loftiest of our wishes. God is great, God is great. (*Allah ghayatuna Al-rasul za'imuna. Al-Qur-'an dusturuna. Al-jihad sabiluna. Al-mawt fi sabil Allah asma amanina. Allah akbar, Allah akbar.*)[20]

All or parts of this chant were often used in mixed public gatherings. It was used to great effect during demonstrations on the march. It was most often a part of the proceedings of the meetings of the Brothers in the headquarters, especially the Tuesday-night meetings, when its recitation by the massed audience dramatized a collectively intense renewal of the oath of loyalty to the principles of the Society.[21]

Here again Hudaybi violated the traditions of the Society. Frowning on this form of vocal exercise, he seemed, in effect, to be dampening the ardour of the members. Besides issuing official requests that chanting should be confined to the beginning and end of meetings, he also, at the meetings, used his own authority to disparage the practice, particularly at times when such behaviour could be regarded as inflammatory. His objection was not to the chants as such—these had come to be regarded as integral parts of the paraphernalia of the movement—but rather to the more uncontrolled uses to which they had been traditionally put. In resisting the chants, Hudaybi was being consistent with his broader policy of bringing under firmer control the excesses of the past.

Beyond the chants (and certain verbal and social mannerisms), there were few if any overt signs by which a Brother could be identified. In the early days of the movement in Cairo, members on the higher levels (and thus the higher classes) sported a short cape, over the shoulders only, which was marked with a badge of cloth bearing the name of the Society. The badge changed from green to white in the mid 1930s, and then the costume disappeared in the early 1940s. Mosque speakers from the Society used a similar cape, more elaborately decorated with gold braid and supplemented with a special pocket over the heart to carry the Qur'an, but this disappeared when the other cape did.[22] In the

[20] For some detailed explanations of what these meant for Brothers, see Khuli, *QDIHB*, pp. 12–18; and 'Assal, *BKA*, pp. 107–27.

[21] For some pictures of a particularly tense meeting at the end of 1953, see *MAS* (2 Dec. 1953), 8–9. So well known was the chant that the government made full use of it in 1954 to discredit the Brothers; in one cartoon in *MTH* (11 Nov. 1954), 3, noted personalities of the Society were shown in caricature carrying the deposed Faruq on their shoulders and in their hands bearing placards reading: Power is our goal (*al-hukm ghayatuna*); Faruq is our leader (*Faruq za'imuna*); deception is our constitution (*al-tadlil dusturuna*); the secret apparatus is our path (*al-jihaz al-sirri sabiluna*); death in the path to power is the loftiest of our wishes (*al-mawt fi sabil al-hukm asma amanina*).

[22] Banna, *TIWMI*, pp. 35–6 and pictures therein.

1930s, also, members were ordered to wear on the little finger of the right hand an identifying silver ring, which was to be sold through the headquarters.[23] There seems to have been little success in the matter, and ring-wearing became an optional and little-used privilege. Those who wanted them had them made privately.

The ring bore the device early adopted and still accepted as the badge of the Society: two crossed swords cradling a Qur'an. This appeared on every official publication of the organization; on all the green banners which hung on the windows, walls, and doorways of all its buildings and were carried in parades and demonstrations; on the goods produced by its economic projects; and on the various pictures of Banna, calendars, and desk memorandum pads which appeared over the years. In 1953 the insignia was put on a little pin button and sold to members outside the headquarters by itinerant booksellers, apparently without much success. The button was one of the many enterprises which sought to make the fullest possible economic use of the membership on the basis of the insignia of the Society.[24]

INDOCTRINATION

Newspapers, magazines, meetings, and other paraphernalia of organization could not, in the long run, do more than supplement the work of the institutions within the Society dedicated to creating and sustaining inner loyalties. These institutions, we have already seen, were primarily the family system and the rovers; also, to a limited but no less real extent, the secret apparatus.

Family Section

The system of 'families' was regarded by the Society as 'the active fulfilment of the meaning of Islam among the Brothers', and the most fundamental of its 'educational' (*tarbiyya*) instruments.[25] What information has been made available about it is a consequence of the Brothers' desire to correct what, in their opinion, is the erroneous image of the system identifying it with the more notorious 'cell';[26] an image fostered by the extensive press

[23] *Mudh.*, pp. 218–19.

[24] See *JIM* (23 July 1946), 2; (29 Dec. 1946), 2, for warnings from the headquarters to the members against merchants and salesmen who were distributing and selling goods—especially textiles, books, and even medicines—under the insignia of the Society without authorization.

[25] *RNUNA*, pp. 3–4.

[26] See Ahmad, *Mizan*, p. 45; and more recently Halpern, *Politics of Social Change*, p. 141. Harris, *Nationalism and Revolution*, p. 191, we assume

campaign launched by the government in 1949. The new leadership made a special attempt to define, for the Brothers and for the public, the roots of the system and its purposes.[27]

The creation of firm bonds both between the member and the Society and among the members called for devices more effective than mere verbalizations of an oath of loyalty. For the Society of the Brothers, it became an issue when membership outgrew the bounds within which it could be realistically expected that loyalty to Banna's person would satisfactorily solve the problem of loyalty—i.e. when it became physically impossible for Banna to supervise members' education.

In the pristine stages of the Society, membership loyalties were expressed informally and personally. Members were related to the organization without breakdowns as such, and simply took 'the oath of brotherhood' (*bay'at al-ukhuwa*) to be loyal to each other. During the winter of 1936–7, after an influx of new members especially from the university, there took root the idea of unit breakdowns for purposes of instruction in the aims and meaning of the movement. The first groups were units of ten, some of which were given personal instruction by Banna himself. The 'oath of brotherhood' remained the primary verbal expression of loyalty. At the same time, Banna began formulating the 'battalion' (*katiba*) system, consciously designed to generate a total physical, mental, and spiritual absorption in and dedication to the Society, its ideas, and its members.

In the autumn of 1937 the 'Battalions of the Supporters of God' (*kata'ib ansar Allah*),[28] were launched. Three groups numbering forty in each—for workers, students, and civil servants and merchants—met separately one night a week for training which involved a rigorous and sustained night vigil, with a minimum of sleep and a maximum of common and private prayer and meditation. Led by Banna himself, a high point of every session was 'spiritual instruction' from him on subjects which ranged from Sufism to sex. The essence of the commitment required of members was described in three words: 'action, obedience, and silence'. The unfolding of the ritual at night was consciously

interpretatively, translating the word (family) *usra'* as 'cell'. The Brotherhood publication cited there does not use the word 'cell' nor were they 'secret'.

---

[27] For the brief summary which follows, and on this subject, see the articles by the head of the family section in 1952 in *MDA*, 15, 22, 29 Apr., 27 May, and 3 June 1952. See also the most important official publications of the section, *RNUNA* and *RNURT*.

[28] Qur'an 61: 14.

patterned after Prophetic Tradition recording that the Prophet took pleasure in such activity.

The night meetings were scheduled to number forty in the year, but in the very first year the programme went uncompleted, very likely because of a lack of clarity of purpose in the minds of both leaders and members.[29] Banna's disillusionment was great; the failure had disrupted the schedule of growth which he anticipated for the battalions, and thus for the Society. As a movement, we have already seen, this was expected to pass through three stages: (1) of making known the ideas and goals of the Society, among its members and outside (*ta'rif*); (2) of forming and sustaining an effective organization which would embody those ideas (*takwin*); (3) in which the organization would put into effect the ideas of the Society (*tanfidh*). The battalion system was the signal that the second stage had arrived—Banna hoped to gain 12,000 recruits for the battalions so that they might not 'be defeated for lack of members'. The failure of the battalion system indicated not only that the second stage had been prematurely inaugurated, but that the third stage was to be subject to even longer delay.

The experiment, however, was instructive, paving the way for later, more effective formulations of the ideas which had come into play. In the atmosphere of the war years, the twin factors of rapidly increasing membership and growing external pressure on the organization inspired a new and more successful attack on the problem of membership loyalties. In September 1943 the 'family system' was established. First officially called 'the co-operative system' (*nizam al-ta'awuni*), it was soon popularly referred to as 'the family co-operative system' (*nizam al-usar al-ta'awuni*), and finally, popularly and officially, 'the family system' (*nizam al-usar*).

The general regulations of the Society noted that the 'active members' of the branch would be divided into 'families' of no more than five (later changed to ten) members each.[30] One of the members was elected chief (*naqib*) and represented his family before the leadership of the branch. The family was regarded as 'a complete unit, collectively responsible' for its acts. Four families combined to form a 'clan' (*'ashira*) headed by the chief of the 'first' family. Leadership rotated among the members and chiefs of each family and clan. Five clans joined together to form a 'group' (*raht*), and five groups to form a battalion (*katiba*).[31] In effect, Banna

[29] Banna saw a relationship between this failure and the defection of the activist group in 1938–9; see *RNUNA*, pp. 12–16.

[30] *LD* 9: 5 notes that the number of members is five, but the special regulations drawn up for the section (see *RNUNA*, pp. 18–23) divide the members into groups of ten.

[31] *RNUNA*, pp. 18–19.

had abandoned the idea of creating battalions as distinct units in the Society running horizontally (the rovers could fill this need) and adopted a more effective mobilization of the entire membership into categories which placed them all in battalions. The new system, the structure within which it operated, and the ideas which it transmitted to its members were in fact the real basis of the power of the Society of the Muslim Brothers; permitting, as it did, authority to express itself through a well-recognized, clearly defined, and tightly knit chain of command, the system became the fundamental instrument through which the leadership expressed its will. Along with the scout system and the secret apparatus, it perfected the devices through which the vision of the future was to be realized.

The high command of the family system was located in the general headquarters in the family section. From it issued a special set of regulations governing the internal operation of the families.[32]

Meeting weekly with his 'family', the member had prescribed obligations defined as 'personal, social, and financial'. Personal duties included the sincere and industrious practice of the rituals of the faith; the avoidance of the recognized 'evils' (gambling, drinking, usury, and adultery); continuous striving towards the Islamization of the home and family; and the continuous reaffirmation of loyalty and dedication to the organization, its principles, and its leaders. Socially, the Brothers were advised to make the most of the 'brotherly relationships of the family', i.e. to attend the weekly meetings outside the branch headquarters, preferably at the homes of the members in rotation, to spend at least one night of the month together, in the open, sleeping and partaking of common meals, and to pray jointly the Friday prayer and if possible, the morning and night prayer. Financially, members of the family were made 'mutually responsible' for each other, sharing each other's burdens, needs, and gains. A 'co-operative treasury' was to be established to which each Brother contributed a part of his income. One-fifth of the treasury was to be sent to a general fund in the headquarters to be invested in 'the Society for Islamic Social Insurance'.[33]

The ideas which underpinned the system were summed up in

[32] The following is a summary of *RNUNA*, pp. 18–23.

[33] See *RNUNA*, p. 15, for the story which Brothers regard as illustrative of the economic mentality which the system tried to create: one Brother, having given half of his income to his unemployed Brother, was asked how he could arrange his own affairs with only half of his earnings; he replied: 'But how can my Brother live with no income at all?' There was no further information available on the Society for Islamic Social Insurance mentioned in the text above.

three words which Banna called 'the pillars': 'familiarity' (*ta'aruf*); 'understanding' (*tafahum*); and 'responsibility' (*takaful*)'—all three, as will be noted, couched in the form of the verb indicating mutuality. 'Familiarity' meant 'the strengthening of brotherhood among the Brothers', the concept derived from the Qur'anic verse which reads 'And hold fast, all of you together, to the cable of Allah, and do not separate',[34] and from the Prophetic Tradition which said 'The believer to the believer is like the building [held together] one part with another'. 'Understanding' meant the true understanding of Islam and willingness to abide by its teachings and be personally responsible before one's fellows. 'Responsibility' was defined as 'the essence of brotherhood' and the meaning of Islam; in the Prophet's words: 'It is better that ye pursue the needs of your brother than to isolate yourself in my mosque for a month, and whoso brings happiness to the house of a Muslim, God will reward with no less than Paradise.'

The reading and study material for the family was limited, in Banna's time, to the *rasa'il* which he had compiled for the battalions, and to other general literature of Islam. The object of the instruction was the reconstruction of what may be called the member's 'Islamic personality', the reaffirmation of the 'total' Muslim in the multiple areas of man's behaviour—religious, ethical, social, economic, and political. While the approach was thus general in theory, in practice, an inordinate amount of the instruction was focused on the daily moral and social behaviour of the members; these were aphorisms, usually with a textual base in the Qur'an or the Traditions, which pointed to set forms of phrase and behaviour for appropriate times of the day and on various occasions.[35]

In the post-Banna period, the section leadership assumed a more direct hand in the training programmes for members. The new programme of activity included the publication of special pamphlets authored by the section leaders on the history and aims of the family system and its essential teachings,[36] as well as specific study programmes.[37] Emphasis continued to be placed on the personal and social behaviour expected of the 'good Brother and good Muslim'. These pamphlets more effectively than others made the

[34] Qu'ran 3: 103.

[35] There were many forms in which these 'lessons' appeared but almost always under the title *al-Ma'thurat*. The best of the numerous editions of this work, which reproduces Banna's writing with commentary and exact references to texts is Radwan Muhammad Radwan, ed., *al-Ma'thurat* (1952).

[36] Besides the already quoted *RNUNA*, see *RMAUK* and *RNJM*.

[37] See the pamphlets entitled *al-Minhaj al-dirasi al-Islami li-Ikhwan al-usar*, used in Cairo with the authorization of the family section. A more general series was called *al-Minhaj al-dirasi al-Islami li-madrasat al-jum'a*.

point so essential to the whole spirit of the Society (and one of Banna's guiding principles) that the problems of Egyptian or Islamic reform could never be solved unless individual Egyptians or Muslims were first rehabilitated or reformed.

The increasingly active role of the family section after Hudaybi assumed the leadership, was, as has already been related, a result of the struggle within the Society over the issue of its activist past. As Hudaybi saw the situation, the proper emphasis in the Society was reformist and spiritual; the proper instrument for giving members the right training was the family section. Hudaybi's problem, it will be recalled, was to correct in the history and thought of the Society the undue weight given to the physical and the martial. In the struggle with the leaders of the secret apparatus, Hudaybi used as his prime instrument an expanded and more active family section, hoping that it could successfully win over the members and thus automatically dissolve the secret apparatus. He intended to make the family section and the section for the propagation of the message the primary channels for membership indoctrination. In both sections, he successfully appointed men favourable to his leadership and enlarged their terms of reference; and he reorganized and enlarged the sections sufficiently to perform the new tasks being imposed on them.[38] On the assumption that re-oriented instruction meant reoriented teachers, he also set in motion training schools for the teachers of the family, their leaders.[39] The effect was to create not only a more clearly defined body of learning but a more efficient system of teaching and teachers; the latter result, incidentally, also helped to fill the gap, made so apparent by the death of Banna, in secondary and tertiary leadership.

However, as with all the other facets of the internal dispute over the new directions in the Society, these developments served only to exacerbate the situation and hasten the day of the Society's demise. A critical element in the situation was the relationship of the family institution to the rovers.

The Rovers (jawwala)

The rover units were perhaps the oldest of the institutions created and passed on to the Society by Banna. The idea had religious roots, and was based on the importance attached to the

[38] An Indian Muslim visitor describing his visit to the Brothers (Nadawi, *Mudhakkarat*, p. 21) correctly reflected the new orientation with his description of the head of the family section as the 'cultural supervisor' (*al-muraqib al-thaqafi*). See also Zaki, *Ikhwan*, p. 137.

[39] See *Ila al-Ikhwan*, no. 7 (n.d.), 2–3, 7; no. 8 (n.d.) 2; and *RMAUK*, pp. 11–12.

inseparability of the healthy body from the healthy mind.[40] While still in Isma'iliyya, the Society saw the birth of the 'excursion groups' which became the focus of athletic activity and physical training. After the move to Cairo this first group (which remained in Isma'iliyya) was deliberately reorganized on the model of the Egyptian national scout movement. It was renamed 'the rover troops' (*firaq al-jawwala*), and given an official leader. After the third general conference (March 1935), it was made an arm of the central headquarters by the appointment of a leader to supervise and to unify the activity of the various local units.[41]

About 1939 the retired army officer Mahmud Labib (who was later involved, it will be recalled, in liaison with the secret group of army revolutionaries) came into contact with the Society. He became, thereafter, an important figure in the training and development of the rover movement; his coming set in motion the first major drive to enhance its growth. It should also be noted that the effort was made following the unsuccessful attempt to create the 'battalion' system in 1937–8.

In the new policy, a special class of leaders were to be almost exclusively concerned with the rovers and to this end were to receive special training; at first they were to be the nucleus of rover membership and later its primary leaders. In each branch there would be a scout group of at least ten men to be trained for a minimum of three years. Provision was made for the increase of members in groups of five. To supervise the affairs of the scouts, a 'higher committee' of seven was founded with Banna himself as its supreme head, and Mahmud Labib as 'inspector-general'. The other members were those who had been prominent in the movement from the beginning.

This concerted effort on the part of the leaders was auspiciously timed with the war years, which brought to the Society waves of new members and thus new recruits for the rovers. As a result, by the end of the war, the Society had the most powerful and effective of the many youth groups which competed for the centre of the political stage in Egypt.

In the light of that development, Banna, who had hitherto

[40] According to Zaki, *Ikhwan*, p. 121, the idea derived from the Prophetic Tradition which said: 'The strong believer is better and more loved by God than the weak believer.' See *MDA* (11 Mar. 1952), 9, for the argument that organized athletics was the partial solution for the necessarily frustrated sexual urges of the adolescent youth of Egypt. 'Scientific' and 'neutral' observers at the university regarded the great success of the Society there as a function of this theory.

[41] *Mudh.*, pp. 110, 206, 256; Hajjaji, *RWR*, p. 327. Cf. Zaki, *Ikhwan*, pp. 123–4. Zaki's treatment of the scouts (pp. 121–30) is the most extensive we have used.

remained aloof from the official Egyptian national scout movement, was prepared to review his attitude towards it. By registering with it the Brothers' scouts could profit from the official privileges extended to it, such as reduced prices on uniforms, subsidies, and use of national facilities. With a rapidly increasing membership these were matters of no mean economic import. Equally important was the possibility, made real by the successful recruitment and training programme, of now having some influence, ideologically and politically, in the councils of the national scouting organization. Thus Banna registered his rovers officially at the end of the war, and by 1948 they were the most active and numerous part of the Egyptian scout movement.

Banna's conception of a scout movement was many-sided. First and foremost, to whatever size it grew and to whatever other functions it lent itself, the Brothers' rover movement had as its major activity ordinary outdoor scouting activity: hiking and camping. It also partook of the general spirit of practical 'public service' which permeated the movement as a whole. Thus, by the early 1940s, informally, the rovers came to be regarded as the active instruments of the welfare and social services of the Society. This was especially true at first in the countryside, where, from 1943, an organized and inclusive 'social project' was inaugurated for the villages of Egypt, designed to stimulate local initiative in matters of education, health, sanitation, and welfare. The rovers also rendered assistance to the authorities at times of national emergency, such as the malaria epidemic of 1945 in Upper Egypt; the floods of the same year in that and other areas; and the al-Wajh al-Bahri cholera epidemic of 1947, also in Upper Egypt.[42]

The most important function of the rovers, however, was perhaps the preservation of order within the Society and its defence against enemies from outside. During the celebrations of King Faruq's accession in 1936 the scouts played a prominent, and for Banna a praiseworthy, part as a 'police force' for the maintenance of order within the ranks.[43] All mass meetings and special functions before 1948 were 'ushered' by them.[44] And throughout the 1940s, as the Society entered the political arena, they were ever vigilant in the protection of its interests and prestige, especially as it moved into hostile competition with the Wafd. It will be recalled that the Wafd called upon the Sidqi government to dissolve the Brothers' 'troops' or risk having the Wafd 'take the law into its own hands', after the youth groups of both organizations

[42] Zaki, *Ikhwan*, pp. 126–30; and *MDA* (3 Feb. 1951), 22.
[43] *Mudh.*, pp. 252–6.
[44] See e.g. *JIM* (23 Aug. 1946), 4; (1 Sept. 1946), 1.

clashed in the Canal Zone. The Wafd and others contended[45] that this group of Brothers was not a scout organization 'in its clear meaning' but rather the façade for 'uniformed troops' upon which the Society could depend. In the 1948–9 crisis with the government, the great majority of those arrested were rovers. Nuqrashi Pasha's assassin was a member of the secret apparatus and a graduate rover. The arguments of the government in the Nuqrashi murder trial centered, as we have already seen, on the charge that the rover system of the Brothers was their prime source of power, the machine by which the alleged revolution was to be effected, and that its spiritual-military training programme was a prime inspiration to violence.

In 1948, just before its dissolution, the Society claimed 40,000 members in the rover section.[46] In 1951 and 1952 the scouts were again active in the national movement by joining the battalions which were sent into the Canal Zone, but the events of 1948–50 had reduced them to an estimated 7,000 in 1953.

The uneasy relationship between the Brothers' rovers and other Egyptian scouts, born of the insistent claim of the Brothers to leadership, became a subject of immediate concern after the 1952 revolution. Developments in this field confirmed for many people the question of ties between the RCC and the Society, both inside and outside the Society. At the Brothers' request the RCC set on foot the reorganization and reorientation of the national scout movement. An assembly of interested parties was called in August 1952, out of which came a temporary committee to direct scout activities until a permanent directing council began operations in September. Both on the temporary committee and the final council, the Brothers were represented; in the final hierarchy the director-general of the Muslim Brothers' scouts ('Abd al-Ghani 'Abidin) was named secretary-general of the national group. In the spring of the following year a prominent leader of the Society's rovers (Sa'd al-Din al-Walili) was named head of the Egyptian delegation to the international meeting of scouts held in Switzerland.[47] However, the crisis which from that time on marked the relationship of the Society with the government brought the Brothers' ascendancy to an end. By the end of 1953 government measures had effectively brought their scouts under strict surveillance.

[45] See e.g. Ahmad, *Mizan*, pp. 100–1 and, explicitly or implicitly, almost all other observers of this movement. We agree, except that we have tried to show above the existence of an important non-military dimension to the rovers; and in our reading of their history, that most groups on the scene had similar para-military organizations, if less effective ones.

[46] See *MDA* (15 Apr. 1951), 5; Zaki, *Ikhwan*, pp. 124–8.

[47] For a description of the meetings of the scouts after the return from the international meet, see *MDA* (17 Mar. 1953), 10.

In effect the rover movement virtually ceased to exist. The main reason for this was not government hostility but the group's own failure to attract members, partly because of the different atmosphere in the Society after 1950 and the absence of official encouragement. More than anyone realized, the death of Hasan al-Banna and the appointment of Hasan al-Hudaybi meant the end of an era. The new regulations issued in 1951 made no mention of a rover section. The continued existence of that section can only be explained in terms of Hudaybi's general struggle to purge the Society of the forces which had been responsible for the violence of the 1940s. Though this struggle centred on the secret apparatus, it was also concerned with the general concept of physical training and athletics which was to underlie the 'creation of a new generation of Muslims'.

It will be recalled that Hudaybi's plan for the abolition of the secret apparatus involved the family section taking over the function of indoctrination, with an intellectual and spiritual rather than physical bias. Moreover, while Hudaybi accepted without question the need for a healthy body, he proposed to achieve this by more exclusively athletic methods. The 1951 regulations created a new section called 'bodily training' (*al-tarbiyya al-badaniyya*) to replace the rovers. Though these seem to have continued to exist informally under the auspices of the new section, Hudaybi hoped, on the whole, to have restrained both the secret apparatus and the rover group, both by administrative reorganization and ideological re-orientation.

That problem was by no means solved as was evidenced by the announcement in the autumn of 1953 that henceforth rover activities would be separated from the section for bodily training. Hoping to soothe the feelings of 'Abd al-Rahman al-Sanadi, the intransigent leader of the secret apparatus, the leadership had made him chairman of the section; the separation of the scouts from the section reflected the failure of that policy. The section then passed into new hands more responsive to Hudaybi; its aims were redefined as the promotion of athletic activities in the countryside —hiking, camping, and the organization of athletic meetings. As if to emphasize the new direction, the section began the publication of a series of *rasa'il* on the rules and regulations for different sports, the first of which was on cross-country running.[48]

Partly as a result of the policy disputes in the section for bodily training, a new focus of athletics, one firmly in the hands of leaders loyal to Hudaybi, was also created in the section for the propaga-

[48] Qism al-Tarbiyat al-Badaniyya (al-Sayyid Hasan Shaltut), *Musabaqat ikhtiraq al-dahiyya* (Cairo, [1954]); see also *Ila al-Ikhwan*, no. 8 (n.d.), 2.

tion of the message. The choice was justified by the regulations of the section, which gave it a hand in the physical training of members; the task was assigned to 'the department of clubs and troops' whose activities were governed by a new set of 'general regulations for athletic activity'. Three committees were established to carry out the new policies for a reinvigorated athletic programme.[49] All these programmes, and the issue itself became academic, however, in the wake of the crisis of 1954.

Militancy, Martyrdom, and the Secret Apparatus

The family and rover sections were the two major institutions for membership organization and indoctrination; they alone reached the membership as a whole and provided the cement in the fabric of the Society's power. Of only peripheral—though more dramatic—relevance to the question of indoctrination and power was the 'special section' (*al-nizam al-khass*) or the 'secret apparatus' (*al-jihaz al-sirri*). Although the secret apparatus was primarily responsible for the violence charged to the Society, and brought it ruin, in the wider context of the power of the Muslim Brothers it was secondary to the tightly knit, well-disciplined, and co-ordinated membership-at-large. The importance of the secret apparatus here is that it logically derived from, and was sustained by, the 'tone' of the training in the Society at large. While it was true that before 1948 few members indeed knew about the secret apparatus, those who did—and after 1948 this number included most of the articulate members—found few if any reasons to resist it. Thus while the secret apparatus had relatively few members, it had, as a concept, large if inarticulate support. The principal reason for this, as suggested, lay in the peculiar emphasis chosen by Banna for membership indoctrination (see below, pp. 206–8).

About the organization and operation of the secret apparatus there is little reliable information. Between the elaborated and exaggerated stories in the press and official releases and the categorical dismissals of the subject by the Brothers, there have been few references indeed to the subject of moderately convincing tone. To begin with, one must speak of two organizations: that which existed prior to 1948 and its remnants up to 1954; and that which came into existence in 1954. Except for the attempted assassination of the prime minister in October 1954, the later secret apparatus never had the time to develop a history or any institutions. Consequently, the story of the secret apparatus

[49] See Qism Nashr al-Da'wa, *al-La'ihat al-'amma li'l-nashat al-riyadi* (Cairo, [1954]).

largely belongs to the instrument left as a legacy from the Banna period.

Although 'organizational charts' have been made public,[50] I believe that they represent a fact of a moment in time (1948 and 1954) and that fluidity and informality of structure reflected the actual state of affairs. The only constants appear to be (1) the existence of a leader or leaders; (2) the enrolment of members in various kinds of armed formations trained to perform espionage and to commit violence; (3) a relationship to the open organization through selected leaders whose control over the apparatus in both 1948 and 1954 was uncertain; and (4) a set of rules, symbols, and paraphernalia appropriate to its clandestine nature. Once selected, the member was given suitable training in religion, history, and law and in such 'practical' matters as first aid, urban communications and transport, weaponry and military training. After reaching a prescribed level of efficiency, he was then admitted to inner circles with an appropriate oath of 'obedience and silence' before a Qu'ran and pistol.[51]

With even less certainty than for the open organization is it possible to determine accurate membership figures. Estimates by responsible sources for the period of 1948 put the figure at about 1,000. In 1954, while members testified to figures ranging from 1,000 to 3,000, the government placed it at 400.[52] While the number of those tried came closer to the larger figure, those who, by the evidence of the trials, seemed to be really involved appeared to be less than the smaller one.

With the foregoing discussion of the organization, function, and place in the Society of the family, the rovers, and the secret apparatus, it is necessary to conclude with a word about the tone of the training which gave to the Society its distinctive qualities. If the Muslim Brothers were more effectively violent than other groups on the Egyptian scene, it was because *militancy* and *martyrdom* had been elevated to central virtues in the Society's ethos. Its literature and speeches were permeated with references

[50] We included them and made an extended effort to reconstruct from multiple sources a meaningful discussion of the secret apparatus in the original version of this study. In retrospect, we now consider that story to be not so much wrong as so incomplete as to justify our excluding it. For another short (and, we think, incomplete) account, see Husayni, *Moslem Brethren*, ch. 13. Among the source materials we used are the official proceedings of the Jeep and Nuqrashi trials; Kira, *Mahkama*, i and ii; press accounts in *MRY* (7 Dec. 1953, 7 Nov. 1954); *MMB* (12 Dec. 1950); *MAS* (1 Dec. 1954); *MMR* (12 Nov. 1954); *MTR* (3 Nov. 1954).

[51] The most famous description (with pictures) of the oath-taking is still Sadat, *Safahat*, pp. 154–6.

[52] *MTR* (3 Nov. 1954), 7; *JJ* (16 Nov. 1954), 10; (23 Nov. 1954), 4.

identifying it and its purposes in military terms. Banna told members again and again that they were 'the army of liberation, carrying on your shoulders the message of liberation; you are the battalions of salvation for this nation afflicted by calamity'. They were 'the troops of God' whose 'armament' was their 'Islamic morality'.[53]

The most specific illustration of the militant quality of the movement is to be found in the use of the concept of *jihad*. While members very often insisted that *jihad*, properly, was a variant of *ijtihad* and connoted intellectual effort, as used in the Society's literature it more correctly conveyed the sense of *qital* (fighting), leading, if necessary, to death and martyrdom. '*Jihad* is an obligation on every Muslim'—a duty as firmly established as any of the other pillars of the faith. This view, argued Banna, was supported in Qur'anic texts, the Traditions, and the four schools of law. Those who minimize 'the importance of fighting [*qital*] and the preparation for it' are not true to the faith. God grants a 'noble life' to that nation alone which 'knows how to die a noble death'.[54]

The certainty that *jihad* had this physical connotation is evidenced by the relationship always implied between it and the possibility, even the necessity, of death and martyrdom. Death, as an important end of *jihad*, was extolled by Banna in a phrase which came to be a famous part of his legacy: 'the art of death' (*fann al-mawt*). 'Death is art' (*al-mawt fann*). The Qur'an has commanded people to love death more than life. Unless 'the philosophy of the Qur'an on death' replaces 'the love of life' which has consumed Muslims, then they will reach naught. Victory can only come with the mastery of 'the art of death'.[55] In another place, Banna reminds his followers of a Prophetic observation: 'He who dies and has not fought [*ghaza*; literally: raided] and was not resolved to fight, has died a *jahiliyya* death.'[56] The movement cannot succeed, Banna insists, without this dedicated and unqualified kind of *jihad*.[57]

[53] *JIM* (1 Sept. 1946), 3; (14 Sept. 1946), 1, for two out of hundreds of possible references.

[54] See the special *RJ*, *passim*; also, *RTH: IASNN*, pp. 19–20. For two 'unofficial' studies of the question of *jihad* read by Brothers, see Muh. Fahmi al-Tammawi, *al-Mujahidun* (1952); and Ahmad Nar, *al-Qital fi'l-Islam* (1952).

[55] The article using the phrase was first written in 1937 in the context of the Palestine question and was *sina'at al-mawt*; when reprinted in 1946 the title was changed to '*fann al-mawt*' because it was 'closer to the style of the age'. For the reprint article, see *JIM* (16 Aug. 1946), 1; see also Ghazali, *FMD*, pp. 143–5.

[56] *RNURT*, p. 10.

[57] 'Abd al Mun'im Ahmad Ta'lib, *al Bay'a: sharh Risalat al-Ta'alim* (Cairo, 1952), p. 56.

It is an understatement to note that such themes were an important aspect of the formal as well as informal training of the members. In the families, along with the 'theoretical' study of *jihad*, the student's 'history lessons' dwelt on the martial glory of early Islamic conquests.[58] They also included an important section called 'the legality of fighting' (*mashru'iyat al-qital*); in substance, these lessons were exhortations to Muslims to resist the imposition on them of non-Muslim and anti-Muslim ideas and values.[59] Similarly, one of the important aspects of holiday celebrations was the recollection of the famous military events in Muslim history. Of special significance was the annual celebration of the anniversary of the battle of Badr, during which speakers extolled the spirit of *jihad*. The battle of Badr and its significance for Muslims was the subject of one of the few theatrical productions performed by Brothers for Brothers.[60]

That militant *jihad* and the concept of the 'art of death' had as a necessary corollary an emphasis on martyrdom needs no further elaboration. By fighting and dying in the name of Islam in the Canal Zone, in Palestine, or on the gallows in Egypt, the Brother was sure that his 'noble' death had elevated him to the ranks of the pious heroes of Islam.[61] It was in this spirit that a Brother could calmly observe: 'It is the shortest and easiest step from this life to the life hereafter.' It was this spirit which Hudaybi was unable to conquer, which fellow Egyptians—Muslim and non-Muslim alike—fear, and which, coupled with political activism, Egyptian governments of all shades have been unable to tolerate.

[58] See variously in the series called *al-Minhaj al-dirasi al-Islami li-Ikhwan al-usar*.

[59] See e.g. ibid., no. 9, pp. 50–60.

[60] See below, pp. 292–3.

[61] See e.g. Buhi, *MSI, passim*; and numerous small pamphlets on individual 'martyrs', victims of the fighting of 1951–2 in the Canal Zone.

PART III · IDEOLOGY

VIII

THE PROBLEM

THE very active and often violent history of the Society should not obscure the fact that its ideas and non-political activity were to most members the most important part of their membership and, to even the most political of them, matters of vivid concern. While it spent much time doing battle with the government, it spent even more in the service of the multiple needs of its members, not the least of which were 'ideological'. Hence we turn to the complex of notions which in combination produced what the Brothers called the *fikra*—ideology. We shall attempt to reproduce here a coherent statement of these notions which bore the membership along into an all-embracing and passionate commitment to the Society and its leaders, and which, at the same time, set it at odds with all organized authority in Egypt.

Intimately related to this set of ideas was the Brothers' image of the world in which they lived. In general terms this image had three separate facets: Egypt, Islam, and the 'West'. Out of the conglomeration of attitudes and beliefs which informed the perception of these three images was woven the group of ideas which in turn inspired the activity of the Brothers. In so far as what men believe to be real, is real, our concern here will be not the validity of these beliefs, but only the fact of their existence. In the next three chapters we will deal in turn with (1) the image of the world in which the Brothers lived—the problem as it was perceived; (2) (2) the consequent response to that problem in theoretical terms—the ideological solution; and (3) the practical response to the problem—the activity of the Society in the multiple areas of behaviour.

IMAGE OF ISLAM

Muslim History

Like so many of the modern Muslim reformers, the Brothers accepted the view that Islam's decline set in after the end of the period of the first four caliphs. The state which was ruled by the orthodox caliphs (*al-khilafat al-rashida*) was 'truly representative of Islam as a faith and a system'. The ruler was selected from among the people because of his qualifications: 'competence' and the confidence of the mass in him'. The people knew that they alone were 'the source of authority', ultimate arbiters, with Islam, of their ruler. The ruler was pious, learned in the spirit and the law of Islam. The treasury was at the service of the people, for the people had a 'right' to demand that the ruler and state be responsible for the satisfaction of their needs. And in this state there was unity in the 'brotherhood of religion' and 'equality in rights and duties'.

Unhappily for Islam, 'by mischance', political control passed into the hands of the house of Muʿawiya. The Umayyad period of Islamic history saw: the caliphate become a 'kingship' belonging to one family with arbitrary power, indifferent to the popular source of authority, the rulers with no sense of Islam; the treasury become the private purse of the ruler to the detriment of the needs of the people and the interests of the nation; the 'tribalism' of the *jahiliyya* Arabs reawakened and 'factionalism' become a tool of the ruler to maintain power; 'morality' and 'obedience to God' despised and neglected; and individual rights and freedom sacrificed. Throughout the Umayyad period only the rule of ʿUmar II evidenced the 'inner strength' of Islam.

The ʿAbbasid successors of the Damascene rulers provided the unhappy climax to the disintegration of the Islamic community. Under them, hereditary rulership evolved into a 'divine right of the sultanate'. Adulation, servile flattery, and praise of the ruler, right or wrong, became the rule. The caliphs wallowed in luxury, pomp, wealth, silks, and, 'some say', drink; they lived off the public purse, their private lives related in no way to their mission as leaders of the message of Islam. They played on Persian and then Turkish tendencies in the milieu, thereby aggravating the dissensions in the Arab community begun by their predecessors.[1]

The 'height' of Islamic world power was only a façade which concealed bitter political disputes and factionalism. Religious and 'school' (legal) disputes led to an Islam of words and phrases rather than 'faith and action'; 'fanaticism' replaced discussion and debate; 'stagnation' overtook the religious community; and the 'practical sciences' were neglected for theoretical philosophies. Complacent in its power, the state remained ignorant of the 'social development' of other nations; and when it became alerted, the only response was one of 'imitation'. Meanwhile, the power focus

[1] Ghazali, *IIS*, pp. 172–9, 196–8; Qutb, *AIFI* (Hardie tr.), p. 229, 176–232.

shifted and leadership was transferred to 'non-Arabs—Persians, Daylamites, Mamlukes, and Turks', none of whom ever 'tasted the real Islam' because they could not perceive (presumably because of the language) its true meanings. In this setting the first catastrophes struck and then multiplied—the Crusaders, the Tatars, the Carmathians, and the push of Europe against Islam in Spain, and on the peripheries of the Islamic world as Europe opened its era of discovery.[2]

The Turks who had now become political leaders in Islam only staved off the day of doom. In a historic sense, the shift of power from the 'Abbasids to the Turks was tantamount 'to treating one disease with another'. The Turks, in the first part of their reign, were like the orthodox caliphs in their faith; their early successes both among Muslims and East Europeans can only thereby be explained. But 'the emotions [of the Turks] . . . towards Islam were greater and more intense than their understanding of its law, and their warmth for it stronger than their understanding of its spirit'. After Sulayman, *al-qanuni*, the empire disintegrated. The evils of inherited authority set the stage for decline; luxury, internecine power struggles, seclusion of crown princes, and female usurpation of power all added to the picture of decay and left the Ottoman Empire a prey to resurgent Europe. By the end of World War I, 'the enemies of Islam' had utterly wrecked the Islamic state[3] and ensured its impotence in the face of future encroachments on the peoples of its lands. Zionism aided by imperialism in the Arab world—'the heart of Islam'—and imperialism all over the Muslim world continue with impunity to act at will in the land of Islam.[4]

al-Azhar

It will be recalled that Banna, after his first experiences in Cairo, suffered a profound shock at the religious state of the capital; eventually he found his way to the leaders of the Azhar and poured out his anguish over the debased condition of Islam and Muslims. His revulsion at the sense of futility in the Azhar in the face of the currents battering away at Islam can be said to mark his disenchantment with it as a citadel of defence for the faith. Unlike the leaders of the Salafiyya movement, who had influenced his thinking and who also challenged the efficacy of the Azhar's 'defence of Islam', Banna chose, as we saw, to take this cause directly to the people, an attitude consistent with his own Sufi training. Without in any sense associating itself with the secularist attack on the

[2] *RBAWY*, pp. 9–13; *RNJM*, pp. 15–16. [3] Ghazali, *IIS*, pp. 211–18.
[4] *RNJM*, pp. 17–18.

Azhar, his movement was a direct challenge to Azhar authority and a demonstration of its impotence.

In his personal contacts Banna was, of course, friendly to Azharites at all levels. Azhar students came to form an important and active core of the membership of the Society. From the leaders of the Azhar there was no active challenge—except in 1948 and 1954, both instances being politically inspired. During the second rectorship of Mustafa al-Maraghi (April 1935–February 1942) there was even close contact, a fact related to the rise to power of ʿAli Mahir. Maraghi continues to be one of the most highly esteemed by the Brothers of the recent Azhar leaders—an example of a man with 'correct' attitudes about revitalizing both Islam and the Azhar.[5] He seems to have taken a favourable view apart from politics—of Banna and his movement; during the late 1930s, in fact, he supported 'active co-operation' between the Azhar and the officials of the Society.[6] Even so, the Society's basic approach to the Azhar was hostile, though Banna was restrained in his public statements. Once, when commenting on the decaying state of the Muslim world, he merely noted that 'the *ʿulama*' saw and observed and heard and did nothing'.[7] He and his followers often took pains publicly to dispel the belief in Egypt that there was tension between the two groups. One writer, however, observed, more to the point, that there were two Islamic groups in Egypt, the 'officials' of the Azhar and those of the 'Islamic societies', and they 'do not co-operate'.[8] Yet another observation, that the Muslim Brothers have become the champions of the 'Islamic idea' in Egypt, goes to the heart of the matter: the repudiation of the Azhar as the voice of Islam.

The charges levelled at the Azhar by the more articulate and vociferous Brothers were many-faceted, but fundamentally two: (1) that the leading voice of Muslims in the world had failed in its assigned role of spokesman for a living and dynamic Islam; and conversely (2) that it had not been vigorous enough in its resistance to encroachment on the Islamic preserve by foreign ideas and values. The Brothers' special and immediate motive for making these charges was the belief that the Azhar had permitted Egypt to fall into religious, cultural, political, economic, social, legal, and moral decadence and impotence.

[5] See e.g. Anwar al-Jundi, *al-Imam al-Maraghi* (1952). See also *COC*, iii (1946), 511, for a summary of Maraghi's life on the occasion of his death, 21 Aug. 1945.

[6] See Heyworth-Dunne, *Modern Egypt*, pp. 32–4; *Mudh*, pp. 273–4; *MDA* (12 Feb. 1952), 2. Boehm, 'Les Frères musulmans', 217–18, generalizes, we think incorrectly, that the Azhar was favourable to the Brothers because of the prestige they brought to Egypt in the Muslim world.

[7] *MS* (14 Nov. 1947), 3–4.

[8] Ghazali, *IMABSR*, pp. 26–7.

The first set of attitudes had to do with the question of Islam in the modern world and the role attributed to the Azhar as intellectual keeper of the faith. The consensus was that it had failed to represent Islam to Muslims—ruler and ruled alike—as a vital, living code of life; it had failed 'to lead' and 'to teach', and with the abdication of these duties came the corruption of Muslims. When the *'ulama'* of the Azhar 'went to sleep', the Muslim community followed.[9] This situation was a betrayal, not only of historical Islam, but also, even more seriously, of the living Muslim community. For the Azhar had persisted in a time-worn, anachronistic approach to Islam and its teachings—dry, dead, ritualistic, and irrelevant to the needs of living Muslims. Its failure to bring Islam abreast of the times was pinpointed and most readily observable in its medieval system of learning: stagnant teaching; the absence of new learning and research; reliance on memory instead of reasoning; the study of ancient and obsolete texts without reference to modern disciplines and new techniques.[10] Banna notes that the failure of the Azhar was that 'it graduated religious literates, not . . . spiritual guides'.[11] The Azhar *'ulama'* are thus seen as inefficient teachers of an irrelevant doctrine.

The second general criticism followed from the first: having failed to understand their positive mission the *'ulama'* failed in their negative one—the 'defence of Islam'. In Egypt the Azhar failed to resist the governments of Egypt—'the occupier', the palace, the parties—and had thereby contributed to their corruption of all aspects of life in the country. Worse still, the *'ulama'* had not fought the imperialists. Indeed, the dead, resigned, submissive Islam of the Azhar was the Islam 'supported and maintained by the imperialists'; 'if the voice of religion is not heard in the battle for freedom, then whose will be heard?'[12] The *'ulama'*, further, had joined hands and found common cause with the ruling classes and landed interests; they had, thereby, sold their chances to speak out on the great causes of 'exploitation' and 'social justice'. Said Ghazali, 'I know men among the shaykhs of the Azhar who live on Islam, as do the germs of bilharzia and ankylostomiasis on the blood of the wretched peasants.'[13] For these *'ulama'* who became the servants of a foreign occupation and

[9] Ghazali, *FMD*, p. 12; Hajjaji, *RMM*, pp. 56–9; 'Awda, *IBJAWAU*, pp. 22–3, 36, 60–4.

[10] For a succinct summary of this view, see the article entitled 'The Mamluke Era continues in the Azhar', *JIM* (1 July 1954), 12.

[11] 'Abd al-Majid Fath Allah al-Bajuri, *Hasan al-Banna'* [1952 or 1953], p. 26. Father Ayrout, Catholic teacher and student of Egypt's peasantry, in conversation, compared the Brothers' attitude to the Azhar with that of St Ignatius Loyola's protest against the unfeeling religion of the Book.

[12] Ghazali, *IIS*, pp. 6–7, p. 210.

[13] Idem, *IMABSR*, p. 27.

of tyrannical economic and political overlords, the Brothers had a name: 'civil-servant *'ulama*''—the agents of the government which paid them.[14] Loyal to their salaries above all, they had failed to honour their obligations and had thus dishonoured themselves and the religion in whose name they spoke.

Sufism

Banna, it will be recalled, passed his youth saturated with the symbols, literature, and practice of Sufism, a fact of continuing, negative as well as positive, importance in his life. He did not maintain his formal links with Sufism after the creation of his own organization; but, unlike many of his followers, he never violently attacked or openly broke with it, nor did he ever lose his faith in the validity of 'pure' or 'true' Sufism.

His views[15] on the historical development of Sufism conditioned his response to full participation in its practice as he grew older. He argued that following the extensive spread of Islam and its accompanying material enrichment, a reaction against the worldliness of the Muslim community set in, with the reassertion of the piety and asceticism of the Prophetic and early post-Prophetic days. Once begun, the reaction was institutionalized into formal practices which came to be called Sufism; in their 'pure' form, these practices—the *dhikr*, asceticism, worship, and the intuitive and mystical perception and knowledge of God—were of 'the core and essence of Islam'.

After the first century, however, Sufism went beyond this limit, and it was harmed by elements, foreign to it, like 'the sciences of philosophy and logic and the heritage and thought of ancient nations'; the effect was that 'wide gaps were opened for every atheist, apostate, and corrupter of opinion and faith to enter by this door in the name of Sufism'. This led to factionalism and the setting up of many different Sufi orders; new divisions were thereby created in the Muslim community. While recognizing the part that Sufism had played in the historical spread of Islam, especially in Africa and Asia, Banna nevertheless felt that whatever benefit Islam and Muslims might derive from it was worthless in the light of the greater evils consequent on its corruption. He urged, therefore, a serious reform effort designed to save 'pure' Sufism from its later accretions, and to combat the competitiveness of its organized groups, with an eye to restoring Sufism to all Muslims as a universal and transcendent way of living within Islam.

[14] *MDA* (6 Feb. 1951), 13.

[15] The following is a summary of those views from *Mudh.*, pp. 16–19.

This, Banna explains, was why he made no effort to present his own organization as an order (*tariqa*). After the Society took root, he continued to enjoy visits from, and disputes with, the leaders of the local orders when they passed through Isma'iliyya; he sought to persuade them of the need for reform so that all might unite and work together for the salvation of Islam. For the Society of the Brothers, he preferred another organizational form: 'I did not want to enter into competition with the other orders; and I did not want it to be confined to one group of Muslims or one aspect of Islamic reform; rather I sought that it be a general message based on learning, education, and *jihad*.'[16]

Banna's views of Sufism were shared by his followers who, however, only in passing recognized the positive spiritual qualities he saw in it. It was perhaps necessary to do this because of Banna's well-known early links with formal Sufism; Banna, of course, became a pure example of this acceptable 'spiritual Sufism'.[17] But the esteem accorded the leader in this aspect of his personality did not minimize the widespread revulsion and contempt felt by the articulate and the urban Brothers for Sufism.

Members' views on the origins of Sufism were variants of Banna's theme. In one reported discussion among Brothers, Sufism was seen as a consequence of the failure of the caliphate to discharge its dual function of 'administrative—spiritual guidance'; when the caliphate became a mere political operation, Sufism filled the gap as a community-wide 'reaction'. Again, Sufism was seen in origin to be 'un-Islamic', because its orders were 'based on a class system'. Finally, it was seen as a Greek–Hindu phenomenon which had 'no relation to Islam'. All present agreed that Sufism was a temporary and limited treatment for 'the problems resulting from the absence of a true Islamic life'.[18]

The members of the Society shared, with more conviction, Banna's religious and institutional objections to Sufism: that the orders led to community factionalism inspired by an irresponsible struggle for power and prestige among their shaykhs; and that they had permitted the multiplication of 'innovations' (*bida'*)—superstitions, talismans, witchcraft, and saint worship—in violation of the laws of Islam.[19] But for Banna's followers there appeared

[16] Ibid., pp. 68–9. Banna's use of the phrase 'the other orders' (*al-turuq al-ukhra*) suggests some foundation for the view of some members that there was much more Sufism involved in the founding of the Society than any care to admit.

[17] See e.g. Hajjaji, *RMM*, pp. 59–60; and *IMAM*, ii. 25: 'There is nothing wrong with it [Sufism] provided it remains within legal bounds.'

[18] See Nadawi, *Mudhakkarat*, pp. 83–5.

[19] With the reference in n. 17, above, see Ghazali, *IIS*, p. 183; Bajuri, *Hasan al-Banna'*, pp. 26–27.

to be other more compelling economic and social objections to Sufism: it was a remnant of the 'feudal ages' used by the unscrupulous 'to drug the masses'; the Sufi shaykhs were corrupters of the countryside, the major obstacles to progress and reform, and 'tools' of the politicians for 'the exploitation of the people'; finally, Sufism inspired and justified a spiritual withdrawal from life which leads to the evil of the socially useless existence. Exploited by shaykhs whose influence over them was complete, victimized Muslims 'resigned' themselves to their economic and social 'fate'. Sufism was the first blow which struck at Islamic thought, and, indeed at the existence of the Islamic nation.[20]

This latter view of Sufism stemmed from the 'activist' mentality Banna inspired in the Society; in particular, it had to do with a distinction in Sufism made by him. In the essay written at Dar al-ʻUlum in which he discussed his preference for teaching as compared with the way of the mystic, he addressed himself to the question of the social value of mystical practice, drawing a distinction between 'isolated spirituality' (*al-ruhaniyya al-iʻtizaliyya*) and 'social spirituality' (*al-ruhaniyya al-ijtimaʻiyya*). For men, beside the mystical aspect of the ritual and the spiritual discipline gained thereby, the obligation was to enter the world and exert 'effort' (*jihad*) towards the solution of social problems.[21] In a general sense this attitude dominated the Society's outlook on the problems its members faced, and it militated against any sympathetic understanding of Sufism. The definition of the Society by a member as a movement of *effendiyya*[22] was a negative one, admittedly designed to dissociate from the perceived stigma of the mystical orders, and especially from the sense of futility which they represented.

Sects and Schools

One of the constant elements in the attitudes of the Brothers to the Azhar and its *'ulama'* and Sufism was their concern with Muslim disunity. This was because disunity, i.e. disputation and factionalism, was contrary to the prime duty of every Muslim to live in loving 'brotherhood' with his fellow Muslims; and because it induced and perpetuated the subservience of Muslim states and peoples to foreign ideas and controls. Disunity was not only sinful; it promised to be fatal to the Muslim community. Hence the Society's image of the sects of Islam and its schools of law.

Banna's memoirs clearly indicate his early concern with the division of Muslims into competing and conflicting groups, and

[20] See Ghazali, *IMABSR*, pp. 47–8; *IMI*, p. 174; and Qutb, *MIWR*, p. 96.
[21] See Zaki, *Ikhwan*, pp. 41–2, and above, p. 66.
[22] Hajjaji, *QDHRTM*, p. 84.

he describes his attempt, once established in Isma'iliyya, to combat this by preaching the essential unimportance of the differences which permissibly exist within the body of Islam. These were, he felt, another element in the decline in the Muslim community; and as a first step towards its regeneration, their importance must be minimized. The Brothers, Banna insisted, belonged to no sect or school. Differences of opinion were, of course, necessary and even desirable, but carried beyond their legitimate function they became harmful to Islam. 'Each of the four schools is respectable', and the difference among them should be debated in an 'atmosphere of love'. The word 'schoolman' (*madhhabi*) is properly a term of derision.[23] Banna's favourite plea for unity was often recalled by his followers: 'Let us co-operate in those things on which we can agree and be lenient in those on which we cannot.'

Two groups within Islam, it should be added, were openly excluded from this proposed tolerance of diversity: the Qadiyanis of Pakistan and the Baha'is of Iranian origin. Both were repudiated because of their founders' pretensions to prophecy and the subsequent developments within the 'apostate' groups 'conflicting with Islam'.[24]

IMAGE OF EGYPT

Egyptian History

Egypt's relation to Islam, felt the Brothers, was unique. From the beginning of Islamic history the destiny of Egypt had been irrevocably bound to the destiny of Muslim peoples. The centre of the oldest civilizations of mankind, Egypt was the logical and historically right place for Islam to base itself. It was Egypt that had carried high the banner of Islam, in the period of the dissolution of the Arab Empire, against the Crusaders and the Tatars. Because Islam had penetrated deeply into the 'conscience and emotions' of Egyptians, because Islam had become 'its faith, its language, and its civilization', Egypt had a unique role to play in Islam's resurgence.[25]

But first Egypt must recover from the blight which had affected her as well as all other parts of the Muslim world. The 'men of religion' bore the chief initial blame for their failure to bring into

[23] See *Mudh.*, pp. 65–7; *RBAWY*, p. 9; *RTH: D*, pp. 26–8; *RNURT*, pp. 6–7.

[24] See *Mudh.*, p. 69, and the pamphlet widely distributed among the Brothers by Lajnat al-Shabab al-Muslim, *al-Mas'ala al-qadyaniyya* (1953), written by abu al-'Ala' al-Mawdudi of Pakistan.

[25] See e.g. *RDFTJ*, p. 24.

effect the 'true' Muslim life and thereby check if not prevent the corruption of Muslim society. If the 'men of religion' were negatively responsible by failing to act, the positive cause of decay was imperialism, which had imposed itself and its civilization on Egypt. There were two kinds of imperialism: 'external' (*al-isti'mar al-khariji*), the brute force of the occupying foreign power, and 'internal' or 'domestic' (*al-isti'mar al-dakhili*), the forces which consciously or unconsciously—at best by indifference, at worst by 'treason' to the needs and will of the Muslim community—served the interests of that power. 'Domestic imperialism' spread 'dejection and moral defeat' and diverted Egyptians from their traditional faith to 'a dead pacifism, lowly humiliation, and acceptance of the *status quo*'.[26] It was in this context of dual imperialisms in Egypt's history that her political, economic, and social problems were viewed.

Politics and Parties

Political parties, political leaders, and 'partyism' were the first and most vehemently objectionable aspect of the Egyptian scene. The parties were guided by personal greed and interests; there were no programmes and no goals; and their activity was governed by men, not ideas. In reality the parties were 'a front for capitalism', the political instrument by means of which the capitalist exploited the workers and used the legal and administrative apparatus of the state to serve his own ends. Instead of being their servants, the parties had 'ruled the people' illegitimately because they neither reflected the will of the nation nor served its interests.[27]

These attitudes about parties were largely governed by specific and secular considerations. An even more important facet of the image for the Society was the picture of the parties and their leaders as tools of British and Western ideologies—the leaders of cultural 'domestic imperialism'. The parties, according to this view, followed Western patterns of organization and thought. As such, they were supported and maintained by the military and political might of the occupier, and served and reinforced each other for their mutual gain. The historic mistake of Egyptians, observed one Brother, was in accepting independence, a constitution, and a parliamentary system 'before we expelled England from Egypt'. The corollary to this view, which was, as has been suggested,

[26] Ghazali, *MHN* (Faruqi tr.), p. xiii. See also Smith, *Islam in Modern History*, pp. 41–7, esp. p. 47.

[27] See for this well-worn theme, and its counterpart that the Muslim Brothers were just the opposite, Ghazali, *TFDWH*, p. 159; and *IMABSR*, p. 119; *RMFDNI*, pp. 55–8.

cultural as well as political in inspiration, was that the leaders were incompetent Muslims; trained in Western ways and thoughts they were inadequate to the task of leading Muslim countries because 'they forgot their glory, their history and their past'.[28]

Mentally separated from their countrymen and lacking any common cause with them, the party leaders and their tools, the parties, became the agents of division and disunity. The party system weakened the national strength during the crucial battles for political freedom and internal reform. Divided into irresponsible and conflicting groups, the nation forfeited its unity and therefore achieved neither independence nor progress.[29]

Corruption in the parties and party leaders had a crucial political consequence: parliamentary life and democratic government failed. The 'upper class', the seat of politico-economic power, 'monopolized' government. The people were 'compelled' to choose the parliament from among their 'oppressors': the landlord commanded the votes of his tenants; the 'lord of finance' those of his debtors—'the hungry ones'. The people were victimized by a political-economic social tyranny. Though the granting of the parliament of 1923 by the British was intended to mean that the nation would 'rule itself by itself', that very same parliament became a 'cover' for plundering the rights and wealth of the people. It was only a natural—and for the Society and Egypt extremely important—extension of this view of Egypt's parliamentary life to say that 'all the elections since 1923 . . . are spurious'.[30]

The administration of government had also been the victim of political corruption in the parties. The hallmarks of the bureaucracy had been inefficiency, muddle, and corruption, abuse of authority, and personal power; appointments had been made without regard to the qualifications of the appointee. This situation led to inexcusable complications in dealings with the government: anyone who wanted to send his children to school, enter a hospital, facilitate the completion of government business, leave the country, or get appointed to a job was either 'in need of intercession' (*wasita*) or thought he needed it. This had two fundamental explanations: (1) 'the loss of confidence in the law' and of respect for it as it had been administered by 'corrupt officials'; and (2) the centralization of authority in the hands of the 'powerful leaders' to the point where the subordinates dared not take upon

[28] Ghazali, *IIS*, pp. 3, 17–19; Hajjaji, *IMAM*, ii. 20–3; 'Awda, *IBJAWAU*, p. 25.

[29] See *JIM* (19 July 1946), 4. For an extended brief against the parties, see three works by Anwar al-Jundi: *Faza'i' al-ahzab al-siyasiyya* (n.d.); *Munawarat al-siyasa* (1947); and *Ta'rikh al-ahzab al-siyasiyya* (1946).

[30] Ghazali, *IMABSR*, pp. 118–19; *MDA* (1 Apr. 1952), 18.

themselves responsibility and had become 'tools with neither will nor opinions'.[31]

In this political picture the monarchy figured only slightly before 1952, for obvious reasons. It has already been suggested that Banna through much of his life as leader seemed not to have lost his loyalty to the monarchy, but the forces turned loose in the movement inevitably set it against the palace. The works of Muhammad Ghazali, the first of which appeared in 1948, could be regarded as indirect assaults on monarchical authority and reflections of the spirit of the membership, if not of the leaders. This fact seems to have been clear to the palace, as the 1948 decree of dissolution shows. The 1952 revolution freed the movement's writers from earlier restraints and launched the great campaign to discredit Faruq as the source of all corruption in the country.

Only one other point is worth noting here about the historical image of the monarchy—one which reflected an important contradiction in the Brothers' thinking. Muhammad 'Ali, the founder of the last Egyptian dynasty, received a variety of interpretations. One view extolled him as the 'leader of Egypt'—'the great man who had rejuvenated a great people'. With only three million people he set the nation on its modern path; not only did he build factories, navies, and armies, he also raised Egyptian dignity and prestige. This positive nationalist and secularly patriotic view of Muhammad 'Ali was balanced by a negative religious picture of him as the instrument of the penetration of Western ideas and the further destruction of Islam. Though the validity of his work was grudgingly admitted as 'proving' that Egypt was 'a nation alive', it was none the less felt that he missed the point of all modern reformers and failed to establish Islam as an operative 'socio-political system'.[32]

A similar blend of praise and anger was directed towards the Turkish revolution and its leader Mustafa Kemal: on the one hand, praise for the work of consolidating and unifying the nation; on the other, anger at his disestablishment of Islam. The conflict of motives correctly mirrored the complex of factors which underpinned the Society's appeal, a subject which will conclude this study.

Capitalism and Foreign Economic Domination

The economic image of Egypt comprised two main factors: (1) the maldistribution of wealth and land—i.e. Egyptian capital-

[31] *JIM* (26 Sept. 1946), 1, and Ghazali, *IMABSR*, pp. 67–70.

[32] See *JIM* (11 Aug. 1946), 1, for the first view; for the second see Ghazali, *TFDH*, pp. 28–30, and Hajjaji, *RWR*, pp. 46–8.

ism and what were deemed to be its evil consequences for the economy and people of Egypt; and (2) foreign economic exploitation—deriving from the imperialist but also from his internal counterpart among the 'domestic imperialists', the foreigner in Egypt.

The image of Egyptian capitalism centred on the land-holder: 'the few' who still owned most of the land as in 'the most oppressive ages of feudalism', and exploited it and its peasants for their own personal interests without regard for the true function of their position as a 'social charge' (*wazifa ijtima'iyya*). But the image of capitalism encompasses much more. Money needed for developmental projects is in the hands of the capitalists who evade their duties towards the state and the people because the government represents them and not the needy masses. The poor people pay the taxes. The capitalist, placing his own interests before those of the nation, fails to use wisely the natural and human resources of the state. The constitution in theory freed the masses from the slavery of feudalism, but in fact slavery continues without the virtue shown by the feudal lord of concern for the body and soul of his slave. The exploited populace lives in a continual economic crisis, with an intolerably low standard of living; its existence is marked not only by poverty but derivative filth and disease. The labourer lives in a home without the water, light, and other facilities necessary to maintain a decent level of life and health; he lives amidst 'piles of sweepings', smothered with flies, in alleys and streets of the city which 'deserve nothing better than destruction by dynamite' so that they may be rebuilt from the foundations.[33]

This situation leads to many evils: (1) it 'paralyzes the strength of the nation in work and production'; (2) it 'destroys human dignity and rights'; (3) it 'corrupts the character and the conscience'; (4) 'it denies individual security'; (5) it 'pushes people into the arms of the communists'; (6) it 'violates the spirit of religion'. In short, the situation cannot and must not last, because it rejects 'all principles of humanity, of the age, the nature of things and the simplest economic principles'.[34] These views were a graphic demonstration of how far ahead of the leader the members were: Banna, never so direct in his attacks on the

[33] Ghazali, *IMABSR*, p. 106 and *passim*; *IMI*, pp. 153, 159–65, for the bitterest of the attacks on landlords. The same author in *IMI*, pp. 107–8, reveals part of his motivation when he asserts that the irresponsible sale of land by large Arab landowners in Palestine was one of the long-range causes of the loss of that country.

[34] Qutb, *MIWR*, p. 7; pp. 9–27 and 47–66, where the author details his case against the leading Egyptian capitalist, 'Abbud Pasha.

economic order, confined himself to denunciation of the gap between the rich and the poor.[35]

The Brothers' views on Egyptian capitalism were not, of course, separate from their views on foreign economic domination, but the latter had a special and important non-economic aspect. It will be recalled how, early in his life, Banna had expressed his dismay at the extent of foreign control over Isma'iliyya, and how shocked he was to see street signs, even in the popular quarters, written in 'the language of the economic occupation'. The feeling of resentment at the inferior cultural, social, and economic position of Egyptians as compared with the foreigner was enshrined in the words of the labourers who came to Banna and launched the movement.[36]

Unlike so many other issues, this one moved Banna to only slightly less vehemence than his followers. 'The foreigners', he observed—both the imperialists who have occupied Egypt and those who have assumed 'Egyptian nationality'—have taken for their own and for their native country's interests the best of the natural resources of the country; industry, commerce, and utilities are in their hands; and all of them 'continue to view the Egyptian citizen, the Egyptian worker, and the Egyptian rulers without esteem and without justice'.[37] In no discussion of this matter by Banna or his followers was the economic question of control separable from the cultural, religious, societal, or personal question of inferiority and humiliation—an angry response to the conspicuous contempt of the foreign 'economic overlord' for the Egyptian and to 'Muslim servility' before the foreign master'.[38]

The importance of this attitude cannot be over emphasized; strongly felt and widely held, it remained a constant in the movement's dynamic. Its implications were many, for the foreigner—the *khawaja*—was invariably a Christian or Jew; the posture of the Society 'in defence of Islam' led necessarily to a view of the foreigner which included religious and cultural as well as political and economic objections. And not the least of the implications of this view was the identification of the foreigner with the *local* Christian or Jew, a relationship between majority religious and cultural inferiority and the minority. We will return to this point again.

[35] See e.g. *RMFDNI*, pp. 71–2.

[36] See above, p. 8, and Nadawi, *Mudhakkarat*, p. 47, for comments by Banna's father on this subject.

[37] *RMFDNI*, p. 73; see also *RMK*, p. 30; and *RBAWY*, p. 26.

[38] Ghazali, *FMD*, pp. 198–9, and *IWAI*, pp. 72–83, 137–8 for an extensive discussion.

Society and Morality

The evacuation of the British troops from Egypt in 1954 meant for the Brothers the end of 'the military-political-ethical-social invasion'. Here again, in the social order imperialism was seen as the fountain head of corruption. When the armies of Europe came to Egypt, they brought with them their laws, schools, languages, and sciences; but also their 'wine, women, and sin'.[39] The introduction of the traditions and values of the West has corrupted society, bred immorality, and destroyed the inherited and traditional values of Muslim society. Social and family life is corrupted by the 'cheap' cinema, stage, radio, and music. The moral and sex problems of youth are related to the 'naked' women in the streets, the 'dirty' films, the 'suggestive' popular music, the 'uncontrolled' press and its lewd pictures, and the permissibility of wine.

Indiscriminate mixing of the sexes has led to debauchery. Women have lost their Muslim virtues by their immodest participation in the partying and dancing which marks so many of the official and unofficial functions. Why? Because 'European women do it and we want to be like Europe in all respects!!' As a consequence, the nation is torn in its personal and home life between an Islamic and a Western pattern; some have remained Muslim while others have 'outwesternized the Westerners'.

This ethical duality has entered into other important areas of the social order; law and education. The nation has a dual system of schools: a religious education leads to the Azhar; a civil education to the university. Each is separate from the other, one a remnant of Islamic heritage, the other an imitation of the West. This anarchic, contradictory, and conflicting situation has led to intellectual backwardness and confusion, chaos and atheism.

Finally, the introduction of Western codes of law has corrupted and perverted the nation's thought, mind, and logic. When imperialism introduced the foreign laws it was not resisted by the 'incompetent '*ulama*'' or by the leaders, law-makers, and lawyers of the country, who were both ignorant of the nature of the *shari'a* and shackled by a 'self-imposed bondage' to the opinions of Europeans in legal matters. Thus the law of Egypt has no relation to its citizens, is not supported by their beliefs, and does not spring from their hearts. It is man-made law transferred from the laws of the European countries, existing side by side in a dual legal system with a revealed religious law. The inharmonious relation of

[39] *MDA* (17 Aug. 1954), 1.

revealed and man-made law has served to shatter the 'unity' of the nation.[40]

The image of Egypt is thus a distressing one. Religious indifference and imperialism and the multiple facets of both have left Egypt in psychological chaos, a prey to 'deadly desperation, lethal indolence, disgraceful cowardice, despicable obsequiousness, effeminancy, miserliness, and egotism'.[41] In the weakened state of the Muslim community, European civilization has invaded, 'strongly and violently', and left it in ruins:

> European 'civilization' . . . has developed in us a morbid mentality, a morbid taste and has made of us a morbid community that looks upon its own morbidity and decay as a thing of virtue and a sign of progress. . . . Once corrupt, the greatest corruption is to regard one's corruption as good and desirable.[42]

IMAGE OF THE WEST

In so far as the ethos of the movement was in such large part a response to the 'enticement' of the Western values and ideas which accompanied the movement of Western power to the East, the image of the West—Western civilization—held by the Brothers was important. It has already been noted by one writer that the Brothers distinguished between Western civilization 'in its own environment' and the Western civilization which was 'thrown at the East'.[43] It might further be observed that the Brothers, although distinguishing between its various parts, in general defined 'the West' so as to include both the 'free world' and the communist world.

Western Civilization

Western civilization, as it unfolded in its own environment, had both negative and positive qualities. The 'free world'—primarily England and the United States—had much to commend it so far as its internal way of life was concerned. Its respect for individual freedom and the right of workers to take action to protect their interests was particularly noteworthy. There were effective democratic processes in the West and a truly representative parliamentary life. Related to this was the sense of responsibility of the

[40] See almost any issue of *MDA*, esp. those of 27 July, 17 Aug. 1954; any issue of *JIM*, esp. those of 19, 21 Sept. 1946; Qutb, *DI*, p. 85; *RMBBM*, *passim*, esp. pp. 112–14; *RDFTJ*, pp. 27–8; see also Gibb, *Modern Trends in Islam*, p. 42. For the law see 'Awda, *IWAQ*, and by the same author, *IBJAWAU*, *passim*.

[41] *RTH: D*, pp. 31–2.

[42] An Azhar appeal for reform quoted in Ghazali, *MHN* (Faruqi tr.), pp. 82–3.

[43] Husayni, *Ikhwan*, p. 173.

rulers to their peoples, and the widespread 'social spirit' (*ruh ijtima'i*) in Western nations. The 'infidel nation' of England compared favourably with some Muslim countries as regards justice and equality.[44]

The virtues of the communist world, though only of 'outward appearance' and largely theoretical, were, nevertheless, noteworthy: concern for the poor, 'equality', 'mutuality of responsibility' among classes, 'brotherhood', and 'humanitarianism' without distinctions between peoples.[45] These qualities conduced to 'potential' social justice on a 'material' level—a spiritually barren satisfaction of bodily needs. This was Russian communism and perhaps was the path for Christian Europe: 'we have no good grounds for any hostility between Islam and the thought of social justice such as the hostility which persists between Christianity [the West] and communism'.[46] 'Irreligious' and 'absolute', Russian socialism, because of its emphasis on social justice, is the only alternative to an 'Islamic socialism based on the cardinal points of monotheism and the brotherhood of man'.[47]

One analogy, which was often made in the Society to demonstrate Islam's priority of possession of the fundamental ideas of the West, neatly summarizes some of its positive attitude to the West; incidentally, it makes a revealing and concise observation about the Brothers' attitude towards Nazism, or more broadly, totalitarianism. The statement is as follows. The truly 'practical social order', which all world systems have touched in part, is found in Islam. The prayer of the Muslim is the best example of this truth. Communism preaches 'equality, the abolition of classes, distinctions, and pride in property'; the Muslim feels this completely, for when he enters the mosque, he knows that the mosque belongs to God, that there are no 'great' and no 'small' within its precincts. The *mu'adhdhin* cries out, prayer begins, everyone follows the *imam* in his actions; there is 'unity and discipline', the best qualities of dictatorship. But the *imam* is no tyrant, for if he errs he must stand corrected by anyone in the congregation who may choose to do so; this is the best aspect of democracy.[48]

The negative views about the West in its own milieu are as instructive and predictable. The Western democracies may have

[44] See esp. Qutb, *MIWR*, p. 25; Ghazali in *IIS*, p. 162; in *IMABSR*, pp. 68–9; in *TFDH*, p. 131; in *IWAI*, pp. 86–94.

[45] *JIM* (17 July 1946), 1, written at the peak of its anti-communism.

[46] Qutb, *AIFI* (Hardie tr.), p. 14.

[47] Ghazali, *MHN* (Faruqi tr.), p. 135.

[48] *MS* (14 Nov. 1947), 30–1. See also *JIM* (26 Dec. 1946), 3: communism arranges 'economic matters and social life'; democracy stabilizes the life of 'representative government'; and fascism inspires 'martial strength and military preparedness'.

created satisfying political processes, but democracy has led to the corruption of individuals and thus of societies. An excess of 'individualism' has led to licence and has set man against man and class against class; it has led, too, to moral irresponsibility, 'degeneracy', and 'social chaos', all of which have precipitated crisis in the home—the debasement of women and the weakening and destruction of the family. On another plane, democracy has become synonymous with capitalism and its exploitive basis of legally recognized usury. And, finally, in the leading democracy of the West, failure has marked efforts to solve the 'race issue on the basis of equality and justice'; America has become the defender and leader of 'the empire of the white man'.[49]

The communist world—the 'peoples' democracies'—is equally at fault. There, 'atheism', internal 'political tyranny', and 'international dictatorship' are the hallmarks of the system. 'Freedom of work, speech, and thought' are consistently denied; the Russian 'concept of equality' is so materialistic as to be meaningless; and the guiding principle of the system is 'destructive' and 'incites to revolution'.[50]

The common denominator of all the Western systems is materialism: 'The Western world, during [recent] centuries, has been materialist in tissue and fibre . . . resulting in a deadening of human sentiments and sympathies, and in the extinction of godly endeavours and spiritual values.'[51] And the basic problem is that their values are limited and confining because their goals are finite: 'The criteria of justice and equality and other human virtues are in the hands of humans [as against God] who define their limits.'[52]

These negative views of the West were summed up in an early indictment by Banna: 'The civilization of the West', proudly strong in its science, and for a period able to subjugate the world, is now 'in bankruptcy and in decline', its political fundamentals destroyed by dictatorship, its economic systems racked by crisis [written in 1936], its social order decaying. 'Revolution is in process everywhere'. 'The people are perplexed'; greed, materialism, and oppression have destroyed the relations between states [reference is to the failing League of Nations]; 'all humanity' is 'tortured' and 'miserable'. Leadership of the world, first Eastern, moved westwards with the Greeks and Romans and eastwards again following the Semitic prophets [*sic*]. And finally with the

[49] *RBAWY*, pp. 19–20; *JIM* (19 July 1946), 1, 4; (23 Oct. 1946), 1. See also Qutb, *MIWR*, p. 31, and *DI*, p. 107.
[50] Qutb, *MIWR*, pp. 23–7; Ghazali, *IMABSR*, pp. 36–8.
[51] *RDFTJ*, p. 10.
[52] 'Awda, *IWAS*, pp. 78–9.

Renaissance it passed into the hands of a 'tyrannical' and 'oppressive' West. The time has come for the East to rise again.[53]

'Materialism' and 'greed and tyranny' were the keys to the Brothers' negative attitude to the West—consistently both before and after World War II. This reflected the two important and related levels of thought among the Brothers: resistance to Western secularism (i.e., materialism) and resistance to Western occupation. Since the former was seen as a derivative of the latter, a keystone in the structure of ideas was the question of imperialism —Western civilization in the East.

Imperialism

The hatred and anger felt by the Brothers about the occupation need not be described in detail. What they felt it meant for Egypt has been summed up as 'slow annihilation and profound and complete corruption'.[54] As an 'international' movement the Brothers were of course concerned with imperialism as it affected every Muslim country, and they accordingly publicized persistently inflammatory attacks on the 'imperial powers' for their international 'political immorality'. This was directed at the traditional imperial powers of the West—Britain and France and the earlier cases of Italy and the Netherlands. And reflecting the post-World War II line-up of nations, attention in these later years focused on the United States as leader of the 'free world' and on Soviet Russia.

Russian imperialism was seen in a historical and purely Muslim perspective: 'Tsarist Russia was one of the most violent in its enmity to Islam and Muslims', a fact intimately connected with 'Christian Crusading fanaticism' (to which reference will shortly be made again). Under the auspices of the Bolsheviks Russian imperialism continued unabated with even greater venom and more terrible bloodshed. For enslaved Muslims the Russian empire became 'a slaughterhouse of religion'.

American imperialism shared with the Russian variety the charge of having been responsible for the outcome of the Palestine question. Palestine was the beginning of the identification of the United States with political imperialism: 'After Roosevelt', the United States joined 'the ranks of the imperialists with the creation of Israel', and began to support imperialism 'wherever Muslims were occupied'. 'Truman', 'four million votes', 'Zionist pressure', and 'Jewish gold and Zionist influence'—these were the explanations for American support of Israel. America, which 'theoreti-

[53] *RTH: NN*, pp. 87–9.
[54] *JIM* (24 Oct. 1946), 3, as an example. Qutb, *DI*, pp. 96–8, 207–14, and the columns of the daily, *JIM*, esp. e.g. 23 July 1946.

cally' believed in the 'rights of man', 'social justice', and the United Nations Charter, belied her principles by joining England in support of the 'Zionist aggressors', and 'gave Palestine to the Jews'. And among those things which most inflamed opinion were the effect of the American 'Zionist-dominated' press, radio, and films in destroying 'the reputation and honour' of everything 'Muslim and Eastern' in the campaign to win Palestine, and the related Zionist fund-raising drives, which at one point allegedly featured the slogan 'Pay a dollar and kill an Arab'.[55]

The Palestine question became the starting-point for attacks on the United States. Other sore points were that country's alleged support of England in Egypt and France in North Africa. Because of the 'violations of freedom by the free world' in Muslim countries and because of 'racism' in America, the United States was seen to be the new defender and leader of 'the empire of the white man'. Occasionally, these attitudes were qualified by the notion that the United States was only stupid rather than evil. Mostly it was simpler to explain the policies of the world's leading 'capitalist state', both as regards to 'colonial countries' and to the continuing 'cold war' with Russia, in terms of imperialism.[56]

America's capitalism was also the type image of economic imperialism. Before World War II consideration of economic imperialism by the movement was confined to indignation over the 'exploitation' of the nation's resources by 'the imperialist oppressor'. With the emergence of the 'cold war' and the concomitant wooing of Asia by both parties to it, the issue crystallized more firmly around the theoretical question of capitalism and communism, both of which the Brothers rejected. As we have observed, economic reasons were not the only ones for this rejection: capitalism was equated with licentious individualism and

thus with social chaos, communism with atheism, and both with materialism. Moreover, bitterness towards Egyptian capitalism and its abuses predisposed the Society to come to regard the 'capitalist West', especially the United States, as the real enemy, seeking through the technical and economic aid programmes to pervert the political independence of the countries aided, and to establish this 'commercial dominance' by 'glutting the local markets'.[57] Israel, it should also be noted was seen as a device to

[55] See Qutb, *MIWR*, pp. 41–2; Hudaybi in *JA* (25 Nov. 1953), 6, 11; and *MDA* (22 Nov. 1955), 1, for a statement about the Zionist fund-raising campaigns and this slogan.

[56] Qutb, *DI*, p. 107, and *SAWI*, pp. 157–64. Qutb, in the USA before the Korean war, was enamoured of the view that war in America has become 'a necessity of national life'. His position as head of the section for propaganda of the message made him an important opinion-maker at the time.

[57] Qutb, *SAWI*, p. 164, and Hudaybi in *JA* (25 Nov. 1953), 11.

establish commercial hegemony over the Middle East. Thus, along with the Brothers' religious interpretation—communism has no religion and capitalism has a hypocritical religion—there was a clear political view of 'economic imperialism': communism is a threat 'at the gates of the nation', capitalism is a threat 'within its boundaries'; 'we believe that purging the nation of its painful economic oppressions is its protection from both red and white imperialism'.[58]

The movement also concerned itself with another kind of imperialism not always the object of nationalist attack: cultural imperialism. This was the imperialism which 'entered the minds of the people with its teachings and thoughts' and which tried 'to dominate the social situation' in the country.[59] On this important level, the response of the Society was very revealing.

This attitude to cultural imperialism became more conspicuous during and after the Palestine war. For example, United Nations activity in Palestine was seen as 'a new declaration of Zionist-Crusading war against the Arab and Islamic peoples'. The full identification of Zionism with crusading Western imperialism was indicated by the interchangeable use of terms such as 'European crusading' (*al-salibiyya al-urabbiyya*) and 'Jewish crusading' (*al-salibiyya al-yahudiyya*).[60] There was, of course, a specific historical foundation for this attitude, and the same implications persisted. In so far as the Brothers saw religion not as a mere facet of society or culture but as synonymous with these, 'crusade' had both political and cultural connotations for them. 'Western imperialistic crusading' thus appeared as an attempt not only to conquer Muslim lands but to subvert Muslim society. In statements stronger than those usually made on this issue one writer says:

> The West surely seeks to humiliate us, to occupy our lands and begin destroying Islam by annulling its laws and abolishing its traditions. In doing this, the West acts under the guidance of the Church.
>
> The power of the Church is operative in orienting the internal and foreign policies of the Western bloc, led by England and America . . . . A hundred years ago the situation was one of enmity between the State and Christianity. Today, however, the relationship is obviously a cordial alliance.[61]

The historical Crusades succeeded in unleashing in Europe 'a

[58] Ghazali, *IMABSR*, p. 10.

[59] Hudaybi in *JA* (25 Nov. 1953), 6.

[60] See e.g. *MS* (14 Nov. 1947), 86–8; and Nadawi, *Mudhakkarat*, p. 43.

[61] Ghazali, *MHN* (Faruqi tr.), pp. 22, 15, xvi–xvii; see also the pamphlet circulated by the student section of the Society, Qism al-Tullab, *al-Muslimum bayn al-tabshir wa'l-isti'mar* (Cairo, 1952), *passim*, esp. p. 19. Ahmad, *Nahda*, p. 49, sees the 'religious renaissance' of Islam as a function of 'Western Christian imperialism'.

hatred and a sinister fury against us that has raged unappeased to the present day'. Today, 'the old hatred combines with covetousness and fanaticism' to produce 'Christian imperialism'. Combining this thought with the attitude towards 'aggressive Zionism', Qutb could logically conclude by saying: 'General Allenby was no more than typical of the mind of all Europe when, entering Jerusalem during World War I, he said: "Only now have the Crusades come to an end." '[62]

On the question of how the crusading spirit could still exist in a 'Europe which has discarded Its Christianity', Qutb answers:

> Crusading was not confined to the clangor of arms, but was, before and above all else, an intellectual enmity.
>
> European imperial interests can never forget that the spirit of Islam is firmly opposed to the spirit of Imperialism. . . .
>
> There are those who hold that it is the financial influence of the Jews of the United States and elsewhere which has governed the policy of the West. There are those who say that it is English ambition and Anglo-Saxon guile which are responsible. . . . And there are those who believe that it is the antipathy between East and West. . . . All these opinions overlook one vital element in the question . . ., the Crusader spirit which runs in the blood of all Westerners.

In this sense, there is no distinction between Russia and the United States. Both share in a common crusade against 'the spirit of Islam'.[63]

What is at stake is not the advance of the *religion* of Christianity at the expense of Islam, but the retreat of Muslim *civilization* before Western *civilization*. Banna warned his followers early and often that 'formal political independence' was worthless unless accompanied by 'intellectual, social, and cultural independence'.[64] And one of his most frequently quoted sayings (one adopted by Hudaybi) was 'Eject imperialism from your souls, and it will leave your lands'. Subsequent writers adopted the same tone. Ghazali deplored 'this age, created by the cultural invasion, which bears Muslim names, but has not a Muslim heart or a Muslim mind'. 'The cultural invasion . . . makes Muslims ignorant of their religion and loads their minds with limited truths, then leaves their hearts a vacuum.'[65] And Qutb warns the Brothers that 'spiritual and mental imperialism is the true danger' for unlike military or political imperialism which inspires opposition, this type dulls, calms, and deceives its victims. 'Holy war' must be declared against 'the apparatus which directs the operation of deception': the 'modern' techniques of the imperialism of the 'free world'—

[62] Qutb, *AIFI* (Hardie tr.), p. 235.

[63] Ibid., pp. 236–40.

[64] See *JIM* (9 July 1946), 4.

[65] *MDA* (27 July 1954), 3.

foundations, technical aid, UNESCO, and the 'pens and tongues' of the 'people's democracies'.[66]

The most dangerous operators of this apparatus, for Qutb, were the missionaries and the researchers—orientalists and social scientists who were 'probing the most sensitive parts of our country'.[67] Concern with the work of orientalists was a recent development and derived from an increased awareness of, and sensitivity to what Westerners were saying about Islam and Muslims, and about the Muslim Brothers. Attention focused on Western scholars for what were regarded as misrepresentations of Muslim history, and for the critiques which destroy Islam's 'sacredness'; indeed the latter point was the most serious objection raised against Western research.[68] Egyptian writers who shared or adopted the 'false ideas' of the orientalists about Islam were regarded as having abetted, 'intentionally or not', the cultural imperialism of the West. Well-known writers accused of this tendency were Taha Husayn, 'Ali 'Abd al-Raziq, Khalid Muhammad Khalid, and Amin 'Uthman.[69]

The missionary, however, was the major 'agent' of cultural imperialism and the chief object of the Brothers' criticism. 'It was natural', recalls Banna, 'that there should be a clash between the two [Brothers and missionaries] in view of the fact that one of them defends Islam and the second attacks it.'[70] There was no clearer and simpler statement of the Society's image of missionaries.

One other aspect of this problem is worthy of note here. Missionaries were normally identified as 'Western' Christian missionaries from whom not only Muslims but Eastern Christians were to be protected. This distinction between Eastern and Western Christians was an important one for the Society (p. 271). Here it need only be said that the Brothers encouraged and supported both Christian and Muslim writers who attacked Western, especially Protestant, 'subversion' of the local Orthodox and Coptic heritage.

[66] Qutb, *DI*, pp. 163–6; for another recognition of this problem, see F. S. C. Northrop, *The Taming of the Nations* (1952), p. 67. Out of this mood was generated the futile 'book-burnings' (see above, p. 50).

[67] Qutb, *DI*, p. 163.

[68] See esp. *RNJM*, pp. 19–22. However, the hostility to orientalists was not unrelieved: *JIM* (2 June 1954), 13, in an article by a 'non-political' member, Muhammad Yusuf Musa, admits the 'service' of the orientalists to Islam and Muslim culture. A book circulated among, and discussed with interest by, English-reading and speaking members was Gibb's *Modern Trends in Islam*. In our own research, we encountered more than once the articulated hope that this study would not 'abuse Islam'.

[69] See Ghazali, *MHN* (Faruqi tr.), pp. xiii–xvi.

[70] *Mudh.*, p. 157; above, pp. 6, 13.

IX

THE SOLUTION

THE RETURN TO ISLAM

THE image of the world in which the Brothers lived was one vividly characterized by decay and humiliation: the corruption of the faith was serious enough, worse still, it resulted not only in the abuse and disregard of its teachings, but in their headlong replacement by foreign values brought by the invader and incompetently resisted by the political, intellectual, and spiritual leaders of the country. Egypt, wrote Banna to Faruq, is 'at the crossroads'. It is facing in two directions: 'the way of the West' and 'the way of Islam'. Advocates of both summon the nation to follow one or the other. The Muslim Brothers, true to the faith, plead that the nation be restored to Islam. Egypt's role is unique, for just as Egyptian reform begins with Islam, so the regeneration of Islam must begin in Egypt, for the rebirth of 'international Islam', in both its ideal and historical sense, requires first a strong 'Muslim state' (*dawla muslima*).[1]

This Islam to which we beckon—this pure Islam is 'the Islam of the Muslim Brothers'. Not a new Islam,[2] it differs from many of the incorrect historical interpretations given it by Muslims. There are those who see Islam as mere worship and ritual—'that is the widespread meaning among the mass of Muslims.' Others see it as 'noble virtues' or 'spirituality' protecting them from material things. Yet others see it solely in its earthly 'practical' aspects. And finally, there are those who see it merely as an 'inherited faith'—'untroubled and unprogressive'; these are 'disgusted with Islam and all that has to do with Islam'. This view is found mostly among those with foreign education who are unfamiliar with Islam in its original state or know it only from the 'defaced picture' presented by those who do not practice it correctly.

We believe the provisions of Islam and its teachings are all inclusive, encompassing the affairs of the people in this world and the hereafter. And those who think that these teachings are concerned only with the

[1] *RTH: NN*, p. 85; *RDFTJ*, pp. 11–12.

[2] Much was made of the point that the movement represented no innovation: see *RMKH*, p. 8, *RDFTJ*, pp. 30–1, and *RD*, p. 3.

spiritual or ritualistic aspects are mistaken in this belief because Islam is a faith and a ritual, a nation (*watan*) and a nationality, a religion and a state, spirit and deed, holy text and sword. . . . The Glorious Qur'an . . . considers [these things] to be the core of Islam and its essence. . . .[3]

The ideologies of the West must be resisted: they are the forward arm of corruption, 'the silken curtain' behind which hide 'the greed of graspers and the dreams of dominators'. There is 'no salvation for the Arabs and the Muslims, and no self respect for the East' until it rids itself of all of them 'rising from itself', and depending 'on the grace of God'. It is possible for Muslims to resist the foreign ideologies because they do not need them. Islam includes in its teachings the best features of all of them:

> Internationalism, nationalism, socialism, capitalism, bolshevism, war, the distribution of wealth, the relation between producers and consumers, and whatever is related to these topics . . . which have occupied the leaders of nations and philosophers of society—all of these, we believe, Islam has penetrated to the core. Islam established for the world the system through which man can benefit from the good and avoid dangers and calamities.[4]

And again:

> If the French Revolution decreed the rights of man and declared for freedom, equality, and brotherhood, and if the Russian revolution brought closer the classes and social justice for people, the great Islamic revolution decreed all that 1,300 years before. It did not confine itself to philosophical theories but rather spread these principles through daily life, and added to them [the notions of the] divinity of mankind, and the perfectibility of his virtues and [the fulfilment of] his spiritual tendencies.[5]

Islam then includes all the virtues of other systems, it is sufficient in itself for the renaissance of the nation: 'Its history has testified to its fitness and has exhibited to humanity as a whole . . . one of the strongest, noblest, most merciful, virtuous, and blessed of nations'. In building our lives on our own principles, not on others, we are asserting, as with our political independence, our truly 'social and existential independence'. The Islamic way is 'complete and total', establishing itself on both 'practical and spiritual' foundations—a fact unique to Islam as a system. Islam can give a nation that is being reborn all that it needs. It gives 'hope'; it creates 'will and determination' without which life cannot be rekindled. 'Despair is a road to blasphemy, and despondency is an expression of error.' Finally, it gives 'national self-respect',

[3] *RMKH*, p. 10 and previously, pp. 8–9. This has been one of the most enduring of Banna's statements and was often reproduced.

[4] *RIASNN*, p. 30.

[5] *JIM* (19 Sept. 1946), 1, 4.

for every nation must respect its own nationhood, its glories, and its history.[6]

The essential step in the renaissance, and more important than 'practical reform', is a vast 'spiritual awakening' among individuals. 'Verily God does not change a people (*qawm*) until they change what is in themselves' (Qur'an 13: 12). A people cannot be saved until individuals are. The reason for 'the weakness of nations and humiliations of peoples' is that hearts and souls become weak and emptied of 'noble virtues and the qualities of true manhood'. The nation which is overwhelmed by 'material things' and 'earthliness', and which has forgotten 'hardship and struggle on behalf of truth', has lost its self-respect and hope. 'Material strength', which the East so obviously needs, is secondary to a mobilization of its 'spiritual strength'. Once the individual regains his spiritual balance, then the effect of his reform will find its way to his family and thence to the nation at large. The nation will continue to suffer so long as its individuals lack the qualities necessary to make it great.[7]

The Prophet Muhammad placed in the hearts of his followers three principles: (1) they have received final Truth in a final Revelation; (2) since they are the possessors of Truth, their mission in life is teaching; (3) because of these facts, 'God stands with them'. The Muslim Brothers preached these cornerstones also, even before the five pillars: 'Faith in the grandeur of the message, pride in its adoption, and hope for the support of God.'[8]

Therefore, until Muslims return to what inspired the first Muslims, there can be no salvation. 'The noble Qur'an is an inclusive book in which God has gathered the fundamentals of faith, the foundations of social virtues and all worldly legislation.' If Muslims have deviated from these truths: 'Our mission is to return—ourselves and whoever will follow—to the [true] path'.[9] This is a call to return to Islamic principles and not a literal return to the seventh century; those who say this are confusing 'the historical beginning of Islam with the system of Islam itself'.[10]

AL-NIZAM AL-ISLAMI

The ultimate goal of the Muslim Brothers was the creation of an 'Islamic order' (*al-nizam al-islami*). In practice, this phrase was

[6] *RTH: NN*, pp. 85–91, esp. 89–91.

[7] *RMKH*, pp. 4–5; and esp. *RIASNN*, pp. 25–9; *RDFTJ*, pp. 21–4. If any single idea could be said to have been a keystone in Banna's 'system' it was this one; it was so regarded by the membership.

[8] *RDFTJ*, pp. 18–20.

[9] *RIASNN*, pp. 3–4.

[10] Qutb, *MIWR*, pp. 84 ff. Hudaybi (*RD*, pp. 3–4) records his surprise that people at large believed the Society to advocate 'the abandonment of most of the characteristics of civilization and a return to the life of the *badu* in the desert'.

sometimes loosely used to mean a 'Muslim state'; mostly, however, it referred to a set of legal (not political) principles which were regarded as fundamental to Muslim society whatever the particular form of political order. The *shari'a*—its implementation or non-implementation—was the determinant in the definition of a true Islamic order.

The distinction between an 'Islamic order' and a 'Muslim state' in a medieval sense is a fundamental one and distinguishes our analysis of the Society from most others, which view it as a reactionary movement fanatically dedicated to re-creating a seventh-century political order. Apart from the question of revolutionary intent, such a view does not explain its relative indifference, as we shall soon see, to such issues as the caliphate. It makes impossible an analysis of the complexity of motives which prompted membership. Quite apart from the secularist and nationalist members, few even of the 'traditional' Brothers, let alone those who had entered in varying degrees the 'modern' world, would have considered this a possible goal if even a desirable one. We take essentially at face value the view attributed to Banna and expressed by Hudaybi, and in writings by members of the Society, that the existing constitutional parliamentary framework in Egypt, if reformed, would satisfy the political requirements of Islam for a 'Muslim state'.[11]

If this was true, then the political activism of the Society meant something other than an attempt to overthrow the existing order in the name of a 'theocracy'. The truly important 'religious' aspect of this was the larger question of the imperatives of Muslim society: the centrality of the *shari'a* to it. A Muslim Brother could, and indeed did, concede 'development' of specific aspects of community or political organization, but he could not remain true to his image of Islam and deny the ultimate validity of God's law as revealed in the Qur'an. The rejection of the religious foundation of Muslim society which was symbolized in the rejection of the *shari'a* for Western codes, and in the consequent separation of religious and secular authority, not only violated Muslim history

[11] We are not saying this statement is true. Safran, *Egypt*, p. 290, points out, in challenging this idea as a camouflage for the call to revolt, that obviously Egypt was not an Islamic state. This is true if the referent were the caliphate of the seventh or eighth century; our referent, and why we think the statement important, is what articulate Muslim Brothers probably actually felt to be the case. Hudaybi made this abundantly clear in his letters to the government in 1954. Harris, *Nationalism and Revolution*, pp. 162–3, follows Husayni, *Moslem Brethren*, who believes that 'religious government' was a primary goal of the Society. We are not sure what Husayni intends. Our attempted distinction here is between religious government (a 'Muslim state') and a government inspired by religion, the 'Islamic order'.

but destroyed the essence of Muslim society. In setting the state apart from the revelation, Muslims had rebuked God by the creation of a *shirk*. Thus to return to the distinction just made, the immediate concern of the Muslim Brothers was not the organization of a 'Muslim state' (although, as we shall see, this was considered), but rather the more profound issue of the nature and destiny of Muslim society in the twentieth century—'the Islamic order', the most important elements of which were: (1) the *shari'a* and its validity for modern times; and (2) the related question of 'the separation of church and state'.

The Shari'a

It would be difficult to overstate the intensity of the Brothers' conviction that while other civilizations could dispense with religious institutions (because of multiple roots), Muslim civilization without the *shari'a* as its central inspiration was meaningless, a 'loss of cultural direction' and 'a contradiction in terms', leaving 'a society of cultural mongrels and spiritual half-castes'.[12]

This belief emphasized the indispensability of the *shari'a* to the healthy Muslim community, what Professor Wilfred Cantwell Smith has called the 'theological imperative' in current Islamic social reform. 'It has two sides: the community's external relations and its internal order. Islam being what it is, Muslims feel that they must solve the problem or perish. It is not only the welfare of the community which is at stake but the validity of the faith.'[13]

To live by the *shari'a* was both religiously and socially necessary. The Qur'anic injunctions to rule 'by what God has revealed' are sufficient to make putting it into effect an 'obligation'. 'Thus we will satisfy our Lord, who said, 'Rule with what God has revealed'; he did not say with what resembles what God has revealed.'[14]

The religious sanctions were obviously important; equally so, however, was the social sense of disorder and disequilibrium and historical dislocation. The point was often made that the people of Egypt were being subjected to laws foreign to their history, traditions, and spirit with a consequent social demoralization. 'Law does not perform its function unless it rests on principles accepted by the people and in which individuals and societies have faith. . . . Unless it is this, it cannot fulfil its function.'[15] Banna warned those who were being enticed by Western ideas of the

[12] *Arafat*, i/1 (Sept. 1946), 32. Although Pakistani in origin, this magazine reflected well some of the positions of the Brothers.

[13] 'Trends in Muslim Thought', *MW* (Oct. 1952), 322.

[14] *RD*, pp. 5–6, 11.

[15] *MDA* (22 Apr. 1951), 8–9.

rootlessness of the foreign values ('without father or mother') that they were accepting, whereas what these values replaced was 'deep of root and firm of bond with our history, our society, and the needs of our environment'.[16] Indeed, the intensity of feeling among Brothers on what might be called the 'social or cultural imperative' involved in the establishment of the *shari'a* perhaps outdid the theological imperative.

Given the necessity of the *shari'a*, the next important consideration for the Brothers was its definition. Banna himself was restrained on this question. Confining himself to generalities, he felt no need to elaborate on the obvious; or, from another view, to discuss matters which would provoke divisiveness. He was undoubtedly less concerned than his followers about the intellectual assumptions of the movement, especially after 1952. He would agree that the *shari'a* was first and foremost a derivative of the Qur'an; that of about 6,000 verses in this, 500 are concerned with legislation on which was built the science of jurisprudence. To this would be added the deeds of the Prophet—the Traditions, 'purified' and taken from 'trustworthy' authorities.[17] To emphasize Islam's 'flexibility', Banna recalled that the legist Shafi'i gave different rulings in similar-type cases in Egypt and Iraq, and that another famous judge decided differently from season to season.[18]

Banna may have believed but never made it an issue, as did his followers, that the *shari'a* is not and never was inclusive of the four schools of law. Qutb, for example, notes the confusion between the *shari'a* and 'the historical origins of Islamic jurisprudence'. The rulings of the legists of the Islamic tradition are obviously inadequate, he says, for the needs of society through time. Because jurisprudence ceased developing when Islamic society failed, this does not mean the *shari'a* is dead.[19] The most widely circulated 'legal' book among the Brothers deplores the confusion between the 'words of the legal scholars' and the *shari'a*, and connects this confusion with the decline of Islamic society.[20] The legal scholars, as *mujtahidun*, are important historical and substantive guides to the present, but Muslims today are free 'to do as they did for our times and our situations'.[21] The Brothers expressed themselves just as frankly about the corpus of exegesis transmitted from the past. Thus, without denying the validity of the exegetical legacy

[16] See Hajjaji, *RLAT*, pp. 20–1.

[17] *RD*, pp. 4–5; *RNURT*, p. 3. In his own works he used the 'most dependable' of the records—al-Bukhari and Muslim (*RJ*, p. 11).

[18] See e.g. *RMFDNI*, pp. 19–20, and Ta'lib, *al-Bay'a*, p. 16, for a more restrictive view.

[19] Qutb, *MIWR*, pp. 84–7.

[20] al-Sayyid Sabiq, *Fiqh al-sunna* (1954), i. 17–24.

[21] See *JIM* (29 July 1954), 14; see also Samman, *IM*, pp. 18–19, 92–4.

of Muslims, one Brother expressed the view that most of the works are irrelevant or meaningless, that the 'concise' exegesis are good 'dictionaries of the language', and the 'lengthy' studies are 'sources for researchers', full of 'wearisome padding, tiring debate, and distorted repetition', and that neither type satisfies the need of the Muslim community for clear pronouncements about the 'vital meanings' of the Qur'an.[22]

The Traditions, finally, were felt to need serious re-study. Delayed in their collation, subjected to the vicissitudes of partisan and internecine struggle within the Muslim community, they inevitably suffered corruption. In this light, Muslims must not be bound by the books of Tradition simply because they are ancient. There must be a serious re-examination of the Traditions to determine the true from the false; new books must be written in the light of these studies; and the great books of Islam examined for new Traditions and new light on the Traditions. A common belief among Brothers was that no more than a handful of Traditions would survive such a study; an extreme form of this view held that only one Tradition would survive, and that this would have the Prophet say 'Take from me only the Qur'an'.[23] The following observation by a member of the Society is not typical in its literal implications but is characteristic of an attitude: speaking about the *sunna* he noted that 'it is a kind of supplement to the legal injunctions of the Qur'an, but mostly it is a spiritual inspiration and guide to the whole Islamic system'; it could be described, he concluded, as 'a fallible man's experience in society guiding fallible men'.

This, briefly, was the conception of the *shari'a*: its two fundamental sources were the Qur'an and *sunna*; the former requiring new and clearer interpretation and the latter, expurgation of falsity in order to give both more relevance to the life of the Muslim. And by depriving the legists and their *fiqh* of a popularly attributed sacredness and insisting only on their historicity, the Brothers claimed to offer the contemporary Muslim freedom from tradition: 'the attribution of sacredness to the old stands always in the path of every renaissance';[24] rejection of the 'slavish worship of tradition' was necessary if Islam was to keep abreast of the times and be true to its nature of 'renewal' (*tajdid*), not 'imitation' (*taqlid*).[25] A *shari'a* so viewed was eminently less difficult to cope with, for

[22] Samman, *IM*, pp. 86–92, esp. 86–7. Samman observes that no useful exegesis exists except those of Muhammad 'Abduh and Rashid Rida, and Ibn Kathir.

[23] We were unable to trace this Tradition. For the preceding, see Samman, *IM*, pp. 94–6. We found oral sources considerably more useful here than written ones.

[24] Samman, *IM*, p. 92.

[25] *JIM* (29 July 1954), 14.

insistence on freedom from the past was a necessary prelude to the assertion that the *shari'a* was 'general', 'flexible', 'developing,' and 'universal' in scope, that it prescribed the 'principles of action' necessary for progress and happiness in all times and places.[26]

The first of these 'principles of action', in line with the rejection of tradition, was the 'opening of the door of *ijtihad*' for the endeavour of present-day Muslims to meet the needs of the community.[27] Then, of course, there were the traditionally accepted principles of 'analogy' (*qiyas*) and 'consensus' (*ijma'*) for bringing Islam abreast of the times. And to these devices were added the 'powers' given the Muslim ruler to legislate for the 'general welfare'.[28]

Two of the most widely read of the Society's writers pay special attention to this last aspect of the issue. Sayyid Qutb argues that the 'wide powers' given to the head of state to legislate for the general welfare include: (1) the 'public interest' (*al-maslaha al-mursala*); and (2) the 'blocking of means' (*sadd al-dhara'i'*). 'Any measure which has no specific detailed authority to support it is known as a measure of public interest' and can thus be legislated. The 'blocking of means' was more complicated. 'A means is that which leads to an end and to "block a means" is to remove it. The sense of the phrase is that anything leading to a forbidden end is itself forbidden while anything leading to a desirable end is itself desirable.' Qutb explains further and concludes:

These two principles . . . both derive from a common root, that of ensuring the welfare of society. They are integrally connected with the established laws of Islam and with its general purposes. It is these two principles which can give guidance for the legislation necessary to ensure a sound form of Islamic life including comprehensive social justice in its scope.[29]

Muhammad Ghazali, the other writer who discussed this problem, also suggested that Islam gave the ruler rights (established in

[26] Samman, *IM*, pp. 13–17; *RD*, p. 8; 'Awda, *IBJAWAU*, pp. 13–17; Qutb, *MIWR*, pp. 77, 108; and Ghazali, *MHN* (Faruqi tr.), pp. 18–19.

[27] See Samman, *IM*, pp. 92–3; Sabiq, *Fiqh al-sunna*, i. 19–20.

[28] Qutb, *AIFI* (Hardie tr.), p. 248; and Ghazali, *IMABSR*, pp. 104–5. *Ijma'* was more often chosen than *qiyas* by Brothers as a 'principle of movement'. We think that to the younger Brothers it had pleasing 'democratic' and thus political overtones rather than legal or religious ones.

[29] Qutb, *AIFI* (Hardie tr.), pp. 260–6. In a briefer treatment of this subject in a pamphlet put out by his section, Qutb lists as some of the 'new matters' which could be treated with this concept of the public interest new types of companies, contracts, and food and drink at hotels; see Qism Nashr al-Da'wa, *al-Tashri' al-Islami* (Cairo, 1953), pp. 8–9. Banna briefly mentioned the concept of the public interest in *RNURT*, pp. 18–19, but was clearly not as preoccupied as his followers with this question.

'principles upon which Islamic jurisprudence was founded') to legislate for the welfare of the community. Without going into detail, he listed the devices mentioned by Qutb and suggested numerous others; and he went further to suggest that Islam gave the ruler power 'to interfere' in some of the behaviour permitted to a Muslim by the Qur'an and Prophetic Tradition if behind the interference was a 'sound purpose', i.e. in accordance with the general welfare. An illustration of this point for Ghazali was the effort made by the former rector of the Azhar, Shaykh al-Maraghi, to mitigate divorce and polygamy even though both are 'textually guaranteed by the Qur'an'; the objections raised were not legal—for al-Maraghi, according to Ghazali, was within his rights—but social, all turning on the decadent state of Egyptian society.[30] This power of the ruler was discussed, incidentally, in the context of an argument for the necessity of controlling private ownership, and pointed out the importance of the secular economic and social, as well as religious, motivation for ideas of reform in Ghazali as well as in Qutb. That this was true of the articulate movement as a whole was an important factor in its success.

If all this was true, then the *sharīʿa* was eminently adaptable to the times. But the issue of establishing it as the fundamental code of the nation always compelled the Brothers to meet 'objections' to it which focused on certain provisions in the fields of criminal and commercial law—the much discussed punishments for theft and adultery, and the question of usury. The question of usury will be discussed later; here it is sufficient to note that the Brothers remained true to traditional thinking on the matter though with some slight qualification. The more emotional issue of the punishments of stoning for the crime of adultery and the cutting off of the hand for theft aroused less intellectual activity than extensive sensitivity. The provisions of the law could not be gainsaid, but, in the face of universal criticism, they could be, and were, 'explained'. As the Brothers saw it, these matters had simply been 'misunderstood'. On the punishment for theft, the real position of Islam is that a thief is sentenced to the ultimate punishment only if he commits his crime *after* society has provided him with all his needs; the state protects itself and its citizens from theft by assuring for every man sufficient food, clothing, and shelter; the citizen

[30] Ghazali (*IMABSR*, pp. 103–7) argues that the devices he mentions are sufficient to permit progress and development without denying the faith; he specifically repudiates the secularist idea—based on the Tradition which says 'You are more knowing in the affairs of your world'—that religion has no say in worldly matters. This same Tradition, used by secularists to defend the notion of the separation of church and state, was used widely by university Brothers especially as an example of one of the important and valid Traditions which would in fact pave the way for movement in the Islamic community.

does not steal, because his wants are supplied. In this light, the question of punishment for theft is academic, for as long as there is no 'truly Muslim society' there is no application of the law.[31] This attitude was best expressed in the strongly worded condemnation of the implementation of the law of cutting off hands in Saudi Arabia 'while the rulers swim in the gold stolen from the state treasury and the wealth of the people'.[32]

The explanation for the texts requiring the stoning of adulterers was less expansive but equally interpretive: since either confession of one or both of the guilty parties or the evidence of four witnesses is required for effecting the punishment, it is virtually unenforceable.[33]

On a more general level, and reflecting the obvious need to recognize the existence of the regulations, these punishments were seen on the whole as 'preventive' and 'just', because they could not be applied except in a truly Islamic society. They were 'severe' because of the need to protect 'the safety, security, and stability of society'; 'fear of punishment stops the commission of crime'. As though further to meet the objections raised to this aspect of the Muslim law, Hudaybi also suggested exploring the possibilities of the concept in jurisprudence known as *ta'zir*, a non-Qur'anic tradition of punishment whose precedents were built on the discretionary rulings of judges.[34]

Separation of Church and State

Curiously enough, on different occasions, the two leading legal minds of the Society, Hudaybi and 'Awda, observed that the law imported into Egypt and Islamic countries, apart from a few exceptions (already noted, in the fields of criminal and commercial law), 'was in agreement with the text of the *shari'a* and did not violate its general principles'.[35] If such was the case, why then

[31] See *RD*, pp. 10–11; Ghazali, *IWAI*, pp. 43–4; 'Awda, *IBJAWAU*, pp. 53–4. Qutb, *MIWR*, p. 105, had another variation: if there are 'social or individual justifications which compel the act, then there is no punishment'. Banna was not so apologetic and made the traditional case in *JIM* (16 July 1946), 3. Illustrative of the increased sensitivity in the Society, when the above article was reproduced later (*MMN*, Feb.–Mar. 1954, p. 24), it contained a footnote explaining the proposition in the above terms.

[32] Ghazali, *MHN* (Faruqi tr.), p. 8. See also Samman, *IM*, pp. 20–3, for criticism of the 'synthetic staidness' of the Yemen and the Hijaz and of the falsity of attempting to recreate the 'externals' of the first century.

[33] References as in n. 31, above.

[34] *RD*, p. 11; and Qutb, *AIFI* (Hardie tr.), p. 67; see 'Ta'zir', *Encyclopaedia of Islam*, iv. 710–11.

[35] 'Awda, *IBJAWAU*, p. 23; *JJ* (19 Nov. 1954), 7, for an expression along the same lines by Hudaybi at his trial. See also Husayni, *Ikhwan* (Beirut Eng. ed.), pp. 138, 150.

insist on the *shari'a*? The question as such was never raised by the Brothers, but their apparent answer had two related aspects: (1) dismay at the current of 'imitation' of the West by Muslims; and (2) the theological and social imperatives involved in being Muslim. Imitation of the West was one of Banna's principal anathemas:

> We want to think independently, depending on . . . Islam and not upon imitation which ties us to the theories and attitudes of the West in everything. We want to be distinguished by our own values and the qualities of our life as a great . . . nation which has its past.[36]

Another Brother notes that the West has its virtues and evils which must be seriously considered, but

> if imitation is founded on the basis of a sloughing off of all our valuable heritage and useful traditions in the sense that everything we have is corrupt and everything Westerners have is good, then imitation is destructive of our meaningful existence—national, historical, and religious.[37]

Banna revealingly observes that just as the Soviets regard the basis of their state as 'communism' and Anglo-American governments base themselves on 'democracy', so every Muslim state has the right to build on 'Islamism'.[38]

The tone of this last argument reflected the deeply felt need for cultural identity: the establishment of the *shari'a* would help preserve the 'national pride' and its 'integrity'; and it would give 'active expression to the treasured heritage that history has transmitted'.[39] The tradition of Islam met the spiritual and emotional as well as the legal needs of the community, a tradition which was not merely of law but of sacred law. 'Positive law' was a necessary part of any nation's legal structure, but man-made law, it was argued, merely reflects a society's development; the *shari'a*, God's law, performed the even more fundamental task of 'the organization of society and its direction'.[40] For Islam this meant primarily the total unity of man, and thus of society. The establishment of the *shari'a* would assure the primacy of God's law and thus the application of the only criterion whereby man's behaviour could become genuinely, totally moral.

For the Brothers, the argument focused on the question of the 'separation of Church and state', the ultimate question for those who would actively restore the *shari'a* as the arbiter of men's lives.

36 *RDFTJ*, p. 24. 37 *RMBBM*, p. 112.

38 *JIM* (5 July 1946), 2. In this respect, Ghazali, *MHN* (Faruqi tr.), p. 22, expresses his admiration for Zionists for returning to their past, unashamed of their religion, to call themselves Israel; 'What evil must we not expect to befall Islam at the hands of such adversaries.' 39 *RD*, p. 11.

40 'Awda, *IBJAWAU*, pp. 8–18.

The question was stated simply, but the answer was complex. If there was revelation which contained a law governing man's relation to man (as well as to God), how was this fact to be given expression in the modern world of secular nations and states? What was to be the relationship of the 'religious' to the 'secular' in man's life, and how would this relationship once defined, govern, if at all, men's behaviour? To formulate an answer to this question had immediate political implications, for this could be a way of setting aside the objections to this 'religious' organization's involvement in 'politics'. But even more fundamental was the ideological issue for Islam in the twentieth century: for to insist on the *shari'a* was to insist on a complex of corollaries which appeared, even in terms of Egypt, anachronistic; but to insist on less would have been to repudiate what was regarded as the 'essence' of Islam.

The question of 'separation of Church and state' always raised the issue of 'theocracy'; could a state, organized and directed by revelation, escape being an 'ecclesiastical tyranny'? The Brothers' answers to this question revolved around two points. First, there is no 'religious class' in Islam, and because this is so there can be no fear of theocracy as it was known to 'Christian Europe'. Banna put it another way: 'Men of religion are different from the religion itself.' And in the same vein, Qutb argues: 'The rule of Islam would not be effected because a religious class was in power—if Islam recognized a religious class—but rather because Islamic law would be established.[41]

The second point was a simple and non-traditional political one: in Islamic political organization, authority to rule derives from men, not God; the ruler receives this authority from 'the people', who grant it because he will obey the law. The concept of 'consultation' (*shura*) in Islam assures human control of human affairs within the bounds of the law.[42]

Apart from the political aspect of theocracy, the very concept of the 'separation' of religion from state—of the *din* from the *dawla*—was inadmissible. The word 'Islam' was not synonymous with 'religion'. Rather, 'Islam' was a word including in its total meaning religion, politics, economics, society, etc. In other terms, *dawla* is not the equal or opposite of *din*; both are expressions of Islam.[43] But since the issue was most often discussed in the

[41] Ghazali, *MHN* (Faruqi tr.), p. 7; *RTH: NN*, pp. 108–9; Qutb, *MIWR*, p. 91.

[42] Qutb, *AIFI* (Hardie tr.), pp. 87–99; 'Awda, *IWAS*, pp. 77–80.

[43] Qutb, *DI*, pp. 202–3, argues the existence of the Society as proof of this point: the Muslim Brothers are not a 'religious society' in the Western sense of the word.

Western terms of church and state—God and Caesar, it was answered in those terms. It is not of our making, Banna argued

that politics is a part of religion, that Islam encompasses the ruler and the ruled. Thus there is not in its teachings a rendering to Caesar that which is Caesar's and to God that which is God's. Rather . . . Caesar and what belongs to Caesar is for God Almighty alone.

In another place, he adds:

there is no authority in Islam except the authority of the state which protects the teachings of Islam and guides the nations to the fruits of both religion and the world . . . . Islam does not recognize the conflict which occurred in Europe between the spiritual and temporal [powers] . . . between the Church and the state . . .[44]

Two reasons for this situation in the West were described by Qutb: (1) the differing circumstances of origin—Christianity appeared on the scene when Roman law and custom were already firmly established; (2) the difference in intent—Christ 'came to preach only spiritual purity, mercy, kindness, tolerance, chastity, and obedience'. Christianity thus developed as a religion primarily concerned with man's relation to God. Relations between men, and between man and the state, were left to temporal law. Islam, on the other hand, in the circumstances of its origin could and did command a 'unity of life'; to impose upon Islam the Christian separation of loyalties was to deny it its essential meaning and very existence.[45]

This belief was pursued to its conclusion: 'Rule is in the nature of Islam', for if the Qur'an gives a law, it also requires a state to enforce the law.[46] There are certain duties incumbent on Muslims which they cannot pursue individually; the state is necessary to facilitate these duties. 'Where Islam is dispossessed of power, the greater part of its teachings remain as mere ink on paper.' Moreover, besides being necessary for the fulfilment of individual duties, the state was necessary to 'protect' Islam.

Faith should not be left without a political stronghold to give it protection, . . . and to champion the cause of believers everywhere. . . . Seldom, if ever, has Islam needed the state more than today—not merely because the state is an integral part of it, but also because Islam itself is threatened with extinction in a world where only the strong can survive.[47]

[44] *Mudh.*, pp. 102–3; and *JIM* (12 May 1946), 1, 4. For a similar position taken by Shaykh Maraghi, former rector of the Azhar, see Gardet, *La Cité musulmane*, p. 25.

[45] Qutb, *AIFI* (Hardie tr.), pp. 2–4, 7–8; 'Awda, *IWAQ*, pp. 104–7.

[46] 'Awda, *IWAS*, pp. 55–63.

[47] Ghazali, *MHN* (Faruqi tr.), p. 26, 14–15.

That there was felt to be a political as well as religious need for the state requires no emphasizing but the strength of the purely ideological issue should not thereby be minimized. Every aspect of the 'renaissance' of Islam in the twentieth century focused on this central problem of the *shari'a* and its corollary, the 'unity of life'. As already suggested, for the Brothers to deny the problem was to deny the essential meaning of ideal Islam; if history had only briefly shown the ideal in practice, this was the fault of man, not of God's work. It was incumbent upon Muslims to restore the community which God had intended, to redeem their history.[48]

THE ISLAMIC STATE

The *shari'a* was the distinguishing characteristic of the 'Islamic order'; within this order would exist the 'Islamic state'. We have already indicated our belief, generated in part by the paucity of 'official' organization literature about it, that the precise nature of a Muslim state was not a burning question. The absence of material on the subject also reflected the absence of thought and imprecision in the Society's ideology, a fact which became apparent after Banna's death. With the loss of his charisma, it became necessary to attempt to formulate, in its fullest implications, the characteristic outward forms of a Muslim state. Consistent with the other areas of the Society's thought, the attempts were confined to generalities which would 'unite the words and hearts of men'. But generalities were also used because history had not bequeathed to Muslims an immediately discernible theoretical legacy. Qutb was one of the few who recognized this: 'When we come to discuss political and economic theory from the practical point of view of the state, we find that the course of history shows an exemplary failure in the life of Islam.'[49] Thus, with only the short period of the orthodox caliphate as an acceptable source of example, would-be theoreticians were compelled to emphasize the 'principles' which would guide an Islamic state; the 'specifics' would be left to 'time, place and the needs of the people'.[50]

[48] Smith, 'Trends in Muslim Thought', 321–2; and the same author's sensitive study, *Islam in Modern History*, ch. 1.

[49] *AIFI* (Hardie tr.), p. 175.

[50] On no other issue were Brothers with whom we talked less certain. The above formulation was widely used, and reflected in our mind, the general acceptance of the political and legal development of modern Egypt. It could also be argued further that indifference to the forms of the Muslim state inspired the generalities and uncertainties. Professor R. Bayly Winder has suggested, quite correctly, that this condition may also have resulted from historical indifference to political forms.

Political Organization

The political structure of the Islamic state was to be bound by three principles: (1) the Qur'an is the fundamental constitution; (2) government operates on the concept of consultation (*shura*); (3) the executive ruler is bound by the teachings of Islam and the will of the people. Founded on these three principles, the Islamic state would have a just and efficient government, be consistent with the traditions of the society, and be capable of securing the general welfare. The details of organization would follow from these principles.[51]

The name given to the executive in the Islamic state would be unimportant. *Khalifa*, *imam*, king, governor (*hakim*)—these and any other words used in the Qur'an are acceptable, for the idea of 'ruler' principally refers to the idea of 'leadership' (*ri'asa*) in its 'general meaning' and indicates no 'specific system' of government. If he governs with 'obedience to the commands of God' and with respect for the limitations placed on him by the concept of 'consultation', then the name given him is a matter of indifference; without these conditions, whatever Islamic name be given him, the system is not Islamic.

There were two acceptable types of central authority, Banna felt: (1) on the British pattern, 'ministerial' or 'delegated' (*tafwid*) authority; (2) on the American pattern, 'executive' (*tanfidh*) authority. Banna and most of his followers seemed to incline to the latter form, a fact clearly related to the revulsion from irresponsible ministerial government in Egypt.

Whatever the form of rulership, its occupant must have certain qualities: he must be Muslim, male, adult, sane of mind, and healthy in body; he must be knowledgeable in Muslim jurisprudence, just, pious, and virtuous; and he must be capable of leadership. He need not be—contrary to the traditional view—a member of the Quraysh. Unless he resigns or is removed for legal, moral, or physical reasons, his tenure may be for life; this decision is left for 'the nation' (*al-umma*) to make as it sees fit.

'The nation', 'the people', in fact, are the source of all the ruler's authority: 'The nation alone is the source of power; bowing to its will is a religious obligation.' The ruler has no legal existence and

[51] 'Awda, *IWAS* is the most detailed and 'original' of the very few works available on this subject. Our outline of the political aspects of the Muslim state is based largely on this work, which has been summarized and in part translated by F. Bertier, 'L'idéologie politique des Frères musulmans', *Temps modernes*, 8th yr. (Sept. 1952), 540–6. Bertier makes the point (p. 543) that 'Awda was trained in French law. For the very limited thoughts of Banna on this question, see *RMFDNI*, pp. 40–4, and *RD*, p. 8. *MDA*, 7, 21 June 1955, contains important statements on this question of political organization.

deserves no loyalty except as 'he reflects the spirit of the society and is in harmony with its goals'.[52] Banna described the relationship of ruler and ruled as a 'social contract' (*'aqd ijtima'i*) in which the ruler is defined as a 'trustee' (*'amil*) and 'agent' (*ajir*). This view immediately and automatically excludes the possibility of hereditary leadership; religious texts and historical experience from the time of the Orthodox caliphs repudiate this possibility.[53] Since the ruler is the 'agent contracted for' by the nation, he is 'elected' by it. The Qur'an designated no specific ways of holding elections. Hudaybi believed they could be held in any way seen fit by the people concerned, perhaps even 'directly by the people'.[54] 'Awda suggested that it could be done by *ahl al-shura* (see below, pp. 247–8) in three stages: (1) 'nomination', either by he previous ruler or by one of the *ahl al-shura*; (2) 'selection and acceptance' by the *ahl al-shura*; and (3) *bay'a* (oath of loyalty), during which the ruler swears to govern 'by the Book and *sunna* and in truth and justice', and the *ahl al-shura* swear to obey him as long as he rules by God's laws. The people of the nation are then bound by the oath sworn in their name by their 'representatives'. A government established 'by force' should not command the loyalties of the people, for the ruler will have violated the principle—symbolized in his selection by the *ahl al-shura*—that 'the authority of the ruler must come from the nation'.[55]

The ruler, as the chosen agent of the people, is responsible to them for all his acts—political, civil, or criminal; to his person attaches no special privilege, and if necessary he is subject to trial by ordinary courts. His chief function is the establishment and maintenance of Islam and the execution of its laws, a duty which automatically ensures the general welfare. Obedience derives from the execution of the law—'that is the contract with the ruler'; failure to do so frees the nation from loyalty to him. If he deviates from his assigned tasks, he must be 'warned', 'guided', and then removed.

The practice of 'consultation' (*shura*) is a mandatory and fundamental part of the Islamic state: 'He [God] commanded consultation among themselves' (Qur'an 42:38). The institution whereby consultation operates is the *ahl al-shura* (or *ahl al-hall wa'l-'aqd*);

[52] Cf. Ghazali, *IIS*, pp. 52–4, 162–3.

[53] Qutb, *AIFI* (Hardie tr.), pp. 176–83; 'Awda, *IWAS*, p. 73; Ghazali, *IIS*, pp. 180–7; and *FMD*, pp. 109–28 for a statement by Muhibb al-Din al-Khatib on the subject. It was this position which *inter alia* set Faruq in opposition to the Society and won the enmity of the then king of Saudi Arabia, Ibn Sa'ud.

[54] *MMN*, iii/1 (Nov. 1953), 7.

[55] It is one of the many ironies of this Society's history that the author of that thought, 'Awda, died on the gallows in 1954 for his alleged role in a plot to overthrow the regime by violence.

as representative of the people, this body commands the obedience of both ruler and ruled; in it lies the real power in the state, for it represents the real source of power, the nation. Since its members represent the people, they too, would be 'elected'; the question of how, and of their numbers, is a 'secondary' matter not defined by Islam and therefore left to the circumstances of each age and place. Whatever procedures are used for elections, they must be 'universal' in scope, 'reaching the opinion of all' so that the nation is truly reflected. The system used by no means necessarily involves the use of political parties.[56]

Who would be eligible for election to the *ahl al-shura*? Banna felt that it should consist of two types of people: (1) 'legists', with a background of 'general knowledge'; and (2) men practised in leadership—heads of families, tribes, and other organized groups. Elections are only desirable if they lead to the selection of such people.[57] 'Awda was only slightly less specific: the *ahl al-shura* would comprise people most of whom would be knowledgeable in the law; the demands of the modern scientific world would make desirable the addition of specialists and technicians, but the final word would rest with the legists. Precise arrangements on this matter could be left to time and place.

As the 'true rulers of the Islamic state', the *ahl al-shura* would have the right to expect all matters to be submitted to them for deliberation and decision. A majority opinion would be required for a decision; after a period of free expression and debate on any issue, the minority should support the majority decision; this is the valid procedure because the Prophet has already said 'My community cannot agree on error'. In its deliberations the body may concern itself with every matter but two; (1) 'the facts of the sciences'; and (2) 'the principles of religion'. In other words, the principle of *shura* applies everywhere except for certain matters which 'admit only a single view'.[58]

There are five 'powers' in the Islamic state; executive power belongs to the ruler alone; legislative power is shared between the ruler and *ahl al-shura*; judicial power is exercised by judges nominated by the ruler who, because of their role as interpreters of the law are 'absolutely independent'; financial power by officials appointed by the ruler but responsible to the community; and the power of 'control and reform' belongs to the community at large in the persons of the *ahl al-shura*.[59]

[56] Cf. Qutb, *MIWR*, pp. 92–9.

[57] *RMFDNI*, pp. 60–1.

[58] This concept was also used in a discussion of Banna's role as leader of the Society; see e.g. Hajjaji, *IMAM*, ii. 62.

[59] Besides 'Awda, see Ramadan, *MT*, p. 66.

The Islamic state thus outlined would be unique; as already noted, it would not be a theocracy because the authority of the ruler derives from men not God; it would not be a dictatorship because the ruled may remove their ruler if he breaks his contract; and it would not be a monarchy because the ruler has no hereditary authority.

The individual in such a state has a set of guaranteed rights. From the time of its revelation, Islam has contained guarantees for the protection of the 'personal rights'[60] of all individuals encompassed by it. These rights were designed 'to raise the standards of individuals, permit their participation in activities which would serve the welfare of society, safeguard human dignity, nurture individual talents, and aid in the exploitation of their physical and intellectual resources'. These rights are inclusive. *Equality* is guaranteed 'absolutely' by the revelation and the tradition of Islam. No individual, group, race, or colour is superior to another. Muslim and non-Muslim share equally in rights, duties, and responsibilities. Muslim and *dhimmi* are equal in all respects except those relating to 'faith'; in those areas the *dhimmi* is governed by his own law.

Freedom in all its aspects is clearly proclaimed by Islam—freedom of thought, of worship, of expression, of education, and of possession. *Freedom of thought:* Islam encourages man to think freely and clearly, liberated from 'fear, superstition, and imitation', and to accept nothing 'which is not acceptable to reason'; Islam frowns on the man who 'abrogates his reason and sets aside thought'. *Freedom of worship:* 'Islam's was the first law which permitted freedom of worship; in accordance with the *shari'a,* each man may accept the faith he wishes and no one can compel him to leave his faith for another; in the face of 'error', one may only persuade or advise. 'There is no compulsion in religion' (Qur'an 2:256). *Freedom of expression:* This is not only a right but a duty for every Muslim; each person must 'say what he believes to be the truth, and defend this belief with tongue and pen'. He may speak on all matters pertaining to morals, the general welfare, and the 'general system', subject only to the restriction that what is said should not violate 'the text or spirit of the *shari'a*' and should be devoid of 'evil intent and hostility'. Within these limits, freedom of expression is 'beneficial to individuals and the nation, leads to the growth of brotherhood and respect between individuals and between groups, unites the people in truth, creates a state of constant co-operation, and limits personal and factional disputation'. *Freedom of education:* Islam not only decreed the right to education

[60] See 'Awda, *IWAS*, pp. 195–201 for what follows.

but made it a 'religious obligation'. Both God and the Prophet elevate learning to a divine level; it is, indeed, 'the path to God'. The provision of education so defined is an obligation of the Muslim state. *Freedom of possession:* Islam has decreed that a man may own what pleases him, within the limits set by the law—that property be owned in proportion to its usefulness (without excessive deprivation or luxury), and that excessive wealth be distributed according to Islamic law.

Economic Organization

Within the framework of political organization so conceived, the individual was to be a full participant in the political life of the community and was to have a share in the decisions which would affect his own life. That much of this political thinking was intimately related to political frustration in Egypt seems obvious. The same might be said of the economic thought of the Society, which had much the same blend of pragmatic response to the actual world and concern with issues of ideological import for twentieth-century Islam.

Banna, perhaps more than his followers, was single-minded about the 'moral' dimensions of economic behaviour, an approach admittedly inspired by the Muslim view of the indivisibility of man's morality. It was in this framework also that the concept of 'social justice' was applied: economics without reference to 'social justice and the principles of morality' violated the fundamental teachings of God. This moralistic approach was matched by other constants in Banna's economic thinking. His concern with 'unity' in the nation led to a strong affirmation of Islam's revulsion from 'economic class conflict'. And the problem of 'foreign economic control' in Egypt led him to emphasize the 'duty' of Muslims to build a strong 'national economy'. These points were the essentials of the 'Islamic economic system' as discerned by Banna and elaborated upon by his followers, who placed them in a more coherent if still vague relationship with one another and with other economic issues.[61]

As in all other human affairs, Islam confines itself, in the area of economic thought, to the establishment of 'general principles'. Specific economic institutions 'develop with every age and change with the progress of sciences and the ways of life'. Thus Islam leaves it to 'human thought' to provide 'what is needed for the realization of a people's interests within the framework of its general legislation'. This adaptability to all time and place is a

[61] See the outline in *RMFDNI*, pp. 74–82, reproduced in *MDA* (24 Feb. 1953), 7.

fundamental, then, of Islamic economic theory. It is matched in importance only by the characteristic which makes the Islamic economic system unique in human history; the moral imperative which guides it and the social justice which is its goal. 'Islam does not treat economic activity independently of its moral principles.' The life of man is 'a spiritual and material unity', a view in direct opposition to the image of the 'economic man' held by 'the Western doctors of economics'. In this respect, Islam is consistent with the latest scientific analysis of the economic behaviour of men in terms of 'psychological motivations'; 'there is no measure for them in the material world'.[62]

The corollary, or end, of moralistic economic behaviour is social justice—the important foundation of the Islamic state.[63] Social justice in Islam derives from two of its principles: 'the absolute, just, and coherent unity of existence; and the general, mutual responsibility of individuals and societies'. Its most fundamental quality is that it is

> a comprehensive social justice, and not merely an economic justice; that is to say, it embraces all sides of life and all aspects of freedom. It is concerned alike with the mind and the body, with the heart and conscience. The values with which this justice deals are not only economic values, nor are they merely material values in general; rather they are a mixture of moral and spiritual values together. Christianity looks at man only from the standpoint of his spiritual desires and seeks to crush down the human instincts in order to encourage those desires. On the other hand, communism looks at man only from the standpoint of his material needs; it looks not only at human nature but also at the world and at life from a purely material point of view. But Islam looks upon man as forming a unity whose spiritual desires cannot be separated from his bodily appetites and whose moral needs cannot be divorced from his material needs. . . . In this fact lies the main divergence between communism, Christianity, and Islam.[64]

The principles of economic theory are placed in this setting.[65]

Property. All 'wealth' (*mal*) belongs to society and ultimately to God. Man merely utilizes it, within the limits of the law, in the role of 'steward'. The acquisition of wealth is possible only

62 Ramadan, *MT*, pp. 42–3.

63 We will follow here the best-known work on this subject, Qutb, *AIFI*. See also the less well-known works of Ghazali, *IMI* and *IMABSR*.

64 Qutb, *AIFI* (Hardie tr.), pp. 24, 25, 100.

65 For a short statement, see Ramadan, *MT*, pp. 44–51. Like the Brothers, we have confined ourselves to general propositions. Especially in this area, the bulk of writing of the Brothers was vague and largely uninformed. We were told in mid-1954 that the committee for economics in the headquarters was charged with the responsibility of harmonizing 'the views of Islam and the scholars ['*ulama*'] of economics'. This development was another sign, in this period, of dissatisfaction with the slogans which had carried the Society so far.

through 'work of any kind or variety'. Those enumerated by Islam include hunting, fishing, mining, raiding, working for others for a wage, and the like. All ultimately point to the fact that 'labour' is the only genuine foundation for possession. This means, in Islam, that there are no class distinctions based on material possession; whatever differences exist between men are of a mental and spiritual nature.

Every person has the right to private ownership. But unlike capitalism, which defends this absolutely (thus inspiring chaos), and communism, which denies it absolutely (thus restricting individual freedom), Islam recognizes the principle of possession but hedges it with controls in accordance with its primary concern 'the general welfare'.[66] 'Islam . . . ratifies that right of private property but along with it, it ratifies other principles which almost makes it theoretical rather than practical.'[67] For the Brothers the historical figure symbolizing these views was the Prophetic Companion, abu Dharr. Although he was viewed by the 'official *'ulama*'' (the Azhar) as a 'communist', the Brothers saw his teaching as a 'reaction', 'in the true spirit of Islam', to the corruption of Islam in his day.[68]

Inheritance procedures in Islam are a device for controlling large properties and the monopolization of wealth; they have been formulated with the express purpose of doing justice to all the heirs. The regulations surrounding inheritance are only part of the large scheme of control over the augmentation of wealth. Men may increase their possessions, but only within legal bounds. Forbidden practices for the accretion of wealth include *dishonesty*, *monopoly*, and *usury*.

Dishonest practices not only 'defile the conscience' but they are contrary to the principle of acquisition of wealth by work. Similarly monopolistic practices, especially in the area of 'necessities of life', are forbidden as an abhorrent and illegal method of gain. Usury, a sin comparable to 'thirty-six acts of adultery', is absolutely condemned. Besides being harmful to men's human relations, usury in the present age leads to the 'amassing of a vast amount of capital wealth which does not depend on effort or labour'. This fact leads to two 'social ills': the growth of 'unlimited fortunes'; and the 'division of society into two classes'.

To those who need it, money should be loaned 'freely'. Loans 'to encourage production' are made on the principle that 'the profit

[66] Ghazali, *IMABSR*, pp. 96–102. In a later chapter, pp. 142–7, Ghazali takes a critical view of the former mufti of Egypt, Shaykh Muhammad Hasanayn Makhluf, for rejecting the view of Islam as a 'socialistic religion' and for making an unwarranted defence of 'capitalism' in Egypt.

[67] Qutb, *AIFI* (Hardie tr.), pp. 104–16.

[68] Ibid., pp. 214–16.

is made rather by the effort expended than by the money borrowed, for money cannot make profits except by effort', and it is that effort which is the important thing in the eyes of Islam. In all loans it is incumbent on the creditor to be 'indulgent' if the debtor is in 'adverse circumstances'; it is equally incumbent on the debtor 'to spare no effort to pay back his debt'. In these terms the financial problems of a Muslim community would be negligible. And Islam would not be out of harmony with the times, for the Soviet Union has made the abolition of usury a cardinal point in its doctrine.[69]

Zakat is 'the outstanding social pillar of Islam' and 'the most essential part of the economic theory of Islam'. 'Payment of the poor tax is a duty.' Because Islam disapproves both of 'people being in poverty or need' and of 'the existence of class distinctions', it necessitates the payment of the tax on the basis of 'a statutory level of property'. The principle of *zakat*, along with the general powers given to the head of the state 'to assign levies on capital—that is to say, forced contributions from capital at a reasonable rate'—provide the state with adequate means for maintaining the welfare of all in the community and the stability of society.[70]

If 'labour' is the foundation of property, then it is 'a fundamental economic and social value'. Because of this, Islam invests labour with 'sacredness' and 'dignity'. Consequently, Islam has established certain rights and duties for the worker. His relationship with his employer is governed by the principle governing all human relations—'a mutuality of duties and rights' based on mutual 'respect and sympathy' and ordered by the 'spirit of brotherhood'. He has the right to a healthy and clean home, wages adequate to provide the needs of life and 'punctually' paid, and limited hours of work. The worker is forbidden to 'allocate any part of his wages' to his leaders. In return for these rights he shall 'perform his work fully and faithfully', thus respecting the rights of management and fulfilling his own responsibilities.[71]

[69] Qutb, *AIFI* (Hardie tr.), pp. 116–24; Ghazali, *IMI*, pp. 111–21, 134–40. Ghazali, like most other Brothers, does not go much further than stating the illegality of usury. Qutb, *AIFI* (Hardie tr.), pp. 272–5, has a suggestion for the problem of capital development in the form of 'share-issuing companies' which are permitted by Islam. The issue was a lively one in the Society but more effort was expended in justifying the injunction because it was Islamic than in offering proposals to alter the world-wide use of interest.

[70] Qutb, *AIFI* (Hardie tr.), pp. 133–8, 221–5, 267–76; Qutb, *MIWR*, pp. 51–4, is at particular pains to deny that the emphasis on *zakat* was essentially charity, a criticism very often made of this aspect of the Society's thinking.

[71] See Ghazali, *IMI*, pp. 142–59; and *JIM* (20 June 1946), 3. For this view, the Society won the wrath of communist and other radical groups in Egypt and confirmed the view of those groups (already noted) that its labour activities were designed to further the interests of capital and the ruling classes. The earlier

Social Organization

'The foundation of every healthy society is the virtuous individual.' For this reason Islam paid heed to the individual's needs for education, made individuals 'responsible for themselves before God', made them responsible for the 'liberation of the soul from superstition and depravity', and taught the preservation of the delicate balance between 'the demands of the body and the demands of the spirit'. The renaissance of the nation and the successful preservation of society is impossible without a fundamental concern for the state of the individual.[72]

If the family is the cornerstone of the social structure, its salvation lies in the salvation of the individual; and the nation can be saved only if the family is; for the nation's values and morals are born and nurtured in the bosom of the family. Islam has structured the family relationship to assure a tranquil and stable society, but this has been misunderstood, says Ghazali, by Westerners and Easterners alike.

> Some of us constrain woman with the traditions of the East; others give the licence of the West. On one side it is narrow-mindedness and chains; on the other, absolute freedom and libertinage. Both factions use the holy books of Islam for support and authority. In truth, Islam is far from either side. . . .
>
> The most important Oriental traditions . . . can be summarized as follows:
>
> (1) Because of her physical constitution, woman occupies an inferior position. Man is unconditionally superior.
>
> (2) Woman's *raison d'être* is limited to sensual pleasure and reproduction. Hence, her rights and duties should not transcend the emotional and intellectual scope of this *raison d'être*.
>
> (3) The standard of woman's personality and moral worth shall be her chastity alone, whereas in the case of man, the standard shall include other and more important values.
>
> These three traditional principles give rise to a whole system of detailed manners and customs to which woman is inevitably and ruthlessly subjected. The tragedy of this system is that its adherents think it is part and parcel of Islam itself.

view of the Society was expressed in lectures given by Banna to union groups in which he taught workers their duties towards 'God, himself, and the owner of the plant'; see *JIM* (24 Aug. 1946), 5. While obeisance to the principle of 'mutuality' in labour–management relations continued to prevail, the shift leftward in a widely read Qutb was very real. For a more comprehensive statement of the question of labour in Islam, see Jamal al-Din al-'Ayyad, *Nuzum al-'amal fi'l-Islam* (1952). Both he and Ghazali make extensive use of the economic studies of Rashid al-Barrawi, regarded in some circles in Egypt as 'liberal' in his economic views.

---

[72] Ramadan, *MT*, pp. 30, 31–2.

The women's organizations that presumably are opposed by Islam are really opposed by these traditions which they mistake as being those of Islam.

On the other hand, the Western traditions are:

(1) Absolute equality of men and women in everything.

(2) The foundation of society upon the free and complete association of the sexes.

(3) The consideration of the sexual life as something absolutely private and subject to the person's own free choice and natural inclinations.

These Western traditions have many admirers among us who enthusiastically spread them about. Our society is gradually being dragged down by them.

Islam . . . should be . . . distinguished from both Oriental and Western nonsense.[73]

In the eyes of Islam women are the equals of men. Islam resisted the early tribal notion that 'a girl child was a disaster', and raised her status, giving her, *inter alia*, rights of inheritance, possession, and administration of property; she also has the right to reject or accept a husband.[74] Unlike the Western world, Islam never debated the existence of a soul in women. What discrimination exists (in inheritance, legal hearings, prayer) is a function of the greater responsibility devolving on men and of the difference in the mental and emotional attributes of the sexes. Because mental power and emotional stability belong in larger measure to men, they are placed in a position of 'leadership'—'a fact' confirmed by history—and thus, 'one step' above women. This is a leadership of 'responsibility' and 'experience'—his are greater—and is not a priority of maleness over femaleness. Thus the only qualification to equality between male and female is a consequence of the 'practical' needs of living; this 'limited superiority', one based on larger responsibility, is 'purely a dictate of worldly efficiency'. This does not preclude, e.g. in the family, that husband and wife 'work together' in their respective areas, sharing and consulting on joint problems 'to fulfill the mission of life'.

[73] Ghazali, *MHN* (Faruqi tr.), pp. 106–7.

[74] Qutb, *AIFI* (Hardie tr.), pp. 51–2. In this section on the family and women we follow primarily *RMBBM*, *passim*. This *risala* was written by al-Bahi al-Khuli, an old and respected member of the Society, and published in 1953 as a commission by the Society with a preface by Hudaybi recommending its contents to members. Its appearance reflected the importance the new leadership attached to classifying the organization's social attitudes; it also reflected pressure from within the organization for comprehensible guidance on the perplexing problems of adolescence, sex, and marriage in a changing society. The result is an 'official' manual for the happy life, both frank and comprehensive. See also Ghazali, *MHN* (Faruqi tr.), pp. 108–28; Ramadan, *MT*, pp. 32–4; Qutb, *MIWR*, p. 111.

Women's 'rights' in society are well defined; they create a role contrary to that of woman's role in the West where she has an open invitation to 'licence and debauchery'. The West has surpassed Islam in its treatment of woman only in granting her 'freedom of recklessness'. Islam, on the other hand, has granted woman her 'rights', consistently with the axiom that the natural place for the mission of women is in the home.

The mixing of the sexes should be controlled and confined to 'necessity' and for 'logical reasons'.[75] Conversation and discussion are appropriate occasions for this. In the home, the woman must never be alone with any man other than her husband; she may go out to visit, to lectures, to prayers, or to the market; she should have holidays and go sightseeing; in getting from one place to another she should walk if possible, take a taxi if the distance is far and money is available, and use public transport only when necessary. Husbands who do not take their wives out, or if they do, permit a wife to walk behind for fear of being shamed, show a 'disgraceful ignorance' of the teachings of Islam.

The woman who leaves her home should be 'decently dressed'. 'The clothes of which virtue approves are well known. They mirror the moral state, dignity, self-respect of the person who wears them. Categorically, Islam does not tolerate the uncovering of arms, legs, and breast, or the wearing of transparent or semi-transparent clothes.' The veil has not been commanded by Islam although recommended by some Traditions and jurists in order 'to keep women from undue interference and avoid the possibility of temptation'. 'We do not think this is a very efficient means of precaution and we consider that Muslims have adopted it in a time of weakness and indecision. Training men and women for virtue requires a more comprehensive and positive programme.'[76]

Properly dressed, a woman may pursue her 'lawful' interests outside the home. This must include education and may include gainful employment. Education is not only desirable but necessary in the same measure for women as for men, the training should be addressed to preparing the woman for her primary function in life as wife and mother. Girls may study such things as agriculture, law, chemistry, and engineering, but in so doing they sacrifice some of their 'femininity' and 'sensitivity'. Medicine and teaching are desirable objectives for women students. No subject of study is forbidden to women by Islam, but the 'welfare' of society poses

[75] Qutb, *SAWI*, pp. 57–60, accepts as an ideal the notion of mixing the sexes but, taking the United States as an example and discussing divorce and infidelity, he insists that the concept is impracticable because of 'the nature of man and woman'.

[76] Ghazali, *MHN* (Faruqi tr.), pp. 117 ff.

questions about absolute freedom of selection and suggests specialization in those fields of endeavour which accord with the character and role of women in society. As to the question of accommodation at the university, there would be no harm in co-education were Islamic values understood; until they are, there should be special universities or special classes for women.[77]

Islam does not prohibit a woman from being 'a merchant or a doctor or a lawyer' or anything else which will bring lawful gain, provided it is necessary, that it be done in 'noble surroundings', and that the woman be rigorously decorous in behaviour and dress. Even under these conditions, however, the desirability of such a goal for women is questionable. 'True female progress' is not measured solely by a woman's right to become a merchant, doctor, or lawyer. Rather, the more genuine progress is in the development of her 'humanity': 'the education of her mind, the elevation of her character, and the purification of her heart and nature.'[78] Her Western model is devoid of 'honour and dignity'. The West has capitalized on woman as female; their beauty and femaleness have become primary elements in the market-place, 'instruments' of 'increased profits'. The prominent place of 'the beautiful secretary', 'the cashier hostess' (*sic*), 'the salesgirl', 'the model' in advertisements is an instance of 'the employment of the sex instinct by the tycoons and potentates of the merchant world'.[79]

Woman's real job is still the home and family: she creates 'for the son his manhood'; she is 'the spiritual source of love and kindness for her husband'; she alone creates 'the future of the nation'. These are the most noble of tasks. 'Religion does not forbid woman to work, but it does forbid her to flee from her natural place without excuse'.[80]

The same propositions apply to women's 'political rights' with added emphasis on the time dimension: 'in the present political, social, and legislative circumstances', political rights for women, recognized by Islam, should be left in abeyance until both men and women are more educated—intellectually and spiritually—and more faithful adherents of the principles and practices of the faith. Before granting political rights to women, society should be purged of its corruption; when the community begins to abide by 'religion

[77] Hudaybi in *MMR* (27 Nov. 1953), 25. See also Ghazali, *MHN* (Faruqi tr.), 125–8.

[78] *RMBBM*, p. 122.

[79] Qutb, *AIFI* (Hardie tr.), pp. 52–4.

[80] *RMBBM*, p. 127, and pp. 128–35 for similar observations about government and military service. In a by-the-way to this problem, and on another level, it was suggested (see Banna in *JIM* (8 Aug. 1946), 3) that concern about the 'right' of women to work be set aside until the problem of unemployment for family men be solved.

and reason', the way will have been prepared for the creation of the 'noble society' in which women will exercise their political rights.

The question of women's rights was one more and more frequently put to the spokesmen of the Society in its later years. Hudaybi, on a number of occasions, summed up these views in a way that was not possible for many members of the Society:

> The woman's natural place is in the home, but if she finds that after doing her duty in the home she has time, she can use part of it in the service of society, on condition that this is done within the legal limits which preserve her dignity and morality. I remember I left my daughters freedom to choose the kind of education which fitted them. The elder entered the faculty of medicine, is now a doctor and practises professionally. The second is a graduate of the faculty of science and is now a teacher in the faculty. Both are married and I hope that they have found harmony between their homes and jobs.[81]

The question of women's rights in Islam was, of course, intimately bound up with the two fundamental issues of *polygamy* and *divorce*. The prevailing view in the Society was the modernist, apologetic one which held that the Islamic attitude to the institution of polygamy was an historic advance over prior social practices, in that it limited men to four wives. But this limitation was even further qualified so as to make its literal application difficult. The warning that a man must be equal in treatment to all wives (Qur'an 3: 4) or confine himself to one is a virtual prohibition because it is impossible of fulfilment. Besides, the entire complex of problems arising from multiple wives and competing families in effect violates the more basic directives of Islam about marriage as an act of love, kindness, and mercy. The principle was preserved, however because of the times when 'necessity' demands its practice. These occasions are clear: when the wife is sterile; when the wife is chronically ill, in which case it would be better to marry again in 'purity and chastity' than to seek out a prostitute or commit adultery as is done in the Western world; and when the woman is 'unique', i.e. has a 'negative nature which does not harmonize with men and does not respond to the desires of her mate'. To these personal cases would be added the possibility of

[81] *MMR* (25 July 1952), 13. See also *MMR* (27 Nov. 1953), 25; *MDA* (29 Apr. 1953), 3. See *JJ* (18 Mar. 1954) 1, for a much more alarmed Azhar view of female political activity on the occasion of a hunger strike of women in March 1954. 'Awda, on the other hand, was closer to the Azhar. While serving on the 'committee of rights and general freedoms' as a representative of the Society in the constitutional committee set up by the RCC in 1953 he fought against political rights for women. When asked why, he defended his position in terms of male precedence in political leadership. Admitting for argument the right of women to vote—he did not accept it as a given in Islam—he felt it could serve no useful purpose. See *MDA* (1 Sept. 1953), 3; (24 Nov. 1953), 6.

other kinds of needs: economic need, 'as in underpopulated parts of the countryside' where extra 'working hands' are needed; social and moral needs, in the case of the decimation of male populations and the problems arising therefrom ('as in Germany after World War I'). The real objection to polygamy is not the principle but the abuse of the spirit in which it was intended by its use as a device of 'lust' and 'sin'. The answer is not the abolition of the principle, which can and does have its function, but the education and training of the people in the truths of the faith. The problem will 'solve itself by itself'; as in urban centres, polygamy will continue to decrease until it is confined to the real 'area of need'.

'Divorce is the most hateful to God of the lawful things.' This Prophetic Tradition, according to the Brothers, should be the guide to Muslims on this problem. The answer to its evil consequences is a more profound dedication to the principles of the faith and a more sincere application of the devices provided by Islam for the settlement of marital disputes. Divorce is not mentioned in the Qur'an as a final solution of marriage disputes—even if the man 'hates' his wife. This is consistent with the sacredness with which Islam has invested the marriage bond. Woman is helpless before the constant threat of divorce only because of the abuse of the institution, and this is so because of the repudiation of the genuine Islamic spirit in life. The answer is not 'the abolition of what is permitted' but a return to the fundamentals of Islamic life.[82]

[82] Qutb, *SAWI*, pp. 64–9 in addition to *RMBBM*, pp. 60–76.

X

THE SOLUTION: REFORM AND ACTION

THE Muslim state, the Muslim order, as conceived by the Brothers was, however, far from realization. But if the country could not be 'Islamized' overnight, much could be done to pave the way towards the final goal. This meant a total reform of the political, economic, and social life of the country by the government from the top, and by the people from below. The government was to be 'guided' by a series of reform programmes advocated by the Society; and these were to be given substantial support from the ever-increasing circle of Muslims converted anew to the truths of the faith. Thus, besides advocating reform programmes, the Society attempted to create a milieu conducive to the 'truly Islamic life', by undertaking on its own initiative numerous projects designed to demonstrate the viability of Islam as a coherent programme of social organization.

GOVERNMENT AND POLITICS

Political, Legal, and Administrative Reform

The first and most important of the political reform measures was the reform of the constitution. Banna's conception of constitutional reform was embodied in the slogan his followers shouted: 'The Qur'an is our constitution'; this indicated his undifferentiated approach to law and politics, for when listing political reforms he called for the 'reform of the law' in general so as to harmonize it with the *shari'a*. After him, reform programmes announced by the Society tackled the issue of legal reform less directly, apparently assuming that conformity with the *shari'a* would emerge automatically from effecting specific reform measures in all areas of society.[1] Constitutional reform, as such, was seen as a specific issue and in slightly more secular terms. Thus the Egyptian constitution was intolerable because it was the product of 'the age of English imperialism' and of 'political tyranny'; the 'gaps' left

[1] See *RTH: NN*, pp. 113–14, and *RIASNN*, p. 32; cf. *al-Bayan*, *passim*. A law committee in the headquarters was at work on an 'Islamic civil code'; see *Ila al-Ikhwan*, no. 3 [1953], 6–8.

in it because of this made it appear to be 'a grant from the king and not derived from the will of the nation (*umma*)'. The time had come (August 1952) to call a convention to draft a new constitution which would be 'an expression of the faith of the nation, its will and its desires, and a shield for the protection of its interests'; its 'principles should derive from the principles of Islam . . . in all matters of life without exception'. Such a constitution would enunciate the fundamental principle that ruler and ruled alike were equally responsible before the law for all behaviour.

Constitutional reform would lead to the reform of parliamentary life. From the beginning of Egypt's parliamentary life, Egyptians have known neither 'fit nor genuine representation'; corrupted parliaments have been impotent expressions not of the popular will but of party intrigue and monarchical will. Genuine parliamentary reform will come with the abolition of political parties; the parliament, during the period of 'partyism' (*hizbiyya*) has been little more than 'a device which has given legality to the appetites of the rulers and the tyrannies of authority'.[2] Parties are not necessary for a representative form of government; democracy requires only that there be guarantees of freedom of opinion and the participation of the nation in government. Without 'partyism', parliamentary life is perfectly compatible with the teaching of Islam; further, because parties create 'disunity' in the nation, they are incompatible with Islam.[3] Banna expressed what was later only implied: the abolition of political parties should be followed by the creation of a single party with an 'Islamic reform programme'.[4]

Suggestions for the reform of parliament and parties included: (1) the establishment of a catalogue of 'qualities' which should inhere in candidates whether they are representatives of an 'organization' or not: (2) the definition of a limit to electioneering; (3) the reform of election schedules and voting procedures to free them from the tampering of vested interests, and compulsory voting; (4) 'harsh punishment' for election 'forgery and bribery'. Banna also suggested election 'by list' rather than 'by individual with party affiliation'; this procedure would 'liberate the representative from

[2] *al-Bayan*, pp. 8–10; Hudaybi made it clear that his opposition was not to parliaments as such but to the way they operated in Egypt; see *MMR* (25 July 1952), 12–13.

[3] *RMFDNI*, pp. 41–2, 47–8, 53–5. Banna felt that the United States and Britain were successful examples of united communities with two-party systems; while they competed at times of elections, on national issues they were as one party (ibid., p. 55). The importance to the Brothers of the idea of national unity on fundamentals cannot be overstated. The same idea clearly dominates the thinking of the present regime.

[4] *RTH: NN*, p. 113. As successful single-party systems, Banna points to Russia and Turkey; see *JIM* (22 July 1946), 4; (25 Dec. 1946), 1.

the pressure of those who elected him', and ensure that public rather than personal interests were served.[5]

The other field of governmental reform was public administration, particularly the civil service. One aspect of this question was the Islamization of the civil service in a moral sense, the other covered matters of work and procedures. Banna had more to say about the first. He advocated: (1) the diffusion of the spirit of Islam in all departments of government; (2) control over the personal behaviour of the civil servant so that there would be no dichotomy in his behaviour as a civil servant and as a man; (3) reorganization of working hours to facilitate work, and to prevent the worker from 'staying up late at night'; (4) control of all government functions to conform with the spirit of the teachings of the faith; and (5) employment of more graduates of the Azhar in military and civil posts.

These attitudes were characteristic of Banna's approach to the problem of reform in general. He also addressed himself to the more mundane problems of the civil service which directly concerned his followers, and which were the focus of later reform programmes. Reform measures along these lines included: (1) the selection of civil servants on the basis of ability and not kinship; (2) the stabilization of working conditions and the simplification of work procedures by clarifying responsibility and abolishing centralization; (3) the improvement of the conditions of minor officials—raising salaries and bonuses, thus closing the gap between them and the higher officials, guaranteeing 'legal and financial security', and protecting the lower officials (*mar'us*) from 'the tyranny and whims' of the higher officials (*ra'is*); (4) the reduction of the number of civil-service posts and the more equitable and responsible distribution of work to those remaining; and (5) the cessation of the practice of 'excepting' (*istithna'*) favourites, friends, and families from the rules.[6]

The civil servants' subcommittee of the section for the professions undertook much of the programming of civil-service reform in the Society. Practical help, in the form of paying the cost of university education for the children of civil servants earning less than £E30 a month, was given by the special committees which were set up after World War II in the large cities (and were planned for the provinces) to 'fight the high cost of living'. The work of these special committees was in addition to

[5] *RMFDNI*, pp. 63–4. See *MDA* (7 June 1955), 1, 12, for an argument for parliaments without parties. Rather typical of the new mood in later years, *al-Bayan*, p. 10, confined itself to calling for reform of the electoral laws on a 'healthy foundation'.

[6] *RTH: NN*, pp. 114–20; *JIM* (2 July 1946), 4; and *al-Bayan*, p. 12.

that of the Society's general advocacy of reform—especially in the realm of salary and social security—which filled the pages of the Society's press. The obvious importance—from the point of view of attracting members—of this championing of the civil servant will be dealt with later.

Because political salvation from 'imperialism' was so closely related to political reform, the latter always included notions about military reform. The militancy which was part of the training programme of the Society's members has already been noted; Banna advocated such an approach on the national level when he preached 'the strengthening of the army and the kindling of its zeal on the foundation of Islamic *jihad*'.[7] 'Defence of the homeland' and 'defence of the truths of Islam' were the themes of repeated articles in the Society's press advocating military reform, themes which assumed even more importance after the revolution of 1952. At that time the Society proposed: (1) that the army should be strengthened and expanded without reference to the expense involved; (2) that the training of personnel should be conducted so as to 'establish relationships between its members on the basis of brotherhood'; (3) that recruitment should be expanded so that 'after a defined period there should not remain in the nation any one able to carry arms and not doing so'; (4) 'military training' including 'the arts of war and the techniques of real fighting' should be made 'compulsory' in universities and schools; (5) a 'reserve army' (*jaysh iqlimi*) should be established for those not in the regular army; and (6) the government should found armament industries.

Police reform was a matter advocated emphatically and specifically only after the first dissolution of 1948 and the subsequent death of Banna, and it had an obvious political and personal (i.e. Societal) quality about it. The reforms proposed included the abolition of corruption, tyranny, prison terror, and the political police, and the raising of police pay.[8]

Political Attitudes and Action

The role played by the Brothers in the national movement and in the internal politics of Egypt brought much condemnation from groups and individuals in Egypt and abroad. What, it was asked, does a 'religious society' have to do with 'politics'? The answer the Brothers gave has already been indicated: the view that 'religion' is a mere set of rituals to be practised in a house of worship is of Western origin and is in violation of the unity of life

[7] *RTH: NN*, p. 114.
[8] *al-Bayan*, pp. 14–15.

taught by Islam; 'politics' and 'religion' (*din*) are not opposite and incompatible spheres of activity but, like all other types of human behaviour, aspects of the indivisible Islam. Political action, then, was inseparable from the movement by definition. Such a view, however, raised some ideological questions about the nature of political loyalties in a Muslim community set in a world of nation states. In what terms was political action to be explained and justified: Given the 'internationalist' interpretation of Islam by the Society, what was the Brother to feel about other and more immediate commitments to Egypt and to the Arabs? The views of the Society on this matter were clear—at least intellectually.

Nationalism

'Nationalism (*qawmiyya*) in our minds attains the status of sacredness.' This was patriotism for Egypt, an unqualified commitment to defend the 'nation' (*watan*) and struggle on its behalf. Not Egypt as such, but because Egypt is a Muslim land. Patriotism was sacred because it was in the service of the faith; patriotism for Egypt was all the more possible and desirable because of Egypt's historically important relationship with Islam. Thus patriotism demanded, as a first step, 'the struggle against imperialism', for the salvation of Egypt is 'the first link in the anticipated renaissance'; Egypt is 'a part of the general Arab nation, and . . . when we act for Egypt, we act for Arabism, the East, and for Islam'. In this nationalism, protecting the nation from aggression is a 'religious duty' because only in a free nation can there be 'religious self-respect'.[9]

But this is not nationalism in the Western sense of the word. This 'new emotion' has established 'modern states' but it has destroyed the unity of the Muslim world and left it a prey to Christian and Zionist imperialism. While the whole world moves towards internationalism, Muslims with a tradition of internationalism are regressing to regional and provincial loyalties. Worse, this 'narrow nationalism', which is a Western product, has established 'a new object of worship', the materialist nation, destructive and incompatible with the 'nationalism of divine principles' decreed by God in Islam. The modern nation has become 'a partner with God'; the secular nationalist is guilty of *shirk*.

The ultimate and only real relationship possible to men is with God, not with other men; 'there is no higher self-respect (*'izza*) than this'. Man, if he is bound primarily by the God–man relationship, and thus free of narrow partisanship and factionalism,

[9] *RDFTJ*, pp. 11–12; *RS*, p. 14; *RIASNN*, p. 40; and variously in *JIM*.

is free to unite with other men under the single banner of God.[10] Islam, then, repudiates nationalism narrowly defined by secular and material interests, preferring rather that patriotism serve the larger—and only valid—divinely inspired goals of the community. Nationalism without religion is inconceivable: 'So long as nationalism [patriotism?—*wataniyya*] is loyalty to the nation (*watan*), then religion is its gate, for no loyalty is possible for him who has no religion.'[11]

The use of words in the matter of nationalism was not always consistent in the literature and speech of the Brothers. *Watan*, *qawm*, and *umma* were used interchangeably for 'nation'; 'nationalism' was variously described as *wataniyya* or *qawmiyya*. Banna, in one of his early messages to the Brothers, attempted a clarification of the words both for the Brothers and for those outside who raised questions about the political loyalties of the Society. He distinguishes between *wataniyya* ('devotion to one's country') and *qawmiyya* ('devotion to one's people'), and sees in each a variety of qualities of which some agree and some conflict with Islam.[12]

> *Wataniyat al banin*, i.e. the love for one's country and place of residence, is a feeling which is hallowed both by the commands of nature and the injunctions of Islam. Bilal . . . and the Prophet himself approved of this kind of *wataniyah* when they expressed their tender love for their home town of Mecca.
>
> *Wataniyat al-hurriyya wa'l-'izza*, i.e. the desire to work for the restoration of the honour and independence of one's country is a feeling approved by the Qur'an (63. 8/8; 4. 141/140) and by the Ikhwan.
>
> *Wataniyat al-fath*, i.e. the desire for conquest and world domination has its basis in Islam, which directs its conquerors towards the best system of colonization and conquest, as is indicated by the Qur'an (2. 198/189).[13]
>
> *Wataniyat al-hizbiyah*, however, i.e. the love for party-strife and the bitter hatred of one's political opponents with all of its destructive consequences, is a false kind of *wataniyah*. It does not benefit anybody, not even those who practise it.

Islam, then, teaches *wataniyya* but one which is contingent on

[10] Ghazali, *MHN* (Faruqi tr.), pp. 35–7; Ramadan, *MT*, pp. 13–14; *RIASNN*, pp. 11–16, 39–40; Rosenthal, 'Muslim Brethren', 284.

[11] *MS* (14 Feb. 1947), 75; the article is a blistering attack by Sa'id Ramadan on secular nationalism. See the discussion of the difference between 'religious nationalists' and 'religious anti-nationalists' in E. Marmorstein, 'Religious Opposition to Nationalism in the Middle East', *International Affairs*, xxviii/3 (July 1952), 356 f.

[12] We follow here the rendering by Rosenthal, 'Muslim Brethren', 283–7, of the *RTH: D*, pp. 14–23, from which the above is taken. Rosenthal's notes are omitted.

[13] The 'moral and good' 'imperialism of Islam' is discussed at length in *RIASNN*, pp. 3–6, 20–3, 37–8.

religion rather than geographical boundaries; its goal is not only, as in Europe, 'the promotion of a country's material well-being,' but also, and primarily, the spread of the word of God across the face of the earth.

If *wataniyya* is in Islam, so also is *qawmiyya*, the devotion to one's people. There are various kinds of *qawmiyya* also.

> *Qawmiyat al-najd*, i.e. the pride of the young generation in the glory of their forefathers and the desire to equal them is a praiseworthy feeling which was approved by the Prophet. . . .
>
> *Qawmiyat al-ummah*, i.e. the special interest of a person in his particular group and people . . ., is also a genuine feeling.
>
> *Qawmiyat al-tanzim*, i.e. the realization of the common aims of freedom and salvation achieved by the work and struggle of each individual group, is another legitimate aspiration.
>
> All of these are legitimate expressions of *qawmiyah*, and are approved by Islam. However, *qawmiyat al-jahiliyah*, i.e. the desire to re-establish old '*jahiliyat*' customs and to replace Islam by an exaggerated nationalism and racism, is a highly contemptible and dangerous sentiment. Under its influence some states have destroyed the outward signs of Islam and Arabism and have gone so far as to change proper names, the letters of the alphabet, and the vocabulary. . . . This kind of *qawmiyah* tends to destroy the heritage of Islam and its most sacred possession, the religion of Islam. . . .
>
> Likewise, *qawmiyat al-'udwan*, the desire to gain dominance for one's race (*jins*) over all others, is a contemptible and false sentiment. It is exemplified by Italy and Germany, and in fact, by any other nation which would claim to be superior to all other nations (*fawq al-jami'—über alles*).

This approach to *wataniyya* and *qawmiyya* led to the repudiation of the movements which had vied for Egyptian and Arab loyalties in the last quarter-century: 'Pharaonicism' in Egypt, 'Phoenicianism' in the Lebanon, and 'Syrianism' in the Fertile Crescent as a whole; even 'Arabism',[14] when it becomes 'secularist and racist', is erroneous. The idea of Pharaonicism which divided Egyptian intellectualist nationalism in the 1920s was a matter of special concern for Banna: 'We welcome', he says, 'ancient Egypt as a history in which there is glory, pride, science, and knowledge.' But, he adds, Muslims (i.e. the Muslim Brothers) would resist 'with all our might' the view that Egypt should be recreated in its image 'after God has granted to her the teaching of Islam'.[15] As the quotation indicated, Pharaonicism, as well as the others noted above, was resisted not so much for what was advocated as for what was omitted—the fact of Islam. It was on this ground that the Society resisted with some bitterness the notion advocated by

[14] *RTH: RD*, p. 23. [15] Ibid., pp. 12, 23.

Taha Husayn that Egypt was not Eastern (Oriental) but rather part of 'Mediterranean culture' and therefore 'Western'.[16]

Of the other movements, Phoenicianism was largely Lebanese and relatively insignificant. Syrianism, however, was very important, because of its scope and because its ideas were embodied in the effective Syrian Social National party founded by Antun Sa'ada. For the Brothers, it was necessary to repudiate Syrianism, both because it posed a direct challenge to Arabism which (as will be seen in a moment) was an important element in the hierarchy of Muslim loyalties, and also because it was the most vigorous of the increasingly large number of groups which, if not 'anti-religious', advocated secularization of community loyalties.[17]

Arabism

The problem of secularization was perhaps the most significant of the objections raised to some forms of Arab nationalism (*qawmiyya*). The Brothers felt that the advocates of non-sectarian Arabism (the chief spokesman being Sati' al-Husari) were just as misguided as those of Syrianism, because they failed to understand the unique place of the Arabs and Arabism in the scheme of things.[18] 'Arabs are the first Muslims', the Prophet has said; further, 'If the Arabs are humiliated, then so is Islam.' From the Persian Gulf to Tangier, the Arab nation is gathered in one faith and unified by one language. That language is 'the tongue of Islam'. Thus the necessary prelude to a truly Islamic renaissance is not only the liberation of each Muslim land (the practice of *wataniyya* and *qawmiyya*), but the 'unification of the Arab nations', the goal of Arabism. In serving Arabism, the Muslim Brothers are 'serving Islam and the welfare of the entire world'.[19]

This view of Arabism generated a special intensity about the major question facing the 'Arab nation'—that of Palestine. If the Arabs were the 'first' Muslims, then Palestine had a significance transcending purely geopolitical considerations. Palestine was 'the first line of defence of the Arab nation (*watan*)', but more, it was 'the heart of the Arab world, the knot of the Muslim peoples, the first of the two *qiblas* [direction in which Muslims turn to pray] and the third of the holy places [of Islam].'[20] However, even the Brothers could argue secularly for the resistance to

[16] See *MDA* (3 July 1951), 7; (8 Nov. 1955), 1, 6–7, 12.

[17] See esp. Qutb, *DI*, pp. 167–71.

[18] Ibid.; on Husari and his thought, see Hazem Zaki Nuseibeh, *The Ideas of Arab Nationalism* (1956), p. 49 and n. 23, 24.

[19] *RDFTJ*, pp. 12–13.

[20] See *MS* (14 Nov. 1947), 86; *JIM* (13 Aug. 1946), 1; Sharif, *IMFHF*, p. 9; Ghazali, *TFDH*, pp. 145–6.

Zionism in Palestine: 'If religion provides no sufficient reason for combating [Zionism] . . . then the purely worldly interests of Palestine's neighbours amply does.'[21] But this argument was one of a hierarchy; the reasons for opposing Zionism, in order of importance, had to do with 'the interests of Islam, the interests of Arabism and the limited interests of the nation [Egypt]'.[22]

Attitudes towards the first attempts to institutionalize Arab unity also had an Islamic quality, but in more mundane terms. The Arab League received only qualified approval: it was seen as 'a creation of England', and England had not lent her support to the idea because of 'the blacks of our eyes'. Its questionable paternity, however, should not preclude the use of the League with vigilance and constant attention to the possibility of changing its character to serve 'our own [i.e. Arab] interests'. In so doing, Arabs could benefit from this already existing formal structure of Arab unity—however faulty, and whatever its original intent—as a first step towards genuine organic union.[23] As one step towards this goal, and in answer to alleged external political manipulation of the structures of Arab unity, the Society advocated and supported measures designed to facilitate economic unity among the Arabs, chief of which would be a company capitalized with purely Arab money to support commercial, financial, and industrial endeavours in the Arab world.[24]

Involved in this generally doubtful feeling about the League, and related to the larger issues of Arab unity, was a deep mistrust of the Hashimite family, widely regarded as British 'stooges'. The Sharifian revolt against the Turks was viewed with mixed feelings, but basically as an error; not so much because it brought independence from the Turks (although the disruption of the caliphate created for the Brothers ideological confusion and complicated attitudes), but because it brought subjection to the British and French. Hostility to the Sharif of Mecca focused largely on his heirs in Iraq and Jordan, especially the late King 'Abdullah. The feeling toward the latter was reflected in the Society's opposition

[21] Ghazali, *MHN* (Faruqi tr.), p. 94.

[22] Sharif, *IMFHF*, p. 9; and a good statement in 'Abd al-Rahman al-Banna', *Thawrat al-damm* (1951), pp. 23–7. Secular nationalists, especially but not only communists, regarded the Society's enthusiasm about Palestine as traitorous incitation about a problem which was none of Egypt's concern. From this it was argued that the Society served British interests in Egypt (see Ahmad, *Mizan*, p. 62). See also Qutb, *DI*, pp. 102–7, for an answer to the partisans of the 'Egypt first' thesis. We would assume that despite Egypt's apparent whole-hearted current commitment to Arabism, there are those who continue to believe in 'Egypt first'.

[23] Ghazali, *MHN* (Faruqi tr.), p. 21; *IIS*, pp. 218–19; cf. Zaki, *Ikhwan*, pp. 59–60.

[24] See *JIM* (14 July 1946), 3.

to the 'Greater Syria' scheme: the idea of Greater Syria was good if it meant a union of Arab Muslims (in some measure, this plan was identified with Syrianism); but such a move, inspired from Jordan (i.e. 'Abdullah) would be merely an attempt 'to enlarge the area of occupation of Trans-Jordan until it includes other Syrian lands—in the name of Greater Syria'.[25] 'Abdullah's reputation was not enhanced by what was regarded as his 'treason' to the Arab cause during the Palestine war—a feeling shared and still held by most Egyptians; at the time of his assassination the editorial comment by Brothers was unsparing.[26]

Islamism

The final and only enduring loyalty possible to a Muslim is to the 'Islamic nation' (*al-watan al-islami*)—'every bit of land on which there is a Muslim who says "There is only one God and Muhammad is his Prophet"'.[27] The justification for serving the limited national interests of Egypt (or other Muslim states), and the larger but yet confining interests of Arabism is Islam and the unity of the Muslim peoples, and, in the final analysis, the welfare of humanity. Islamic nationalism transcends 'geographic boundaries, political divisions, and the varieties of colours, races and languages' because it is founded on the notion of 'the unity of humankind'; unlike 'limited nationalism', Islamic nationalism is divinely inspired by the triple principles of 'Godliness, humanitarianism, and internationalism'. These objects alone are worthy of the attention of divinely created man; their dissemination as purposes for human existence is the duty of all Muslims. Thus Islamic nationalism is in the service of all humanity.

Its object, the renaissance of the Islamic nation, was, however, a matter for the distant future. The task required prior steps: the liberation of the separate Muslim nations, and the unification of the Arab world. The symbol of Islamic unity, the caliphate, could be 'seriously considered' as the bonds between the Islamic and Arab nations grew stronger.[28] These bonds could be strengthened by greater concern and mutual support among Muslims for each other's problems and needs.

[25] Ibid. (30 Nov. 1946), 1. The point was made in a play called *Greater Syria* written by 'Ali Ahmad Bakthir and published in *JIM*. The 'plot' involves a young Arab girl who seduces a young *shaykh* into marrying her but who admits —after being caught in an act of unfaithfulness with an Englishman—to being an English spy involved in a design to usurp the wealth and possessions of the young man's family by marrying into it. See *JIM* (8 Dec. 1946), 4.

[26] See *MDA* (24 July 1951), 1.

[27] Ramadan, *MT*, p. 71.

[28] *RTH: NN*, pp. 18–19. We have already noted the Society's relative indifference to this question. For the best statement see *RMK*, pp. 50–1. See also *RTH: NN*, p. 114.

The Society responded to this last belief by making its magazines, newspapers, and books platforms for 'Muslim causes' all over the world, and claimed to have sent material support to some of these. The Society's formal instrument for strengthening bonds with other Islamic countries was the section for liaison with the Islamic world, whose headquarters, as already indicated, played host to Muslim missions and delegations to Egypt or to the Society, and sought to assume the role of headquarters for an 'Islamic movement' which would sweep the Muslim world. An effort was made—and partly brought into effect by the revolutionary government of Egypt in 1954—to make the pilgrimage the occasion for an international conference of Muslim leaders in Mecca. The Society each year in the mid-1940s set aside special areas in Mecca and put up tents to greet and entertain and convert pilgrim delegates from all over the Muslim world.[29] It was also formally represented at the Islamic conferences held in Karachi in 1949 and again in 1951; one of its then leading members, Sa'id Ramadan (now in exile), was elected secretary-general of the group[30] which came into existence in their name.

'*Easternism*'

Islamism—effort on behalf of the Islamic nation—should be the final goal of all Muslims, but there was another dimension to supranational activity. 'Easternism' (*sharqiyya*) was a concept recognized by Banna in passing; for him, the bloc of Asian nations referred to as the 'East' was important primarily as it reflected a Western state of mind, summed up in Kipling's phrase that 'never the twain shall meet'. As a phenomenon on the world scene, Banna was sure it would disappear when the West established just relations with the world at large. But, meanwhile, there were problems for Asian nations, and in so far as the Brothers were 'Muslims and Asians' they were bound to strive for the restoration of the 'honour and dignity' of the Asian nations in every way possible.[31]

Banna, however, lived before the era of Bandung and the serious involvement of Asia in the cold war. Thus, among his followers, Easternism was transformed into the question of loyalty to the 'Afro-Asian bloc'. The Brothers found it possible to be warm but still reserved: it was desirable to work within the group; but as a

[29] See *JIM* (13 Nov. 1946), 3; Husayni, *Ikhwan*, p. 137; Khuli, *QDIHB*, pp. 40–4.

[30] See *MDA* (6 Mar. 1951), 2 and *passim*; (13 Mar. 1951), 4, for a rebuttal of communist charges that the conference was in the service of 'Anglo-American imperialism'.

[31] *RDFTJ*, pp. 14–15; see also Zaki, *Ikhwan*, pp. 60–1.

bloc, it could only be regarded as temporary and transitional because it lacked common long-range interests. The more realistic expression of Asian unity of action was in the 'Muslim bloc' which, because of its similarity of purpose and inspiration, could alone survive the rigours of the cold war.[32] The cold war, in fact, was the chief reason for the limited support given to the Afro-Asian bloc—as long as it was not possible to have a Muslim 'third bloc' through which to counterbalance the two antagonists of the cold war.

The cold war, it should be noted, was seen as an opportunity for Islam to serve humanity by mediating between the capitalist and communist worlds. Islam was neither capitalist nor communist and was sufficient unto itself, and for this reason rejected the possibility of alliance with either camp.[33] Muslims, too, were warned to be wary of the efforts made by the West through Christianity to ally itself with Islam against communism; Islam and Christianity indeed, have much in common against the atheistic system of the communists, but a 'union of the crescent and the cross' is possible only between those who genuinely believe in and practise the teachings of Jesus and Muhammad.[34]

It should also be noted that the cold war was seen as an opportunity for Islam and Muslim nations to save themselves in the predicted cataclysm between the two forces by mediating between them or as a situation to be exploited for the end of national liberation or domestic reform. While recognizing that the Soviet camp was ultimately as great a threat to Islam as the Western it was possible to see the fear generated by the Soviet Union as useful: 'We are in temporary need of the communist power', says Qutb, in order to frighten 'oppressors' and 'exploiters' into instituting social reform.[35]

A complete discussion of the political action and attitudes of the Society might properly, in this section, include the important questions of political violence and revolution. Because these matters are so closely related to the meaning of the Society for Egyptian political life, they will be deferred to a concluding chapter.

[32] Qutb, *DI*, p. 167.

[33] See e.g. *MDA* (25 May 1954), 1; Qutb, *SAWI*, pp. 128–56.

[34] See Ghazali, *MHN* (Faruqi tr.), p. 90. The Brothers made much of this point. See Qutb, *DI*, pp. 116–19, for a repudiation of 'American Islam'—the Islam about which Americans learn and which they try to win over to the fight against communism. For partially adverse reaction on this basis to the conferences of Christians and Muslims sponsored by the American Friends of the Middle East see *JIM* (20 May 1954), 11; and *MDA* (22 Feb. 1955), 7.

[35] Qutb, *SAWI*, pp. 167 and 166–9.

ECONOMICS

Economic Reform

Over the years in which the Society had been advocating reform in Egypt, economic measures had slightly changed both in scope and in their relative importance in the total scheme of reform. Whereas for Banna, moral, political, and educational reform were priorities, for some of his followers economic reform seemed not only prior but pivotal; however, even Banna came to pay more attention to the economic problem, a reflection of the concern with and needs of the membership in the increasingly tight economic squeeze in post-World War II Egypt. The Brothers saw economic reform in terms of two factors: (1) economic independence was the foundation of genuine political independence; and (2) economic betterment—some form of economic and social security—for the poverty-stricken masses of Egypt was necessary in order to close the gaps in the class structure and thus avoid further national disunity in the name of the class struggle. Within this framework, the Society proposed certain measures of economic reform to be enacted by the state through legislation or decree; and designed to bring Egypt into harmony with its Islamic heritage.[36]

1. Usury in all its forms should be abolished; the government should lead the way by rejecting interest charges in all its own operations.

> Suppose that the state decrees the abolition of interests on funds in banks, companies, public enterprises, and private loans, what will happen then?
>
> What will happen will be that capitalists will find themselves unable to increase their wealth except by two general methods. First they may put it to some profitable use themselves in manufacture or trade or agriculture. Or second, they may put it to a profitable and helpful use by investing it in share issuing companies, where the share values may rise or fall. Both these methods are sanctioned by Islam, and neither of them will work the slightest injury to economic life.[37]

2. The natural resources of the country should be nationalized; foreign control of public utilities and mineral resources should be broken; and foreign capital should be replaced by local. These

[36] The following is summarized largely from *RMFDNI*, pp. 83–92 and *RTH: NN*, pp. 119–20, which are Banna's work, and *al-Bayan*, pp. 10–13, a programme released in 1952.

[37] Qutb, *AIFI* (Hardie tr.), p. 274, and pp. 250-3, above, for the theoretical views on this question.

measures should be accompanied by extensive exploitation of the country's natural wealth—agricultural and mineral.[38]

3. The nation should be industrialized 'immediately', with emphasis on industries dependent on 'local raw materials' and on 'war industries'. 'Household industries' should be encouraged not only to aid the poor and destitute, but to create 'a door for the change to the industrial spirit and the industrial era'; such work could be established in spinning, weaving, and soap, perfume, and preserve making.[39]

4. The National Bank of Egypt (*al-bank al-ahli*) should be nationalized as a further step towards financial independence; Egypt should have a press for printing her own money and found a mint (*dar sak al-nuqud al-ma'daniyya*).

5. The bourse (*bursat al-'uqud*) should be abolished, and 'cotton policy' should be reformed.

6. Taxes should be reformed so that a levy of *zakat* was applied 'progressively' on capital as well as profit. The taxes should be used for the general purposes of the state and to raise the standard of living and serve the welfare of the people. Among the goals of taxation should be the control of conspicuous spending and luxury.

7. Land reform should be pursued vigorously: (*a*) a ceiling should be placed on the amount of property which could be owned; the remainder should be sold 'at reasonable prices over a long term' to the landless; (*b*) the national lands should be distributed to small owners and the landless.[40]

8. Farm-rental legislation should be passed to protect the renter from the abusive practice of the owner's taking an unjust share of the farmer's production.

9. Labour legislation should be reviewed with an eye to reforms which (*a*) guarantee to all workers (including 'farm labourers') security against unemployment, injury, illness, old age, and death; (*b*) compel labour organization; and (*c*) assure the wage-earner of a fair share of increased productivity. Agricultural and industrial workers should be trained in their jobs more effectively to insure increased productivity.[41]

[38] The 1952 programme did not officially call for nationalization of foreign companies, and was far more concerned with land development.

[39] According to Banna, the Qur'an commanded Muslims to have heavy industry.

[40] Banna accepted the principle of land reform but seemed indifferent to the question. Not so with some of his followers, notably Ghazali and Qutb, as we have noted. Hudaybi accepted the principle but conflicted with the government on the ceiling.

[41] On the question of labour reform see also Qutb, *DI*, p. 90; and a strong statement in Ghazali, *TFDH*, p. 68.

10. Finally, every worker must be guaranteed 'social security'; if a man cannot find work, or if his work is insufficient or he is unable to work, his needs must be met by the state through *zakat*. The *zakat* must be administered to the needy in the area from which it is collected so that rich and poor alike will have the sense of 'mutual responsibility'. If *zakat* is not sufficient to meet the needs of the poor, then the state has the right to compel the wealthy who do not do so willingly to give more to the poor.

Economic Activity

Much of the reform programme advocated by the Society was beyond its institutional capacity to do more than talk about. However, efforts were made in the fields of 'industrial' enterprise and labour activity to demonstrate the possibility of an Islamic approach to economic affairs. In its 'industrial' and commercial operations, the Society sought not only to demonstrate the viability of 'Islamic economic theory', but also to provide itself and the membership with profitable earnings. In its labour activity, the Society sought not only to demonstrate the feasibility and desirability of harmonious labour-management relations within an Islamic framework, but also, and perhaps more importantly, to establish itself as the spokesman for the needs and expectations of the vast and inarticulate body of Egyptian labour, a fact of great significance in its claim to authority on the Egyptian scene.

Industry and Commerce

The original purpose of the Society's business enterprises was the development of the national economy. Banna was not the originator of the policy; when it was first put into effect he was, in fact, making distinctions, interesting in the light of later ideological developments, between economic activity and the Muslim Brothers' programme. 'The message', he observed, 'was one thing and finance and economics another.' He did, however, go along with the idea as a means not only to contribute to the national wealth, but also to destroy the control of foreigners over the economy.[42]

Foreigners, in the first instance and in a non-economic sense, meant missionaries; the initial inspiration for the Society's enterprises was in reply to missionary activity. One case of conversion in which it interested itself appeared to have come about from economic motives. The Society thereupon organized a 'workhouse-school' (*mashghal*) for women in an effort to provide some means

[42] *Mudh.*, pp. 266–8, 158–9

of livelihood for the destitute of the area involved. Similar attempts were made on a local basis as the Society grew, but all remained local and ineffective ventures. The larger enterprises followed the rise to fame on the Cairo scene.

In 1938 the Society embarked on its first major venture, the founding of the Company for Islamic Transactions (*sharikat al-muʿamalat al-islamiyya*). The original announcement declared the company to be an attempt to provide the means for gain within the framework of Islamic principles. Initial capitalization was to be £E4,000 divided into 1,000 shares of £E4 each; stock could be purchased in one payment or over a period of time not to exceed forty months at a minimum of PT10 monthly. Management was to be in the hands of a board of directors composed of a chairman, treasurer, and seven other members; members of the board had to have at least five shares in the company, and the chairman and treasurer at least ten. The Society was to take 2½ per cent of the capital and profit of the company annually for purposes of *zakat*. The company was to embark on 'investment activity' when the funds became available from sale of stock, buying at 'wholesale prices' in accordance with the 'requirements of the Brothers' and selling at 'appropriate prices'. Profit would be distributed annually on the following schedule: 10 per cent for directors' fees; 20 per cent for the reserve fund; and 50 per cent for the shareholders, paid on their initial purchase of stock.

The first sale of stock was rapidly completed and the company expanded from its initial capital value of £E4,000 to £E20,000 in 1945; in 1946, a new issue of stock was advertised which was to increase the capital to £E30,000. In 1947 the company was combined with another enterprise called the Arabic Company for Mines and Quarries (*al-sharikat al-ʿarabiyya li'l-manajim wa'l-mahajir*) which had a capital value of £E60,000. The various activities of the two groups included moving and trucking, automotive repairs, and the production of cement, tiles, and gas-cooking equipment. In 1947 the quarrying end of the merger decided to modernize traditional techniques and placed orders in Europe for equipment for cutting and polishing marble. The equipment was sent, but remained on the docks of Alexandria and deteriorated during the crisis of 1948 which brought an end to the economic activity of the Society; after its return to legality in 1950, the Society sued the government for its losses.[43]

A larger enterprise, earlier in inspiration but later in fruition,

[43] Zaki, *Ikhwan*, pp. 165 ff. There was little information available on the workings of this enterprise or any of those to be discussed below. We rely on Zaki and on some bits from *JIM* in 1946 and 1947.

was the Society's printing press. It will be recalled that the second general conference of the Brothers authorized a small company for the establishment of a press. In the pre-war period the venture failed to achieve either continuity or permanence, largely, it would seem, because of inefficient distribution.[44] The growth of the Society in the war years, however, changed the situation and in the post-war years the enterprise flourished. In 1945 publishing operations were separated from press operations and two separate limited companies founded: the Brothers' Printing Company (*sharikat al-ikhwan li'l-tiba'a*) and the Brothers' Journalistic Company (*sharikat al-ikhwan li'l-sihafa*), initially capitalized at £E70,000 and £E50,000 respectively. The Journalistic Company was responsible for producing the Society's daily founded in 1946, which provided it with a firm economic basis; the Publishing Company, on the other hand, was hampered by lack of equipment, which was ordered from abroad but which did not arrive in quantity before the 1948 dissolution of the Society and the curtailment of its multiple economic activities.

The success of the Journalistic Company was apparently related to the establishment of the Arabic Advertising Company (*sharikat al-i-'lanat al-'arabiyya*) in 1947. Heyworth-Dunne reports its capital to be a reputed £E100,000 and sees the company as a 'rival to the Société Orientale de Publicité', a fact which he relates to violence inflicted on the latter in 1948.[45] The Brothers' company included in its operations newspaper and cinema advertising, covers for books and magazines, and sign-painting for business establishments. There seems to have been little doubt among the Brothers that this was the largest and most successful of their undertakings.

In an effort to come to terms with the serious post-war unemployment problems, the Society embarked on a programme of small industry. This included the Muslim Brothers' Company for Spinning and Weaving (*sharikat al-ikhwan al-muslimin li'l-ghazl wa'l-tansikh*), which was founded in 1947 with a capital of £E8,000, of which £E6,500 had been subscribed when it began operations. All the workers in the company were shareholders. The company claimed to have spent in its first ten months of operations £E2,700 in salaries to sixty workers (or almost half its initial capital) and concluded the period with a profit of £E1,400. The Society took much pride in this company, advertising it as an effort to 'revive Islamic socialism', 'liberate the national economy', and 'raise the level of the Egyptian worker'. Its factory was in the Shubra

[44] *Mudh.*, pp. 189–90, 201–2, 250.
[45] *Modern Egypt*, pp. 57–8.

al-Khayma industrial quarter of Cairo, the scene of the great labour depression and unrest of the early post-war years. Most of its stocks were sold through the Shubra branch of the Society as well as through the labour section at the general headquarters.[46]

In Alexandria the Society founded the Company for Commercial and Engineering Works (*sharikat al-tijara wa'l-ashghal al-handasa*) which concerned itself with the construction of buildings, the production of construction materials, and the training of workers in such trades as plumbing, electricity, and carpentry. The company was capitalized at £E14,000 divided into 3,500 shares. Another company founded in Suez as the Company of Commercial Agencies (*sharikat al-tawkilat al-tijara*) expanded largely into the fields of advertising and transport.

These enterprises never recovered from the blow dealt the Society in 1948, although their confiscation was repudiated by the Council of State in the case brought by the Society in 1950 and 1951.[47] A committee was appointed in 1952 to make an effort to revalue the stocks of the various companies in the light of the losses and depreciation of equipment since 1948, but nothing was concluded before the new dissolutions of the Society in 1954. Only one new venture had been established between 1952 and 1954; it seemed to be prospering. In 1952 the Commercial Company (*sharikat al-tijara*) was founded at al-Mahalla al-Kubra; by the end of the year it had sold £E8,000 of capital stock and by February 1953 was advertising to increase its capital to £E25,000. The company produced textiles, household goods, clothing—ready-made men's clothing and accessories, including ties and scarves—notions, office and school supplies, and electrical equipment. It was confiscated with all other assets of the Society in 1954.[48]

Labour

It may be argued that the rise to power of the Society was closely related to the economic and social conditions of the Egyptian worker. This was particularly the case during the periods of post-war economic crisis, but it continued to be true throughout the history of the movement. The Society's recollection of its origins, it will be recalled, emphasized the inspiration it had received from workers, and the Society's writers made much of

[46] It was boasted that £E6,000 of the capital was owned by 530 shareholders, unlike most companies where a 'few capitalists' own the bulk of stock. See Husayni, *Ikhwan*, pp. 92–3.

[47] See *MDA* (15 Apr. 1951), 13, for a list of the companies confiscated and the case in court.

[48] See *MDA* (24 Feb. 1953), 15; (21 Apr. 1953), 14.

the fact that membership, in priority and in quantity, came from the 'labouring class'.[49] Banna's memoirs provide ample evidence that this early solicitude for the worker sprang not only from concern for the salvation of his corrupted Muslim soul, but also, and more immediately, from strong and bitter feelings about 'foreign control of the economy' and the 'injustices'—economic and otherwise—suffered by the Egyptian worker. The opportunities provided by the post-war economic crisis to champion the rights and needs of labour only strengthened a bond already firmly established.

As early as 1932, in Isma'iliyya, foreign management clashed with the Society in the person of Shaykh Muhammad Farghali, who was sent to a local fig firm 'at the request of the workers', to become their 'imam and teacher'. After his arrival the workers demanded and won a mosque from the company; and within a short time the company asked him to leave for unspecified reasons which seemed to be connected with an upset in labour–management relations. Banna intervened to stave off a clash with the police by a compromise solution; Farghali was to leave the company premises after a short period, with a 'commendation', and the company was 'officially' to request a new shaykh from the Society.[50]

This incident was the beginning of the Society's role as 'protector' of the Egyptian worker from 'exploitation' by foreign companies. The Society publicized many cases, all demonstrating a nationalist as well as an economic and social dimension. The following instances are typical but not exhaustive. (1) An English phosphate company on the Red Sea coast was charged with maintaining poor working conditions underground, and with providing inadequate wages, water-supplies (water rations and costs forced the labourer to choose between 'death by hunger or death from thirst and filth'), prayer facilities, housing, and rest and leisure. (2) An Italian phosphate company in Suez, against which similar complaints were made, was presented with the following demands: health insurance as protection against the hazards of the job; a six-hour working day; a minimum daily wage of PT 25 (instead of an alleged PT 8.5); a committee of government officials, workers, and management to settle disputes in the plant and supervise its administration; a contribution by the management of the 'necessities of food' as determined by the ministry of social affairs; the erection of a mosque and school; guaranteed leave on religious and official holidays, annual leave, and a whole day of rest once a week;

[49] See Husayni, *Ikhwan*, pp. 154–5; Hajjaji, *RWR*, p. 236; and *QDHRTM*, p. 139.

[50] *Mudh.*, pp. 110–13.

and, finally, free water supplies sufficient for drinking and washing, additional water to be supplied at cheap rates on request. The Society also proposed that a government office should be established in the area to ensure the fulfilment of the proposals. (3) All foreign companies, and especially the Suez Canal Company, were watched for the replacement of Egyptian by 'foreign' workers; in the case of the Canal Company a file on such matters was maintained, and, when necessary, complaints were lodged with the labour section of the ministry of social affairs and with the head of the company.[51] In this connection the Society waged an extensive press campaign in support of the so-called 'companies' law' of 1947 designed to set a lower limit to the number of foreigners a foreign company might hire.[52] (4) Finally, a lesser but no-less intensive watch was kept over the various foreign-owned commercial and luxury establishments in the major cities to see that the 'rights' of the workers were not overridden. In pursuing these activities the Society was fulfilling one of Banna's earliest demands: that the 'masses' should be protected from 'the tyranny of the monopolistic [foreign] companies'.[53]

The war years, as has already been indicated, provided a unique opportunity for the Society to increase its labour support. Unemployment resulting from the closing down of Allied establishments and the higher cost of living which followed inflation were the major problems which inspired 'waves of members', as the Society boasted, to descend on the headquarters. The opportunity was seized, and the Society played a major and active role in the politico-economic agitation of the early post-war years. As we have already seen, some of its commercial and industrial enterprises were set up with a view to relieving unemployment. The real centre, however, of its post-war activities was the labour section at the headquarters. Here workers were invited to meetings to protest against the government's in activity and to hear proposals for solving some of their economic problems. In this section a 'committee of the unemployed' was created to organize pressure on the authorities and to work out solutions to the issues at hand. Most of these solutions included as a central element a massive government drive to industrialize the economy.[54] One proposal

[51] *JIM* (10 June 1946), 4; (16 July 1946), 4; and (23 Dec. 1946), 3.

[52] See ibid. (30 Oct. 1946), 3 for a column headed 'The Bitter Truth' (*al-haqq al-murr*) which thereafter carried the case for the companies' law. See also ibid. (24 Dec. 1946), 3, for publication (without comment) of a report of a letter sent to the Director of Socony-Vacuum in Alexandria threatening him with death if foreign clerks were not replaced by Egyptians.

[53] *RTH: NN*, p. 119.

[54] See *JIM* through the summer and fall of 1946. Among the proposals in *JIM* (18 Aug. 1946), 5, was one to return to their villages some of those workers urbanized during the war who could not be classified as 'technical workers'.

forwarded from the labour section to the Guidance Council for approval recommended that the Council should appoint a 'preparatory committee': (1) to survey, in conjunction with the ministry of commerce and industry, the country's industrial needs and potential; (2) to found 'limited stock companies' to supply the industrial need out of the capital of 'the rich'; and (3) to deduct weekly from the wages of the workers amounts sufficient ultimately to purchase ownership of the company and to reimburse original investors. If this were done, two major problems would be solved at once: unemployment and the continuing conflict between management and labour.[55]

The labour section accompanied its 'economic research' with services to its members of a more pressing nature. It retained a panel of lawyers who were 'specialists in labour affairs' to deal with individual issues as they arose. It also served as a clearing house for jobs for the unemployed, a service made possible by maintaining contacts with both the department of labour and private industries. And, finally, it conducted a 'labour school' designed to instruct workers in 'their rights' and to explain labour legislation.[56]

The Society's press was, of course, the chief instrument by which it publicized its case for labour. Unemployment, the high cost of living, and the general 'insecurity of life' were the themes with which it castigated the government and, indirectly, Egyptian capitalism. The unceasing and uncompromising attack was made even more telling by daily reportage in regular columns detailing individual and personal accounts of country-wide economic misery. At the same time it was actively participating in violent labour agitation.

Consistent with its terms of reference, the labour section was active throughout the 1940s forming labour unions inspired by the ideas of the Society in every possible area. In the mid-1940s its efforts showed conspicuous success among the transport[57] and textile workers,[58] especially those of the major cities, and had some

[55] *JIM* (12 July 1946), 3.

[56] Zaki, *Ikhwan*, pp. 115–16.

[57] See *JIM* (19 June 1946), 3, reporting the decision of the Associated Transport Workers to create a union 'in the light of the message of the Muslim Brothers', with its centre in the labour section in the headquarters building of the Society. See also Handley, 'Labor Movement in Egypt', 283.

[58] See W. M. Carson, 'Human Relations Research: an Egyptian Textile Mill', in Middle East Institute, *Report on Current Research, Spring 1956* (Washington, 1956), pp. 45–7. T. B. Stauffer, 'The Industrial Worker', in S. N. Fisher, ed., *Social Forces in the Middle East* (1955), p. 86, argues that 'urban or specialized concentrations of factory workers . . . are not the great sources of recruitment' for groups like the Muslim Brotherhood. Earlier, the same writer says in an article, 'Labor Unions in the Arab States', *MEJ*, vi (Winter 1952), 86, 'fanatic nationalist groups such as the Muslim Brotherhood have more influence within Egypt's unions than do overt communists'.

success among workers in public utilities and the refinery workers in the Canal area. Well established in critical areas, the Society was in a position to play a crucial role in the strikes which gripped Egypt between 1946 and 1948, and it did so. The most vivid of the strikes was the long, bitter, and often bloody disruption of the industrial area of Shubra al-Khayma in Cairo, the area chosen by the Wafdist–communist coalition to make its stand against the palace-supported minority governments. We have already seen that the withdrawal of the Society-dominated unions from that front weakened it and brought upon the Society the wrath of all 'progressive' forces involved, who saw the action as predictable and further evidence of the 'servitude' of the Muslim Brothers to the 'capitalists' and 'exploiters' of Egypt. In the circumstances, evidence that the Brothers aided the government's intelligence in its drive against communists only exacerbated the group hostilities further.[59]

In all these areas of labour activity, not the least of the Society's successes was the commitment of large numbers of workers to its ideas. The obvious interest of the Society in labour affairs helped to confirm it as a leading, if not the leading, voice of the voiceless masses. In terms of the political situation, the Society was effectively challenging the attempt of the Wafdist–communist alliance of the time to pre-empt the role of leadership of these economically disenchanted masses. Even more importantly, in attacking a government which was seemingly indifferent and impotent in the face of economic malaise, the Society was also raising fundamental questions about the economic and thus the social and political order, questions whose answers were in a real sense inseparable from the very existence and dynamic of the Society. This fact primarily explained the breakdown of the semi-cordial relations which Banna in 1946, in the light of the leftward swing in the country, tried to establish with authority. As we have already noted and emphasized, in 1948 three of the counts levelled at the Society had to do with disrupting the socio-economic *status quo*. In 1946, however, the major evidence of the reality of fundamental antipathy between the movement and the ruling groups was to be found in the Society's defence of the cause of labour.

After the dissolution of the organization in 1948, it never again regained the influence it once had. The labour section continued on a lesser scale to give instruction on 'labour and unions'; a new series of pamphlets was prepared for distribution to workers and peasants on these matters. The combination of the two sections

[59] See above, pp. 46–7; see also Alexander, 'Left and Right', pp. 124–5; Badaoui, *Les Problèmes du travail*, p. 156.

for workers and peasants foreshadowed increased agitation for unionization of the agricultural workers and was part of a larger effort to extend union coverage to more areas, including servants both in homes and in ministries and among teachers.[60] Influence among unionized workers was largely reduced in most areas, with the notable exception of the textile area of Mahalla al-Kubra, which the government, in 1954, described as the area 'of the most dangerous activity of the Brothers in the country'.[61] Evidence of the decline of the Society's power among unions was dramatically demonstrated by the support of organized labour for Gamal 'Abd al-Nasir in his conflict with Neguib and the political parties in 1954. Having carefully and quietly established rapport with the unions from the beginning of the revolutionary period, Nasir effectively unleashed them in 'popular demonstrations' which successfully carried the day—the only time since the beginning of the revolution that elements of the former regime, with Neguib as their champion, almost toppled him. To this extent, the decline of the influence of the Brothers in labour affairs was all the more significant.

The Question of Overpopulation

The public attitude of the Society towards Egypt's pressing problem of overpopulation was conditioned in part by nationalist sensitivity. The oft-repeated assertion of Western students on the subject raised for the Brothers (and others in Egypt) the prospect of an evil Western manœuvre designed to reduce Egypt (and Islam) to impotence.[62] The subject was not often, however, treated solely in such unrealistic terms. In general terms the Society argued for a solution of the population problem through 'positive' rather than 'negative' means. Egypt, felt the Brothers, was not lacking in resources to meet the needs of her people; the problem was more that of a more equitable distribution of wealth and a more efficient exploitation of agricultural and mineral resources. If the country took positive action in these fields—extended its economic horizons— it would not need to resort to the 'negative' devices of delayed marriage and birth-control.[63]

[60] See Qutb, *DI*, p. 90; *MDA* (17 Mar. 1953), 12; and *JIM* (20 May 1954), 12.

[61] *MTR* (30 Nov. 1954), 12–13, 44, for the 'exposure' of a 'plot' by the deputy director of the weaving section, a Brother and allegedly of the secret apparatus, to kill Salah Salim, the then minister of national guidance, and then to destroy the factory!

[62] See e.g. *JA* (25 Nov. 1953), 6, 11.

[63] For a summary of the Society's position, see Zaki, *Ikhwan*, pp. 50–3. See also Ghazali, *MHN* (Faruqi tr.), p. 143, a position which is subjected to a critique in the above reference to Zaki.

The Society did not differ fundamentally in its views about the desirability of marriage and large families from the traditional spokesmen of the Azhar. This was especially true in the time of Banna.[64] However, it responded in later years to the increased interest in birth-control by taking a position which conceded that under certain circumstances this was permissible. What appeared initially to be merely a concession was formalized in 1953 in an official publication dealing with the problems of marriage and women. In a chapter on birth-control, the writer makes his initial point that Islam advocates 'many offspring', but that in 'certain circumstances' it is permitted to prevent pregnancy. As to method, precedent existed in the days of the Prophet, for he did not oppose *'azl* (lit. separation, *coitus interruptus*). Modern science has since provided other means to prevent pregnancy, namely 'sterilization' and the use of contraceptives. 'There is no harm in using these devices because they are less harmful to the man and the woman than *coitus interruptus*.'

There must, however, be good reason for preventing pregnancy. These would include those cases where there is the possibility of injury to the woman's health or of a threat to her life; where the woman would be burdened in the work she must do; and where the husband feels the need of lessening the cost of living by reducing the number of children. In no case is birth-control permitted for the sake of the leisure and pleasures which would be possible in a childless marriage.[65]

These relatively untraditional views about birth-control appeared in the context of a study of the role of women in modern Islamic society, and were not anywhere, to our knowledge, projected in the Society's views on the economic implications of overpopulation. Nevertheless, that the Society had moved from its earlier position was demonstrated by the appearance of this study, and by a proposal concurrently pending in the headquarters for a study of Egypt's overpopulation problem with reference to the feasibility of migration to Iraq.

SOCIETY

Education

In its social-reform programme, the Society's greatest activity was in the field of education. The great emphasis on recruitment of teachers and students was quite naturally linked to the view

[64] *RTH: NN*, p. 116. See a typical Azhar view in a press interview of the former mufti of Egypt, Shaykh Muhammad Hasanayn Makhluf, in *MJJ* (7 Sept. 1952), 18.

[65] *RMBBM*, pp. 87–91 (see above, p. 255 n. 74).

that in their hands lay 'the future of culture in Egypt'. This was more than an assessment of a national future; it also envisaged the nation's historic and cultural identity and destiny. Qutb puts it thus:

> No renaissance of Islamic life can be effected purely by the law or statute, or by the establishment of a social system on the basis of the Islamic philosophy. Such a step is only one of the two pillars on which Islam must always stand in its construction of life. The other is a production of a state of mind imbued with the Islamic theory of life, to give permanence to external forces leading to this form of life and to give coherence to all the social, religious, and civil legislation. . . .
>
> And the natural method of establishing that philosophy is by education.[66]

What caused the Society most concern was the secularization and fragmentation of the school system of Egypt, the low educational standard, and the lack of educational opportunity. It tackled these problems by (1) propaganda and agitation for reform of the existing school system, and (2) the founding of supplementary or alternative educational facilities. Perhaps in no other field except politics was the Society more persistent in the pursuit of its aims.

As early as 1935 the organization formed delegations to visit the ministry of education and the prime minister, and 'parties' were held for members of parliament; these occasions provided the opportunities to publicize the need for reintroducing religion in the schools of Egypt as a necessary prelude to the reconstitution of the schools on a truly national and Islamic basis.[67] The Society bitterly resented the fact that the government of Egypt, whose official religion was Islam, permitted Christian missionary schools to function freely, but would not allow the teaching of Islam in the government schools, and allowed European rather than Islamic history to be taught.[68]

[66] *AIFI* (Hardie tr.), pp. 249–50.

[67] See *Mudh.*, pp. 268–72; see also *RTH: NN*, pp. 117–18, for Banna's early reform notions.

[68] See 'Awda, *IWAQ*, p. 55. On the occasion of the sixth annual meeting, on 1 March 1948, of the Catholic Association for the Schools of Egypt where the annual report was heard, the Society's daily launched a two-week attack on the catholic schools, arguing the thesis that (1) schools are the moulders of future generations; (2) if schools are teaching matters contrary to the nation's patriotism and religion they are 'corrupt' and should be closed or at least curbed in recruitment. Father Henri Ayrout wrote a letter of protest to the daily but received no answer or acknowledgement. Through a friend in the Society, he succeeded in August in meeting Banna to discuss the matter. On 5 August the daily carried a report of the meeting and discussion which focused on the need of revealed faiths uniting in the struggle against atheism and for the welfare of Egypt. The paper reported that Ayrout belaboured Banna for the attack on

Implied in the resistance to mission schools—that they were teaching matter contrary to patriotism and the nation's religion—was the problem of the duality of the school system: the division between religious and secular schools and what this meant for the unity of outlook of the citizens of Egypt. Just as the missionary schools were alleged to be creating Egyptians lacking in contact with Egypt's main social and political currents, so the division in the educational system between mutually exclusive religious and secular schools was creating a schism in the body of the cultural or ideological life of Egypt and further disrupting its unity.

In 1938 the minister of education, Muhammad Husayn Haykal, proposed to the rector of the Azhar a programme for uniting religious and secular education. The Brothers joined in the ensuing public debate; a letter to the minister of education stated the views of the Society, which in essence summarized the kind of argument thenceforth made on this issue.[69] The introduction of Western secular education, contended Banna, alongside the traditional Azhar-type education had created formidable conflicts between the two groups, a situation dangerous for a nation seeking 'rebirth', since the greatest need was a 'unity of culture'; the path taken by Iran and Turkey which was advocated by the secularists was not for Egypt because of the indestructible bond between Islam and Egypt. 'Religious people' are misguided in thinking that they will be done with the evils of secularism by ignoring it; secularism will be conquered only by mastery of the fields of 'science and learning'.

Banna therefore suggested that education should be neither purely Islamic nor purely secular (i.e. Western), but should harmoniously blend religious character and moral training with scientific training. The syllabus should be consistent and balanced in its parts. Kindergarten education should be related to the 'child's perception' and his 'emotional needs'. In the primary schools no foreign languages should be taught but only the 'language of the nation', an emphasis to be supplemented by character training. The secondary schools would teach two foreign languages (one Western and one Eastern), Islamic history, 'patriotism', and related subjects; they would also lay the foundation for future 'technical, specialized, or teacher-training schools'. Higher training

the schools ('We desired only . . . the good', said Banna), and for the failure to acknowledge the letter of protest (it was 'unintentional' said Banna). This material was made available to us by Father Ayrout from his files and consisted principally of clippings from Cairo's French-language press.

[69] The letter was reproduced in *JIM* (17 July 1946), 4, and the next two issues.

would be in the Azhar or Egyptian universities with similar general courses in subjects related to Islam and history so far as these could be fitted in with the student's other non-religious academic needs. The Azhar would be expanded and developed in the areas of 'research, criticism, writing, composition . . ., and Islamic sciences'. Studying the Qur'an would depend on the student's specialization; a student in arts and Islamic studies in higher learning would be required to know the whole of it. Non-Muslims would deal with selected parts of their own religious literature.

These suggestions were important, not as a 'programme' for Egyptian schools—the Society never thought out the issues in such specific detail—but rather as another reflection of the deeply felt national disunity, not only or even primarily on a political level but on a cultural one. When describing the Society's image of Egypt we noted its disillusionment with the intellectual and political leaders of the nation who, trained in the secular tradition (or converts to it), were seen as having betrayed the national history and tradition. The political leaders were felt to be even more guilty, since political betrayal had also meant the legal perpetuation of an un-Islamic situation: expressed succinctly, this view held that 'there are those who learn religion and do not rule and there are those who rule but know no religion'.[70] No less important, it will also be recalled, was the Society's flaying of the religious authority, the Azhar, for its failure to rise to the challenge posed by the champions of secularism and give its traditional education the spark necessary to restore it to life and its mission among Muslims.

This complex of ideas, first charted by Banna, remained central to the Society's thinking on education, but, after Banna, its official reform programmes put less emphasis on the Muslim aspect of the problem. Thus in 1952 its reform brief to the new revolutionary government included the demand for opportunities for 'all citizens' for an education aimed at creating a 'new generation' imbued with 'religious, moral, and patriotic spirit'. As an aside, it was felt that some effort should be made to rewrite national history purged of the influence of 'imperialists and orientalists'. As a second point, the Society urged full support for, and the expansion of, all 'institutes and universities' in their needs for 'libraries, laboratories, and instruments of research' so that Egypt might launch out on a 'new scientific renaissance' which would sustain and support the 'economic and social renaissance'.[71]

In part to give meaning to their advocacy of reform in the school

[70] Nadawi, *Mudhakkarat*, p. 125. [71] *al-Bayan*, p. 8.

system by example, in part to compete with and undermine missionary educational enterprise, and in part to help fight the massive problem of illiteracy in Egypt, the Society organized its own educational facilities. The Brothers' first project in Isma'iliyya after founding a mosque was the establishment of a school for boys and then of one for girls. As the Society expanded this pattern was repeated throughout the country, but this schooling, such as it was, remained largely informal and haphazardly organized. The really significant school movement began only after World War II with the tremendous increase not only of members needing education but also of those able to give it—teachers and students. In May 1946 the 'committee for the founding of primary and secondary schools for boys and girls' was established; in the following month the 'committee for cultural care' was established to aid the already existing 'education committee'.[72] These three bodies were primarily responsible for the Society's educational activity.

School projects were financed in a number of ways. First, the branches to which the schools were normally attached undertook, whenever possible, to maintain the school out of their own budgets. This was the usual arrangement. Another major source of finance was private contributions from inside and outside the organization. One list of contributions in the Society's newspaper included a gift of £E5,000 and a promise of £E1,000 more for every ten schools the Society opened.[73] A third source of aid came, in certain periods, from the government. In the autumn of 1946, the education minister, Muhammad Hasan al-'Ashmawi, sent a formal letter to the Society enlisting its support and its educational apparatus for a programme then being launched by the government to fight illiteracy. It was agreed that the ministry of education would pay PT 75 per student educated by the Society, one-third to be paid when it had ascertained that the student was between the ages of 12 and 18, that his attendance was regular, that the schoolroom was located in a healthy place in a branch, and that there were teachers. The ministry undertook to provide books and materials and then to complete the payment of the subsidy after it was seen that the schools were operating success fully. Thenceforth, the student was registered, with details and photographs, at the headquarters of the Society and the ministry of education.[74] The fact that 'Ashmawi was a close friend of the Society and its ideas may have been a factor of importance in this co-operation; the Society undoubtedly profited in terms of converts from this opportunity to join in the battle against illiteracy.

72 *JIM* (10 June 1946), 4; Zaki, *Ikhwan*, p. 148.
73 *JIM* (25 June 1946), 4. 74 See Husayni, *Ikhwan*, p. 85.

Finally, money came from the sale of stock. In 1946 an 'unlimited stock company' was founded in Cairo to help finance the building of schools by the time of the first advertisement for the sale of stock, half of the proposed capital of £E8,000 (2,000 shares at £E4 each) had been subscribed. A similar company was founded in Alexandria in 1948 with a capital of £E4,000; by the time of the dissolution of the Society at the end of 1948, the company had established a kindergarten, a primary school, and part of a secondary school.[75]

The training in the schools of the Society had a variety of purposes. In the villages and urban primary schools emphasis was on religious and moral training patterned largely on the traditional *kuttab*. At the higher levels of the primary schools, the fundamentals of literacy—reading and writing—were taught. Basic education was the theme of night schools organized for adults—peasants and workers alike—and was the chief instrument in the illiteracy programme. In the rural areas farmers received agricultural guidance as well, with the help of students from the university colleges of agriculture. Similarly, urban workers received supplementary instruction in matters pertaining to unions and labour from students of economics. Special classes were provided for youths deprived of education because of economic compulsion to enter the labour market, and other classes were established for training youths for trades and industrial and commercial work. Boys at the primary level could attend 'private schools' and similarly there were special schools for girls. These latter establishments, called schools for the 'mothers of the believers', reflected the ideals that inspired the organization of the Muslim Sisters: mothers were the true and primary source of a child's character and outlook; and girls who really understood their religion would be truly Muslim and thus truly emancipated. The ranks of the Muslim Sisters provided the teachers for these schools. Finally, the Society offered special kinds of schooling, such as a 'tutorial service' for prospective applicants for the civil-service examinations and for students whose success in university examinations was in doubt. For all these operations the Society called upon its members for instruction—university professors, teachers in primary and secondary schools, and students—each of whom contributed his work freely for the cause of illiteracy and for that of the Society.[76]

[75] *JIM* (16 July 1946), 4; and Zaki, *Ikhwan*, p. 149.

[76] In addition to *JIM* of June, July, August 1946, see *MDA* (17 Nov. 1953), 8–9. The Society was a consistent advocate of the use of the armed forces as an instrument for training workers and wiping out illiteracy; see *JIM* (19 July

Little information, apart from incidental references in the Society's daily is available on the nature of the curriculum in the general educational scheme of the Society's schools. On the whole they seemed to have broadly followed the pattern of the Egyptian school system with, however, more emphasis on the Islamic and national heritage. English was prominent among the foreign languages taught. There is a similar paucity of information about the number of students served by the system and the number of schools (in the widest possible sense of that word) that existed. In 1948 Banna claimed (perhaps correctly if the word 'school' is loosely defined) that each of the 2,000 branches had one or more types of school attached to it.[77] In 1953 a friendly student of the Society surveyed the Cairo–Giza area and found thirty-one schools—mostly kindergarten and night schools—with about 3,500 students,[78] an expected decline and part of the general slow-down in the Society's activity after 1948, but probably not a reflection of the facts before that time.

Public Health

In his early reform messages Banna made public health an important part of social reform concentrating especially on the dissemination of information and the increase of facilities and personnel to tackle the vast national health problem.[79] The Society's programme of action adopted the same approach.

The first Societal groups used to disseminate hygenic knowledge and bring medical care to the countryside were the rovers. Local rover units undertook the actual work of cleaning up the streets and alleys of the villages, encouraged villagers to use hospitals and clinics and provided simple first aid. These activities were part of a general 'social programme' established for the rovers in 1943 in revulsion against the filth and the sanitation and health problems of the mass of Egyptians, rural and urban. Although this kind of activity gradually passed to the medical section of the Society, the rovers continued to be a useful medium for dealing with the medical problems of the villages. It will also be recalled that Banna offered the services of the rover groups to the ministry

1946), 5. See also Caskel in von Grunebaum, ed., *Unity and Variety in Muslim Civilization*, p. 346.

[77] *Qawl fasl*, p. 33.

[78] See Zaki, *Ikhwan*, pp. 150–1. *MDA* (17 Nov. 1953), 8–9, describes the activities of the branch in the 'Abbasiyya quarter of Cairo, with special reference to its educational set-up. A late addition to the concept of education was the boarding-school—one was established in this quarter. Students of the Society's schools also wore the 'official' badge on their school uniforms—the Qur'an surrounded by two crossed swords—and rode in the Society's buses to school.

[79] *RTH: NN*, p. 119.

of health during the epidemics of 1945 and 1947 to serve in the stricken areas where needed.[80]

This largely educational programme of the Society was augmented in November 1944 by the establishment of a 'medical section' by the doctors in the organization. Its objectives were defined as the establishment of dispensaries, clinics, and hospitals, the intensification of the programme for 'spreading the message of hygiene' and the 'raising of the health level of all classes' by all means available. The first dispensary was opened at that time in the offices of the leading doctor member (Muhammad Ahmad Sulayman), and within a month it was transferred to the Society's headquarters. In 1946 the clinic moved to its own building near the headquarters and added to itself a pharmacy headed by a registered pharmacist. This clinic, which soon professed to be a small hospital, claimed to have treated 21,677 patients in 1945, 29,039 in 1946, and 51,300 in 1947. From the time of its opening smaller clinics were started wherever possible, and by 1948 the medical section had an annual budget of £E23,000.

While most of the equipment and material of the clinics and dispensaries was confiscated in 1948, activity was resumed in 1950. In 1953 it was claimed that each province of Egypt had at least one dispensary and that sixteen clinics in Cairo had treated over 100,000 patients.[81] In January 1954 the government of the revolution formally took over all the clinics then operating;[82] what has happened to them since is not clear.

Welfare and Social Services

The medical section, although conceived independently, was very rapidly made part of the larger 'welfare and social services section', organized in 1945 to take the place of the former 'social-assistance office'. The new section was organized 'independently' of the Society in order, as already indicated, to benefit from government aid. In 1946 the Society registered with the ministry of social affairs 102 branches of the welfare agency. In 1948 it claimed 500 branches all over Egypt.[83]

Besides its medical services the welfare and social services

[80] We have just noted that the armed forces were seen as an instrument for wiping out illiteracy; similarly, the army was seen as a means of combating the diseases with which so many of its peasant conscripts were afflicted—bilharzia, trachoma, and ankylostomiasis—and as a school for hygiene, whose message of cleanliness would be carried by the soldiers as 'messengers of reform in the Egyptian village' as they returned to their homes; see n. 76, above.

[81] Most of the above summary is from the daily and from Zaki, *Ikhwan*, pp. 169–72. On the medical activity of the branch in the 'Abbasiyya quarter see reference in n. 78, above.

[82] *JJ* (15 Jan. 1954), 1.

[83] Zaki, *Ikhwan*, pp. 110–12.

section was basically concerned with help in money or in kind to poor families, especially those without breadwinners, the aged, the homeless, and the orphaned. In some of the branches 'social treasuries', to which members contributed monthly, sometimes supported these activities; mostly the situation was less formalized, and aid (usually in the form of food, clothing, and soap) was distributed on religious holidays either by the branch or by leading members of the particular community who were 'influenced' by the Society.

While much of this effort benefited the urban membership, its initial orientation was towards the rural areas and was seen as a contribution to the greater purpose of rural reform. In the eyes of its members the organization was dedicated to the 're-birth' of the Egyptian village. The work of the rovers in the villages was one facet of this. Banna also made it a central part of his reform programme that the problems of the village—its organization, education, 'comfort', and 'development'—must be given their due by the central authorities.[84] Hence the society's dailies continually reported on the issue of 'village reform'. Among subjects treated at length was the problem of the physical reconstruction of the village, with special reference to architectural design, to accessibility of roads, fresh water, and lighting, and to the establishment of village industries.[85]

Another rural problem taken up by the Society was that of local government as symbolized in the local leader—the *'umda*. An article given prominence in the Society's daily made the following points: (1) the *'umda* should be a 'responsible civil servant' under 'constant supervision' to see that he served the needs—especially economic and social—of the community; (2) he should not only have a higher education but he should also be trained in agriculture and husbandry; (3) agricultural schools, for their part, should introduce into the curriculum studies in 'administration and sociology'; (4) village councils of local people should be established to help the *'umda* govern. A successful village council—one that was genuinely allowed to participate—would be able to curb all the excesses and abuses on which the old system thrived.[86]

Social Reform and Morality

While welfare and social services dealt with the externals of a better society. Education was the most effective means of

[84] *RTH: NN*, p. 119.

[85] See a special series of articles in the daily beginning in *JIM* (4 June 1946), 5, entitled 'Rural Reform'. Zaki, *Ikhwan*, p. 110, reports the efforts of the Society to establish a 'co-operative model farm'.

[86] *JIM* (18 June 1946), 1.

establishing the groundwork for the good society of the future. But the immediate problem was that of ever-present sin in a corrupted society. Thus demands for government curbs on moral and social abuses formed an integral part of the Society's reform programme. These demands varied in intensity and quality as between Banna and Hudaybi, but basically they were the same: legal proscription of what 'God had forbidden'—wine, gambling, and dance halls. In later years the demand for censorship of films and the press and magazines was noticeably less vigorous than Banna's earlier demands for controls over all media of communication—theatres, films, songs, radio, press, and magazines—and the use of these media to promote nobility and virtue. And Banna also went further in demanding strict surveillance over such places as coffee-houses and summer resorts,[87] heavier punishments for crimes against morality, the abolition of prostitution, and the prosecution of adultery.[88] If this were done, if the family bonds were strengthened, and if education were given the proper direction, then social behaviour would be revolutionized and Islamic morality would once again begin to hold sway.

As with other things the Society demanded, it could only make appeals for government action and try to set examples. Its press and magazines were regarded as examples of 'edifying' journalism. 'Sensationalism' in both news and advertising was frowned upon. The non-news columns were given over to economic reportage, sports, literary criticism, and book reviews, the latter two items dealing with the Islamic and Arabic heritage in history and poetry. Short stories were included in the literary contributions to *Majallat al-Da'wa*. And the last of the Society's papers, the weekly *Majallat al-Ikhwan al-Muslimin*, added columns on Islamic art and the cinema. The cinema column dealt with the problem of the art of making films, and 'currents of reform' in the substance of films. In itself, the column reflected a development from opposition to films as evil to the hope that they could be reformed and 'used' for the renaissance.

The Society also condoned 'Islamic drama' (which was also 'edifying') of two types: political satire and religious. Written usually by 'Ali Ahmad Bakthir, the plays, normally of one act, were published in the daily to be read, but on occasion they were

[87] There was no official mention of this point in Hudaybi's time. The new leader was himself a beach-goer and indeed, as we have noted, was criticized from within the Society for doing so.

[88] Cf. *RTH: NN*, pp. 115–16, with *al-Bayan*, p. 8. The differences were due in part to the less puritanical attitudes in the Society in its later days to which we have alluded and to which we will refer again, and in part to increased sensitivity to unpopular ideas which the Society nevertheless held.

also produced and acted by the members. Typical titles included the following: 'King of the Sudan'—an attack on British policy in the Sudan; 'Greater Syria'—an attack on British policy in the Fertile Crescent; 'The Message of the White Man'—an attack on Western racial policies. The religious drama most frequently featured was one entitled 'The Raid of Badr' which dealt with that event in Islamic history with a fervour matched only by the Society's attachment to its militant importance.[89]

Finally, in their own personal lives, members sought to demonstrate both the possibility and desirability of 'correct' behaviour seeking thereby to reconvert others to the 'true' morality. It was in this field that the Society suffered one of its major unresolved dilemmas—whether example and advice would suffice to reverse the un-Islamic tide, or whether the problem was of such magnitude as to require the 'force of the hand', the Society's hand. We have already seen that this issue was a partial cause of a major defection in the late 1930s which led to the creation of a splinter group. Banna then brought Qur'anic texts to bear against Prophetic Tradition to make his point and presumably to settle the dispute against 'forceful' or 'negative' reformist action. Nevertheless, his passionate and dramatic 'exposure' of problems inspired attempts at solution of which he was not always aware and which, presumably, he would himself have opposed. The will of some members to act, combined with the militant sense of righteous power he inspired, led almost inevitably to sporadic but continuous acts of intolerant violence and interference by members in the name of Islam and its morality, acts which only confirmed the concern felt by other citizens at the Brothers' rise to power. This is one of the important aspects of a greater issue to which we will return in our conclusion.

'*The Virtuous City*'

Approximately in 1951 a co-operative society was founded by some members of the organization to begin planning a city which was not only to be virtuous, pious, and peaceful, but would also provide economic security in terms of co-operative ownership of the land

[89] After the crisis between the Society and the government, Bakthir was taken over by the government-sponsored daily, *al-Jumhuriyya*, and advertised as a writer famous for his 'treatment of Islamic and Arabic questions'; see *JJ* (30 May 1954), 10, and subsequent issues over the next few days. Sometimes these productions appeared in Cairo theatres (see *JIM* (2 Aug. 1946), 4, for a show at the Ezbekieh Gardens theatre), but the headquarters also had a theatre group which travelled to the provincial capitals and towns for branch performances; see *JIM* (11 Aug. 1946), 5. For the plays see respectively *JIM* (9 Nov. 1946), 5–6; (8 Dec. 1946), 5–6; (28 Dec. 1946) 5 f.; (20 Aug. 1946), 4; and also (4 Nov. 1946), 4–5.

and planned facilities.[90] Some 400 feddans of land were chosen in an area of old Cairo (close to the Muqattam hills) and £E20,000 was paid to the government as initial costs. Once the regulations governing the co-operative society were accepted by the government, an 'administrative council' was elected and work on the area was started. Land surveys and contour and geological studies were made, and then water pipelines were laid and electric-power stations started. It was expected to serve 2,000 families in the area. It was at this point (1954) that the organization collided with the government and work stopped. There was no evidence at the time that the government confiscated the co-operative society's assets. This may have been in part because large numbers of its members were not members of the Society (indeed, the co-operative was not advertised as a project of the Brothers); and in part because most of its leading figures were those who in the Society had clashed with Hudaybi, had escaped arrest, and who thus were regarded as under government 'protection'.

[90] Zaki, *Ikhwan*, pp. 120–1, describes some of the objectives of the co-operative society. This short statement is the only written account available to us. Our own short summary comes from Zaki and from oral sources. Ironically, the idea for the model city was inspired by the precedent of the Pakistan village, Rabwa, established by the much detested Qadiyanis; for a description of Rabwa, see Stanley E. Brush, 'Ahmadiyyat in Pakistan', *MW* (Apr. 1955), 145–71.

PART IV · CONCLUSION

XI

CONCLUSION

IT now remains to focus on some of the special questions raised by this study of the Muslim Brothers and to attempt an assessment of its meaning. Accordingly, in this chapter, we will look more closely at the organization, especially the leadership phenomenon so integral to the Society's dynamic, the question of political action and the related motif of violence, the place of the Society in Islamic modernism, and, finally, the type of member who responded to the appeals of the Society and the significance of these data for a final evaluation.

ORGANIZATIONAL DYNAMICS

Leadership

The description of the Society's organizational hierarchy noted the tripartite division of authority between the leader and two other bodies—the twelve-member Guidance Council and the larger (usually 150 members) Consultative Assembly—both theoretically responsive to and reflecting the will of the membership. However, as the description of the history and activities of the organization has shown, the leader—whether a Banna or a Hudaybi—was in fact the centre of all power. The organizational regulations, however potentially 'democratic', were in practice superseded by authoritarian direction. This was true in Banna's time because of Banna and the circumstances in which the Society grew; the extent to which this continued to be true in Hudaybi's time was due largely to the momentum, or inertia, which perpetuates traditions.

As we have seen, there were challenges, however ineffectual, from within the organization to this centralization of power, in the earliest crises of the Society in Isma'iliyya and Cairo, at the time of the Sukkari and Ibrahim Hasan dismissals and departures in 1947, that of Mu'min's dismissal in 1951, and in the last years of the Society's conflict with the military rulers of Egypt. Each of these episodes contained other elements of overriding importance, but each also attested to the persistent—if small—current of uneasiness at the absolute decision-making power which was vested in the General Guide.

Under Hudaybi there were some changes which slightly altered the mechanics of the leadership role. Perhaps because Hudaybi was less energetic, but also, we think, less headstrong and insistent on the absolute prerogatives of leadership, there appeared to be an incipient expansion in the directive role of the Guidance Council (the new regulations in 1951 foreshadowed this change), and an increase in the administrative scope given to the secretary-general. While there was little practical change in the locus of power, there were clearly more fingers in the pie. (It might be argued that this element greatly contributed to the decline in the power of the organization.) Similarly, under Hudaybi, the more intense activity which marked electioneering for high posts and the more frequent meetings of the Consultative Assembly—meetings sometimes marked by discordant expression of differing opinions—suggested an understanding from within that power was no longer the monopoly of the leader, that the leader could, with impunity, be challenged. We will return to this point in a moment.

Banna, on the other hand, was and remained, in full measure, the final and unqualified authority in the Society. We have noted changes in the Society's regulations in 1945 and 1948; in both cases (especially after Sukkari's dismissal in 1947), Banna was responding in a limited way to the internal pressures for 'democratization'. It was a sufficient gesture to provide the possibility of change by revising the constitution. Real change in this respect was perhaps impossible for Banna, in view of his image of himself and his mission, and of the concept of authority and discipline in the relationship between leader and led which he made the basic element in the strength of the organization.

The solution put forward by Banna for the problems of Islam and Egypt, as he defined them, included the appearance of a spokesman who would analyse Egypt's ills and successfully prescribe the remedies which would guide her out of her multi-dimensioned wilderness. The sense that he was that person permeates his own recollection of how teachers and friends had recognized his ability to bring strong influence to bear on men and to unite their divided counsels. His very youthful inspiration of, and commitment to, reform associations which he always came to direct, attests not only to his powerful urge towards organized action but also to administrative and organizational talent. His final choice of 'teaching and counselling' as a life goal, as the highest of possible services to his community, reflected again (especially as he tells it in retrospect) a purposeful and self-conscious sense of mission.[1]

If, however, Banna was modest in confining the description of his aim in life to that of a mere *murshid* (a humility which was of great moment to his followers, as we shall shortly see), those he led were uninhibited and unstinting in their acclaim of 'the man of the hour'—'the Muslim leader, the spiritual brother, the Arab struggler, the social reformer, the powerful believer'. It was always said by the Brothers that the unique fact about the Society was that it transcended personalities and peoples; yet they would probably all agree with one of their leading writers that 'the secret of [the] success [of the movement] was in the personality of the preacher [Banna]'.[2] During his lifetime, it inspired a virtually unlimited personal veneration. Husayni says: 'His mastery over his followers was complete and inclusive, almost approaching sorcery.'[3] One Egyptian newspaper commenting on Banna's relationship with his followers observed: 'If Banna sneezed in Cairo, the Brothers in Aswan would say "God bless you".'[4] In a more personal and dramatic testament, one follower thus dedicated himself to the memory of Banna: 'I will live and die in loyalty to you.'[5]

Some of the elements in Banna which inspired this devotion to his person emerge from the limitless eulogies and encomiums written after his death. Chief among them are his personal and oratorical eloquence and his ability to convey a sense of sincerity, humility, and selflessness. Far and wide in Egypt, in or out of the organization, few have failed to observe that Banna was one of the great speakers and writers of his time. One of his enchanted followers ascribes his success to his ability to create 'a spiritual bond between himself and his listeners'; this he did by feeling the meaning of the words before uttering them and then speaking simply but forcefully, thus reaching out to lift his hearers to his own level of perception, understanding, and emotion.[6] Given an Arab world enamoured in any case of the gift of eloquence, the point need not be laboured and needs emphasis only to underline the transcendently persuasive external circumstances in which the dialogue between leader and led took place.

As important as was Banna's eloquence in an external sense, this

[1] See esp. *Mudh.*, p. 60, and above, pp. 1–6.

[2] The quotations above are respectively from 'Assal, *BKA*, p. 46; Hajjaji, *RWR*, p. 215.

[3] Husayni, *Ikhwan*, p. 54.

[4] Quoted in Nadawi, *Mudhakkarat*, p. 26.

[5] Hajjaji, *RLAT*, p. 4.

[6] See Husayni, *Ikhwan*, pp. 54–6, for an excellent statement and quotations from the followers; also 'Assal, *BKA*, pp. 58–63; Buhi, *IWR*, pp. 50–9.

fact was matched by an equally telling skill, at a personal level, in appealing to Egyptians of every level of life and learning. One friendly writer describes Banna as a man who knew the language of the Azhar and of the Sufis, who knew the dialects, the traditions, and the problems of the cities and towns, of the provinces, of the delta and the desert, and of Upper and Lower Egypt; he knew the speech of the butcher and the little girl and the various types of people who inhabited the cities, including the thieves and murderers—he spoke to them all, says this observer, and 'always his knowledge astounded his hearers'. In this manner 'he won individual after individual', binding them in an unbreakable bond to him as representative of an idea and as a personal friend.[7]

This sense of personal friendship between Banna and his followers was of great importance for his image. No other facet of his personality aroused such warmth, and a discussion of the subject was invariably accompanied by a story which highlighted a meeting, a separation in time and place, another meeting, and Banna's recollection and spontaneous use of the facts of the personal life of his 'friends'.[8] One story told of him goes as follows: In 1946, when the Society was negotiating the purchase of its headquarters, it found in the treasury only a small amount of the necessary money; Banna went ahead with the contract to the dismay of those around him and when asked how he would solve the problem of the deficit he reportedly said, 'I know 10,000 Brothers personally who will give me whatever I ask'; in a week, it was said, he had raised the money.

Banna's success in personalizing his relationships went beyond his ability to communicate to his power of conveying a sense of sincerity, selflessness, and humility about himself and his activities. There was little doubt in the minds of the rank and file that he was different from other leaders in the country, that he sought nothing for himself from those who rallied to his cause. Similarly his boundless expenditure of time and energy for the message—travelling, speaking, making contacts—were evidence to his followers of the fullest possible expression of sincerity and selflessness for the cause.[9] It was this quality of committed selflessness conveyed to his followers which perhaps accounted for his widely hailed prowess as a mediator and harmonizer;[10] convinced of the absence of ulterior purpose, a member could and did place trust in the justice of his judgements.

7 *MR* (28 Apr. 1952), 463.

8 See Husayni, *Ikhwan*, pp. 51–2; Hajjaji, *RWR*, p. 204.

9 See Hajjaji, *RWR*, pp. 190–5, 202–3, 245–8, 255–64, 278–80; 'Assal, *BKA*, pp. 17–18, 24; Banna, *TIWMI*, pp. 20–1.

10 See esp. Baquri's statement, in *MDA* (12 Feb. 1952), 14.

And, finally, not the least of the qualities admired by his followers was the sense of humility he conveyed—his open-hearted response to the humblest of his followers in the meanest of circumstances and his apparent denigration of self in the advocacy of the cause he led. To his followers, his choice for his title of *murshid* rather than *qa'id* or *ra'is* exemplified this characteristic and demonstrated for them conclusively that he sought primarily to establish a relationship between himself and God rather than with other men.[11] In no small measure, Banna's successful assumption of the role of the indispensable leader was directly related to his success in eschewing it.

Banna's death was a tragedy of incalculable proportions for members. Nothing that befell the Brothers as individuals and groups at the hands of authority had a more debilitating effect on the movement than the loss of its leader. A Western commentator is not far out in observing that 'the memory of Hasan al-Banna has assumed a messianic character and the tragedy of his death is recounted in terms reminiscent of the crucifixion of Christ'.[12]

Outside the organization Banna's personal reputation was also high. A friendly commentator said of him:

he made love of country a part of the emotions of the soul, for he raised the value of the nation and glorified the measure of freedom. He created between the leader and the led a bond of co-operation not domination, and between the rulers and the people [the principle of] responsibility not authority.[13]

A bitter critic of the organization, Muhammad al-Tabi'i, noted that 'he will take his place at the side of the leaders of the masses like Mustafa Kamil and Sa'd Zaghlul'. Ihsan 'Abd al-Qaddus, another leading journalist and writer, and a critic of the organization, said:

I have never met in my journalistic life a leader or politician more firmly persuaded of his mission than Hasan al-Banna. I used to meet him in a mood of challenge, intent on crushing his logic with my logic. I would part from him convinced of his faith, the honesty of his mission, and the strength of his determination to reach his goals.[14]

11 See 'Assal, *BKA*, pp. 7, 41, 47–50, 112; Hajjaji, *QDHRTM*, pp. 41, 95–105.

12 Middle East Institute, *Newsletter* (6 Mar. 1955), 1. Banna's father has been most active in circulating stories about 'miraculous' events in Hasan's early and youthful life; see e.g. *MMR* (29 Aug. 1952), 16–17.

13 *MR* (28 Apr. 1952), 463.

14 Both quotations are from Khuli, *QDIHB*, pp. 67–8. See also the commemorative issues of *MDA*, esp. 12 Feb. 1952, for other observations by non-members.

Hasan al-Hudaybi did not—could not—live up to the extraordinary image that Banna bequeathed to the Society. He himself is said to have warned the Society of the futility of a comparison when he first took over Banna's job. The curt, phlegmatic judge who publicly noted his distaste for the ebullience of political demonstrations, who curbed excessive enthusiasm at public meetings, who spoke quietly—neither visibly moved nor visibly moving—failed to fit the mantle passed on to him, partly because it might have been impossible for any man to do so. While some of the support—a majority of the organization—that Hudaybi mustered in his conflict with the government and the dissidents came from those genuinely committed to him and the new spirit he represented, much more came from those still bound to the *murshid* by the residual glow after the flames had died down. Hudaybi was ready to admit at his trial in 1954: 'I was unfit to lead the organization.'[15] The importance of this fact lay in the breakdown of the concept of authority and discipline.

Authority and Discipline

The consequence of the personal veneration for Banna for the life of the organization was the fullest and widest acceptance by the members of his conception of leadership and discipline. The regulations of the Society formalized this concept in the oath of loyalty to the General Guide required of all members; *inter alia*, it will be recalled that this required a member to swear 'complete confidence in the leadership, and absolute obedience (*al-sama' wa'l-ta'a* [lit. 'hearing and obeying']) in what one likes or dislikes to do (*fi'l-manshat wa'l-makra*) (*QA* 4: 9). The most elaborated statements of these points appeared in the often-mentioned *Risalat al-Ta'alim*, written for the use of the battalion system founded in 1937 but which came to be the primary indoctrination text for the membership-at-large. There Banna listed among the ten pillars of the oath of loyalty 'obedience' and 'confidence'. Under obedience Banna described three stages of loyalty to the organization, three stages which we have already met as degrees of organizational perfection: 'acquaintance, formation, and execution'. In the first stage, which applied to the generality of membership in its most general activity, 'complete obedience is not compulsory'. In the second stage, of 'formation', those prepared 'to carry the burden of *jihad*' unite on the basis of Sufi 'spirituality' and military 'action' under a strict rule of 'obedience (*'amr wa-ta'a*) without hesitation, question, doubt, or criticism . . .'. The third stage is the stage of 'execution'—the time of *jihad* which

[15] *JJ* (19 Nov. 1954), 8.

means 'uninterrupted labour to reach the goal'; it means, further, complete and unqualified acceptance of the duty of 'absolute obedience'.[16]

Complementing the concept of obedience was that of confidence in the leaders, for there could be no 'obedience and respect' from the soldier if there was no confidence 'in the ability and the sincerity of the leader'; 'the leader is a part of the message, for there is no message without a leader, and in the measure of mutual confidence between the leader and the soldier will lie the strength of the Society, the wisdom of its plans, and the successful achievement of its goals.' The leadership of the Muslim Brothers would have the authority of father, professor, shaykh, and leader. The Brother, on the other hand, could test the extent of his confidence in the leadership by asking himself the following questions: Does he know his leader, his life, his abilities, his sincerity? Is he prepared to accept the orders of the command without 'insubordination', dispute, or debate? Is he prepared 'to assume error on his part and correctness on the part of the leadership if he opposes what he has been asked to do'? Is he prepared to place his 'vital interests' at the disposal of the movement and permit them to be weighed against its interests? The answers to these questions would determine the readiness of the member for higher levels of membership.[17]

From the earliest days of the movement Banna made these qualities of obedience to and confidence in the leadership cardinal features of the dynamic of the organization in the minds of his followers, and was able to make the success of the movement's ideas conditional on their unqualified acceptance. To furnish the necessary organizational impetus to their acceptance, a system of disciplinary procedures was built into the doctrine. At the third general conference, when membership categories were first formalized, Banna impressed upon the field leaders the need for exacting 'punishments' from the Brothers for deviations from the duties prescribed, in accordance with their magnitude, and that 'strong measures' should be taken with every 'negligent' member.[18] In the course of events, these punishments came to be embodied in the regulations of the Society, and although the degree of emphasis and the enforcement procedure varied at different levels of the hierarchy they nowhere significantly varied from the sanctions established for the lowliest branch member: in progressive stages, warning, fining, suspension, and finally dismissal.

[16] *RNURT*, pp. 11–13.
[17] Ibid., pp. 15–16; cf. Ahmad, *Mizan*, pp. 26–7, 53.
[18] *Mudh.*, pp. 203–5.

Information on how these sanctions were put into effect is totally lacking, except, of course, for those instances already described of conflicts with the leadership that resulted in dismissals. It would seem rather, from these cases and from members' recollections, that rarely, and only on the grand scale, were the devices at hand invoked; the degree to which Banna commanded the obedience of his followers was in no sense a function of any of the punitive actions open to him. Banna's real success lay not in commanding obedience but in having it willingly given; his followers time and again made the point explicitly that their obedience to Banna, their loyalty to him, was a matter given, not demanded; and because it was a deliberate act it was not a blind one.

The ease with which obedience was given followed primarily from the nature of the movement. The membership, believing in the religiously defined goals, accepted without question the corollary of religious missions—that there was no disputing either the message or, by implication, the voice that uttered it.[19] The religious aspect of the case was most clearly described by one member, who said: 'obedience is one of the forms of worship (*'ibada*) which brings [Muslims] closer to God'.[20] In purely Islamic terms (in answer to the question of the applicability to Banna's authority of the theoretically democratic, and thus confining, concept of *shura*) one of his followers made the following point: 'And there are matters which cannot be submitted to the principle of *shura*; I mean that [in these cases] one is compelled to act [or think] in only one way.'[21] His point was made specifically as regards Banna's authority and reflected best the total loyalty of the membership to the leader, reinforced over and over again by Banna's personal prestige and the widely accepted view of the sacrosanctity of his mission.

Banna, in his conception of the relation of the leader to the led, placed the two facets of loyalty—confidence and obedience—on the same plane. His followers, however—and the difference became ominous for the movement's survival—predicated obedience on confidence; when the leadership no longer commanded the respect and confidence of the membership, it ceased to have its obedience or even loyalty. While this fact, as we have seen, did not apply to the majority of members after Hudaybi took power, it did

[19] See Hajjaji, *QDHRTM*, pp. 72–80, for a typical view.

[20] 'Awda, *IBJAWAU*, p. 8.

[21] Hajjaji, *IMAM*, ii. 62. In a friendly dispute (or so it was presented) with his Guidance Council about the obligation to accept the limitations of *shura* in his dealings with them, Banna agreed to submit to it although he did not believe himself bound; see *MDA* (12 Feb. 1952), 4.

affect an important core of people so significantly placed in the order of things, in and out of the Society, as to precipitate a crisis fatal to its life. It was among this group that a movement for organizational 'reform' was inaugurated which had as its goal the 'democratization' of the movement. For the first time, at all publicly, members (for whatever reasons) were raising questions about the traditional cornerstone of the Society, absolute obedience; the demand was raised to replace 'blind' (*'amya'*) with 'deliberative' (*mubsira*) obedience.[22]

While the question of obedience was of course primary, of equally intimate concern to the disputants, all of whom were aspiring and ambitious members of the leadership élite, was the question always related to that of obedience, the distribution of power in the organization—the office of General Guide, the Guidance Council, and the Consultative Assembly. The question which lay at the root of all dismissals effected by Banna, and which inspired his formulation of the constitution of the Society in 1945 and his subsequent revision of it in 1948, finally emerged as a crucial matter of debate when he was no longer present to invoke confidence in his own person as the final arbiter. This fact was accompanied by (had as a consequence?) another metamorphosis in the ethos of the Society: its transformation from a Society whose function was largely based on the spiritual and personal ties between the leader and the led to one in which the constitution suddenly emerged as relevant. As one member of Hudaybi's opposition put it: 'Banna governed the Brothers like the head of a family; Hudaybi governed them like the head of a Society or of a party.'[23] The ultimate consequence, as we have seen, was the disintegration of the Society's common front against its enemies and its fatal weakening; the immediate consequence of this state of mind was the agitation for reform of the Society's constitution and practice.

The impetus for the reform movement, it will be recalled, was the feeling of Hudaybi's antagonists that only the Consultative Assembly, strengthened, could reverse both the decrees of dismissal that had rent the Society in November 1953, and the policies which seemed to be responsible for the implacable hostility which in 1954 separated the army junta from the Society.

[22] See *MDA* (5 June 1954), 16, for one of many articles after May 1954.

[23] This view was conversely echoed by a Hudaybi partisan who, during the crisis of November 1953, rose to attack the dissidents in this way: after noting their 'error' in thinking that 'the Society is like a state in which it is possible to make insurrection', he reminded them that the organization of the Brothers is 'a message before it is a formation and a . . . spirit before it is a Society' (see *JA* (29 Nov. 1953)). He was right—at the wrong time.

The basis for the feeling, it will be further recalled, was the antipathy with which some of the older members viewed the new leader, his entourage, and his policies, especially the one concerning the dissolution of the secret apparatus.

The first attempts to solve the disputes which racked the inner circles of the Society were in the form of suggestions made to the leadership to change the title of the General Guide (in order to preserve for Banna his unique place in the memory of the membership), to make effective provision for real elections of the Guidance Council, and to create devices by which the 'active' members (presumably the 'old' members of the secret apparatus) might have a hand in the formulation of policy and the selection of the hierarchy. These suggestions were obviously made in the early stages of Hudaybi's arrival, since none of them reflected much more than the bruised feelings of the older members as they viewed the arrival of the new leader. But they did hint at an important change in the distribution of power in the hierarchy effected by the new regulations attached to the statutes immediately after Hudaybi's assumption of power in 1951. With the issuance of those regulations the Guidance Council emerged with theoretically increased authority.[24] This fact was important not only for the history of the development of the Society's administrative apparatus, but also for the history of its inner power struggles; for while Hudaybi did not abdicate his power, he was prepared, given a favourable series of elections which confirmed his choices, to share his authority. The opposition, on the other hand, sought first to bring the Guidance Council under control by controlling its elections and then, failing this, to bypass it completely.

The proponents of the 'reform' ideas received their first concession only after they were expelled from the Society in November and December 1953. At that time, following upon the public airing of the internal schism, it was announced to the membership that a committee of five was to be established to revise the regulations. The committee's composition, mostly 'neutrals', assured a hearing for the position of the dismissed members, but before anything serious was undertaken, the Society was subjected to its first dissolution in January 1954. Not only was the question of revision pushed aside, but, because of the confused nature of the pattern of loyalties following that event, partisans on both sides took more extreme positions. Among the 'reformists', for the remainder of that year, an inflexible position was adopted and held: resistance to what was called Hudaybi's 'dictatorship' by increasing the power of the Consultative Assembly at his expense

[24] Cf. *QA*, pp. 16–21, with *LD*, pp. 12–20.

and at that of the Guidance Council, his 'tool'.[25] By September 1954 'Ashmawi, the spokesman of the opposition, was prepared to say that the Consultative Assembly possessed all authority'.[26]

This view was contrary to all but the broadest of the interpretations of the constitution of the Society and its history. The internal regulations of 1951, which expanded the role of the Guidance Council, added hardly a word to the already vaguely described functions of the Consultative Assembly. Historically, that body had been the repository of people of 'prestige'—old and respected members, and people who, Banna had hoped, attracted by this offer of status, would in turn bring prestige into the Society itself. With the death of Banna began the pressures really to 'elect' members of the Assembly; as one Brother put it, 'There was no one of great enough stature left to make such selections.' With the public eruption of the disputes within the Society, further demands were heard for a power which it had never had. In the circumstances, there was no other body to which the dissidents could turn to redress their grievances.

By September 1954 when the issues had really boiled over with the government and the organization's activity and leadership were paralysed, it was accepted by all parties to the dispute that something had to be done, and that the logical place to begin was the Consultative Assembly, which leaders of both groups hoped to make more 'representative' of the opinions of the membership on the issues at hand. In effect, both groups hoped to win a vote of confidence for their views by convening a new Assembly. Thus it was agreed to dissolve the old Assembly and institute procedures for forming another. At the meeting of the Assembly on 23 September, Hudaybi's supporters successfully pushed through resolutions which, on the one hand, beat down attempts to limit the term of office of the General Guide to three years (if passed, Hudaybi's term would have automatically ended), and, on the other, called for the rewriting of the constitution for the purpose of dissolving the Consultative Assembly and replacing it with a newly elected body.

These basic resolutions were carried with the support of the 'neutrals', who added to the discussions which surrounded the passage of the resolutions other recommendations which took account of the dissidents' complaints. Among these were the following: that the Consultative Assembly should be elected every six years; or that every three years half its membership should

25 See esp. *MDA* (12 Jan. 1954), 11.

26 See *MDA* (28 Sept. 1954), 1; see also the similar approach taken in the discussion of the Assembly powers in Zaki, *Ikhwan*, pp. 99, 103 f. Cf. above, ch. VI.

stand for election; that it should meet every three months to keep more closely in touch with the affairs of the Society; that it should have a special secretariat to study the recommendations made to it; and that it should found a 'legal' committee to deal with matters relevant to its work, without reference to the General Guide. The tenor of the proposals was revealed in another recommendation which held it to be a principle that the work of the Guidance Council was to be 'supervised' by the Consultative Assembly.

Immediately after the meeting procedures were begun in the branches throughout the country for elections. The electoral law provided for a Consultative Assembly of 120 members. As originally conceived, the plan was that thirty of this number were to be appointed by the General Guide, but this was later changed to provide for selection by a committee to be established from among the other ninety members of the Assembly. Those ninety members were to be chosen by indirect election. In balloting supervised in each branch by its administrative council, seven members of each branch would be elected, who in turn would join with other branch 'electors' to elect the ninety members of the Assembly. As in other instances when it faced questions of parliamentary elections, the Society remained consistent to its abhorrence of the allegedly 'corrupting' concomitants of 'party-like elections', and refused, therefore, to countenance the direct voting techniques identified with them. Those not in charge of the voting procedures—the pro-Hudaybi forces, clearly in the majority, controlled the apparatus of organization—inevitably felt abuses of another kind, and voiced their complaints that the elections could not but be 'staged', because the power to appoint the regional officers still resided in the office of the General Guide, and that this power assured pressures in the branches incompatible with truly free elections.[27] However, by the time the debate began really to centre on the crucial questions of what in fact constituted free choice in elections, the matter became academic, for within weeks the final collision occurred between the Society and the government which brought both the crisis and the Society to an abrupt end.

POLITICS AND VIOLENCE

For whatever the Society of the Muslim Brothers may be remembered in Egyptian history, its political role will probably remain dominant, both for what it did or did not do politically and

[27] This information is summarized from the trial proceedings; and *JAY* (23 Oct. 1954), 7; (25 Sept. 1954), 1, 8; and *MDA* (19 Oct. 1954), 5.

for what its activity reflected about Egyptian politics. To our earlier discussion of the political attitudes and actions of the Brothers we will now add some considerations about the central questions of the Society's political role: (1) its attitudes and intentions towards the assumption of political power; and (2) the problem of political violence.

Political Power: Evolution or Revolution?

In the two major instances when the Society was legally dissolved and physically repressed, in 1948 and 1954, the major official justification for the action was that it was plotting an imminent revolutionary assumption of political power. If the material in this study bears any resemblance to reality (we again note the assumption that in both cases the government concerned made available all the evidence at its disposal), then the charge levelled at the Society is not precisely true. In 1948 the mass of documents showing discontent with the order of things, organization open and secret, and training for military operations did not conclusively show evidence of an imminent overthrow by force of the government of Egypt. It would be doubtful, further, to assume that Banna, given his shrewd, even cunning caution, would have 'come out into the open too soon',[28] with the bulk of his activist followers in Palestine, away from the expected scene of action.

In October 1954 the situation was clouded by a premature and propagandistic charge of revolution in January of that year followed by a reconciliation which was an obvious power deal. When the assassination attempt on Nasir was made in October, the case for revolutionary plotting was stronger than in 1948. There was clear evidence of the existence of plans and attempts by certain groups of Brothers to make contact with other dissident—especially army—groups in the hope of replacing the army junta with another, less hostile group. As our earlier presentation suggests, it was not proved that these lesser goals, including the assassination attempt—let alone plans to assume power as an organization—were conceived and executed by the Society's leadership.[29] In both 1948 and 1954 accumulated tensions between the Society and the government were relieved by an event—in both cases assassination attempts—which provided the government with the occasion to put an end to dissidence which was incompatible with internal stability and even the sovereignty of the state. We are saying in

[28] Majid Khadduri, 'The Army Officer; His Role in Middle Eastern Politics', in Fisher, ed., *Social Forces in the Middle East*, p. 167, and above, ch. III, pp. 78–9.

[29] Above, pp. 157–60.

effect that however well-trained and disciplined were the para-military forces of the organization, they would have been no match for any serious resistance by Egyptian security forces, with or without any support from other opposing groups. The capacity for terror is not coterminous with the capability for revolutionary action which would have involved sufficient power not only to mount a revolt but to maintain it. It is not even likely that the activists in the organization would have so miscalculated the real power position of the Society either in 1948 and certainly not in 1954.

This assessment of the two dramatic points in the Society's clash with authority does not, however, address itself to other pertinent questions about the Society's attitude towards political power or to the question of whether, if they did not in fact try on two occasions, they did ultimately intend to seek power by revolutionary means. The theoretical position of the Brothers on the question of the relation of Islam to government and politics has already been noted; political power is one, if not the fundamental, aspect of Islam, for the revealed law requires a state to enforce it. In so stating the Brothers were not only restating the classical Islamic view of the unity of life, but also justifying their right to political action.[30]

Banna emphasized in clear terms that the power to reform was inextricably tied up with the power to rule; but he also took care to make clear that officially the activity of the Brothers was not to come to power but rather to aid in the reform of society. At the organization's fifth conference in 1939, he made an explicit and detailed statement on the subject: (1) the kind of Islam in which the Brothers believe makes government an important cornerstone of their programme; (2) without the power to legislate, the voice of the reformer would be as 'a scream in the wilderness'; (3) thus, shirking the quest for governmental power (*hukm*) is an 'Islamic crime' (*jarima islamiyya*); (4) the Brothers do not seek power for themselves and are prepared to be the 'troops' of those who would carry this burden in an Islamic way; (5) before anything can happen, there must be a period during which the principles of the Brothers are spread.[31] The last point remained the essence of the official position throughout Banna's time and especially in Hudaybi's: the principal role of the Society was to be one of education (*tarbiyya*) of the people to the truth; 'when the people have been Islamized, a truly Muslim nation will naturally evolve'.[32]

[30] See Ghazali, *MHN* (Faruqi tr.), pp. 3–4, which is translated more strongly than the Arabic (pp. 18–19) warrants.

[31] Hajjaji, *IMAM*, ii. 93–7; see also *JIM* (15 Oct. 1946), 1.

[32] See the foreword in al-Sayyid abu al-Hasan al-Nadawi, *al-Islam wa'l-hukm* (Cairo, A.H. 1372), p. 3.

This position, plus the Society's sweeping condemnation of the existing system of parliaments and parties, created an ambivalence—both ideological and tactical—in its attitude towards the assumption of political responsibility via established political institutions such as parliaments and cabinets. This ambivalence towards parliamentary participation and elections was observable throughout the history of the movement and more often than not raised the question of political duplicity. Thus the decision in 1941 to participate in elections, in order 'to record our opinions in the official parliament', was followed in 1942 by entrance into the campaign and a subsequent withdrawal under Wafdist pressure. The effort in 1945 to join the election rolls foundered on what appeared to be government manipulation of the results against the Wafd as well as the Brothers. Charges of forgery, cast in the form of denunciations of parties, partyism, and anything related, required denials that the initial ventures of the Society into organized politics within the system were ever 'in the name of the organization'.[33] The situation could not but heighten the current of extra-legality, which in any case was a basic element in the growth of the Society and was part of the larger picture of the breakdown of the Egyptian political processes. At the same time, however, as the Society was heaping abuse on the system, it continued to participate in local elections and claim victory for candidates running 'on the principles of the Society'.[34] That these victories occurred in 1946, during a period of collusion with the Sidqi government (a fact which prompted Wafdist election protests),[35] probably did not encourage any long-range appreciation of the virtues of the electoral processes and parliamentary life, although at the end of 1946 the paper of the Society began a campaign to encourage the registration as voters (it was a 'national duty') of members at all levels of the organization on reaching the legal age.[36]

In the Banna period the Society's attitudes towards elections reflected both the unique situation in Egypt itself (the steady movement towards political breakdown) as well as Banna's tactical manœuverings among the political forces (especially the palace and the Wafd). Following his death, the Society's public attitudes towards the political processes became even more ambivalent, a fact reflecting not only tactical considerations but the divided opinion which followed the succession of Hudaybi. The election proposed for the spring of 1952, for example, initially found the

[33] See *MMB* (23 Jan. 1951), 4; *JIM* (15 Oct. 1946), 1; and *JIM* (4 July 1946), 4. [34] See *JIM* (19 Sept. 1946), 3, and subsequent issues.
[35] See *JSU* (25 Sept. 1946), 3. [36] *JIM* (8 Dec. 1946), 3.

Guidance Council appearing to agree to participate in March, with the proviso that neither the organization as such nor its members would do so unless the electoral laws were revised; and in April it was decided not to participate whether the law was changed or not. The arguments put forward by the members were varied: that the Society could realize its mission without elections; that elections cause 'hates' and 'national disunity' which were at that time incompatible with the needs of the national struggle; that in the light of martial law and the continued incarceration of political prisoners elections would be meaningless.[37] The variety of the answers reflected both official and unofficial opinion on the principle of elections, the Society's participation in elections, and its participation in this one. The ambiguity of the position reflected the fact of agreement with the government over restraining national passions while the heat of the fire of Cairo cooled and the fact of a new leadership which was itself uncertain about the political role of the Society.

For Hudaybi, two traditional positions of the Society *vis-à-vis* politics remained valid: the commitment to education (*tarbiyya*) as a first and necessary step; and the hostility to partyism. In interviews in the first period after the revolution, he made the first point in answer to questions about the unwillingness of the Society to participate in the elections planned earlier (which in any case never took place).[38] However, the importance of the second point —corruption in the system—was underlined in another interview a few months later. When asked whether the Brothers still held to their view of non-participation in elections, Hudaybi answered that the days of corruption were one thing, 'but now it is probable that the Brothers have another view'.[39] There was no opportunity, as we know, for the Brothers to test the new situation, but in the one instance when it was possible for Egypt to go back to the old parliamentary system (in the 1954 Neguib–Nasir clash), the Society chose to throw the weight of its influence against such a prospect, despite the fact that its leaders were in the midst of a new repression by the government in which it had reposed so much trust. That in its decision the Society weighed its own power position in the country (actual release from prison for some, including Hudaybi), does not, we think, alter the importance of the ideological issue.

The opportunity to assume political responsibility through cabinet appointment was a reality only in Hudaybi's time. We have already observed that Banna, in the period 1946–7, was not

[37] See *MDA* (1 Apr. 1952), 1. [38] *MMR* (25 July 1952).
[39] Ibid. (24 Oct. 1952), 15.

averse to working with the government against his Wafdist and communist enemies, and that such a liaison reflected—at least for himself—a loyalty to the monarchy as a channel of power. It is a real probability that much might have been different in the history of the movement had Banna been offered a cabinet post. Information is too sparse to speculate on the matter, but what is known about the period and Banna makes it seem not unlikely that he would have welcomed some such recognition of the role of the Society in the political life of Egypt despite its official hostility to the corruption of the existing parliamentary life.

The issue of cabinet participation in the Hudaybi era has already been treated at length. The issues of the power struggle between the Society and the RCC in September 1953, combined with the ambivalence in the Society's position *vis-à-vis* both political power and the RCC itself, brought to naught the apparent plan of the revolutionary officers to involve the Brothers in the political process of government and thereby (presumably) awaken them to the burdens and the costs of political power. Hudaybi's mistrust of Nasir and his works overcame the momentary decision to consider participation in government, a mistrust which was, in any case, fed by ambivalence about the wisdom of political participation on any but the most favourable of the terms necessary for the fulfilment of the message of the Society. Even if the new era had been spawned by the 'blessed liberation movement', it was necessary for commitment to be followed by fulfilment.

It was not, however, a question of whether to participate in the political processes although this is what it seemed to the Brothers; it was a matter of when and on what terms. When the Society split on the issue of whether it was to define itself as a political party in the fall of 1952, the issue was not whether the Society could be so designated but when it should so state this fact—when, in its own terms, it had passed beyond the stage of education—and could effectively assert its right to compete for political power. And although Hudaybi effectively lost his battle to prevent the Society from registering as a party, he continued to formulate his position in the Society's traditional terms: 'When the day comes that the people believe that they must be governed by the constitution of the Qur'an . . . then we, or someone like us, will become the governors.'[40]

This ambivalence towards the definition of the political role of the Society and towards the problem of the use of the existing political channels to influence the situation was, as has been suggested, partly ideological and partly tactical in provenance; it

[40] Ibid.

was also motivated by the frustrations built into the Egyptian political scene, frustrations which underlay much of the widespread resort to political violence in Egypt at large. This frustration reflected, above all, a mistrust of the available 'legal' forms of political expression and inspired a commitment to those forms which was nominal only.

We will return in a moment to the question of political frustration as it related to violence; its relevance here is in the relationship to the problem of political ambivalence within the Society. It was this frustration which fed and sanctioned the current of extra-legal action which persisted, for the activist members of the Society, as the only alternative to elections and cabinets. This current within the Society was what belied and, from within, undermined the official protestations of pacific 'education' as the primary goal of the Society and the necessary prelude to full political involvement. It was a current which took on revolutionary implications from the founder of the movement, although Banna seemed to be no political revolutionary himself. Revolution came through his all-encompassing public denunciations of the social order and in his informal talks with the questioning youth which flocked to his banners.[41] Revolution was expressed in his emphasis on militant preparedness and secrecy in every facet of the organization's activity, and especially in the para-military formations and the secret apparatus.[42] And revolution was dramatized in clandestine contact with groups of similarly disenchanted officers in the armed forces of Egypt, a contact which brought the Society, on the volition of others, as close as it ever came—or perhaps could ever have hoped to come—to political power.

The revolutionary aura which clung to the Society won for it the unending enmity of government after government, enmity which was based as much on its spirit of and potential for revolutionary activity as on the fact of this. Similarly it aroused the fears and passions of other competing and conflicting groups—the political parties and forces, the minorities, the Westernized press and literary men—and could not but widen the gap between them and the Society. In many respects the existence or absence of an intent in the organization became academic, in view of the wide belief inside and outside the Society that the forcible overthrow of the political order was in fact its goal. Inside the organization, no difference was discerned between the political and social order. Outside, it was not readily perceived that the organization's

[41] See Hajjaji, *RLAT*, *passim*; and above, p. 31, n. 64 for comment on this work.

[42] Hajjaji, *RLAT*, pp. 16–18 and esp. 64–5.

politics were inseparable from the problem of Islamic cultural and social disintegration. The consequence of the undifferentiated confrontation was almost inevitably blind fear—and violence.

Violence: Political and Social

The political violence for which the Society is most widely known was, in its fundamental expression, not unique to it. In our analysis of the history of the movement we have suggested the theme, which will be considered further here, that the Muslim Brothers shared with fellow Egyptians a common disdain for law and order and accepted, in more or less degree, a rationale for violence which hastened the end of Egypt's parliamentary life. Perhaps the share of the Society in the process was more telling because it was more effective, but it is important to note, nevertheless, the universality of the contributions to political disorder in the decade before the revolution of 1952.

World War II, as we saw earlier, propelled the Society into a position of prominence in Egyptian political life. The immediate material situation—economic disorder and social and political pressures—might of itself have been sufficient to explain the Society's spectacular post-war popularity, but the explanation had a larger ramification: for the growth of an organization like the Muslim Brothers confirmed the fact that the organized and recognized political groups in the country were no longer capable of serving the political and other needs of many sectors of the community[43] and that the spirit of revolution—a spirit non-directed and in many respects as yet subterranean—was at large in the country.

Of the tensions which made Egypt's post-war adjustment chaotic, perhaps the most important was the vast sense of political malaise which gripped a national movement made all the more turbulent by war-time suppression. The existing and relatively simply defined nationalist hostility to continued British control of Egyptian affairs, a control so obviously exercised during the war,[44] was complicated by new and more complex inner tensions out of which was spawned the stuff of revolution. In its political frustration, the national movement began to define internal as well as external enemies. The consequence was to hasten the demise of governmental authority and the breakdown of what orderly development of the political processes existed. Egypt in 1923 was

[43] See esp. *JIM* (20 Oct. 1946). See also A. Hourani, 'The Anglo-Egyptian Agreement: Some Causes and its Implications', *MEJ* (Summer 1955), 247; and Colombe, *Égypte*, pp. 265–6.

[44] See G. Kirk, *The Middle East, 1945–1950* (1954), p. 118.

granted a constitution along with her 'independence', and up to 1952 she practised a kind of parliamentary life. The evidences of its weakness were apparent from the start, but only in the 1940s did nationalist political frustration begin to focus indirectly on internal political life and in effect challenge its very basis. In retrospect, as has been noted, it can now be seen that the violence which marked the period 1945–52 was the prelude to the burial of the parliamentary system that followed the 1952 army revolution, itself a product of the national political disenchantment.

In Egyptian terms, the political frustration was not with parliamentary processes as such, but with their undemocratic development in Egypt. The constitution of 1923 was in effect an affirmation of the royal power, with British backing, despite the provisions for an operating parliament. The elections held in 1923 and all those held down to 1950 were won by the popular Wafd, though it actually led only five of the seventeen governments formed in those years; two of these came at a time of national reconciliation and unity inspired by fears of Italian adventures in 1936.[45] The constitution of 1930 and the new electoral law of that same year (promulgated by the palace and administered by Sidqi) were designed to curb continuing Wafdist successes at the polls, and did so until the re-establishment of the constitution of 1923 in 1934. To Wafdists—the majority party—the impression of royal, pasha, and British resistance to the 'popular will' was strong. It was not perhaps mere coincidence that the first appearance of paramilitary groups—the Wafdist 'Blue Shirts' and the 'Green Shirts' of the Young Egypt party—coincided with extra-legal manipulation of the constitutional processes by the palace in the early 1930s. If it is true, as alleged, that the 'Green Shirts' were supported by the palace, then another dimension is added to the tale.[46]

Faruq's assumption to power in 1936 slightly but only temporarily altered the picture of royal despotism; for although he adopted as his own the anti-Wafd position of his father, he mitigated its effect by identifying himself with anti-British and thus 'nationalist' pashas who, as we saw earlier, attempted to counter Wafdist power with the new forces like the Muslim Brothers. But Faruq's popularity as a monarch and a person waned in the war and early post-war years as he responded to increased social pressures in the country by appointing repressive and non-representative governments to execute his will.

[45] See Heyworth-Dunne, *Modern Egypt*, pp. 5–6, 18–19; Colombe, *Égypte*, App. II, pp. 331–52.

[46] See RIIA, *GBE*, pp. 27–38, 48–52, 189–90. See a forthcoming study of this movement by James P. Jankowski, *Young Egypt*, University of Michigan doctoral dissertation.

The previous paragraphs have attempted to depict the sense of majority frustration as it focused on the Wafd, the symbol of the Egyptian 'masses' and Egyptian parliamentary life through the early war years. It was not surprising perhaps that the Wafd should resort to extra-parliamentary devices like the para-military 'Blue Shirts' in defence of palace-usurped rights. And it is worth considering the impression of the example on other, less securely established groups like the Muslim Brothers, especially since, even when in power (1936–7), the 'Blue Shirts' were effectively used against opponents of the Wafd. And in elaboration of the theme of the undemocratic quality of Egyptian life, it could further be noted that in 1942, after the Wafd had been summoned to power by the British, the Wafdist press hinted that 'once the Wafd was in power, there might be no further need of party government, since a multiplicity of parties, found necessary in some countries, was harmful to others'.[47] The view of Marlowe, that Egypt's politics 'oscillated between the personal rule of the Palace . . . and the party dictatorship of the Wafd.',[48] is a fair reading of basic elements in the decline of Egyptian parliamentary life. Symbols of authority and democracy, the palace and the Wafd, respectively, both contributed by their abuses to the undermining of political order. The tarnishing of these symbols by the event of 4 February 1942 merely speeded up the process whereby they would be replaced by less orderly political forces.

In itself, a corrupted parliamentary life might have produced nothing more than a chronic instability, which might have gradually become more stable as the nation grew more practised in the expression of its will. However, the demise in Egypt of the parliamentary process in favour of extra-legal violence was not self-generated but grew out of two other elements: (1) the increasingly uncontrollable economic and social pressures for change; and (2) the fact that Egypt's parliamentary experience coincided with a struggle for genuine national independence. As a stimulus to revolutionary violence, socio-economic pressures for change will not here detain us.[49] The second element—the development of parliamentary experience in the midst of a nationalist struggle—needs further consideration.

One of the important legacies of the British occupation in Egypt was a tradition of mistrust and suspicion which taxed to the

[47] RIIA, *GBE*, pp. 72–3; see also pp. 48–51.

[48] Marlowe, *Anglo-Egyptian Relations*, p. 356.

[49] This has been ably done in Safran, *Egypt*, pp. 193–9. Indeed, the section on 'The Political and Social Failure of the Liberal Democratic Regime' (pp. 187 ff.) covers well, in more detail and with only a slightly different emphasis, the points made above about the political atmosphere.

utmost the institutions of government after the occupation. The situation became even more acute when, as in Egypt, a grant of independence barely concealed more or less continued foreign tutelage and controls, thereby exacerbating among the recipients of national freedom this suspicion and mistrust and complicating the problems not only of running a government (as distinct from an administration) but also of organizing political life on a firm basis.[50] The momentous consequence of this situation for Egypt was the emergence of a rationale of violence which encompassed the ultimate political act—assassination.

We have earlier noted and emphasized that disenchantment with the political processes in Egypt was initially an act of positive rejection not of parliamentary life in general but rather of the manner in which it developed in Egypt. This rejection, more often than not, focused on the political leaders of the country, who became objects of scorn because of their real or imagined 'betrayal' of the national trust for their own, and worse yet, for imperialist interests. The mutual suspicion and mistrust which saw a British agent under every *tarbush* fed the poisons eating at Egyptian parliamentary life (initially and basically unstable because of the Eastern setting) to produce a single phenomenon to be resisted: internal political repression by treasonous leaders in the service of imperialism. If there were no 'democratic' means genuinely to effect the national will, then non-democratic, i.e. violent, means would be used. Bullets replaced the seemingly unresponsive ballot,[51] in the fight against 'internal' as well as 'external' imperialism.

We have already shown at length how widespread was the resort to violence by all groups in Egypt in the period 1945–52. Much of the activity evidenced the mundane jockeying between groups for positions of influence within the power system; and, what was perhaps even more important, it also reflected the violent expression of conflicting views about the identity and purposes of the nation. But even more of the violence perpetrated in this period revolved around the theme of action—'murder and terrorism'

[50] On the problem of foreign tutelage and self-government see Nuseibeh, *Ideas of Arab Nationalism*, pp. 112–15.

[51] Marlowe, *Anglo-Egyptian Relations*, pp. 126–7, makes this pertinent observation: '. . . in a country governed by other than democratic methods, violence is the only way in which a government can be opposed.' G. Young, *Egypt* (1927), p. 182, contains a related proposition about university activism: 'the systematic exclusion of a nation from political education will make their education political.' These explanations seem to us more useful than that of Kirk, *Short History*, pp. 248–9: Frustration in social and economic goals leads to seeking the 'patronage of the political leaders, and those who fail in this rigorous competition tried to seek compensation for their frustration and inadequacy in some form of political extremism'.

against 'the English and their tools'. The words quoted belong to Anwar al-Sadat,[52] who, even after he had come to power with the successful coup of 1952 and in the midst of the conflict with the Brothers (and the official repudiation of violence), defended the resort in the 1940s to extra-legal violence as 'the only path for struggle in the shadow of the British Ambassador Lord Killearn'.[53]

The foregoing is of general relevance for the pre-revolutionary political life of Egypt, and is intended as the basis for the general proposition that much of the violence inflicted by the Society of the Muslim Brothers had an inspiration common to other Egyptians. This statement will be qualified in a moment, but we feel it is worth while to emphasize the important similarity of motivation in a crucial area of political behaviour. To match the mood of a Sadat, consider the rarely mourned murder of Nuqrashi Pasha in 1948. Muhammad Malik, one of the Brothers arrested in the sweep of 1948–9, on his release from prison in 1954, avoided a direct answer to a reporter's direct question: 'Did you participate in the planning of Nuqrashi's assassination?' His vague answer, however, revealed a state of mind. He said in part:

> we desired good for the country. We felt that our nation was eternal and that people are transitory. We asked ourselves frankly what these leaders, succeeding each other to the seats of authority, did for Egypt. It was in their power to do much . . . but they refused because their personal greeds outweighed the interests of their country. Because of this they do not deserve from us today even one word of pity.[54]

Malik was typical. The famous jeep papers showed among other things, 'studies' of the economic, social, and moral state of Egypt in which analysis was confined to blaming the British occupation—'which is supported by our leaders'. Letters in the collection speak of 'the leaders and the rich' who have lost the nation's rights and self-respect and whose collaboration with the British makes them 'unbelievers' from whose grasp the country must be 'purified'.[55] In such circumstances there is only one recourse: 'The people will discipline its erring rulers.'[56]

One final quotation from an editorial will combine and sum up this dual-faceted theme of internal political frustration and national betrayal. Speaking about the alleged repressions by the Nuqrashi government, the writer goes on to say:[57]

> and there was no doubt that out of this oppression would be spawned an explosion and that its first victim be the man who was its perpetrator,

[52] Sadat, *Safahat*, pp. 142–4.
[53] *MTR* (3 Nov. 1954), 3.
[54] *MMR* (17 Oct. 1952), 21.
[55] *Qadiyat al-jib, passim*; see also Ghazali, *IIS*, pp. 15–17.
[56] Ghazali, *TFDWH*, p. 21.
[57] *MDA* (22 June 1954), 6.

for fire always eats him who ignites it. . . . Nuqrashi was killed; and he was killed because it was he who planted in the soul of his killer the thought of his killing. He was killed because it was he who threw himself at this end. For his killing was not the result of prior planning or earlier preparation but was the child of a psychological condition [*hala nafsiyya*] which was created by his terroristic rule, his reckless truckling to imperialism and the king and the political egocentricity which reigned over him and the other leaders of the parties.

The words of the writer make the point in terms of cold, unrepenting bitterness, and unrelenting hatred. He was a bold man who would dare to rule Egypt. And his problem was larger than the Society of the Muslim Brothers.[58]

Nuqrashi was also charged with 'aggression' against Islam when he dissolved the Society, and it was this factor which gave its uniqueness to the Society's otherwise shared approach to violence as a political device. To the Society's political frustration was added a religio-cultural facet which generated its own imperative to violence, a violence which was distinguished from merely mundane political struggle by the greater intensity aroused by crucial questions of cultural and religious survival. We have already discussed at length the urgency with which the Society viewed the problem of social and historical identity and cohesion. It was in this sense that its violence bore the indelible marks of cultural crisis: in its resistance to the 'betrayal' by the secular leaders of Egypt, it saw cultural and religious as much as political 'treason'; in its demands for 'democratic rights' lay the question of who was to define the nature of the nation and its goals; in its struggle against imperialism it saw resistance to another Crusade.

This aspect of the situation was clearly demonstrated in the Society's rationale for its instruments of violence. Obviously its para-military forces were, as Husayni puts it, an answer to the secular 'failure of politics',[59] (a view presumably related to our above assessment that the rise of extra-legal action was as much the effect as the cause of the decline of parliamentary processes). However, as we have seen, more often members consciously saw paramilitary operations as a necessary 'defence' of the organization

[58] Safran, *Egypt*, ch. 14, is slightly less preoccupied with the violence of the Brothers than is Halpern, *Politics of Social Change*, ch. 8. We feel that neither has given sufficient attention to the setting that spawned the universal violence of the time. Our objections on this score are based on the distortions of the Society's role in the political systems both authors are discussing. Our objection does not address itself to the question—a more appropriate one—of whether this Society by definition inspired violence with its teachings. Our argumentation suggests that we think it did but no lesson is learned in a vacuum.

[59] Husayni, *Ikhwan*, p. 97.

and its ideas, bound up with a militant concept of *jihad*. The Brothers, it was said, were 'an Islamic army for the protection of the message'.[60] And Banna warned the opposition: 'If you rise against us and stand in the path of our message, God permits us to defend ourselves.'[61]

It would be impossible, of course, to determine the relative weight of God and mundane political considerations in any particular act of political violence. It is our purpose here to point out the dual inspiration and to urge its importance. It is, however, possible to go on and say that the religious element in the picture had other, wider implications. For out of the fact of power in being, and in use in defence of 'eternal' goals, emerged a self-righteous and intolerant arrogance which opened an unbridgeable gap between the Society and its fellow citizens. This was true because the image the Society had of itself and its mission excluded genuine long-range mutuality in relations with other groups. Co-operation for immediate objectives and alliances there was, but these allowances were all too readily dissolvable because of the deep mistrust with which the two parties viewed each other. The Muslim Brothers almost invariably went it alone; nay, insisted on doing so.

Banna himself set the pattern for this largely (but not solely) self-imposed group exclusiveness by classifying people in Egypt in terms of their attitudes towards the Society. There were four kinds of people, he said: the believer (*mu'min*); the undecided (*mutaraddid*); the opportunist (*nafa'i*); and the opponents (*mutahamil*).[62] While in this theory there was room for an Egyptian to be other than an enemy, in practice the line was sharply drawn around 'believers', for whom it was necessary to be not merely a Muslim but a Muslim Brother. The consequence of this structuring of the social order was to generate within the Society a current of rigid intolerance which transformed mundane political disputes into elemental social clashes. Individual as well as group political opponents became the objects of a violence inspired by a social and religious exclusiveness which could brook no compromise with him who was not a Brother.

This social violence was not, as we have seen earlier in this study, confined to political opponents. It was the sense of group exclusiveness which underlay the unresolved tension in the organization about its role in the face of moral decay—whether to persuade and advise or whether to reform with 'the force of the hand'. We have

[60] See e.g. Jundi, *QDHRTM*, pp. 103–4; and *MDA* (3 June 1952), 3, 15.
[61] *RBAWY*, p. 31.
[62] *RTH: D*, pp. 6–9. See variation of this scheme in *RNURT*, p. 14.

seen that although Banna made the former the Society's official policy, the latter continued to persist in the form of sporadic acts of self-initiated policing of fellow citizens, which took the form of threats and acts of violence in the name of Islam and its morality. Banna's rigorous insistence on legislating for morality—by positive governmental acts and by negative curbs on the inducements to sin—provided justification for the zealot and overcame his strictures against forceful or 'negative' reformist action. In combination with the sense of mission he instilled into the members—and, more importantly, the sense of righteous power (in addition to the existence of real power)—the call to moral reform was almost inevitably answered by some in violent terms.

Violence with the Brothers, then, to sum up, was in many respects a response to the situation in Egypt and had much in common with the violence of other Egyptians. The difference lay in the Islamic dimension which the Brothers claimed as their own, and which precipitated a variety of violence in both political and social life which was characterized primarily by rigid intolerance. The question may now be asked, what was the Brothers' place in Islam's modern history? In the name of what Islam did the Society act?

THE BROTHERS AND ISLAM

From earlier Islamic history, the movement of the Kharijites has been most often evoked as the model for the Muslim Brothers.[63] A similar comparison has been made between the Brothers and the Isma'iliyya movement,[64] especially its latter-day expression in the movement of the Assassins.[65] The comparisons are worth while —the mood of the mysterious and the esoteric and the spirit of exclusiveness which engendered violence are particularly noteworthy. We note these things, however, in passing. The historical periods in question are too disparate to bear extensive comparison. And historical analogies are always potentially misleading, always

[63] See Heyworth-Dunne, *Modern Egypt*, p. 56. In both 1948 and 1954, the government charged the Society with being *Khawarij* and received denials in both cases; for 1948, see *Qawl fasl*, p. 40; for 1954, see *JJ* (18 Nov. 1954), 9; (21 Nov. 1954), 3. See the study of the *Khawarij* (an 'Islamic movement') in *MMB* (12 Dec. 1950), 11, which speaks of their undefined 'errors' but goes on to praise their 'rectitude' and their spirit of 'struggle in the path of God'.

[64] Heyworth-Dunne, *Modern Egypt*, p. 56, and next note.

[65] Husayni, *Ikhwan*, p. 152, who is not so sure; and government comparisons as above (n. 63) in *MTR* (23 Nov. 1954), 7, and *MTH* (25 Nov. 1954), 10. Tabi'i, *Ha'ula'i hum al-Ikhwan*, p. 151, makes the comparison between the Brothers and the Assassins and asserts as evidence the fact that the name of all three leaders was Hasan! See also the interesting comments of Ahmad Amin, *al-Sa'laka wa'l futuwa fi'l-Islam* (1952), pp. 65–70 and 96–8.

potentially destructive of the uniqueness which inheres in each discrete historical event. We pass on to more recent developments, those which shared a more nearly comparable framework.

We need not here recapitulate what has already been brilliantly done by Professors Gibb and Cantwell Smith in their studies of Islamic modernism.[66] It is sufficient merely to note that, in that sweep of developments in the Arab world beginning with the movement of the Wahhabiyya in the late eighteenth century, the Society of the Brothers emerges as the first mass-supported and organized, essentially urban-oriented effort to cope with the plight of Islam in the modern world. This fact complicates the attempt to trace its genealogy, but does not obscure the general harmony of its aims with those of earlier reform movements.

The Brothers saw themselves clearly in the line of the modern reform movement identified with the names of Jamal al-Din al-Afghani, Muhammad 'Abduh, and Rashid Rida. Their view of the particular relationship of the reformers to each other and to 'the renaissance of thought in modern Egypt' is an instructive image of the earlier reformers and also a fairly accurate assessment of their role and that of the Society in modernist developments: Afghani was seen as the 'caller' or 'announcer' (*mu'adhdhin, sarkha*); and Rida as the 'archivist' or 'historian' (*sijal, mu'arrikh*). Banna, however, was seen as the 'builder (*bani*) of a renaissance, the leader of a generation, and the founder of a nation'.[67] The Society of the Brothers, according to this view, was the 'practical' (*'amali*) extension of the previous movements. Among other things, this description implies the Society's belief that, for all the greatness of these men, their reforms were inadequate because of their failure to view Islam in the totality which the Brothers insisted was consistent with the truth of the revelation and the history of the community. Afghani sees the problems and warns; 'Abduh teaches and thinks ('a well-meaning shaykh who inspired reforms in the Azhar');[68] and Rida writes and records. As Banna puts it, all are merely 'religious and moral reformers',[69] lacking the comprehensive view of Islam which characterized the Brothers.

Towards Afghani the Brothers felt a special kinship. Many felt him to be the 'spiritual father' of the movement and to him Banna was most often compared.[70] That this self-conscious sense of

[66] Gibb, *Modern Trends in Islam*; Smith, *Islam in Modern History*. See also the more recent and equally brilliant Cragg, *Counsels in Contemporary Islam*.

[67] *MDA* (20 Feb. 1951), 15.

[68] 'Abduh, it was said, busied himself only with the 'men of religion' (*rijal al-din*) not seeing Islam as a 'comprehensive movement' (see Husayni, *Ikhwan*, pp. 179–80). The above statements were made to us orally.

[69] *Mudh.*, p. 98.

[70] See *MDA* (6 Feb. 1951), 13; see also Zaki, *Ikhwan*, pp. 2–3.

identity with Afghani among Brothers was related to his activism seems self-evident. Professor Cantwell Smith has well noted the importance for later movements of this fiery defender of the faith against both internal corruption and external encroachment.[71]

The identification with Afghani was easy because it was with a spirit or a mood out of history. The attitude towards the 'Abduh tradition was more complicated, because it was both closer in time and in itself more complex. We have already noted evidence of the formal and external aspects of the relationship of the Society to the tradition of 'Abduh as it passed through his heirs in the group known as the Salafiyya. Remember that Banna's father was a student of 'Abduh's; that Banna, in his early years, avidly read the magazine *al-Manar* and patterned some of his own juvenile journalism on it; and that, in his Cairo student days, he sought out in admiration some of those regarded as disciples of the master, such as Farid Wajdi and Ahmad Taymur. In a similar category of things was his close relationship with another student of 'Abduh's, the famed rector of the Azhar, Mustafa al-Maraghi.[72] Banna's opinion of Rashid Rida was expressed in his assessment of *al-Manar* under Rida's stewardship as one of 'the greatest influences in the service of Islam for this age in Egypt and in other areas'.[73] After *al-Manar* finally collapsed, despite the Society's efforts to save it, Banna regarded his own magazine, *al-Shihab*, as its successor.[74] Nevertheless, even while Rida was alive, Banna appeared to have closer relations with Muhibb al-Din al-Khatib, the proprietor of the Salafiyya bookshop and editor of *al-Fath*. Khatib remained a continuous contributor to the Brothers' press and magazines and became an editor of their daily in the years 1946–8.

[71] Smith, *Islam in Modern History*, p. 51. Professor Cantwell Smith's description of Afghani (pp. 47–51) could well have been written of Banna. We are not quite sure, therefore, what the difference is between Afghani's and the Brothers' activism, but in Professor Cantwell Smith's study there seems to be one. The answer in part may lie in the theme, partly spelled out in the extensive study of apologetics (pp. 115–56), that somehow modern 'dynamist' movements (i.e. post-Afghani and even Wahhabi) suffer from a corrupted sense of the medieval ethic.

[72] See above, ch. i. On Wajdi, see Smith, *Islam in Modern History*, pp. 132–56; on Taymur, C. C. Adams, *Islam and Modernism in Egypt* (1933), pp. 214–15. See Gardet, *La cité musulmane*, pp. 25–6.

[73] *MS* (Nov. 1947), 9. Banna implied, in *Mudh.*, pp. 272–3, that Rida was about to commit himself to the Society. See next note.

[74] Banna appropriately made the claim in the prefatory comments of his exegesis of the opening verse of the Qur'an, *Muqaddama fi'l-tafsir* [1947], p. 20. The reference is to a version of the work printed under separate cover but which appeared first as the introductory article in *MS*. Maraghi, in an article from *al-Manar* after it was taken over by the Brothers which was reproduced in Banna's memoirs, seemed to suggest (*Mudh.*, p. 273) that it was only natural that Banna should take over from Rida. Safran, *Egypt*, pp. 231–2, has a concise vivid, and excellent comparison between Rida and Banna.

To an Indian Muslim traveller, he identified himself and his magazine with the Society.[75] That Khatib, in his later days, was more influenced by the Society than vice versa seems clear from his writings.

A similarly formal, yet more fundamental, measure of the relationship with the 'Abduh tradition is to be found in an important reading-list distributed to teachers in the Society for their guidance in preparing themselves for creating the 'new generation' of Muslim youth from their students. Under a heading dealing with Qur'anic reading, the list ranked *Manar* exegesis before that of the usually preferred work of Ibn Kathir, and cited no other work except the *fatiha* by Banna. Similarly, the *Risalat al-Tawhid* of Shaykh 'Abduh received a place of honour among a limited number of works (by Banna and Ghazali) in the readings under general studies of faith.[76]

In some general and fundamental points the attitudes of the Society clearly reflected this contact with the 'Abduh tradition. One important point of similarity was the effort to simplify Islam for its adherents and reduce it to the essentials necessary to put an end to the divisive internecine bickering between the sects and schools. Another was that both argued strongly that no external change in the Muslim community was possible without a change in the mentality of Muslims, and that no effective progress was possible without educational reform. Finally, what was perhaps most important, both sought reform from within Islam, on its own terms and by its own dynamic.

Perhaps no other theme so preoccupied Banna as the disunity of Muslims and the consequent weakening of the community. As we have emphasized, he was inspired by political as well as religious motives. Another basic element of his message was the appeal to Muslims for a personal and individual reform, a fundamental change in mentality which would precede, necessarily, a renaissance in the community's life. Like Afghani before him, a central reference in this appeal was the Qur'anic verse: 'Lo! Allah changeth not the condition of a folk until they [first] change that which is in their hearts.'[77] And in the effort to speed the process the Society reserved its most enthusiastic non-political energies for the field of education.

[75] Nadawi, *Mudhakkarat*, pp. 50–1. The government in 1948–9 apparently also thought so since it cracked down on *al-Fath* with other journalistic enterprises of the Society.

[76] *Barnamij thaqafi mihani li'l-mudarrasin* (1952), pp. 6–7. Samman, *IM*, p. 86 (above, p. 238, n. 22) insists that the *Manar* exegesis is the only one 'worthy of God's book'.

[77] Qur'an 13: 11; see also Smith, *Islam in Modern History*, pp. 50–1.

Finally, we have earlier observed at length the major effort expended on the theme of Islam's viability in the modern world, its flexibility, and its potential for development. That effort was futile because it was ill informed about the dynamics, both of its own Muslim society and of that of the West with which it was locked in a battle which by the Society's own definition was a battle to the death. Because this ignorance was combined with an intense spiritual and political malaise, this defence of Islam was structured in terms of an apologetic[78] which obscured a more basic and more real issue which was also central to the Society's message: the historical and cultural imperative to maintain (or restore?) a vital Islamic tradition. We have emphasized earlier at length the strong feelings held in the Society about the need for Muslims to relate their present and future to their past, to seek for Egypt what Professor Northrop, in a more general but related context, has called an 'inner order'—a realistic relationship between the law of the state and the 'positive and living law' of society.[79] In this pursuit the Society saw a major justification for its existence: 'We are protecting for the nation its self-respect and its integrity when we protect the precious heritage which history has bequeathed to it.'[80] This did not mean the return to a seventh-century Islam or a particular Muslim polity, as the Society correctly claimed. (It could not mean this given the advanced state of Egypt's secularization.) Rather, the Society was facing up to a situation well described by a French observer: 'une évolution trop rapide, forcée, pourrait-on dire, a compromis la santé morale de cette société. Il faut revenir en arrière et repartir sur une meilleure voie.'[81] Without providing any reliable intellectual road maps, the Society nevertheless made clear its belief that the starting-point was Islam and its tradition. If the problem of finding the right path was difficult, it was not going to be solved by avoiding the issues (notably the *sharīʿa* and the separation of Church and state) which Islam's history had bequeathed to Muslims.[82]

[78] See Gibb, *Modern Trends*, p. 53; but esp. Smith, *Islam in Modern History*, pp. 115–56. We think Professor Cantwell Smith has slightly overdone his investigation of the Islamic apologetic literature. Given a transitional crisis situation (which Cantwell Smith has brilliantly described) for the Arab world, we wonder whether much else is possible for a period.

[79] *Taming of the Nations*, pp. 5–6.

[80] *RTH: D*, p. 11.

[81] Bertier, 'L'idéologie politique', pp. 555–6.

[82] See in this respect the interesting review of Gardet, *La cité musulmane*, by G. C. Anawati, 'La philosophie politique de l'Islam', *R. du Caire* (Sept. 1954), 104–15. Father Anawati appears to take exception to Gardet's identification of orthodox reformist thinking with the 'real Islam', an identification Anawati would prefer to make with such 'modernists' as 'Ali 'Abd al-Raziq, Taha Husayn, and Ahmad Amin. Gardet (p. 26) refers to Taha Husayn's influence on the intellectuals of the Near East as a 'seduction' compared to the influence of a Mustafa al-Maraghi.

This position did not automatically exclude, as is commonly supposed, any reference to modern Western developments. Rather it was a question of priority and of the maintenance of a point of reference, one which would help to guide inevitable change into channels which would preserve some semblance of social order and cohesion in the process of social transformation. This is the inevitable role of the conservative reformer who sees the need for change but who seeks to control change and give it meaning through the use of stable referents in history and tradition. To paraphrase the words of a Pakistani writer in another context, the problem for the Society was not only to modernize the life of the *milla* but also to Islamize its life on modern lines.[83]

On the other hand, in its relationship to the ʻAbduh tradition, the Society also clearly reflected the progressive change in the character of that tradition as it passed to Shaykh ʻAbduh's heirs—a change from the relatively universalist modernism of an ʻAbduh to the parochialism and orthodoxy of Rida and especially Khatib.[84] Professor Gibb has said of the Salafiyya modernists:

> By carrying the rejection of *taqlīd* back beyond the founders of the schools to the primitive community of the *salaf*, the 'great ancestors', and combining with this the quasi-rationalism of scholastic logic, but without Muhammad Abduh's ballast of catholicity, they naturally gravitated towards the exclusivism and rigidity of the Hanbalite outlook.[85]

While the post-Banna period in the Society's history showed—as we have already noted—some considerable movement towards a change in character, there nevertheless persisted from the Banna era the same quality of rigidity and puritanism which the first leader had indelibly stamped on the organization, and which became the Society's hallmarks on the Egyptian scene.

These qualities were manifest in Banna's unrelenting insistence on being bound by the classical legists on the important question of change through innovation.[86] They appeared as dominant characteristics of the kind of religious revival and campaign for 'moral re-armament' which were leading themes of the movement's message. Profoundly genuine though it was, the call to return to Islam and its code of behaviour was nevertheless vitiated by a sterility born of obedience to inherited forms and a self-righteousness born of sanctimonious claims to omniscience. Finally, as an

[83] See Husayn F. al-Hamdani, 'An Islamic Academy for Pakistan', *Arafat*, i (Mar. 1948), 72.

[84] See Gibb, *Modern Trends*, pp. 34–5. For similar observations about the Brothers, see Anawati, 'La philosophie politique', 111; Gardet, *La cité musulmane*, pp. 18 and 361; Jomier, *Commentaire coranique*, pp. 349–50.

[85] Gibb, *Modern Trends*, p. 34.

[86] See *RNURT*, pp. 6–7.

example of the strong element of rigidity in the organization, it is possible to point to its basic intolerance of dissent. In his critique of the crisis of Islam, Banna reserved some of his strongest words for the 'free-thinkers' and those who would individually interpret the faith.[87] It was with such inspiration that Ghazali could claim extensive freedom in historical Islam from religious compulsion only to qualify it as follows: 'How can Islam be asked to grant life to apostates so that they may participate in its death? The question has transcended the area of the desired freedom of mind and entered . . . that area in which society must defend its interest against reckless personal freedom.'[88] For nations in Asia in process of being transformed into modern political entities, this argument is winning more and more adherents (including the military régime in Egypt); for the Society it was a characteristic and revealing commentary on a basic question of approach. In such fields as the rejection of authority and the opening of the door of *ijtihad* the Society could be charged, with some reason, with limiting those, beyond itself, who could participate in the projected renaissance. We have just discussed in another but related context the violence which was a consequence of the Society's sense of exclusiveness.

The characteristic difference between the Society of the Brothers and the 'Abduh legacy of modernism was in the spirit and mood which informed the Society's ideas. 'Our message', said one Brother, 'means *jihad*, struggle and work . . . it is not a philosophical message'.[89] This preference for 'deed' over 'idea' was demonstrated in the preference for the word 'programme' (*minhaj*) as against 'ideology' (*fikra*) to describe what the Society believed. This outlook, it will be recalled, permeated Banna's early years and dictated his choice of training and work; it was a major dimension of his moulding of the organization. More fundamentally, this outlook reflected a modern and mass expression of classical Islamic thought patterns. Banna was steeped in both the theological and Sufi traditions, and from both he absorbed, and in his teachings demonstrated, the non-rationalist, even non-intellectualist quality which has been observed to be an aspect of Muslim thought.[90] For instance, among the factors listed in his analysis of the decline of Islam is the 'neglect of the practical sciences' in favour of the 'deep, theoretical sciences'.[91] And this

[87] See *RNURT*, pp. 24–5.
[88] Ghazali, *IIS*, p. 119. See also his *MHN* (Faruqi tr.), xvi.
[89] Hajjaji, *RLAT*, pp. 43–4.
[90] See Gibb, *Modern Trends*, p. 7; and W. Cantwell Smith, 'The Intellectuals in the Modern Development of Islam', in Fisher, ed., *Social Forces in the Middle East*, *passim*.
[91] *RBAWY*, p. 10. See also Qutb, *AIFI* (Hardie tr.), pp. 17–18.

non-intellectualist quality expressed itself in the central place given to moral and ethical reform in the programme for religious revival. It was no accident, perhaps, that, with minor exceptions, neither Banna nor the movement produced any work remotely identifiable as theology or philosophy.[92]

The Society's relationship to the 'Abduh tradition thus reflected the progressive change to rigidity which characterized the Salafiyya successors of Shaykh 'Abduh. In its particular methods of approach, rigidity combined with exclusiveness to produce that potential for 'Mahdism' of which Professor Gibb speaks, whose heresy is 'its belief not only that the minds and wills of men can be dominated by force but that truth can be demonstrated by the edge of the sword'.[93] At the same time, the Society's vigorous espousal of the cause of reform through unity and education and within the terms of the tradition brought it into harmony with other more basic, if more general, aspects of the 'Abduh tradition. The non-intellectual (and in many respects uninformed) quality of its appeal only heightened the emotional energies expended on the immediate call for religious revival and moral reform, and constricted the latter purpose to a defensive apologia for Islam in the face of the onslaught of secularism. One other point needs to be made about the Society's relationship with the 'Abduh tradition, a point of difference of another order: the simple fact that its organization was predominantly lay[94] in character and urban in orientation, inspired not only by the Muslim rebellion against the internal corruption of, and external encroachments on the lands of

[92] Banna wrote one 'theological' study called *al-'Aqa'id* which was first published in the *Majallat al-Ikhwan al-Muslimin* of 1932. The study, which dealt with the stages of faith, the names, attributes, and existence of God, was republished later with 'exegesis' (Radwan Muh. Radwan, ed., *al-'Aqa'id* (1951)). Banna, it will be recalled, also did a commentary on the opening verse of the Qur'an (above, this chapter, p. 322, n. 74). Qutb, *AIFI* (Hardie tr.), p. 254, n. 15, promised for the future a study on 'The Islamic Doctrine of the Universe, Life, and Mankind'. We are not sure this was ever completed before his execution in 1966.

[93] We have qualified with the word 'potential' because of uncertainty about the apparently purely religious implication of the word as used by Gibb, *Modern Trends*, pp. 121 and 113 ff. This does not appear to be so much the case with the use of the word 'dynamism' by Smith, *Islam in Modern History*, pp. 89–92, and in the discussion of the Brothers, pp. 156–60. However, even in Smith the tendency to tie activism and violence (which gives rise to the labels) too specifically to the religious phenomenon, Islam, does some violence to the very mundane drives which inspire much of the ferment in the modern Muslim world. Much more rapidly than we believed possible when this study was begun, it will become increasingly more difficult to isolate the religious aspect for purposes of analysing modern Muslims. Hourani (*Arabic Thought in the Liberal Age* (1962), p. 360) suggests the same reservation.

[94] Gibb, *Modern Trends*, pp. 48–9, has already noted the lay character of Muslim modernism, confining it to 'educated laymen' and excluding the *Manar* modernists.

Islam, but also by worldly considerations of bread and status. To that problem we will now turn.

THE SOCIETY: ITS MEMBERSHIP AND APPEAL

It is probably a fair assertion that even the Society itself had no clear idea of the exact number of members who at any one or all times were on its books. There are, however, figures available from the Society and from outside it which, if not exact, are at least indicative. From these figures something of the following picture emerges: 4 branches in 1929; 5 in 1930; 10 in 1931; 15 in 1932; 300 in 1938; 500 in 1940; 2,000 in 1949. In terms of membership numbers these branches have been estimated to represent some 300,000–600,000 in the peak period 1946–8, figures which nearly correspond to the claim by a member that 2,000 branches in 1949 represented 500,000 'active members'. Add 500,000 'sympathizers', and the Society's claim, in 1948, to be speaking in the name of a million Egyptians was not exaggerated.[95] After 1949 membership dropped sharply. In 1953 it was estimated that there were 1,500 branches in the whole of Egypt, a figure estimated to represent a membership of 200,000–300,000.[96]

Precise information on the socio-economic distribution of the membership is just as difficult to amass as on its geographical distribution. But some hard, albeit random, statistical evidence from the numerous legal entanglements of the Society is available to suggest a membership drawn from most sectors of society. In the jeep trials, for example, of the 32 Brothers brought to court, 8 were civil servants, 5 were teachers, 7 were white-collar workers in private industry or business, 7 were small-business owners, 2 were students, and there was one each in farming, medicine, and preaching.[97] Of the 15 tried in the Nuqrashi case, there were 6 students, 5 civil servants, 1 engineer, and 3 small business men.[98] In a list of 'wanted' Brothers published in 1954 by the government, there were 3 lawyers, 3 army officers, 1 police officer, 12 civil servants, 13 teachers, 1 doctor, 9 labourers, 2 carpenters, 38 students, 15 students from the Azhar, 1 soldier, 5 clerks, 8 white-collar workers in private business or industry, 1 doorman, 1 tailor, 2 grocers, 1 architect, 1 engineer, 1 accountant, 1 mechanic,

[95] See *Mudh.*, pp. 150–4; Hajjaji, *RWR*, pp. 199–201; Husayni, *Ikhwan*, pp. 21, 31; Banna, *Qawl fasl*, pp. 23, 39–40; *MDA* (15 Apr. 1952), 5; Rosenthal, 'Muslim Brethren', 278; Heyworth-Dunne, *Modern Egypt*, p. 68; *JIM* (12 Dec. 1946), 3, 4. See also A. S. Eban, 'Some Social and Cultural Problems of the Middle East', *International Affairs* (July 1947), 367–75; Peters, 'The Moslem Brotherhood', 8.

[96] See Zaki, *Ikhwan*, p. 33; *JJ* (14 Nov. 1954), 10; (18 Nov. 1954), 10.

[97] *Haythiyat wa-hukm*, pp. 13–14.

[98] *Qadiyat al-Nuqrashi*, p. 1.

1 journalist, 1 farmer, and 12 unemployed.[99] The point could be affirmed solidly if a chart were to be made of the occupations of the hundreds who came before the People's Tribunal between November 1954 and February 1955.

These listings suggest two things about the membership. First, however large the rural membership (some Brothers, unrealistically we think, put this at over half), it was only important in a statistical sense, for seldom was it true that rural Egypt was more than a backdrop for the urban activists who shaped the Society's political destiny. The same may be said for the urban lower classes who flocked to the organization in the 1940s. Secondly, this random sampling of the membership suggests not only urban activism, but urban, middle-class, *effendi* predominance among the activist membership. One of the writers on the Society self-consciously claimed for the organization as early as 1935 an *effendi* quality in an effort to dissociate it from the 'dervishism' of Sufism: 'the primary manifestation of the message of the Muslim Brothers', he says, 'is that it is the message of the *effendi*'.[100] This may then have been a wishful projection as regards the membership, most of which at that time was rural and working class, but there was much more truth in it as regards the leadership. For example, a listing of these leaders in attendance at the third general conference of 1935 showed that of 112 names, only 25 were classified as shaykhs, most of these being rural in origin.[101] Many years later, in 1953, a listing of the Consultative Assembly showed that of 150 members, only 12 bore the title *'alim*, and 10 others were either 'elders' (*a'yan*) or 'village headmen' (*'umad*) and were rurally rooted; the remainder were of the *effendiyya*.[102] For its part, the Guidance Council, as it last existed, was composed of 11 members: 2 were preachers, 1 was a professor at the Azhar, 4 were higher civil servants (inspectors or directors), 2 were lawyers, 1 a pharmacist, and 1 a professor. We have already seen that the regulations of the organization stipulated specifically that 9 of the Council must be from Cairo, which seems to mean not only urban but *effendi* control of the group.

As the above tabulations from the court records suggest, the *effendi* came to be prominent in the membership also. This fact about the membership is of general relevance, going beyond the activists.

[99] *JJ* (19 Nov. 1954), 1.

[100] Jundi, *QDHRTM*, p. 84. Safran, *Egypt*, p. 199, correctly notes the importance of the lower class to the membership ranks. We prefer to distinguish between rural and urban lower classes and between these and the urban middle class.

[101] *Mudh.*, pp. 194–9.

[102] See *MDA* (13 Oct. 1953), 13; and for a similar, less detailed listing for August 1952, *MAS* (6 Aug. 1952) p. 6.

Over a period of a year and a half, in our fairly regular attendance at the Tuesday night and other meetings of the Society, a fairly regular pattern of attendance emerged. There were those in the traditional, undecorated *galabiyya*—a labourer, a servant, a small merchant, a craftsman; there was the more formal *galabiyya* of the more prosperous merchant shopkeeper and the status-conscious Azharite; there was the scattering of bedraggled and ill-matched uniforms which proclaimed the wearer as a messenger or a coffee server in private or governmental establishments; and finally, in an overwhelming majority, there was the student, the civil servant, the teacher, the clerk and office worker, and the professional in their Western suits.[103]

That this membership largely represented an emergent and self-conscious Muslim middle class is obvious. Sundry aspects of the Society's ideas and programmes demonstrated this clearly. Hostility to foreign economic control which limited the prospects for the new bourgeoisie, a hostility which extended to the local minorities, is one of the most obvious which comes to mind. Another is the political struggle against imperialism (which sustained foreign economic control) and its 'agents'—the internal imperialists, the ruling classes—who buttressed their economic and political power by co-operating with and depending on imperialism. A similar element from a different angle is the 'national unity' theme which so dominated the Society's thinking. In a religious and cultural sense this meant, of course, the re-establishment of Islam as the beacon to guide the nation's destiny; in more secular terms, it was a political call for unity of purpose to protect national sovereignty and to achieve national goals; it was also a call for the unity of classes expressed in the theme of harmony between labour and management, and landowner and peasant; themes which have become the hallmark of middle-class conservative reformism in the Arab world.[104]

The important middle-class segment had also other ramifications. Professor Gibb has astutely observed that one of the most important developments in the modern Muslim world is the appearance of numerous religious associations which perform the function of filling the religious gap in the life of the middle-class

[103] See also Peters, 'The Moslem Brotherhood', pp. 8–10.

[104] Until 1961, and in some respects to the present time, the present régime in Egypt is a good example. In many respects the conflict which developed between the Society and the government in 1954 could be described in terms of differing middle-class conceptions about the nature, purpose, and rate of social change. Professor Halpern's study of the 'new middle class' in *Politics of Social Change* is the most important of recent attempts to give theoretical formulation to the events of recent history in the Middle East.

Muslim.[105] This development is more than an aversion to Sufism, as suggested by Professor Gibb; it also represents an effort to reinstitutionalize religious life for those whose commitment to the tradition and religion is still great, but who at the same time are already effectively touched by the forces of Westernization. For whatever the members themselves felt about their own lives, their Western-type suits meant an inescapable chain of experience in a rapidly modernizing Egyptian society, experience which—consciously or otherwise—was transforming the tradition of which the organization was ostensibly the defender. If the Society could readily accept such externals of Westernization as science and technology, if it could cast its programme in terms reminiscent of Western concepts, if it could in theory admit that Islam might have something to learn from Western philosophy, history, literature, and legislation—if it could do these things, if would also be opening the way to the substantive institutional change which follows the need to adapt oneself to and absorb innovation. In the very process of reaffirming the old, the old is newly conceived and formulated in a way which inevitably reflects the forces which helped to undermine it.

In these terms the movement emerges as one of conservative transition, one which not only sought to imbue the present with some sense of the past (as we have earlier emphasized) but also to redefine the past in terms meaningful for the present. This was what enabled it to combine in membership not only the isolated and traditional groups—men with a stake in history—but also, what was more important, those who had passed through varying degrees of Westernization and had already accepted some of its premises. That the latter group was comprised mostly of men without a stake in society, who in part embraced or tolerated violence to achieve their ends, created the convulsive image of conservative radicalism which will probably remain the image of the Society of the Muslim Brothers in history.

[105] Gibb, *Modern Trends*, pp. 37–8, 51, 55; also in discussion at Princeton University on 12 January 1956, where the ideas were further developed.

BIBLIOGRAPHY

Note: Works cited in an abbreviated form in the footnotes are not listed here but appear in the 'Note on Abbreviations and Transliteration' on pp. xv–xix.

The place of publication, unless otherwise stated, is Cairo.

1. 'OFFICIAL' *RASA'IL* AND PUBLICATIONS

al-Bannā', Hasan. *al-ʿAqā'id.* 1951. Commentary by Raḍwān Muḥ. Raḍwān.

—— *Fi'l-daʿwa.* n.d.

—— *al-Ma'thūrāt.* Various undated editions. See esp. Raḍwān Muḥ. Raḍwān, ed. *al-Ma'thūrāt.* 1952.

—— *Muqaddama fi'l-tafsīr, tafsīr al-fātiḥa.* 1951.

—— *Qawl faṣl.* 1950.

Society of the Muslim Brothers. *al-Aqallīyat fi'l-mujtamaʿ al-islāmī.* n.d.

—— *Hadhihi daʿwatuna.* [1953].

—— *Ila al-Ikhwān.* (Newsletter appearing through part of 1953.)

—— *al-Islām wa'l-ḥukm.* By al-Sayyid abu al-Ḥasan al-Nadawī. 2nd ed., 1372 [1952–3].

—— *Musābaqat ikhtirāq al-ḍaḥiyya.* n.d.

—— *al-Muslimūn bayn al-tabshīr wa'l-istiʿmar.* 1952.

—— *al-Qawl al-faṣl.* 1954.

2. WORKS IN ARABIC

(*a*) *By Muslim Brothers*

ʿĀbidīn, ʿAbd al-Hākim. *Dīwān al-bawākīr.* 1937.

al-ʿArqūsī, Muḥ. Khayr, ed. *Majmūʿat maqālāt Ḥasan al-Banna'.* Vol. i. n.d.

ʿAyyād, Jamal al-Dīn. *Nuẓum al-ʿamal fi'l-Islām.* 1952.

al-Bājūrī, ʿAbd al-Majīd Fatḥ Allāh. *Ḥasan al-Bannā'.* [*c.* 1950–1.]

al-Bannā', ʿAbd al-Raḥmān. *Thawrat al-damm.* 1951.

al-Bannā', Anwar al-Jundī. *Qaḍāya al-aqṭar al-Islāmiyya.* 1946.

al-Būhī, Muḥ. Labib. *Aḥādīth al-jumʿa.* 1954.

—— *Ḥadīth al-thulāthā' li-kibār duʿāt al-Ikhwān al-Muslimīn.* [1953–4.]

—— *Qiṣṣat zawaj.* n.d.

al-Ghazālī, Muḥ. *ʿAqīdat al-Muslim.* 3rd ed., 1952.

—— *Khuluq al-Muslim.* 1953.

al-Hajjājī, Aḥmad Anis. *Ṣawt min al-janna.* 1952.

—— *Thalātha wa-thalāth.* 1947.

—— *Wathā'iq.* 1947.

Ḥatta yaʿlam al-nās. [Damascus, 1954].

al-ʿIssāwī, ʿAbd al-Raḥmān. *Limādha ana Muslim.* 1954.
al-Jundī, Anwar. *Faẓā'iḥ al-aḥzāb al-siyāsiyya fi Miṣr.* n.d.
—— *al-Imām al-Marāghi.* 1952.
—— *Munāwarāt al-siyāsa.* 1947.
—— *Ta'rīkh al-aḥzāb al-siyāsiyya.* 1946.
al-Khaṭīb, Muḥibb al-Dīn. *Awlāduna fi adāb al-Islām.* 1372 [1952–3].
al-Khūlī, al-Bahī. *Tadhkarat al-duʿā.* 4th ed., 1953.
Nār, Aḥmad. *al-Qitāl fi'l-Islām.* 1952.
Sābiq, al-Sayyid. *Fiqh al-sunna.* 5 vols (i and ii, 5th ed., 1954; iii, 2nd ed., 1952; iv and v 1954).
al-Sammān, ʿAbd Allāh. *Arkān al-daʿwa al-Islāmiyya.* 1954.
—— *al-Maʿāni al-ḥayya fi'l-Islām.* 1953.
—— *al-Rusūl ustādh al-ḥayā.* 3rd ed., 1953.
—— *al-Tarbīyya fi'l-Islām.* 4th ed., 1954.
—— *Usus al-ḥukm fi'l-Islām.* 1953.
Shamīs, ʿAbd al-Muʿnīm. *Suqūt al-Qāhira.* 1951.
al-Shurbajī, al-Sayyid. *al-Islām wa dustur al-ḥukm.* 1953.
al-Sibāʿī, Muṣṭafa. *Min wathā'iq al-ṣirāʿ bayn al-Ikhwān al-Muslimīn wa-Jamāl ʿAbd al-Nasir.* Damascus, 1954.
Taʿlīb, ʿAbd al-Muʿnim Aḥmad. *al-Bayʿa: sharḥ risālat al-taʿālīm li'l-imām al-shahīd Ḥasan al-Bannā'.* 1952.
al-Tammawī, Muḥ. Fahmi. *al-Mujāhidūn.* 1953.

(b) By Other Writers

Amīn, Aḥmad. *al-Ṣaʿlaka wa'l-futūwa fi'l-Islām.* 1952.
— *Zuʿamā' al-iṣlāḥ fi'l-ʿasr al-ḥadīth.* 1948.
al-ʿAqqād, ʿAbbās Mahmūd. *al-Islām fi'l-qarn al-ʿishrīn.* 1954.
Khālid, Khālid Muḥ. *Min hunā nabda'.* 6th ed., 1952.
al-Mawdūdī, Abu al-Aʿla. *al-Mas'ala al-qādiyāniyya.* 1953.
Mu'min, Muṣṭafa. *Ṣawt Miṣr.* 1951.
al-Nadawī, Abu al-Ḥasan ʿAli al-Ḥasanī. *Mudhakkarāt sā'iḥ fi'l-sharq al-ʿArabī.* 1954.
—— *Shāʿir al-Islām al-Duktur Muḥammad Iqbāl.* 1951.
al-Tābiʿī, Muḥ., *et al. Hā'ulā' . . . hum al-Ikhwān.* [Cairo, 1954].

3. WORKS IN WESTERN LANGUAGES

(a) Books

Abdel-Malek, Anouar. *Égypte, société militaire.* Paris, 1962.
Adams, C. C., *Islam and modernism in Egypt.* London, 1933.
Ahmed, Jamal, *The intellectual origins of Egyptian nationalism.* London, 1960.
Badaoui, Zaki. *Les problèmes du travail et les organisations ouvrières en Égypte.* Alexandria, 1948.
Binder, L. *The ideological revolution in the Middle East.* New York, 1964.
Bonné, Alfred. *State and economics in the Middle East: a society in transition.* London, 1948.

Colombe, Marcel. *L'évolution de l'Égypte: 1924–1950* (*Islam d'hier et d'aujourd'hui*, x, ed. E. Lévi-Provençal). Paris, 1951.

Cooke, Hedley V. *Challenge and response in the Middle East: the quest for prosperity, 1919–1951*. New York, 1952.

Cragg, Kenneth. *The call of the minaret*. London, 1956.

—— *Counsels in contemporary Islam*. In W. Montgomery Watt, ed., *Islamic Surveys*, 3. Edinburgh, 1965.

Fisher, Sydney N., ed. *Social forces in the Middle East*. Ithaca, N.Y., 1955.

Galatoli, A. M. *Egypt in mid-passage*. Cairo, 1950.

Gardet, Louis. *La cité musulmane* (*Études musulmanes*, i, ed. E. Gibson and L. Gardet). Paris, 1954.

Gibb, H. A. R. *Modern trends in Islam*. Chicago, 1947.

—— ed. *Whither Islam?* London, 1932.

Grunebaum, Gustave von, ed. *Unity and variety in Muslim civilization* (Comparative studies of culture and civilization, ed. R. Redfield and M. Singer). Chicago, 1955.

Halpern, Manfred. *The politics of social change in the Middle East and North Africa*. Princeton, N.J., 1963. (Ref. to paperback ed., Princeton, N.J., 1965.)

Harris, Christina Phelps. *Nationalism and revolution in Egypt: the role of the Muslim Brotherhood*. The Hague, 1964.

Heyworth-Dunne, J. *Religious and political trends in modern Egypt*. Washington, published by author, 1950.

Hitti, P. K. *History of the Arabs*. 4th ed. rev., London, 1949.

Hourani, Albert. *Arabic thought in the liberal age, 1798–1939*. London, 1962.

Issawi, Charles. *Egypt at mid-century: an economic survey*. London, 1954.

Jomier, J. *Le commentaire coranique du Manâr*. (*Islam d'hier et d'aujourd'hui*, ix, ed. E. Lévi-Provençal). Paris, 1954.

Kimche, Jon. *Seven fallen pillars: the Middle East, 1915–1950*. London, 1950.

Kirk, George. *The Middle East, 1945–1950* (Royal Institute of International Affairs, *Survey of International Affairs*, 1939–1946). London, 1954.

—— *A short history of the Middle East*. Washington, 1949.

—— *The Middle East in the war* (ibid.). London, 1952.

Landau, Jacob M. *Parliaments and parties in Egypt*. Tel Aviv, 1953.

Landshut, S. *Jewish communities in the Muslim countries of the Middle East*. London, 1950.

Laqueur, W. Z. *Communism and nationalism in the Middle East*. London, 1956.

Lenczowski, George. *The Middle East in World Affairs*. Ithaca, N.Y., 1952.

Little, Tom. *Egypt*. London, 1958.

Marlowe, John, *pseud*. *Anglo-Egyptian relations, 1800–1956*. 2nd ed., London, 1965.

Neguib, Mohammed. *Egypt's destiny: a personal statement*. London, 1955.

Newby, P. H. *The Picnic at Sakkara.* London, 1955.

Northrop, F. S. C. *The Taming of the Nations.* New York, 1952.

Nuseibeh, Hazem Zaki. *The ideas of Arab nationalism.* Ithaca, N.Y., 1956.

Polk, W. R. *The United States and the Arab World.* Cambridge, Mass., 1965.

Resner, Lawrence. *Eternal stranger: the plight of the modern Jew from Baghdad to Casablanca.* New York, 1951.

Royal Institute of International Affairs. *Great Britain and Egypt, 1914–1951.* 2nd ed., London, 1952.

—— *The Middle East: a political and economic study.* 2nd ed., London, 1954.

Safran, Nadav. *Egypt in search of political community.* Cambridge, Mass., 1961.

Smith, Wilfred Cantwell. *Islam in modern history.* Princeton, N.J., 1957.

—— *Modern Islam in India.* London, 1946.

—— *Pakistan as an Islamic state.* Lahore, 1951.

Speiser, E. A. *The United States and the Near East.* Cambridge, Mass., 1947.

Vatikiotis, P. J. *The Egyptian Army in politics, pattern for new nations?* Bloomington, Ind., 1961.

Wheelock, Keith. *Nasser's new Egypt: a critical analysis.* New York, 1960.

Young, George. *Egypt.* London, 1927.

Young, T. Cuyler, ed. *Near Eastern culture and society: a symposium on the meeting of East and West.* Princeton, N.J., 1951.

(*b*) *Articles in Periodicals*

Alexander, Mark. 'Left and Right in Egypt', *Twentieth Century*, cli (Feb. 1952), 119–28.

Anawati, G. C. 'La philosophie politique de l'Islam', *R. du Caire*, xvii (Sept. 1954), 104–15.

Ansari, Z. I. 'Contemporary Islam and nationalism: a case study of Egypt', *WI.* n.s., vii (1961).

Asad, Muh. 'Islamic constitution making', *Arafat*, i (Mar. 1948), 16–63.

Bertier, F. 'L'idéologie politique des Frères musulmans', *Temps modernes*, viii (Sept. 1952), 540–6.

Boehm, Jacob. 'Les "Frères musulmans"', *Hamizrah Hehadash*, iii (Summer 1952), 222–52. (In Hebrew, Eng. summary; reprinted in French, *Monde non-chrétien*, xxvi (June 1953), 211–25).

Brush, Stanley E., 'Ahmadiyyat in Pakistan', *MW*, xlv (Apr. 1955), 145–71.

'Cinquante ans de littérature égyptienne', *R. du Caire* (Feb. 1953), special issue.

Colombe, Marcel. 'Egypt from the fall of King Farouk to the February 1954 crisis', *MEA*, v (June–July 1954), 185–92.

—— 'Onze mois d'évolution de l'Égypte', *AA*, xxiii/3 (1953), 4–14.

—— 'Où va l'Égypte?', *AA*, i/4 (1948), 29–42.

Eban, A. S. 'Some social and cultural problems of the Middle East', *International Affairs*, xxiii (July 1947), 367–75.

Fakhry, Majid. 'The theocratic idea of the Islamic state in recent controversies', *International Affairs*, xxx (Oct. 1954), 450–63.

Halpern, Manfred. 'The implications of communism for Islam', *MW*, xlii (Jan. 1953) 28–41.

al-Hamdani, H. F. 'An Islamic Academy for Pakistan' *Arafat*, i (Mar. 1948), 63–73.

Handley, William J. 'The Labor Movement in Egypt', *MEJ*, iii (July 1949), 277–92.

Haydon, Douglas. 'Egypt's surprise dictatorship' *National and English R.*, cxxxix (Oct. 1952), 210–14.

Holloway, Owen. 'University students of the Middle East', *Royal Central Asian J.*, xxxviii (Jan. 1951), 10–20.

Hourani, Albert. 'The Anglo-Egyptian agreement: some causes and its implications', *MEJ*, ix (Summer 1955), 239–55.

Kaplinsky, Zvi. 'The Muslim Brotherhood', *MEA*, v (Dec. 1954), 377–85.

Latif, Syed Abdul. 'Islam and social change', *International Social Science Bull.*, iv (1953), 691–8.

Lehrman, Hal. 'Three weeks in Cairo', *Commentary*, xxi (Feb. 1956), 101–11.

Marmorstein, Emile. 'Religious opposition to nationalism in the Middle East', *International Affairs*, xxviii/3 (July 1952), 344–59.

Peters, Donald. 'The Moslem Brotherhood—terrorists or just zealots?', *Reporter*, viii (17 Mar. 1953), 8–10.

Rahman, Fazlu-r-. 'International religious development in the present century of Islam', *Cahiers d'Histoire mondiale / J. of World History*, ii (1955), 862–79.

—— 'Modern Muslim thought', *MW*, xlv (Jan. 1955), 16–25.

Rondeau, Éric. 'Les "Frères musulmans": quarante ans de guerre sainte', *Le Monde*, 30, 31 Aug., 1 Sept. 1966.

Rosenthal, Franz. 'The "Muslim Brethren" of Egypt', *MW*, xxxvii (Oct. 1947), 278–91.

Smith, W. Cantwell. 'Trends in Muslim thought', *MW*, xlii (Oct. 1952), 313–32.

Stauffer, Thomas B. 'Labor unions in the Arab states', *MEJ*, vi (Winter 1952), 83–8.

Sterling, Claire. 'Egypt: Nasser walks the tightrope of power', *Reporter*, xii (10 Feb. 1955), 36–41.

al-Tafahum, ʿAbd. 'A Cairo debate on Islam and some Christian implications', *MW*, xliv (July–Oct. 1954), 236–52.

Winder, R. Bayly. 'Islam as the state religion: a Muslim Brotherhood view on Syria', *MW*, xliv (July–Oct. 1954), 215–26.

Ziadeh, Nicola A. 'Recent books on the interpretation of Islam', *MEJ*, v (Autumn 1951), 505–10.

(*c*) *Unpublished Material*

Brown, John F. 'The Moslem Brotherhood in Egypt'. Unpubl. M.A. thesis, Princeton Univ., 1954.

INDEX

Printed in the United States
20442LVS00003B/151-165